A FIRE WAS LIGHTED

EARLY PORTRAITS

ROSE HAWTHORNE LATHROP

CARING FOR HER FIRST CANCER PATIENT

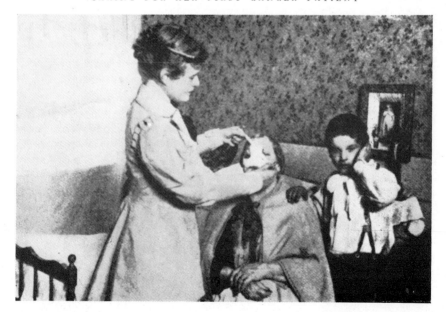

A Fire Was Lighted

THE LIFE OF

ROSE HAWTHORNE LATHROP

by

THEODORE MAYNARD

The Bruce Publishing Company, Milwaukee

To Kathleen

Introduction

It was a perfect love that glowed and grew within the heart and soul of Rose Hawthorne as she devoted herself to the care of the cancerous poor. High thoughts alone, she knew, do not make a woman holy, and her own thoughts gave birth to good deeds in active love of God and the love of neighbor, which alone can save the human race from selfish forces threatening its destruction.

Why will not our unhappy, chaotic world learn the spiritual secret of this valiant woman who sought out the sick and poor to serve them with heroic selflessness and a consuming love of God? She asked no man his creed; she barred none because of his color; and leaders of men and nations who hold the human destiny of mankind in their trembling hands should imitate and emulate her tolerance, her understanding, and her charity!

Beauty of body can easily be disfigured and disappear, but beauty of spirit, Rose Hawthorne knew, was never marred even by cancer as it mercilessly devours the flesh. In tireless devotion she gave of herself to help and tend the pitiful victims of this dread disease, and even the weak heart that in others would have made them falter and fail, Mother Alphonsa would not permit to be an obstacle, as courageously she carried her cross for Christ and for His poor and suffering children.

Sincerely I believe that this biography represents a real contribution in stimulating and extending interest in the work of the *Servants of Relief* who throughout our nation today are perpetuating the boundless, bountiful, merciful work of their foundress — Mother Alphonsa. Such mercy is like unto Mary's — Mother of mankind.

FRANCIS CARDINAL SPELLMAN

vii

Acknowledgments

In the bibliographical note at the end of this book I indicate the many manuscript sources drawn upon and thank those who made them available to me. In addition I have to mention the following who rendered help of one kind or another, some of them a considerable amount of help, some less: Miss Sarah R. Bartlett of the Concord Public Library, Concord, Massachusetts; William L. Reenan of Cincinnati, Ohio; the Rev. Florence D. Cohalan of Cathedral College, New York, New York; Miss Florence M. Osborne of the Essex Institute, Salem, Massachusetts; the Rev. Clement Thuente, O.P., of Amityville, New York; Brother Julian, F.S.C., Manhattan College, New York, New York; Sister Maura of Halifax, Nova Scotia, and Sister Maria Hurley of Wellesley Hills, Massachusetts; Paul R. Byrne, of the University of Notre Dame; Zoltán Haraszti of the Boston Public Library; Miss Mildred Howells of Boston, Massachusetts, and Mrs. Holmes Hinkley of Cambridge, Massachusetts. To Brother E. Ignatius, F.S.C., of LaSalle College, Philadelphia, Pennsylvania, and to the Rev. Matthew Hoehn, O.S.B., of St. Mary's Abbey, Newark, New Jersey, I am indebted for the loan of books, and to Father Matthew Hoehn for other invaluable services too numerous to mention. The manuscript was read by the Rev. Joseph T. Clune and Sister Joseph of Rosary Hill Home. To them I owe a number of useful suggestions. The name of Miss Kathleen Sheehan of Port Washington, New York, must stand alone for the unique services she rendered me. Not only did she copy letters at the Houghton Library of Harvard University (in which task she was assisted by Miss Mary Keefe of Providence, Rhode Island), and the New York Public Library, but she solved what was, for me, the very difficult problem of the transcription of this book, which I was obliged to dictate lying in bed in a sanatorium. It is hardly too much to say that she became virtually co-author.

Contents

Part Three: Mother Alphonsa

Part One: Rose Hawthorne

A fire was then lighted in my heart, where it still burns. . . . I set my whole being to bring consolation to the cancerous poor.

— *Rose Hawthorne Lathrop*

The Rose of the Hawthornes

Little redheaded Rose Hawthorne at three had her own private history. Many of her remarks were prefaced with, "When I was in Morica," though about America she had already forgotten nearly everything. In later life the first memory she was able to record was that of picking a daisy in the garden of the furnished house at Rock Ferry where, on the Cheshire side of the Mersey, the Hawthornes had found a home. About this time her father put down in his notebook that, looking at the moon one evening, Rosebud had exclaimed, "It blooms out in the morning!" To her innocent eyes the sun was the blossom of the moon. Nathaniel Hawthorne was of course delighted, but at that age many children still have something of the poet in them.

One afternoon, when the three young Hawthornes were, as usual, swinging on the garden-gate, two gentlemen arrived as visitors. One of them — jovial, big-bearded, twinkling-eyed Mr. Bennoch — they already knew and liked. But at his companion even ten-year-old Una stared in astonishment. Shabby though he was — his black hat turning green, his coat creased and stained, his boots needing a polish — he carried everything off with a jaunty bearing and a knowing air.

As usual when visitors called, the children's admirable nurse, Fanny Wrigley, quickly applied the corner of a licked apron to rid the little faces of smudges, and then sent them into the drawing room.

Mr. Bennoch beamed upon them and kissed the girls. But when his aged and angular friend, Mr. Jerdan, offered to do the same,

Una drew back, and though Rose submitted to being taken upon his knee, her face resolutely refused to smile but turned upon him the unabashed stare of childhood. It was not easy to embarrass Mr. Jerdan — who afterward turned out to be a professional conqueror of feminine hearts — so he tried his blandishments upon Rose. He dodged from side to side and made funny faces, without the slightest effect; she merely continued to gaze straight into his bleary old eyes. "Why," he said at last, "you would make an admirable judge, and I would not like to be the fellow who would take sentence from your Lordship!"

Something at last amused her, and her face relaxed. "There," he cried, "now I have it; she loves me! she loves me!" He told Sophia Hawthorne that this daughter of hers, who had now slipped away and run over to her father, reminded him of Talley-rand. "And Talleyrand," he added "would have undertaken to stare any man out of countenance."

Dear, impressible Sophia, bubbling as always with enthusiasm, was at first somewhat taken in by the venerable humbug. She decided that he reminded her — of all things in the world! — of Dr. Johnson. But her husband, looking at him with shrewd eyes, set the fellow down as a fraud and wondered how anybody so thoroughly genuine as Bennoch could have brought him there. Though he concluded that it must be because Bennoch wished to exhibit a curiosity to his American friends, his courtesy did not fail, nor did his intellectual charity. Even three years later, after he had read William Jerdan's enormous autobiography — which he called unmitigated trash from beginning to end — and knew things about the man that were not recorded in that work, he continued to be polite to him, though by then, Mr. Jerdan, having about reached the end of his rope, was willing to intro-duce people to Baron Rothschild or the Prince of Wales for the loan of five pounds or even half a crown. But Hawthorne had summed him up correctly by the time the ugly old fellow rose to make his courtly but arthritic bow to Sophia and to bestow his yellow-fanged grimace as farewell on the children. Rose, using her own process, had reached much the same conclusion as that of her father.

Whatever Rose forgot of her early life has been preserved by her journalizing and letter-writing father and mother and brother. From them we know her — in spite of all the admiration all the Hawthornes had for one another — as a child with a temper, easily roused, but also as a child far more than usually charming. According to her mother, she made and perfectly understood jokes by the time she was eighteen months old. Before Rose was two, Sophia wrote to the Peabody grandmother. "Baby was in the highest spirits and conversed for the first time in the most facetious manner, casting side glances and laughing with a great pretense of being vastly amused and of superior insight into the bearing of things." She was always smiling or laughing, at anything or nothing.

Julian, five years older than herself, was especially delighted to have a little sister. Though they were to have their childish quarrels, and in later life something more serious, he delighted Sophia by the way he would say, "Oh, you darling!" to the baby on his lap and give her a look of beautiful and boundless tenderness. Sophia told her mother, "I should as soon expect an angel from the sky to descend to a rough scuffle with a desperado as for Julian to disturb or annoy the little Rosebud."

A radiance of disposition and tireless physical activity — these were as noticeable in her from the start as a head of hair even more violently red than her sister Una's. The Peabodys were disposed to attribute all these things to their descent from Queen Boadicea, though Sophia — perhaps because of the scepticism she observed in her husband's eyes — was not given to pressing these claims. Nor was she always prepared to accept all the grandmother's advice on the bringing up of infants. Mrs. Peabody had suggested that a rug be spread on the ground when the child was taken outdoors. "Why, Mother, I'd as soon think of keeping a wild bird on a rug!" was all Sophia would say.

And how heartily the baby slept! After a nap of four and a half hours Sophia heard her call for the first time, "Mamma!" Running up at something so wonderful she found Rosebud smiling like a constellation of stars.

She was born at Lenox, Massachusetts, on May 20, 1851 — "a child of spring, and spring never vanished from her nature." Though her father pronounced her, as might be expected in the case of one now a father for the third time, to be nothing remarkable, writing to his sister, Louisa, six weeks later he called her "the brightest and strongest baby we have had." He said she was growing prettier but was not "absolutely beautiful." As for her hair he declared it a more decided tint than Una's — and hers was described as Titian.

That "little red house" on the Stockbridge Road was of course unremembered by her. But she had heard so much about it that her imagination saw it; and part of her history of "Morica" was Mr. Melville with his huge black Newfoundland dog, on which even Una could ride; and the famous actress, Fanny Kemble, charging along the country lanes on her tall horse, sometimes with Julian on her saddlebow. At the end of her gallop she would rein herself in abruptly and hand over the small boy by his coat collar saying in her deep man's voice to his father, "There, take him — Julian the Apostate!"

And then there was the house they had rented for a year from the Horace Manns at dismal West Newton — a mere stage on the journey of these pilgrims, though one long enough for the writing of Hawthorne's memories of Brook Farm in *The Blithedale Romance*. The Manns were still there for a while before going to Washington, even the child, now eight years old, of whom its Aunt Sophia had made the classic remark, "I suspect that Mary's baby must have opened its mouth the moment it was born and pronounced a school report." Sophia could be quite acidulous at times.

The brothers-in-law liked each other but, according to the formal fashion of the time were "Mr. Mann" and "Mr. Hawthorne," and Sophia always called her husband "Mr. Hawthorne" when writing to her sisters or even to her father and mother. Before long Horace Mann was to disgust Hawthorne with his extreme abolitionist views, but on this visit only the more harmless fad of objecting to tobacco appeared. Somehow or other it came out that Hawthorne smoked a cigar now and then. Instantly Mr. Mann bristled. "Do I understand you to say, Mr. Hawthorne," he demanded, "that you actually use tobacco?"

"Why, yes, I smoke a cigar occasionally," Hawthorne returned, not at all embarrassed by the admission.

The tall, thin man, with the long, square mouth and the straight, lank hair of the born fanatic, stared in astonishment through his spectacles. He liked Hawthorne as a man and admired him as a writer — but tobacco was too much. At all costs he had to be true to his principles.

"In that case, Mr. Hawthorne," he said at last in a shocked voice, "it is my duty to tell you that I no longer have the same respect for you that I once had." With that he left his brother-in-law excommunicated, but vastly amused.

After West Newton there was Concord, the Concord of the early days of the Hawthorne marriage — sweetest of memories — when he insisted on doing the housework at a time when they were without a servant and Sophia danced to the tinkle of the music box they had borrowed from Henry Thoreau. Well might Hawthorne exclaim, "I have married the Spring! I am husband to the month of May!" This time it was not the Old Manse that they lived in, but the dingy, buff-colored house they bought from Emerson after Alcott had improved it with his esthetic carpentry. They renamed it the Wayside, and as such it was to become world famous.

Though Rose at this time was not, except in the family circle, the main center of attraction, we have a number of glimpses of her. Among the pleasantest, in view of the strong resemblance she came to have to her father, was the one we get of the afternoon Hawthorne arrived back from Washington after seeing President Pierce — his friend from Bowdoin College days — and being appointed the American Consul in Liverpool. Everybody greeted him with enthusiasm, except the baby, and she was asleep. But when she woke and saw Papa who had been away, her eyes, Sophia said, twinkled and closed exactly as if a dazzling sun had blazed upon her. Then when her father went toward her she was so overcome with joy that she burst into tears and hid her little face on Sophia's dress. When at last she subsided, she shook hands with him gravely and got upon his lap with a look of utmost satisfaction.

Sophia also felt the utmost satisfaction that the pinch and strain of their life were to be removed. Writing to her father on March 20, 1853, she told him: "To be able to spend a dollar without painful debate will be a great sense of relief to me — though Mr. Hawthorne is so large handed that the sense of dollars has not been such an incubus to us as to many with far ampler fortunes. . . . I can hardly believe that the world's goods may be added to the golden happiness we already enjoy."* Rejoicing that they would be able to see the wonders of Europe, and at the same time save a substantial amount from the rich emoluments of the consulate, the Hawthornes set out for Liverpool.

Liverpool was at first sight very depressing. Nor, for that matter, did the Hawthornes ever regard it as other than the blackest and most miserable of holes. From the brilliant sunshine

---

* This is the first of many letters at Hawthorne, N. Y., to be quoted here. Ordinarily I shall give no indication of my sources beyond what is in the biographical note. But this book will be largely drawn from such sources, even when direct quotations are not made.

they had had all the way across the Atlantic, they entered under dismal mists into the muddy Mersey, and were carried from the wet decks of the *Niagara* to a sloppy wharf on a soaked and stinking little river tug. From there they drove along streets that seemed a gray stone labyrinth, where everybody walked under umbrellas and with black respirators on their mouths, to the gloomiest of hotels.

There Julian was to remember the solemn meals served "with a ceremonious gravity that suggested their being preliminaries to funerals." But Sophia, always ready to be cheerfully amusing, records that Mr. Lynn, the proprietor of the Waterloo House, out of peculiar respect for the American consul, himself held the soup plate for her and with his own hands presented it to the waiter. At the end of this ceremony Mr. Lynn used to retire with so respectful an obeisance that Sophia was afraid that one day her husband might smile. One of these waiters had so portentous a gravity that Hawthorne called him the Methodist Preacher.

The Hawthornes were all glad to escape from the Waterloo House to Mrs. Blodgett's boardinghouse on Duke Street — an establishment half Dickensian and half Melvillian and altogether unique. Mrs. Blodgett was a plump, comely widow in her fifties, who had once lived in Gibraltar, where she had been well-to-do, and now specialized in caring for American sea captains. This she did so admirably that every one of her guests wondered what manner of man the late Mr. Blodgett could have been to have been so favored by fortune as to have won this paragon as wife. She pressed her good things upon them in such a way that Sophia wondered how she could make any money.

Hers was, Julian gratefully recorded later, the best boardinghouse ever known, before or since.

Hawthorne himself in his *Notebook* — though this was on a later visit — wrote that "the smell of tar and bilge-water [was] somewhat strongly perceptible in it." Though as consul he did not always see the best side of the boarders, at Mrs. Blodgett's he found them "alive to an extent to which the Englishman never seems to be conscious of life." As for Mrs. Blodgett herself, he told James T. Fields, his publisher, he had never known a better woman.

The other member of the firm of Ticknor and Fields — William D. Ticknor — had been their traveling companion. And though his granddaughter somewhat exaggerates in suggesting that Hawthorne could not venture on the journey without him, and needed somebody to tuck him safely into bed, it is true that Hawthorne had a way of getting Ticknor to do a good many things for him that do not ordinarily fall within the duties of a publisher. Ticknor was made the banker of the Liverpool savings and the salvager of whatever could be salvaged of the loans the American consul was forever making to fellow-countrymen stranded on a foreign shore. When Ticknor sailed for Boston he gave Hawthorne a set of razors, with his name engraved in the blades; Sophia a case of scissors especially made for her; and the children gifts that delighted them — little Rose getting a wax doll.

By the time Mr. Ticknor left the Hawthornes had established themselves at Rock Ferry, where, as Hawthorne wrote to Fields, he was as snug as a bug in a rug. It meant his crossing the dirty Mersey twice a day, but he was glad to live some distance from his office as this gave him an excuse for declining at least some of the invitations to the enormous English dinners of that time to which, as American consul, he was constantly being invited.

Their house at Rock Park was one of a score of such houses, all of them two-storied, stuccoed, and all with a little front lawn and a large back garden. Against its walls, topped with broken glass, peach and other fruit trees were fastened. Snails were everywhere, and the little English rabbits so delightfully unfamiliar to the American children. Each of the children had a tiny garden, though Rose did no more than plant a few seeds in a hole and dig them up next day to note their progress in sprouting. Even Julian was to admit that, though assiduous, he did not accomplish much except the digging of a big hole.

The inside of the Hawthorne's house was comfortable but was furnished by Mr. Campbell, the owner, in the most massively ugly Victorian style. Sophia's description of it makes more of its solidity than its lack of grace; the centre table at which she is writing, so she tells her father, is as heavy as a small planet. And she enumerates the carpets and the alabaster and bronze vases and the candlesticks and a lamp "as tall as Bunker Hill Monument" and looking like a lighthouse, without satirical comment. But even Sophia cannot forbear remarking that Mr. John Campbell, the former occupant, whose picture hung over the marble mantelpiece, though not a very lovely looking person, was at least angelic compared to his brother, who hung opposite. In the minds of the young Hawthornes the old song, "The Campbells are Coming," took on a sinister significance. Little Rose was inclined to run whenever she saw those grim visages.

They had plenty of servants, including a butler by the name of King, and a wonderful Mary Poppinesque nurse gratefully remembered by all the children. To her Julian, writing in old age, was to devote the best passages of his final book on his family. Only in England could Fanny Wrigley have existed. They would have liked to have taken her back to America with them seven years later, but they recognized that in that alien air she would have withered away. For her the only things right in the world were English things and she, undoubtedly more than anybody else, came within a few inches — though quite without set design — of turning the young Americans into English children. Her little special aptitudes were all unimportant and Julian calls her "trustworthy and incapable, indefatigable and unproductive, indispensable and futile." She was supposed to be the

children's nurse; she became everything and nothing. They all
loved her for her eccentricities, her irrational timidities, and her
courage, when danger threatened those she loved. A vague, untidy
mass of brown hair, insecurely pinned, protruding myopic eyes,
a little nose and chin overbalanced by a long mouth, walking
always in a fog, trusting to luck and providence — so Julian,
seventy years later, pictured her. Yet he has to confess that her
scarecrow figure was a mirage, and that in spite of her being so
intensely personal, she was not a person at all but "an abstraction
masquerading as an entity." It was she who was always with the
children in the house or when they were playing in the leafy
garden full of hawthorn and yellow laburnum and violets and the
bushes that grow the gooseberries regarded by the English as the
stand-by for dessert.

The Hawthornes, not being English, did vary their desserts
somewhat, and the children were permitted, especially when
there were guests, to come in for the last course, to listen in
silence to the improving conversation, and to partake of whatever
sweet things were on the table. As Sophia did not allow her
children to eat meat, they used to lie in wait in the hall when
the deliciously smelling roasts were being taken into the dining
room, and there maids almost as indulgent as Fanny Wrigley
permitted a surreptitious taste of the dainties. The young Hawthornes used to wonder how grownups could ever bring themselves to leave the table.

At this time Hawthorne, in his attempt to become a good
Englishman, actually conducted family prayers. He never went
to church, nor had Sophia done so since her marriage, though
they were formally Unitarians and quite sincerely — even touch-
ingly — religious in spirit. But whatever good he may have
thought these pious exercises did the assembled servants, they
only the more strongly convinced him that the English "bring
themselves no nearer to God when they pray than when they
play cards." Yet he carried the ritual through, despite his distaste

for it, perhaps in the hope that his children, who had up to this time never attended a service, would somehow or other acquire a tincture of religious sentiment through these proceedings.

They saw little of their neighbors — was it not to escape the demands of society that they had fled to Rock Ferry? However, with one couple in the Park they became rather friendly. This was Mr. and Mrs. Squarey, upon whom Sophia and Una called, liking Mrs. Squarey because she so strongly resembled their astronomer friend, Maria Mitchell. As Mr. Squarey was decidedly square of countenance, with his squareness emphasized by mutton-chop whiskers, and as Mrs. Squarey was inclined to be globular, Hawthorne always referred to her (at home) as Mrs. Roundey — a jest richly enjoyed by infantile minds. It was in the company of these amiable neighbors that the Hawthornes went to see many of the local sights, although they would have preferred to have gone alone.

The closest English friends were the ones they made at once — Francis Bennoch and Henry Bright. Perhaps these were the only two Englishmen of whom Hawthorne was ever really fond, though, to make up for this, of *them* he was very fond.

Both were successful businessmen with literary interests — Bennoch being, as a volume of verse testifies, a poet somewhat in the manner of Burns. But though Henry Bright could turn out a competent set of verses on occasion, he was a critic, or at least a reviewer, for the *Westminster* and the *Athenaeum*. He never wrote any books, however.

He was at least twenty years younger than Hawthorne and unlike him in every possible way, except that both men were Unitarians. Their friendship was of that masculine sort which, if not founded upon argument, at any rate flourishes upon argument. They incessantly debated the respective merits of the British and the American political and social systems, with animation, with perfect courtesy, but without either man ever yielding an inch or liking the other a whit less because of their disagreements.

The most vivid account of Henry Bright is that given by Rose who describes him as so thin and tall that he waved like a reed, with prominent eyes so bright, though shortsighted, that they shone like ice, and a nose that was a masterpiece of English aristocratic formation. His teeth were white and doglike in his very red lips, and his chin, below his pink cheeks, was as deeply dimpled as though an axe had dented it. He wore a monocle and used it as only an Englishman can, says Julian, "to express surprise and curiosity, to wind up a sentence, to point an epigram, to cover embarrassment, to indicate scepticism, to give zest to a joke." It was with him a bodily organ, something alive. Everything with him, Rose decided, added up to a total of ravishing refinement. His peculiar way of laughing particularly entranced his friends; even in retrospect Rose enjoyed the way it invariably ended as a "whispered snort from the great mountain range of his nose."

The children loved him as much as they loved jolly Mr. Bennoch. One scene they never forgot. At high tea Mrs. Hawthorne produced a bottle of raspberry jam. Henry Bright helped himself liberally, saying, "Oh, raspberry jam! Nothing I like better than raspberry jam, Mrs. Hawthorne."

So it would seem. He took it — and then a second helping — eating with an unabashed boyish gusto.

"Where did you get this jam, Mrs. Hawthorne?" he wanted to know. "I've never tasted anything so delicious."

Sophia smiled at his pleasure. Where had she got it? Why, it was very ordinary jam, bought at the grocer's where everything else came from. But just then Sophia looked more closely at the jam pot, and both she and her husband saw something the shortsighted eyes of Henry Bright would never see: it was full of millions and millions of minute ants who had gone there in endless columns and so perished sweetly. It was their brittle little bodies that gave this jam the crunchy taste poor Henry relished so much.

But what to do? Sophia looked at her husband, and he looked at Sophia, and wordlessly they decided. Why spoil Henry's enjoyment? Already he must have eaten a million or so of these little insects; another million or two would hardly make much difference. Making a sign to the giggling children that they were to say nothing, they allowed Mr. Bright to go on and finish the jam, his bright eyes shining more brightly than ever as he pronounced between mouthfuls "Capital jam, Mrs. Hawthorne! I wish we had some more of that jam at Sandheys."

Half in awe, and half in that heartless curiosity children display in what is going to happen — but altogether in amused delight — Una and Julian and Rose watched while Mr. Bright devoured that uniquely delicious jam.

The whole Bright family charmed the Hawthornes. They were connected with the great houses of the Percys and the Stanleys, and by marriage with Mr. Gladstone. Immensely wealthy, and owners of the largest ships afloat, they lived in a combination of state and simplicity in near-by Sandheys. Hawthorne habitually complained that there was too much beef and beer about an Englishman. This was not the case with Henry Bright. Still less was it so of his father, a white-headed old gentleman who looked like an Oriental. Sophia especially was pleased with the elaborate courtesy with which he treated his wife. Writing to her mother she described the pretty scene: "the drawing room, through whose bow windows of plate glass one looked out upon enameled lawns where strutted two stately cranes. Inside the house there was no noise at any time except the angry squall of the cockatoo. When he got angry he tore at his cage and the long feathers on his head became erect like so many swords drawn from their scabbards."

In this kind family, good as well as clever, well educated,

accomplished, and entirely united, Sophia could discover no shadow or flaw. "Health, wealth, cultivation, and all the Christian graces and virtues — I cannot see the trail of the serpent anywhere in that Paradise."

CHAPTER II

Rose and Her Father

To Hawthorne the consulate was anything but Paradise. He not only did his work efficiently and honestly but sometimes showed great courage and generosity in going outside the paths of routine to perform what he felt to be his duty. Work so done must always be some satisfaction; yet Hawthorne groaned in the pain of his harness. To Ticknor he complained, "I cannot express, nor can you conceive, the irksomeness of my position, and how I long to get free from it. I have no pleasure in anything – a cigar excepted: even liquor does not enliven me; so I very seldom drink any, except at some of these stupid English dinners." Again to Ticknor he says more specifically: "What with brutal ship-masters, drunken sailors, vagrant Yankees, mad people, sick people, and dead people (for just now I have to attend to the removal of the bones of a man who has been dead these twenty years) it is full of damnable annoyances."

Occasionally, however, even the damnable annoyances had an entertaining side. When writing *Our Old Home* he gave a most amusing account of a doctor of divinity from New Orleans who was brought into the consulate in delirium tremens after a week's spree and sent home at the expense of the consul. But this account rather carefully expurgates what Hawthorne related to Ticknor and set out in his notebook. He was powerfully eloquent in sermon and prayer, Hawthorne had been told. To Ticknor he says, "He shook in his shoes. Not knowing whether I should ever have another opportunity of preaching to a doctor of divinity (an Orthodox man, too), I laid it on without mercy; and he promised never to forget it. I don't think he ever will."

Rose pictured the consulate in her mind as an ogre's lair, though the ogre was temporarily absent, while her father, like a prince bewitched, was compelled, because of a rash vow, to languish in the man-eater's den for a term of years. Indeed the dingy offices in the smoke-stained Washington Buildings on Brunswick Street almost inevitably suggested as much to a child's imagination. Little Rose climbed up the dark, narrow stairs to an equally dark and narrow passage — often filled with rough and tough looking men waiting for an interview — and then, having passed the outer office where sat the lean, sad looking bewhiskered Mr. Wilding, the Englishman who was the American vice-consul, came at last to the ogre's lair. It was a room about fifteen feet by twelve, made darker by being painted in imitation of oak panels, but disproportionately high. The first thing Rose saw on entering was a hideous, colored lithograph of General Taylor, life size, above the mantelpiece on whose wood the American eagle was painted. On top of the bookcase a fierce and terrible bust of General Jackson, with a military collar that rose stiffly above his ears, glared horribly at any Englishman who crossed the threshold. No wonder that little Rose shuddered. No wonder that she, and all the children, wished that they could always have their delightful father at home.

He carried on his duties grimly but with some humor. It was no laughing matter, however, that almost immediately after their arrival Congress cut down the consular remuneration. Until then the appointees had been paid certain port fees, and Hawthorne found it a pleasant way of making money to get two dollars every time he signed his name — a good price for an author's autograph, he thought. At Liverpool, in the busy season, so Crittenden, his predecessor had told him, he had made as much as fifty pounds in a single day.

The action of Congress changed all this, and the president could do nothing, in the face of its fit of economy, to protect the income of his friend. Sophia wrote her sister, Elizabeth Peabody, that it would mean a loss of $20,000 to them.* More specifically we have the case set out in a letter Hawthorne wrote the president on June 7, 1855, telling him that a consul could not possibly live there and maintain a family at less than $5,000 a year — unless he renounced all social life and the whole advantage of residence in England. Hawthorne went on to point out that the salary allowed under the new law — $7,500 — would leave, after paying his office rent and his clerical staff, a net $2,500 a year. "A man," he concludes, "might be comfortable with this sum in a New England Village, but not, I assure you, as the representative of America in the greatest commercial city in England. For Heaven's sake do not let the next session pass without having the matter amended."

The president did what he could and Cushing, the attorney-general, ruled that consuls might retain their notarial fees. On that basis Hawthorne found that he could hope to clear about $8,000 a year. And as Hawthorne decided that they would limit their domestic expenses to $3,000, they hoped to be able to save the remaining $5,000 for their children's future. Ticknor, acting as Hawthorne's investment broker in America, was able in the course of time to salt away a considerable amount of money for his friend.

There was of course no authorship — except for the keeping of the *Notebooks* from which he salvaged *Our Old Home* and which Sophia published, in a bowdlerized form, after his death. Yet almost every book store contained copies of *The Scarlet Letter* and *The House of the Seven Gables* and *The Blithedale Romance*, all in pirated editions. Sophia came in after seeing a copy of

---

* This is in an undated letter at Hawthorne, N. Y., but one obviously written not long after their arrival. I refer to it because this is an unpublished document that supplements many others already published, making much the same complaint.

Twice Told Tales at the railway station effervescing with mild indignation.

"To see all those books of yours!" she exclaimed, "and you're not getting a penny of royalties!"

At this her husband smiled serenely and lit a cigar. "Neither are that damned mob of scribbling women," he said, "that's some consolation."

"Who are these — well, what you said?" Sophia asked.

She got the answer she expected, "That *Lamplighter* woman — what's her name? — Maria Susanna Cummins. Think of it, Sophia — she has sold seventy thousand copies of her trash!" And both the Hawthornes had to console themselves with the sort of reflections that are still a solace to serious authors. But philosophical though the author of *The Scarlet Letter* might be, he did not fail to make an acid observation in his *Notebook* or to let off steam in a letter to Ticknor. "What is the mystery of these innumerable editions of the *Lamplighter*, and other books neither better nor worse? — worse they could not be, and better they need not be, when they sell by the hundred thousand."

Despite their desire to live economically, the Hawthornes did go into local society. There were obligations the American consul could not always avoid. Moreover as an author Hawthorne felt, as he put it in his *Notebook*, that it would be "ungracious, even hoggish — not to be gratified with the interest they expressed in me." It made him feel like a hippopotamus stared at in a zoo, or an insect imprisoned under a tumbler. Yet, whether as consul or author, he performed the social duties demanded of him. He anathematized all dinner parties, but he went. And what did it matter that he refused to be perfectly formal in the matter of ties? Fields noticed that whenever he entered a room his personal appearance excited a rustle of admiration. Handsome and distinguished to the end, at this time he was still clean shaven. Well might Sophia write to her father, after a visit to the Brights: "I suppose it is useless for me to say that he was by far the handsomest person present and might have been taken for the king of them all." Even better was it — as Sophia related in the same letter — when Rosebud greeted them on their return home, her cheeks glowing, her eyes sparkling, as happy as a child could be, and shouting, "Joy! Joy!"

But much better than country houses or dinner parties were the contacts with friends — old and new. There was Charlotte Cushman, the famous actress, whom they had known in America and who went to see them in the first months of their English stay. Not yet forty, she had already announced her retirement from the stage, though she was not able to put this into effect for twenty years. Tall, dark, with a rather ugly but expressive face, she had immense vitality, and in the appalling drawing room at Rock Park, the Hawthornes discovered how simple, gentle, and sincere she was. During her stay she fascinated Rose, both with herself and the tiny trinkets attached to her watch chain. Seated on her lap, the little girl went over these fairy wonders again and again — an elfin easel with a colored landscape, a quarter of an inch wide; a tragic and a comic mask, made for the smallest of gnomes; a cross of the Legion of Honor; a dagger for a pigmy; two minute daguerreotypes of friends, each encased in a gold locket the size of a pea; a little opera glass; faith, hope, and charity, in their emblems of heart and anchor — such things Rose fingered entranced. And her stories and her songs — these did much the same for Rose's elders.

Hawthorne was at his most genial best during those years in England. At Salem after his father's death in distant Surinam, his mother committed a kind of lifelong suttee, keeping her own room and seeing nobody. Nathaniel and Elizabeth and Louisa showed a similar taste for seclusion, taking their meals alone and going for solitary walks after nightfall. From all this Sophia had rescued him, but even in Lenox, in 1851, Sophia was able to write to her sister, Elizabeth, "He has but just stepped over the threshold of a hermitage. He is but just *not* a hermit still." He was far from being the gloomy man that people often thought him; even less was he morose. But melancholy was one of the elements of his genius. His friend, Hillard, told him, "I should fancy from your books that you were burdened with a secret sorrow," and Melville really believed there was some skeleton in the cupboard. But what Hawthorne himself described as his cursed habits of solitude and what Field called his physical affinity with solitude, seemed, at least for a time, completely to disappear. To the children he had always been a wonderful companion, and here Rose missed something that Una and Julian had enjoyed. The others sometimes had wished wistfully, that their father had not had to write books, as such work bound him to his study. From nine to five every day, while Rose was gathering her first memories, he was in that detestable ogre's lair. Rosebud, or Bab, as her father called her, grew into girlhood receiving hints from the others that made her feel that she was a stranger who had come into that family too late.

Yet to none of his children did Hawthorne impart more of himself than to his youngest child. Looking back she was able to say that if he was at all "morbid," she would recommend morbidity to everybody. She understood that he was often stricken with the sorrow of the world. It was his compassion that she inherited. But though Sophia bubbled and sparkled with gaiety, Rose said, "Even she did not fill us children with the zest of content which he brought into the room for us." If he came into the room at dusk, before the lamps were lit, the place seemed to be illuminated by his face. Sophia's name for him was "our sunlight." Of both parents it was Una who said the last word, "After having had them it will certainly be my own fault if I am not pretty good when I grow up."

That Hawthorne was now so mellowly happy was no doubt partly due to his growing fame, and even more to the fact that at last there really did seem to be some chance of doing something for his family out of what he could save from the proceeds of his consular office. But also it was because, grumble though he might about England and the English, he felt very much at home. "I am getting a little too John Bullish," he told Ticknor, "and must diminish my allowance of roast beef, brown stout, port, and sherry. I never felt better in my life. England is certainly the country to eat in, and to drink in."

The children all agreed that they had the most wonderful of mothers in the small, graceful, vivacious woman whose smile Julian was to call a delicate sunshine. And they were perhaps blessed more than they ever knew in the fact that the marriage of the Hawthornes was one of the most idyllically happy ever known. But it is the measure of Hawthorne's fascination over those who saw him at closest quarters that, after the highest words of praise had been given to the mother, something still higher was to be said of the father.

Of all his articulate children it was the youngest and most gifted who had, at the end, the best to say. Julian does have the fine encomium, "He was beautiful to be with, to hear, touch, and experience," but Julian presents mainly the externals of his father; it is Rose who reaches to the depths of his being. That she was in such awe of him gave their Sunday evening games of blindman's bluff so exquisite a delight. She too had eyes that took in his rolling gait, perhaps inherited, she thought, from their sea-faring ancestors. More important, she noticed that, tender as his actions could be, he was sparing of tenderness and threw none of it away. He seemed, indeed, to be the merriest in that household, but Rose was almost alone in guessing that he was not as happy as he seemed, and also the reason for this. From the time she was hardly more than a baby she perceived that he did not need to speak much, that with him words came almost as an anticlimax. That was why he was so charming a companion: he knew without her telling him what was in her mind, and she knew that he knew.

CHAPTER III

Discovering England

Rose in the bosom of her American family was growing up to be an English child.

But for that matter, all the Hawthornes were becoming English in various degrees. And Henry Bright scored more than a debating point against his friend when he told him, "Hawthorne, we're making you an Englishman."

"Not yet, Henry."

Bright's bright eyes beamed at him, the doglike teeth showed in his smiling mouth, the monocle went an extra large circle in the air; then Bright shot:

"Not yet, perhaps. But you're on the way, Hawthorne, you're on the way." And the climactic, whispered snort came from his aristocratic nose, to conclude his laughter.

It is indeed impossible to grow up in England — so long as one avoids the hideous ugliness of her industrial towns — without having the country close quietly upon one to hold the heart. Other countries may be as beautiful — or have spots as beautiful as anything in England; no other country saturates the imagination or seizes the affections in the same way. Even dear, queer Fanny Wrigley, laughed at and loved by them all, helped powerfully though quite unconsciously in this process. When Sophia visited Norris Green with Henry Bright, she found herself sinking into a downy enchantment, walking those delicate pea-green lawns, which had a luster on them. But all England was lustered, all England was enchanted — except the black, miserable hole of Liverpool where Hawthorne languished from morning to

25

the late afternoon in the ogre's lair. "What a country is Great
Britain!" Sophia wrote in her only book, "Every atom of it is
a jewel." And Hawthorne, writing in mid-March of his first
English Spring, noted that the old-fashioned flowers in New
England gardens here grew wild. Blue bells, primroses, foxglove,
crocuses — these were as common as daisies and dandelions. He
found something very touching and pretty in the fact that the
Puritans should have carried the English field and hedge flowers
across the Atlantic, and nurtured them in their gardens, so that
they seemed to be entirely the product of civilization. He often
took the children with him on walks in the neighborhood and into
their little minds there sank the loveliness of the thatched and
whitewashed cottages of the villages, with their tiny, crowded
gardens of hollyhocks and marigolds.

One of these places, Eastham, was especially dear because of a
yew tree which, already for six centuries, had been famous as the
Old Yew of Eastham. It went back to Saxon England and stood
sturdily there before the Doomsday Book was written, and promised to stand until Doomsday dawned. It had a great gap like a
door on one side, and there on Sunday afternoons the Hawthorne
children "played house" while their father, seated upon one of
its ancient roots, smoked his cigar and meditated.

The children's education may have been somewhat haphazard,
considered from its formal aspect, but it was effectual. Sophia,
who was learned enough to read in one rainy day in her twentieth year de Gérando, Fénelon, St. Luke, Isaiah, Young, *The
Spectator*, and four of Shakespeare's plays while she sewed, and
who knew French, German, Italian, Latin, Greek, and Hebrew,*
supervised the education of the children, with her husband's

* Yet Sophia was clearly accomplished and versatile rather than learned.
There may be reason to wonder how deeply she possessed any formal
branch of knowledge, but there is no doubt at all as to her wide, general
culture.

assistance, and, in the more elementary branches, that of Fanny Wrigley. Later on, English governesses were engaged, all of whom proved grotesquely incompetent; and in the end the first graduate of Antioch College, Ada Shepard, had to take charge of this department. But they had the best sort of education that can be given gifted children — an irregular attendance at classes and the constant association with remarkable people. For Rose just then the richest part of it was the rambles she had with her father or Fanny along the hedge-bordered lanes picking baskets of roses and honeysuckle and daisies. Everywhere, as though in compliment to these children, the hawthorn grew. Rose used to come back with a flowering branch of it on top of the basket.

What there was of actual teaching, at this time, was done mostly by Sophia. She wrote on December 11, 1853, to her sister Elizabeth Peabody — who had been Alcott's assistant in his Boston school and who was regarded as a great authority in all educational matters: "I have not read Dickens' *Child's History*, but Mr. Hawthorne seems to think it very inadequate and bought Mrs. Markham's. I write questions to this and Una, from the questions, writes her own little history. I do not doubt that I shall learn to play as well as Una, and so be able to teach Rose — Madame Hunon asks three guineas a quarter."*

If the religious education of the children had so far been neglected — except for the performance of family prayers, English style — this was not because the Hawthornes were lacking in religious belief or sentiment. Rather it was because Hawthorne and his wife had so idealistic a notion of religion that they were waiting for an opportunity of presenting it in its most perfect form. Though they were Unitarians of the school of "the Pope

* Sophia's idea of learning music to save three guineas a quarter shows how intent she was on the smallest economy. The family lived comfortably, but every possible penny was put by for the future.

of Boston," the great Dr. William Ellery Channing — that is, Unitarians who held what most Protestants today would consider rather old-fashioned Christological views — they had no great enthusiasm for the stuffiness of the services at most Unitarian churches. As Mr. Barzilai Frost, the minister of the first parish at Concord, was a prosy, though worthy, old gentleman, they stayed away from his church.

But now in Liverpool there was a good friend, the great Doctor's nephew, W. H. Channing. When Hawthorne was at Brook Farm this Channing used to visit them and hold memorable open-air services in the woods. Then the Brook Farmers would hold hands in a circle while the eloquent preacher almost made them *feel* the at-one-ment.

But Hawthorne, though he liked Channing personally, was disposed to be what might be called anticlerical. In the days when he was living in the Old Manse he had written: "I find that my respect for clerical people, as such, and my faith in the utility of their office, decrease daily." This attitude of mind is something we should remember when we see him in Italy, looking with a baleful eye on the priests swarming everywhere. His prejudice against them was due to his dislike of Protestant ministers. It was with the aridity of New England Unitarianism in mind that he wrote: "We certainly do need a new Revelation, a new system, for there seems to be no life in the old one."

Sophia went to hear Mr. Channing preach at the Renshaw Street Chapel, and Hawthorne later sent Julian, when Sophia and the girls were in Portugal. The Hawthorne and Channing families were friendly, Julian finding a companion in young Frederick, though his sister Fanny, later to be married to Edwin Arnold, the future author of *The Light of Asia*, was a bit too old even for Una. But Hawthorne continued to worship God in country walks, when his cigar was the only incense.

But soon after their arrival in England, they all attended services in Chester Cathedral, so as to do the thing in the best possible style, or as Sophia put it, "that the children might go to church first in a grand old cathedral, so that their impression of social worship might be commensurate with its real sublimity."

Unfortunately, it did not turn out quite as Sophia had hoped. The service was performed in a stately fashion, and the Book of Common Prayer must have had an appeal for them, as it does for every literary person; but the children were terribly bored during the sermon — which Una wrote to one of her aunts to say was very "tegeuse." Julian even yawned audibly at one point, which so startled his father that he exclaimed, "Good God!" — thus of course making things much worse.

In spite of this disappointment Sophia received communion at the same cathedral the first Easter the Hawthornes were in England, completely disregarding the fact that she was a Unitarian. Indeed the Hawthornes, American though they were, never for an instant forgot their English ancestry. England was, as Hawthorne called it in one of his books, their old home — and in it they made themselves at home, even in the English Church.

It is instructive to note, however, that though the stately Anglican ritual impressed Sophia, she was able to write, "I think the English Church is the merest petrification now. It has not the fervor and unction of the Roman Catholic even (that is dead enough, and will be dead soon). The English Church is fat, lazy, cold, timid, and selfish. How natural that some strong souls, with warm hearts and the fire of genius in them, should go back to Romanism from its icy presence."*

Sophia's husband was equally emphatic after an Easter service at Chester Cathedral three years later when he confided to his *Notebook:* "The spirit of my Puritan ancestors was mighty in me, and I did not wonder at their being out of patience with all

---

* This idea of the Hawthornes of a once perfect Anglicanism, since degenerate, was applied by them to Catholicism, as soon as they encountered it in Italy. It must always be remembered that they judged — perhaps they could hardly do otherwise — the Catholic Church, about which they knew virtually nothing, by their fairly extensive knowledge of Protestantism.

this mummery, which seemed to me worse than papistry because it was a corruption of it." And he went on to comment on "these externals, into which religious life had first gushed and flowered and then petrified."

But though the Hawthornes were disappointed in the Church of England, they felt a very vivid interest in what they could see of the vestiges of Catholic England. One of the first pages of Hawthorne's *Notebook* is a description, made hardly a month after his arrival, of a walk the whole family had one Sunday afternoon to Lower Bebington. What most excited Hawthorne's interest was its church, built in 1100. And though that entry, and some later ones, shows that Hawthorne thinks of the thing as venerable because it was old, it became evident that his sensitive mind, like Sophia's was before long responding to the existence of a Catholicism which, for them, had so far had no real existence.

One of the aspects of Catholicism that appealed most strongly to both the Hawthornes was the veneration of the Blessed Virgin. In his *Notebook* Hawthorne records, as he did also in *Our Old Home*, what Sophia writes in her own book. It was of Lincoln Cathedral. "The Lady chapel is beneath it and here we saw a rich stone, elaborately carved shrine, upon which once stood 'the Virgin of Virgins' holding the infant Saviour; and just before it, a deep place is worn in the stone pavement, by the motion of the foot in making obeisance for ages. The statue is gone, the worship of 'Our Lady' has almost passed away from the land; but the deep print of homage is left indelible."

That feeling about the Blessed Virgin deepened in Italy. But there Sophia's prejudice against monks — fully shared by her husband — was if anything to increase. This blinded Sophia to what should have been obvious. In an old monastery church she thought that the luxuriousness of carving on the choir stalls suggested an "eat, drink, and be merry, for tomorrow we die" philosophy. Six pages later she supposes that the rushing, active life in the stonework expressed "the hopeless longing of the monks to escape from their thraldom." Dear Sophia, at that moment she was not very intelligent, or even very consistent. But what was probably at the bottom of it all was her feeling, as an exceptionally happily married woman, of antagonism to the concept of celibacy. It appeared in a queer form when she saw the tomb of some mediaeval noble and his second wife. To the scandal of the verger who was showing them around she struck the recumbent figure on the head with her parasol asking, "And where's your first — you awful old thing?"

Sophia had quite a way with vergers. Writing to her father on August 27, 1854, she tells of a visit to an old church in company with George Bradford. As she could not find a shilling in her purse she handed out half a crown. The verger, she says, was thunderstruck and looked at her as though she were the Grand Duchess of the Gold Coast. When they left he bowed low and addressed them as "My Lord and My Lady." She enjoyed that, but, both as a good American and a Christian, she was shocked that the Marquis of Westminster's country house of Eaton Hall had in its chapel raised seats for the noble family. She could not forgive the Marquis that, though he did have "an income of £1000 a day" and gold hinges on his doors and even a torque of gold reputed to have been worn by her ancestress, Queen Boadicea.* What the Hawthornes felt was a proprietary right in England. "It is our forefather's land; our land, for I will not give up such a precious heritage." So Hawthorne exclaimed in one of his rare outbursts.

* Hawthorne in his *English Notebooks* also has an account of all this, along with some rather caustic comments on his friend, George Bradford — his lack of dignity, his inane inquisitiveness, his conscientiousness which "seems to be a kind of itch — keeping him always uneasy and inclined to scratch!" Sophia of course left all that out in her edition of his book, not only because it was unkind, but because it was, as she thought, indelicate.

It was in large part because he felt that, in some sense, he was still an Englishman that he was so free (in private) with his criticisms of Englishmen. His favorite complaint was that there was too much beef and beer about them, that they were unspiritual — "gross even in ghostliness." This offended his delicacy; but he resented it all the more because of the glaring contrast between the wealth of the rich and the poverty of the poor. This shocked and hurt him. But instead of hiding from it, as he might have done, and forgetting it entirely in what is called good society, his compassion was constantly driving him to haunts little frequented by American visitors.

He did not attempt to explain how this condition had come about; he was a novelist, not a historian, still less a sociologist. Yet he did ask, "Is it not possible that there may be a flaw in the title deeds?" He felt that there was something gravely amiss, and he was, in fact, on a trail that could have led him to comprehension, had he become aware of England's Catholic past. It could not be expected of him, however, that he would follow the matter further. What he did discover was that gorging and guzzling at the banquets he sometimes attended had an ugly underside in the slums of Liverpool where he saw women gather horse manure with their bare hands into buckets. Of course it was not "nice," and it is understandable enough that Sophia, being so very refined, should edit all such passages away. But the pain Hawthorne felt at such sights does him far more credit than the false delicacy Sophia showed.

Before the first month was out he was writing in his *Notebook:* "Almost every day, I take walks about Liverpool; preferring the darker and dingier streets, inhabited by the poorer classes. The scenes are very picturesque in their way; at every two or three steps a gin shop . . . men haggard, drunken, careworn, hopeless, but with a kind of patience, as if all this were the rule of their life. . . . I never walk through these streets without feeling as if I should catch some disease; but yet there is a strong interest in such walks; and moreover there is a bustle, a sense of being in the midst of life, of having got hold of something real, which I do not find in the better streets of the city."

Then he adds a passage which has exceptional interest in view of Rose's own career, for they corroborate her experience forty years later in the slums of New York: "Doubtless, this noonday and open life of theirs is entirely the best aspect of their existence; and if I were to see them indoors, at their meals, or in bed, it would be unspeakably worse."

Yet it would be unjust to Sophia even to suggest that she was not deeply distressed by the incongruity between these two aspects of England. "The English people," she was to write in a letter, "the ladies and gentlemen with whom we have become acquainted, are very lovely and affectionate and kind. . . . I suppose there is no society in the world that can quite compare to this. It is all stereotyped, crystallized, with the repose and quiet in it of an immovable condition of caste. There is such a simplicity, such an ease, such an entire cordiality, such sweetness, that it is really beautiful to see. . . . Provided that the lower orders could be redeemed from the brutal misery in which they are plunged, there could be a little more enjoyment in contemplating and mingling with the higher. But it seems as if everything must be turned upside down rather than for one moment more to tolerate such suffering, such bestiality."

So it is evident that, though Sophia Hawthorne did not perhaps often actually accompany her husband on these rambles of his in the Liverpool slums, she shared his indignation. Rose drew her compassion from her mother as well as her father.

But one must also commend Sophia for inserting, as an editorial note, a passage Hawthorne had printed in his chapter "Glimpses of English Poverty" in *Our Old Home*. For simply because it had been dealt with there, the plan of her editing of his *Passages from the English Notebooks,* demanded its omission. He had told how during a visit to a workhouse, a sickly, wretched child of six, scabby, and rheumy eyed, asked to be taken up by a gentleman in the party, and how though this was a fastidious and reserved person, he did, after some struggle with himself, embrace the child. And Hawthorne commented, "[I] am seriously of the opinion that he did an heroic act, and effected more than he dreamed of toward his final salvation, when he took up the loathsome child and caressed it as tenderly as if he had been its father."

What he did not say was that *he* was the man. So when, after his death, Sophia published the *Notebooks* he had kept in England, she put that passage in.* Though its date is February 28, 1856, and therefore belongs to a slightly later period, than most of the matters touched on in this chapter, it may be appropriately used at this point.

"After this, we went to the ward where the children were kept, and, on entering this, we saw, in the first place, two or three unlovely and unwholesome little imps, who were lazily playing together. One of them (a child about six years old, but I know not whether girl or boy) immediately took the strangest fancy for me. It was a wretched, pale, half-torpid little thing, with a humor in its eye which the Governor said was the scurvy. I never saw, till a few moments afterward, a child that I should feel less inclined to fondle. But this little sickly, humor-eaten fright prowled around me, taking hold of my skirts, following at my heels, and at last held up its hands, smiled in my face, and standing directly before me, insisted on my taking it up! Not that it said a word, for I rather think it was underwitted, and could not talk; but its face expressed such perfect confidence that it was going to be taken up and made much of, that it was impossible not to do it. It was as if God had promised the child this favor on my behalf, and that I must needs fulfill the contract. I held my undesirable burden a little while, and after setting the

* Even so, with the omission of a few sentences.

child down, it still followed me, holding two of my fingers and playing with them, just as if it were a child of my own. It was a foundling, and out of all human kind it chose me to be its father! We went upstairs into another ward; and, on coming down again, there was this same child waiting for me, with a sickly smile around its defaced mouth, and in its dim-red eyes. . . . I should never have forgiven myself if I had repelled its advances."

Rose was to show in later life how much she was the daughter of the man who wrote that. This passage and the one in the chapter "Glimpses of English Poverty" quoted above — which Rose thought the greatest thing her father ever wrote — molded her mind. In her old age she was still referring to it as the explanation of her life and work.

CHAPTER IV

The Court of a Kinglet

Hawthorne grew strong and stout in England and the children flourished, but Sophia, more and more as time went on, found that she was constantly suffering from bronchial complaints. Toward the end of November of the year of their arrival Hawthorne wrote to Ticknor: "We are all as well as this abominable climate will let us be. You speak of the 'wretched climate of New England.' God forgive you! You ought to spend a November in England."

In the middle of the following May they still had fires in the grates, and Hawthorne was telling Ticknor, "If I could have one week of my Concord hillside, it would do us more good than all the English air that ever was breathed." And when the whole family came down together with the whooping cough, though he and the children suffered no ill effects, Sophia's condition was such that Hawthorne seriously began to think of resigning his consular office.

It was characteristic of Hawthorne that even of the whooping cough he made a jest. Once, taken by a paroxysm while he was standing against the wall, he put his arms against it in such a way that he appeared to be trying to climb up. At this he laughed very much, and so did the others. Therefore to amuse them he often contrived to put the same act on again in his seizures. Then when he had stopped coughing he was ready to join them in laughing. But Sophia's cough was no laughing matter. It was clear that her chest was not built for England. Yet the Hawthornes were reluctant to give up the consulate until they had fully accomplished their purpose of gathering their nest egg. True that the egg was going to be much smaller than they had expected, and Sophia wrote to her sister, Elizabeth, that the bill in Congress had cost them about thirty-five thousand dollars in two years — as those two years, being a period of exceptionally good trade, would have given the consul huge fees had he been able to pocket them all. Even so, what they had contrived to save was a considerable amount, and in a few more years the family would be fairly well provided for — if only Sophia could hold out.

Dear loyal woman! It was wonderful to what expedients she was prepared to resort. A little later she came forward with the desperate suggestion, brightly offered, of staying in her room all through the winter and keeping it at an even temperature and getting what exercise she needed with a portable gymnasium. She hated the thought of her husband's resigning his profitable job on her account.

Fortunately it did not come to that. Sophia and the girls were invited to spend the winter in Lisbon by John L. O'Sullivan, the newly appointed American minister there.

This O'Sullivan was an old friend of Hawthorne's and, in the old *Democratic Review* days, one of his first editors. He was Una's godfather and to the other children "Uncle John" — when they did not refer to him as "the Count," a title which seems to have been not quite mythical though never used. His wife was "Aunt Sue" in the family.

O'Sullivan was a very charming man with, however, one fault that was to cost the Hawthornes dear. As Julian was to put it, with a tinge of bitterness, "He was always full of grand and world-embracing schemes, which seemed to him, and which he made appear to others, vastly practicable and alluring, but which invariably miscarried by some oversight which had escaped notice for the very reason that it was so fundamental a one." Yet that statement of the case is a bit closer to the truth than what Julian permitted himself to say later, when he represented the ten thousand dollars O'Sullivan got out of Hawthorne as a loan. It was simply a very bad investment — in a copper mine in Spain. At the time, when they listened to the eloquent O'Sullivan talking, they were all quite sure that their fortunes were made. A dividend of 1000 per cent was promised from the start.

There was something romantic about the whole family. O'Sullivan's great-grandfather, who was a British officer, had once horsewhipped John Paul Jones. ("How singular it is," commented Hawthorne, "that the personal courage of famous warriors should be so often called in question.") Madame O'Sullivan, as the Count's Italian mother was styled, had in Barbary been carried to the grave and was about to be lowered into it, when her husband insisted on seeing her beloved face once more, and then found her still alive. She was now a beautiful old lady, with delicate lace and dark, kind, weary eyes — the perfect picture of an aristocrat. But the best story of all, one that fascinated Hawthorne, was about Aunt Sue's grandmother. She had died young fifty years before. Later the coffin of one of her children was laid upon her own, in a family vault, and descended hard enough to burst hers open. "This was then found to be filled," wrote Hawthorne in his *Notebook*, "with beautiful, glossy, living chestnut ringlets, into which her whole substance seems to have been transformed. . . . An old man, with a ringlet of his youthful mistress treasured on his heart, might be supposed to witness this wonderful thing." Hawthorne's imagination brooded upon the incident, and he used it in his posthumously published *Dr. Grimshawe's Secret*.

Writing to her father at this time, Sophia says: "Mr. O'Sullivan has taken a vast palace of a house at Lisbon and he wants us all to go there and make a long visit. . . . He says that if by chance we lose sight of one another, we shall wander for years in vain to find one another again." She and the two girls were very

glad to accept this invitation. She was assured that the climate of
Lisbon was a specific for bronchial complaints. Though she and
her husband found it hard to separate, for even a few months, this
seemed to be the only way of his avoiding resigning his lucrative
consulate.

This same letter gives us a glimpse of the children's development. Doctor Peabody had wondered if the letters going to the
West Street house in Boston from Una could be her unaided
compositions. Sophia, bristling a trifle as she always did when
any of her children's performances were questioned, wrote: "You
ask if Una's letters are from her own brain. Certainly they are,
dear father, I never have anything to do with them, but to read
them after they are written. . . . She has quite the cacoethes
scribendi, and composes stories and poems in hexameters and
other meters all the time. . . . Julian also poetizes famously. . . .
There has been no regular study with the children for two
months and more. While the O'Sullivans were here it was quite
impossible, and we did not care much as they were learning
something else from such good society. Mr. O'Sullivan comes
as near perfection of goodness as any mortal I ever knew. Not
a particle of worldliness or selfishness in his disposition."

Sophia, much as she disliked the thought of leaving her husband, reveled in the prospect of the spaciousness of O'Sullivan's
palace and the grandeurs of the Portuguese court. Quite un-
worldly though she was, she took a naïve pleasure in what contacts she had with the great world. In anticipation of this she
writes to her mother about the lodgings at Rhyl in Wales, where
she entertained O'Sullivan. There they had to put up with
German silver and a very ordinary table service. "Ever since our
marriage," she went on, "we have always eaten off the finest
French china, and had all things pretty and tasteful; because you
know, I would never have *second-best* services, considering my
husband to be my most illustrious guest. But now! It is really
laughable to think of the appointments of the table at which

the ambassador to Lisbon and the American consul sat down last Saturday, when they honored me with their presence." She had to remind herself that they had gone to Rhyl, not for high life or the seeing of sights, but simply to get rid of the remnants of their whooping cough.

Now there arrived for Hawthorne, as a kind of anaesthetic to the pain of parting, a delightful September in London, where the family lived at 24 George Street, Hanover Square. During that time he gave himself up to the exploration of the sprawling city, avoiding for the most part ordinary sight-seeing, but instead allowing the great current of London to carry him wherever it would. All day long he wandered in a happy dream, and when at last he was too footsore to go further he would hail a cab and drive home, but only to continue his explorations the next morning. Generally he went alone, but when Julian was with him the boy noticed a marked difference between his father's expression then and on the country rambles around Rock Ferry. Where previously he had looked meditative and introspective, now his glance was alert, his face glowing with pleasure. He noted and observed everything, seldom spending more than a minute or two on any one object, "but with an inspection so comprehensive and searching that one felt sure he carried away the complete image of it with him." So keen were these delights, that he left Sophia and his daughters for the most part to their own little feminine devices. He was drinking in London as a toss-pot drains his tankard and wrote to Field that he wished he could spend a year there.

In Lisbon the eminently sociable Sophia had a time she thoroughly enjoyed, in her own different way. Nobody could be a more charming host than *Señor Ministro*. Sophia danced with the king, gave the princesses drawing lessons, went to the opera and royal balls and, in short, was entirely in her element. Even Rose quickly acquired an imperious demeanor — if indeed that was anything new with her. When some official at court was slow of comprehension she stamped her foot and exclaimed, "Understandy! understandy!" — after which of course the man knew just what to do.

In the letters that passed between Liverpool and Lisbon we get more than one glimpse of the fact that little redheaded Rose was already displaying a quick temper. Writing to Una, her father says: "Tell Rosebud that I love her very much, and that I wrote her a letter a little while ago and sent it to Uncle John, to be sent to her. She is the best little girl in the world, is she not? Does she ever get out of humor? Tell her that I wish very much to know whether she always behaves prettily, as a young lady ought. Is she kind to nurse?" To "his dear little Rosebud," her father wrote: "I hope you are a good little girl; and I am sure you never get into a passion, and never scream, and never scratch and strike your dear nurse, or your dear sister Una. . . . When you come back to England, I shall ask mamma whether you have been a good little girl; and if mamma (I hope) will say — 'Yes, our little Rosebud has been the best and sweetest girl I ever knew in my life. She has never screamed nor uttered anything but the softest and sweetest sounds. She has never struck Nurse nor Una, nor dear mamma with her little fist nor scratched them with her sharp little nails!' . . . And when Papa hears this, he will be glad, and will take Rosebud up in his arms and kiss her over and over again. But if he were to hear that she has been naughty, Papa would feel it his duty to eat little Rosebud up! Would that not be very terrible?"

Somehow one is glad to know, from this and other letters, that this Rosebud had thorns. Children who are too good are a bit painful. Even so, her father was not always obliged to harp upon her naughtiness. Instead we get this charming note: "I have put a kiss for you in this nice clean piece of paper. I shall fold it up carefully, and I hope it will not drop out before it gets to Lisbon. If you cannot find it you must ask mamma to look for it. Perhaps you will find it on her lips."

Meanwhile Hawthorne and Julian made themselves comfortable at Mrs. Blodgett's, in an atmosphere very different from that of the court of Dom Pedro V. And though the man and the boy both, in different ways, missed the family circle, there was much to enjoy where they were. The consul did not allow the fact that he was lodged in a room in which one of his predecessors in office had died in a fit of delirium tremens to disturb him — at any rate the ghost of the former consul did not appear to him. Now, for want of Sophia and the children for company he used to sit every evening in the smoking room playing cards and swapping stories with the American sea captains who were Mrs. Blodgett's guests. At first some of the men were a little shy of him because of his official position — for his literary reputation they cared, of course, nothing. Some had, in fact, met in his office as consul, one who was a good deal sterner than the man who, without any loss of dignity, made himself one with the company and liked by all at Mrs. Blodgett's —

> *Where the noble Yankee Captains*
> *Meet and throng, and spend their evening,*
> *Hairy all, and all dyspeptic,*
> *All of them with nasal voices,*
> *Speaking all through nasal organs,*
> *All of them with pig tobacco,*
> *All of them with Colt's revolvers.*

It was thus that Henry Bright described the scene in the measure of the newly published *Hiawatha*.

Julian was usually permitted to be present at these sessions, and delighted in them. But Julian's mind was turning for the first time to thoughts of love with a young lady of twenty-five, a niece of some other relative of the O'Sullivans. It had somehow come to his ears that this Miss Rogers had been flirting with Dom Pedro. So in the sitting room they had, where during the day Julian did — or was supposed to do — the lessons his father assigned each evening, the boy asked:

"Papa, how do you spell 'reprehensible'?"

"Why that big word, Julian? Who has been reprehensible?"

Julian blushed violently and tried to cover the paper on which he was writing. "Oh, nothing, I just wanted to know."

Hawthorne walked over to the fire to find a live coal with which to light his cigar. The maneuver was one designed to get himself in a position to snatch away the sheet of paper on which Julian was writing. There was his stinging reproof to the faithless Ella Rogers: "Lovely, but reprehensible Madham!" the letter began. Poor Julian! He simply withered under the load of unfeeling parental guffaws.

In the summer of 1856 there was a happy reunion, but not under the most fortunate of circumstances. At Bennoch's advice — which must have been given without any knowledge of the true state of affairs — the whole Hawthorne family, together with Fanny Wrigley, went to stay with a Mrs. Hume who conducted a school for girls at Shirley, about two miles from Southampton. Her pupils were on vacation, and so she had plenty of room.

When she first called on the family at their hotel, Hawthorne thought her "a pleasant and sensible woman," but on the schoolgirl commons she provided they nearly starved to death. So that at the end of three weeks Hawthorne — who had come to this from the groaning board at Mrs. Blodgett's — complained bitterly: "I shall forever retain a detestation of thin slices of buttered bread. She is an awfully thrifty woman, and nobody can sit at her table without feeling that she both numbers and measures every mouthful that you eat; and the consequence is, that your appetite is discouraged and deadened, without ever being satisfied. She brews her own beer, and it is inexpressibly small, and is served out (only to the more favored guests) in one very small tumbler, with no offer or hint of a further supply. There is water in the milk, and she puts soda in the teapot, thereby to give the tea a color, without adding to its strength. . . . I must say that I cordially hate Mrs. Hume — a little, bright, shallow, sharp, capable, self-relying, good woman enough." All that could be said in her favor was that she charged only £4 a week for the six of them — and at that price (two shillings a day a head) they should not have expected much. But how glad they were to leave for London where Bennoch had put at their disposal his house at Blackheath. The only redeeming feature — except the reunion itself — had been visits they had paid to Salisbury Cathedral, Stonehenge, and Netley Abbey.*

But once safely away from the detested Clifton Villa and in Bennoch's comfortable house, Hawthorne's spirits rose. He and Sophia were invited to the home of Mr. and Mrs. C. S. Hall to meet the famous Jenny Lind. The singer said something vague about *The Scarlet Letter* (which she probably had never read), and the novelist said something vague about her singing, which he had never heard.

When they were safely outside, Hawthorne turned to his wife and asked, "Sophia, what did you think of Hall?"

* It would seem, however, that at this time Sophia made — as many Americans did — a pilgrimage to Farringford in the hope of getting a glimpse of Tennyson. Though there is no mention of this in the *Notebooks*, Sophia's drawing of the Farringford Porch is preserved at Hawthorne, N. Y. Such a visit could have occurred at the time Hawthorne was obliged to leave his wife and children and run up to Liverpool for a few days, which would account for its not being mentioned by him.

"Well," she returned, "he was somewhat given to pouring out molasses and butter mixed, don't you think?"

Hawthorne laughed. "He certainly does that! But do you know who Mr. Hall is?"

"I suppose he is Mrs. Hall's husband."

"Worse than that, Sophia! Everybody says that he is the original of Mr. Pecksniff in *Martin Chuzzlewit*."

Sophia stopped and clapped her little gloved hands, "Of course, of course! I kept feeling that I'd met him somewhere before."

"Bennoch took me over to see them several times when you were abroad. I'm afraid the lady is just a bit Pecksniffian too. Do you know what she said at our first encounter? — that it had been the dream of her life to see Longfellow and myself."

Sophia's laughter trilled again, "Dearest, and what did you say?"

"What could I say? What I'd have liked to have said was 'what an object to live for!' At all events she has half accomplished her ambition and as they say that Longfellow is coming over this summer, the remainder may be rounded out. She is a nice woman; though, really, one could hardly be married to Mr. Pecksniff without its having *some* effect."

In the family circle that evening Hawthorne told of another figure of fun he had encountered while they were abroad.

"Of course poor old Martin Tupper," he said, "is a very genuine and likeable person. I can only suppose that God created Tupper to show how easily he could turn a gifted, upright, warmhearted fellow into a laughingstock for persons quite inferior to himself. I liked him and yet I was laughing at him all the time. The very ass of asses!"

"Papa," said Una, "Do tell us about him. What happened?"

"Well Onion" — this was the name Hawthorne had for his elder daughter — "the tubby little man greeted me with, 'Oh, Great Scarlet Letter!'"

The three children shrieked at that and Sophia asked, "How did you answer him?"

"I really don't know, Sophia. I don't think I actually did say, 'Oh, wonderous Man of Proverbs!' or 'Oh, wiser than Solomon!' though had I done so — and perhaps I did — I am sure he would have thought it perfectly appropriate. For in the drawing room he had six lithograph portraits of the Queen's children, as large as life, and all taken at the same age. They appeared to have been littered at one birth like kittens. They had all been presented to Mr. Tupper by her Majesty — and he is the only person to have been so honored."

"But why all at the same age?"

"I suppose, Sophia, that it is when they get to that age that each of the royal children receives a copy of *Proverbial Philosophy*. It is the age at which their minds become capable of comprehending the depths of its wisdom. Tupper is the most harmlessly vain man I have ever met; his vanity continually effervesces out of him, like ginger beer out of its bottle. He is so entirely satisfied with himself that he takes the admiration of all the world for granted. He does not expect you to express admiration; he cannot imagine that you do anything else."

At Blackheath that summer Mr. Jerdan reappeared, it so happened just while Hawthorne was reading the fourth volume of his autobiography, which he found in Bennoch's house. It was wretched twaddle, full of nothing but the parading of names of his famous acquaintances. Seen three years later, Jerdan was more uncouth than ever, and age made him merely timeworn, not reverend. When Sophia came in, her husband told her about the visit from one whom she had thought like Dr. Johnson.

"I'm afraid not, Sophia," Hawthorne told her. "Since we first saw him Bennoch has told me more about him. He's a very disreputable old man — though not less to be pitied on that account."

"What did he want?"

"I know what he wanted. Being at the consulate has made me very keen sighted. I can tell from the hang of a man's coattails if he's going to borrow money. That of course was what Jerdan wanted and I wouldn't have minded giving him a pound or so. I think he was leading up to it when he talked of getting me made a member of some literary institution. I didn't inquire further. It can't be a very high honor if this poor old fellow has anything to do with it. You should have seen his smile at parting — grim with age! Yet as he went down the steps in his shabby clothes I thought I could see some trace of the polished man of society, such as I suppose he must have been at one time. It was like those marble pillars we saw at Netley Abbey, Sophia — they were once smooth and shiny, now all roughened by the weather."

July and August passed pleasantly for them in Bennoch's house with its large garden, where when the sun was hot — and few things can be hotter than one of England's rare warm summers — Hawthorne read *Dombey and Son* in the shade, and in the cool of the evening played bowls with the children on the lawn. And it was at this time that Hawthorne met Miss Delia Bacon and became involved in the most extraordinary and extravagant act of charity of his life.

Miss Bacon had no possible claim upon him except that she was an American and friendless. He was impressed by her sincerity but not in the least convinced by the theory, then advanced by her, that "the old player," as she liked to call him, was an imposter and Bacon the true author of Shakespeare's plays.

Time after time Hawthorne had been imposed on, and each time he assured Ticknor, the careful manager of his funds, that it would be the last. Miss Bacon of course was no imposter, but a woman with a mission, a crank, and one who died insane. But Hawthorne saw that there were some jewels of insight under the vast mounds of her crazy erudition and, as he thought her book should be published, he undertook to pay for its publication, though — such was his delicacy — without letting her know. And when she demanded of him a fuller expression of faith in her theory than he could honestly make in the introduction he had written for her book, he handled her with such courtesy and deference that one would have supposed that she and not he was conferring a benefit. But indeed that was precisely what the mad lady did suppose; she was an enthusiast who had dedicated herself to a cause. As she was asking nothing, she demanded of others that they should be equally selfless. He swore in letters to Ticknor that this would be "the last of his benevolent follies" and in a moment of very mild irritation he called Miss Bacon "the most impracticable woman I ever had to do with — a crooked stick." But even after he had foisted five hundred copies on Ticknor and Fields by letting them know (without giving them the chance to refuse) that he was sending them that number of copies to dispose of in America, he found that he had had to spend about two hundred pounds on giving to the world a crackpot theory in which he did not have a particle of faith. It was all the more regrettable because both he and Sophia were trying to put away every penny they could save for the children's future.

Yet there the two of them sat, while the wondering children looked on, as their father and mother, together under the lamp, tried to puzzle out these, at that time, very novel Shakespearean theories. In a bewildered intentness they read night after night Miss Bacon's turgid and tumid manuscript. It was on the part of both of them pure compassion, and to justify its exercise they searched hard for and made the most of every passage that seemed at all striking.

But with the best will in the world Hawthorne could not make himself believe, though Sophia hit upon the ingenious formula of not disbelieving in Shakespeare but of more highly admiring Bacon. Both agreed to help the fanatical and tragic woman with whose all but unreadable masterpiece they were struggling.

CHAPTER V

Our Old Home

Hawthorne made no attempt to do any writing at this time, except for his official and personal correspondence, and those jottings which, in the end, made several formidable volumes. All this quite accorded with the children's ideas, for even at Concord, where he was always at home, they considered the time he spent in his study as so much time wasted. Una often used to tell Julian, "How nice it would be if Papa did not have to write."

But he still had that ingeniously contrived little desk, which the children were never tired of investigating. The cherubic faces painted on it by Hawthorne himself (one with a pair of black side whiskers), and still more the secret drawers, delighted them. And they often still saw him, sitting in the evening in the dining room, with the two-foot-square desk planted on the table, writing away and stopping every now and then to smear out a word with his finger and then write over the smear. As he told Ticknor, "When once a man is thoroughly imbued with ink, he can never wash out the stain." He also told Ticknor that his journal would be worth a mint of money to both of them, if only he would let him publish it. But he felt his comments much too frank and racy. He had too truthtelling a pen, was how he explained it to Elizabeth Peabody.

He seemed obsessed with horror at the heavy figures of England's women. To his *Notebook* and to Sophia he confided: "They are gross, gross, gross! Really I pity the men I see walking about with such atrocities hanging on their arms — the grim, red-faced monsters!"

Sophia laughed: "I can at least see that I don't have to be jealous."

"You do *not!* I really and truly believe that the entire body of American washerwomen would present more grace than all English ladies put together. Our women may get faded and thin and careworn as they grow old; but these English women — they simply become more earthy. I can't conceive of any grace of soul existing in such creatures; if there is, they ought to be killed so as to release spirits so vilely imprisoned!"

He was given to such outbursts, and Sophia knew she had to take what he said with the requisite grain of salt. But these complaints were too constant to be dismissed as of no consequence. Hawthorne made exactly the same complaint of England's men; and he liked nothing better than when he could charge both sexes with the same fault, as when in the refreshment room, he sat contemplating what was to him an amazing spectacle.

"What are you thinking of, dearest?" asked Sophia at their table, noticing the laughter flicker in her husband's brooding eyes.

"John Bull and his females in full gulp and guzzle," he answered.

Yet he liked Englishmen, and they liked him. As for England, he told Ticknor, he loved it so much that he wanted to annex it. Nor did he think this beyond the scope of possibility, though he hardly expected it to happen in his own time. "I have such a conviction of the decline and fall of England that I am about as well satisfied as if it had already taken place."

Hawthorne, as usual, had a divided mind. He was much too sensitive a man, too much of an artist, ever to be really happy, though one would think that he had as much cause for happiness as any man alive — a wife and children for whom he was the center of the universe, health, creative powers at their height, fame, and even a reasonable amount of wealth. But there was some secret malady in him — and this he passed on to the two children most like himself. It was a malady for which only Rose was to find a complete cure.

Bennoch, who had visited America and was aware that in American eyes Englishmen are extremely reserved, found Hawthorne — a man who was really far more reserved than any Englishman, despite his social gifts — sitting brooding before a fire in the grate. It had sunk low and Hawthorne's spirits appeared to have sunk with it. He was giving the black coals a few feeble and unskilled prods. As Bennoch himself was a bit of a poet he thought he had divined the trouble. "Give me that poker, Hawthorne," he said, "and I'll give you a lesson." Then he thrust vigorously at the center of the mass, which at once shot out a brilliant flame. "Now, that's the way," he exclaimed, "to get the warmth out of an English fire, and that's the way too to get the warmth out of an English heart! Treat us like that, my dear sir, and you'll find us all good fellows." In spite of all this Hawthorne to the end felt as he did when writing to Ticknor on November 9, 1855: "I HATE England though I love some Englishmen, and like them generally, in fact."

He did, however, have a good many happy times. Growl against England as he might, never for an instant did he or Sophia forget their English ancestry. England was theirs, and whatever dividing line there might be in political institutions, there was none whatever when it was a question of English literature. Accordingly they visited the English Boston (among other similar places), but they also visited the Shakespeare country, the Lake District, and Scotland because of Burns and Scott. Usually Rose was left behind with Fanny Wrigley, and occasionally Una as well. But sometimes the girls were brought to a certain point on these pilgrimages — as when they were deposited at Windermere, while the others pressed on to Grasmere and Rydal. But Rose continued to get letters from her father, in the strain of one written at a time when he was away from home. It is evident that she had not yet become a very "good" little girl. "Do you still thump dear Mamma," he had to ask her, "and Una, and Julian, as you did when I saw you last? . . . Be a good little girl, and don't tease Mamma, nor trouble Fanny, nor quarrel with Una and Julian; and when I come home I . . . shall kiss you more than once."*

The family always spent part of the summer, by way of a change from Rock Ferry, at some other little English town. The first of these places was Douglas in the Isle-of-Man. There the children seemed to be more interested in the tailless cats and the carters who gave their horses beer, than even in the fairies who had had here, so their mother told them, their last stronghold. So too had the giants and the enchanters. But when she pointed out a circle of stones to Julian as a place where the Druids had really and truly had a temple, he curled his lips scornfully and said merely, "Is that all?"

Sophia told in a letter of being rowed out to St. Mary's Rock because of its wonderful beach. There they found innumerable pretty pink shells among the pebbles. When Rosebud got her feet wet her mother had to take off her shoes and socks to dry them in the sun. The child's pink toes looked, on the rocks, like a new kind of shell. "You'd better be careful," her mother warned her, "because there's a gentleman over there looking for shells. He'll probably put your toes in his pocket and take them home for his little children." At this the child shouted with mirth.

* The original of this letter (which Rose quotes, but "edits" slightly, in her *Memories of Hawthorne*) is at Hawthorne, N. Y., along with many others of the letters used by her. But others again were sold to the collectors of manuscripts, though fortunately a good many were not so disposed of — especially in the case of those letters not drawn upon by Rose in her book.

Rhyl, visited the next month, proved a disappointment. Hawthorne described it as a most uninteresting place, full of holiday-making English people taking their pleasure sadly.

Southport, where they spent August, 1856, was much livelier, and the climate suited Sophia so well that they spent most of the winter there. Hawthorne, looking out upon a little city of bathing machines on the beach, liked to fancy that it might have been on this spot that the body of Milton's Lycidas, drowned in the Irish Sea, was washed ashore.

Here they engaged a Miss Brown as governess, one of a long line of incompetents. To the children she at once became a figure of fun; and they saw that the little dried-up woman, who looked rather like an insect, was almost totally ignorant of the "branches" she was supposed to teach. Especially was this true of geometry. Even little Rose, though she did not quite understand what it was all about, used to mimic Miss Brown's way of talking about a "parallel-O-gram" and of how the governess would mutter to herself in a mystified whisper, "The square of the hypotenuse is equal to the sum of the square of the two legs."

It was at Southport that the children discovered the delights of sea bathing and the horrors of the English bathing machine. Rose was too small as yet for more than a little paddling but Una and Julian, having undressed in their portable boxes, would be dragged out toward the waves, where a grinning and chuckling ogress, the bathing-machine woman, would thump on the door and when the children appeared, take them, with what seemed to be a gloating glee, to duck them, breathless and cold, deep in the slapping waters. How Julian used to dread to hear the voice of his attendant woman saying with a hideous parody of maternal affection, "Come, come, my little man!"

Here Julian, who had been reading Philip Gosse, acquired a small aquarium. There in a bell-like jar of sea water he had collected prawns and crabs and sea snails and even a small cuttle-

fish, and a pair of soldier crabs that never stopped fighting. All
the children would stand for hours fascinated before this
spectacle.

But one day the cuttlefish died and the water had to be changed,
so Julian sent one of the maids to get a fresh bucketful from
the sea. The next morning there was a ghastly sight inside the
jar. Every form of life it had contained was dead — even the
valiant soldier crabs being on their backs, with their last battle
fought. It turned out that the maid, to save herself the trouble
of going down to the beach, had filled the bucket at the faucet.
It was one of those awful tragedies of infancy, when it comes
home how wicked, how faithless grownups can be.

At Southport Herman Melville came to see them. Rose had
never seen him before, except for his seeing her as a baby at
Lenox, and the other children's memories were growing dim;
but they all felt they knew him well after hearing their mother
tell of one of the visits he had paid them. There he had told
them a wonderful story of a fight between savages on some Pacific
island, and of how one of them had performed prodigies of valor
with his club. He had told it all so vividly that after he had left
Sophia said, "Where is that club with which Mr. Melville was
laying about him so?" They both looked for it but could not
find it, so they asked Melville about it the next time he called.
All he could suggest was that it was still on that island.

When Hawthorne invited him to Southport, he arrived there
with a nightshirt and a toothbrush as his only baggage. Yet they
all saw that he was still very much of a gentleman in his instincts,
except for a streak of heterodoxy in the matter of clean linen.

The two men went out on to the beach and talked metaphysics,
as usual, and Melville announced that he had "pretty much made
up his mind to be annihilated." About him Hawthorne was to
write in a letter, "He can neither believe, nor be comfortable in

his unbelief; and he is too honest and to courageous not to try to
do one or the other. If he were a religious man, he would be one
of the most truly religious and reverential; he has a very high and
noble nature, and better worth immortality than most of us."

But something seemed to have passed away. Though Melville
left his trunk at the consulate, taking only a carpetbag with him
when he sailed a few days later, he made no effort to meet Hawthorne again, and Hawthorne's comment on him was, "The
spirit of adventure is gone out of him. He certainly is much over-
shadowed since I saw him last."

The favorite town of the Hawthornes proved to be Leamington to which they first went in the summer of 1855, to return there
a year later and again just before they left for the United States.
To it Hawthorne devoted a special chapter in *Our Old Home*, one
written with evident affection, though the place would not seem
to have had any very remarkable features, or to have been
specially old or beautiful. It was not much different from, let us
say, Tunbridge Wells, another inland watering place that is
the haunt of half-pay officers and ladies living on an annuity.
Tennyson, who lived there for a while, described Tunbridge
Wells as his abomination, and would probably have said the same
of Leamington. Hawthorne, however, liked it and even declared,
"I do not know a spot where I would rather reside than in this
new village of midmost old England."

Of some of the older places within easy reach — Warwick,
Coventry, Kenilworth, and Stratford — one can understand his
feeling that "he had been there before." Such places were, like
the old church at Bebington, to an imaginative New Englander,
as familiar as a wooden Massachusetts meetinghouse. But perhaps
it was precisely because Leamington issued no challenge and had
no antiquity but was established merely to secure an unpretentious
middle-class comfort that Hawthorne found it to his taste.

Moreover, Hawthorne in the fall of 1857 was at last released from the profitable drudgery of the Liverpool consulate. He was now his own man again and was glad to spend a couple of months unattached in England before going on to the continent. At 10 Lansdowne Terrace he found just what he wanted, "quiet, cozy, comfortable, social seclusion, and snuggery," and pronounced Leamington "the prettiest, cheerfulest, cleanest of English towns."

It was at Leamington that Ada Shepard joined them preparatory to their departure for the continent. She had graduated in June from Antioch, America's first coeducational college, where Horace Mann was president. She joined the Hawthornes on the understanding that she was to get her expenses but no salary. Her position was quite as much companion and interpreter as governess. In this last capacity she was infinitely superior to any of the Englishwomen employed. She was to stay with the Hawthornes for two years and then go back to America to marry her classmate, Henry Clay Badger.*

She did not come a day too soon. So far, the Hawthorne children had never been to school, nor were any of them to go for some years to come. And lessons taught by parents, however cultivated and conscientious, are liable to be somewhat haphazard. It was time that the accomplished Miss Shepard took Julian in hand when he could translate *Itaque conficiunt iter continuo cursu*, as: "So they came to the end of their journey with continual cursing." But with Ada there the children had regular classroom hours and in their instructress, a highly efficient young woman. As their wits had already been sharpened, they made rapid progress in the two years Miss Shepard had them under her charge.

* This she did and taught with him at Antioch College until the faculty resigned in a body. Trouble came upon her. She was not very successful with the girls' school she established in Boston. Then her husband's health broke down, and in 1875 (when she was still only forty) she was "lost" from a boat with at least the suspicion of suicide. Her time with the Hawthornes constituted the golden years of her rather unfortunate life.

It had been part of Hawthorne's charming modesty that he had made no effort to seek out the leading literary men of England, though his fame was such that any of them would have been glad to accept him as an equal. There were, it is true, some chance encounters, in which he ran into men as celebrated as Macaulay and Browning, but even in their cases Hawthorne did nothing to follow up the acquaintances made. So much was this so that Monckton Milnes (the future Lord Houghton) told Julian some years later that he felt that his father did not like him. Nor would the Hawthornes probably have got to know the Brownings as well as they did, had not chance thrown them together in Italy. At Mr. Milnes' famous breakfasts they saw everybody from the Marquis of Landsdowne (whom they mistakenly identified as Thackeray's wicked Lord Steyne of *Vanity Fair*) to Mrs. Nightingale and a daughter — but not the famous Florence. Most of the other literary men Hawthorne met were not of his own stature — Douglas Jerrold, Tom Taylor, Barry Cornwall, and the like. But he did twice seek out Leigh Hunt, perhaps because Hunt was now a forgotten figure and so not formidable to approach. And DeQuincey's daughters wrote asking him to visit them at Edinburgh. But that meeting failed to occur. It would seem that the only writer Hawthorne actually came to know among those whom he specially wanted to know was Coventry Patmore. Hawthorne had read aloud the recently published *Angel in the House* to Sophia and both were deeply moved. "It takes a *truly* married husband and wife to appreciate its exquisite meaning and perfection" was her encomium.

Tennyson they did see once and could have met very easily had Hawthorne not been so reserved. It was at the exhibition at Manchester which the Hawthornes frequently visited in order to prepare themselves, by a diligent study of the paintings there, for the wonders of Italy.

The whole family — even little Rosebud and Fanny Wrigley — were wandering in the galleries when they were told in hushed tones that the poet laureate was in the Room of the Old Masters. Hawthorne describes Tennyson as "the most picturesque figure, without affectation, that I ever saw . . . rather slouching, dressed entirely in black, and with nothing white about him except the collar of his shirt, which methought might have been clean the day before. He had on a black wide-awake hat, with a round crown and wide, irregular brim, beneath which came down his long black hair, looking terribly tangled." The description goes on to tell of the dark, worn, sensitive face, suggesting pain and sorrow, and Hawthorne noted his voice — some people used to call it a growl — "a deep bass . . . but not of a resounding depth, a voice rather broken, as it were, and ragged about the edges."

Sophia gave the rest of the story in a letter to her sister Elizabeth. It was Una who first caught sight of the laureate and cried, "Mamma! There is Tennyson!" There he was, the great poet, romantic and handsome, looking almost too good to be true.

Mrs. Tennyson and some of their children were with him, and as the Tennyson group moved to the next saloon, the Hawthorne group moved too, at a respectful distance. Passing a table where catalogues were on sale, his youngest child, a small boy, stopped with his nurse to buy one. That gave Sophia her chance. "So then," she wrote, "I seized the youngest darling with gold hair, and kissed him to my heart's content." He smiled back at her. For the rest of her life Sophia could boast that she had had Tennyson's child in her arms.

Later Fields, after he had heard of this, told Tennyson about it. "Why didn't he come up and shake hands with me?" The laureate growled, "I'd have been glad to meet a man like Hawthorne anywhere."

CHAPTER VI

The Vision of Europe

It had always been on Hawthorne's conscience to see Italy and to take Sophia there before returning to the United States. He looked upon this as an important part of the children's education. It was to use these opportunities to the full that the polyglot bluestocking Ada Shepard had been brought along. Sophia was in an ecstasy of joy, hardly daring to believe that this had happened at last. "To think," she cried, "of visiting all those places! All my life I have longed to see them."

Yet as so often happens with such things, there was a good deal of disappointment at first. The English Channel was crossed in a state of placid wretchedness, which Hawthorne avoided by the simple expedient of taking a glass of hot brandy and water. Huddled miserably on the sofa in the saloon, Sophia cheered up and smiled when Julian clattered in with the announcement that he could see France and that over there the sun was shining.

"Oh, Ada," Sophia called brightly to Miss Shepard, sprawled on another sofa in the blackest misery, "Oh, Ada, Julian says the sun is shining in France."

Ada never moved.

Paris they hardly did more than pass through. Hawthorne called on the American ambassador, who was worrying about the expected loss of his position under the new administration. As to this the consul who had just resigned said, "Though I am sorry for him, there is no good reason why Uncle Sam should pay Judge Mason seventeen thousand dollars a year for sleeping in the dignified post." A good and sensible man he decided, but "fat-brained."

Far more lively and intelligent was the astronomer Maria Mitchell, whom they had known in America, and who, like them, was on her way to Rome. Mrs. Squarey had reminded them of her, but really nobody was quite like this simple, bustling, hearty little woman, with a weather-beaten face and bright eyes. Humorous, quaint, and with the innocence of a child, they all loved her — especially the children, with whom at once she became another child. To them she pointed out the principal stars and Julian, proud of his new knowledge, at once went to his father and mother to tell them all about O'Brien's Belt. It was in her company that the Hawthornes entered Rome.

This happened on January 20, 1858, after a cold, wet carriage drive. "As we jolted along," Rose was to write long afterward, "my mother held me in her arms while I slept as much as I could, and when I could not, I blessed the patient, weary bosom upon which I lay exhausted. It was a solemn-faced load of Americans which shook and shivered into the city of memories that night."

Julian remembers a little differently that ride from Civitá Vecchia to Rome along a rough road reported to be infested with bandits. As evening fell the occupants of the coach saw or fancied they saw, lurking near the road, men in long cloaks with the suggestion of musket barrels about them. It may be that the Hawthornes were saved only because the mail coach, with guards, was within hailing distance ahead. Hawthorne, though he made a joke of the matter, proposed that they hide their store of gold in places where bandits would not think of looking. One of these was an umbrella, and this of course the children thought to be a delicious combination of romantic danger and humor. Hawthorne prudently kept a moderate number of napoleons in his pocket in case they *were* held up, so as to give the plausible impression of this being all he had. But long before eleven that wet, cold, dreary night, when they got to Rome at last, even Julian's enthusiasm had evaporated.

Rome, where they found lodgings at number 37 Palazzo Larazani, in the Via Porto Pinciana, was at first a bitter disappointment. Hawthorne had a bad cold and sat huddled up in his overcoat before an enormous and draughty fireplace. When he went out, he found the streets windy and cold and filthy; and on the ice-covered pavement in front of Saint Peter's, on which Julian was sliding with other boys, Hawthorne nearly fell down, which did not improve his temper. "Old Rome," he wrote, "lies like a dead and mostly decayed corpse, retaining here and there a trace of the noble shape it was, but with a sort of fungus growth upon it, and no life but of the worms that creep in and out."

Moreover, he and Sophia started with an extremely critical attitude toward the Catholic Church. It was not that they were specially hostile to its teachings or practices — rather the contrary, in so far as they understood them. But they were anticlerical, Hawthorne turning the animosity he felt toward Protestant ministers as a class against priests. And nowhere in the world do priests swarm as they do in Rome. To Hawthorne they would have been, under the best of circumstances, not a very obviously useful class of people; but he encountered several portly and even gross looking monks in the streets, and his distaste flared. "Monks at least should be ascetic," he growled to Sophia. "These fat pigs. . . !"

The one or two priests he actually met while in Italy he liked very much, and it is notable that the individual clerics introduced in *The Marble Faun* are sympathetically — almost sentimentally — depicted. But his dislike of the clerical body was never changed.

Toward the veneration of the Virgin both he and Sophia had

felt drawn when they had encountered its vestiges in England. That attraction now increased. And the mind of Hawthorne, whose compassion and understanding of humanity had already made him the confidant of so many troubled souls, found that the practice of confession in the Catholic Church strongly appealed to him. "What an institution that is!" he wrote. "Man needs it so, that it seems as if God must have ordained it. The popish religion certainly does apply itself most closely and comfortably to human occasions, and I cannot but think that a great many people find their spiritual advantage in it, who would find none at all in our formless mode of worship." But it was the *practice* that he approved; the dogmatic content of Catholicism seems to have been completely outside the range of his interests.

Hawthorne also noted with approval the Catholic use of religious pictures — so violently discarded by the Puritans. "I felt what an influence pictures might have upon the devotional part of our nature. The nail-marks in the hands and feet of Jesus, ineffaceable, even after He had passed into bliss and glory, touched my heart with a sense of His love for us." But there is no indication that he was aware that the center of Catholic worship is Christ upon the altar.

To the Hawthornes the wonders of the art they saw before them and Catholicism were inseparable. They understood that, as even the fifteen-year-old Una was to write to her aunt, there was here "[a] fount of glory and beauty from which the old artists drew so freely." And Rose many years later was to say, "In art, Catholicity was utterly bowed down to by my relatives and friends, because without it this great art would not have been."

How then was it possible for them to worship this Catholic art and reject the Catholicism? They had a formula to hand, one that had already done good service when, in England, they looked scornfully upon the established church as they found it — fat, complacent, and inert — and compared that actuality with an ideal

"Church of England." Over and over again this conversation took place as the Hawthornes gazed at a picture in a church or a gallery.

"What a wonderful thing the Catholic Church must have been in the days when it produced *that!*"

"How we must deplore its present corruption!"

It came to this, that the artistic power that had formerly proved Catholicism to be "true" no longer existed, that it had failed because of the corruption of Catholicism and therefore proved the corruption of Catholicism. But what these corruptions were there is never the slightest indication, unless it was that "those priests," like those Hawthorne had noticed at Amiens, were "jolly, fat, mean-looking fellows." It boiled down to much the same criticism that Hawthorne leveled a thousand times against Englishmen (and still more against Englishwomen), they were gross in appearance.

This criticism was never brought by the Hawthornes against nuns, perhaps because they were not so often seen on the streets, though the Hawthornes could have found fat (and therefore presumably "corrupt") nuns had they looked long enough. But the veiled women who occasionally passed them, always in pairs and with downcast eyes — it was impossible to think of them except as being very good. And Sophia, who took Rose to hear the Religious of the Sacred Heart at the Trinità dei Monti sing Vespers, was deeply moved by the exquisite purity of the singing. And Hawthorne thought "these holy sisters, with their black crepe and white muslin, really looked pure and unspotted from the world."

Rose Hawthorne was too young to have at this time much comprehension of the ideas of her father and mother about Catholicism. What got into her mind was the concrete idea that the monks who so abounded in the streets were so many demons eager for her intellectual blood. But the brotherhood of the Penitents, whose charitable function it was to see to the burial of the dead in a quasimonastic garb, for some reason were supposed to be relatively free from "superstition" — as they were noticed to be clean. And oddly enough — and yet not oddly, because all of us are aware of how we associate utterly disparate matters in the quaintest way — Rose, when she ate one of the brown Lenten pancakes sold in the square under their windows, and found that what looked so richly brown and appetizing was really savorless, at once became convinced that the mental grasp and the religion of the Italians were poor.*

Julian, writing after her death, said rather vaguely of Rose: "My sister and I never discussed religion; and, though we had gathered the impression that the Roman Catholics were somehow in error, we didn't know why, and were affected by the warm splendor of their performances." Probably this comment of Julian's is no more than a gloss upon what Rose herself had to say: "For the year ensuing this life in Rome, I entertained the family with dramatic imitations of religious chants, grumbling out at sundown the low, ominous echoings of the priests, answered by the treble, rapid and trustful, of the little choristers, gladly picturing to myself as I did so the winding processions in Saint Peter's." What is certain is that Catholic life, as witnessed by the observant little girl in Rome, though not in the least understood at the time, did leave upon her mind vivid impressions that were to endure and had much to do with her conversion to the Catholic faith more than thirty years later. In her first draft of the Roman chapter she was to write: "In the churches the chanting monks and boys impressed me differently. Who does not feel, without

---

* So also as is recorded in the manuscript "Rome," a first draft of one of the chapters of the *Memories*, she felt that rice pudding, of which she was strangely fond, was quite spoiled in Italy by the inevitable flavor of lemon peel. On the other hand, she and her father, though they had not agreed on the subject of the Parisian gingerbread, both revelled in the dried chestnuts one bought in the street. Rose thought them "the nicest things to eat that ever challenged young teeth."

a word to reveal the fact, as I did so silently, the wondrous virtue of the Catholic religion. Not told anything of it except what was supposed would shock me, I bowed in spirit before the holy water, and all that was apprehended by the senses."

All the Hawthornes, as might be expected, had their own very definite ideas as to what Catholicism and Catholics ought to be. Nor did they for a moment hesitate to measure His Holiness Pius IX by the standards they had of what was proper. The priests greatly scandalized Sophia by sometimes fortifying themselves, during a long drawn out religious ceremony, by a surreptitious pinch of snuff. And when during Lent the pope appeared in white instead of the violet of the penitential season, she supposed it was because "he is presumed to be beyond penitence and mourning." She considered he would be much better employed if he had the works of the old masters in fresco copied before they quite faded away, instead of wasting his time in the frivolous pastime of "writing encyclical letters." But she thought his face benign and comely and gave Rose a little medallion of him and a gold scudo on which he appeared. "If one could only believe him a perfect saint and virtually Head of the Church, this would have been very impressive," she commented. Her husband was distinctly annoyed with the pope, because he was half an hour late for the ceremony. This seemed to him "particularly ill mannered." The punctual Yankee had not yet discovered that everybody is late for everything in Italy. Hawthorne thought the face of Pius "kindly and venerable, but not particularly impressive." Then he added, "I am very glad I have seen the pope, because now he may be crossed out of the lists of sights to be seen." Rose, by accident, got an even closer sight of him. Walking with her mother one day in the Vatican gardens, they turned a corner and there was the familiar white-robed figure. Smiling benignly, he beckoned the child to him and while Sophia knelt —

for even a New England Unitarian knew that that was good
manners — he placed his hand on the mop of red hair and
blessed her.*

For the Hawthornes the sights mainly meant the picture galleries. Few visitors to Rome could ever have prepared themselves
more honestly to have appreciated its art or to have been more
zealous in getting all the culture they could acquire. Sophia had
some technical knowledge, and also some talent. But Hawthorne,
though earnest, did not display the best of taste, admiring Guido
Reni prodigiously, but concluding that "there is something forced,
if not feigned, in our taste for pictures of the old Italian school."
Yet he preferred even those pictures to the Renaissance paintings
of the nude. Such pictures greatly shocked him, and he felt sure
that those who painted them must have been bad men. From
Raphael's Fornarina he turned away as from "the brazen trollop
that she is."

But — partly because the nude in cold stone was less objec-
tionable to him than warm paint — he preferred statues to
pictures.** Though the painter, Cephas Giovanni Thompson (the
malicious said that he had been baptized plain "Peter John"), was
a friend of his, still more did he associate with William Story,
the sculptor, and even gave him a "boost" in *The Marble Faun*.
But to him John Gibson, the sculptor, was something of a figure
of fun, because he tinted his statues, maintaining that the Greeks
did the same. One rather voluptuously curved nude was profanely
known as "Mrs. Gibson." Sophia tried to argue with this short,
elderly Italianate Englishman one day in his studio, but he merely
smiled and said, "It's all nonsense not to like the tinting of marble;
it makes a richer effect."

* This incident was often related by Mother Alphonsa to the Sisters. It
is not, however, in any of the family memoirs.
** He did say, however, that "old sculpture affects the spirits even more
dolefully than old painting; it strikes colder to the heart, and lies heavier
upon it, being marble, than if it were merely canvas."

"But, Mr. Gibson," Sophia continued to protest, "it's the pure form I look for in sculpture; I don't want it mixed up with painting."

He gave her up as hopeless and started to tell a long, rambling story about a Chinese general. After Sophia felt she could endure no more, she interrupted with, "That is a group of Cupid and Psyche — how lovely!"

"Yes, yes; that's Cupid and Psyche. Well, then the Chinaman said . . . ," and he was off again.

Sophia made another attempt a few minutes later with, "Oh, what an exquisite Flora!"

It was no use. Gibson returned, "Yes, that is Flora — so now that rascally Chinese general declared all the men were respectfully buried." By that time, all Sophia and the girls could do was to glance at a Beatrice Cenci done by Miss Hosmer, an old Concord friend who shared Gibson's studio, and hurry home to dinner.

The Storys were another matter. Beautiful Elizabeth Hoar — who had recently left Rome and whom Rose thought of as a monument of diamonds and pearls, talking so brilliantly and so sweetly, and seeming to know everything about art — wrote from Florence to tell Sophia that she had "always loved them (the Storys) for their thorough kindness to Margaret, and now I have seen them I love them for themselves." The Hawthornes could dispense with the Margaret Fuller recommendation. Julian quotes an opinion Sophia omitted from *The Italian Notebooks* that, "Margaret has not left in the hearts and minds of those who knew her any deep witness of her integrity and purity. She was a great humbug — of course with much talent and much moral reality, or else she would never have been so great a humbug."

They all liked to be at the studio of William Story, famous for his statues of Cleopatra and the Dying Gladiator. Seven year old Rose often wondered how so slight a little man as he was could be so fearless. She was astonished that anybody could carve a new statue when the world was so full of figures carved by men, centuries dead, but whose creations seemed so alive that they seemed about to be surprised when encountered. Her impression of Story's statues, as recorded in later life was: "They looked as if they would take the impress of one's fingers; they seemed to pulsate, so splendid was their faithful vividness." Hawthorne liked this wiry, smiling, nervous fellow Salemite, with his brown beard streaked with gray at thirty-nine and the wrinkles around his bright, alert eyes. But he fixed Story's position accurately when he said: "The great difficulty with him, I think, is a too facile power; he would do better things if it were more difficult for him to do merely good ones." But where Hawthorne divined an underlying melancholy, his children saw only the surface glitter of a lively personality, and thought him the best of good company. Rose was fascinated even more by seeing him at work, and when she could not be in *his* studio, she would linger by the hour watching the men in the marble shops. There the whirring sound of the wheel lulled the senses and worked so efficiently that one got the impression that here the hardest substances yielded to airy forces. She loved the peculiar fragrance that rose from the wet marble lather. And sometimes a workman, hoary with marble dust, could be persuaded to polish for her a fragment of giallo antico or porphyry she had picked up in a ruin. It was magical to see the fresh color come back at a touch of the wheel — yellow, black, red, or green. These she and Julian, often accompanied by ten-year-old Hubert Thompson, the rather timid and undersized son of the painter, used to take home as treasure along with bits of "irridescent glass, of which a single scrap might contain all the glories of Persian magnificence, while pathetically reporting the tears of a Roman girl of two thousand years ago, when the lachrimal was simply white."*

* This is a passage in the manuscript, omitted like much else, from the printed *Memories*. It tells of course what the middle-aged Mrs. Lathrop thought; the child Rose certainly did not have such reflections.

The children, now under the charge of the highly efficient Miss Shepard, had lessons more regularly, though the looking upon beautiful things in churches and museums, and the meeting of celebrated people still remained the main part of their education. Sophia had a way of boasting about her children — without knowing that she was doing anything of the kind — and this her sisters sometimes resented. Perhaps it would be equally correct to say that the slightest word of even implied criticism found Sophia almost morbidly sensitive. She had evidently expatiated so largely to Mary Mann about the advantages the children were now enjoying, that Mary suggested mildly that perhaps too much hotbed culture would not be very good for them. Instantly Sophia accepted the challenge: "You speak of my children's 'hotbed' culture, dear Mary, but this is the very culture I have always avoided. I should say that Ada" — Ada, it must be remembered was a product of Antioch College, of which Mary's husband, Horace Mann, was president; so here Sophia defiantly turned the tables on her sister — "I should say that Ada had had hotbed culture, because I understand by that, a forced and rapid culture, intended to make a precocious bloom or fruit. My plan and principle is *never* to force or stimulate, but to gently aid my human flowers to unfold petal by petal in the way that Nature proceeds. Not a breath of hot steam has ever filled the sails of my young craft. The consequence has been that to Una all knowledge is as the Delectable Mountains to the Christian Pilgrims." From which it will be seen that Sophia, like her sisters — the "Grandmother of the Kindergarten" and Mary whose baby upon being born issued a school report — was herself something of an educational theorist. But Sophia's theories were not very rigid and they did result in her children's all getting a broad culture and avoiding forcing or specialization. The only question that may be raised is as to whether it was not a little too broad and insufficiently formal. In short, it was an education for artists, rather than for any of the learned professions. And the very best part of it all was what they got wandering in picture galleries or in ancient ruins.

Rose found time to sit for her portrait to the incredibly named Cephas Giovanni Thompson, a mild little man, with a philosophic air, a low, slow voice, and a patriarchal brown beard. Rose was to describe him as being "harmlessly handsome," whatever that may have meant. Already, at the age of seven, she decided that he did not paint as well as Raphael, but she liked the smell of his paints.

What she did not like was having to sit still on a high stool all alone, while the artist surveyed her with what she considered a patronizing demeanor. She was not used to being patronized, for Sophia never gave her children commands; and the ordeal of sitting for her portrait filled her with fury. The little portrait, which now hangs in Hawthorne, New York, has a sulky and almost tearful look testifying to her dislike of posing.

Some of the sights she saw — all part of the earnest culture Sophia wished her children to receive — were of course largely lost upon her. The tomb of Cecilia Metella, with its frieze of oxheads — *capo di bove*, the Romans called it — where the ashes of people two millenniums dead were stored in the "dovecot" along with irridescent tear vials, dolls, and other bric-a-brac, was to her far more depressing than interesting. Nor when she was taken into the catacombs had she any glimmering of their significance. (For that matter, not even her father and mother knew how to read all that they told of the ancient Church.) And the Capuchin burial vaults, which were to figure in *The Marble Faun*, where, because of crowded space, no buried monk had more than a short lease on his grave, but was soon dug up to have his skull and bones adorn the walls — these, seen by the light of the *Moccoletti*, seemed to her foolish rather than grisly.

What she and all the children hugely enjoyed was the carnival. Hawthorne himself complained: "Upon my honor, I never in my life knew a shallower joke than the carnival at Rome; and

such a rainy and muddy day, too! Greenwich Fair is worth a
hundred of it." But it was noticed that, after a certain gloominess
at the start, the New England Puritan did thaw and take part in
lively fashion in the fun. Yet the carnival on that not very fair
day, when the flowers fell into the mud, and yet were used again
— crushed, stained, and wilted though they were — might have
been taken by one sufficiently cynical as an emblem of life.
Hawthorne had to shut his eyes to that, to enjoy the proceedings.
The light and innocent heart of a child was needed to take the
tawdry festival at face value.

How much more genuine were their meetings with Frederika
Bremer, the Swedish novelist, who lived in the tiniest of tiny
houses on the edge of the Tarpeian Rock, its courtyard ending
in a parapet from which one looked straight down the precipice.
This was something that gave Hawthorne one of the main incidents of *The Marble Faun*.

How much nicer Miss Bremer was, the children thought, than
the very distinguished and very venerable William Cullen Bryant,
who called on the Hawthornes at this time with his wife. He was,
they saw at once, the kind of man who did not like children. So
they gazed at his long beard with awe but were chilled by his
cold eyes. It was all so different with the bright little Miss Bremer.
She, with a nose hugely disproportionate for her diminutive self,
had a heart as big, and a wise mind. It was a little hard to follow
her correct but oddly accented English — at which of course
Julian and Rose sniggered, despite reproving glances from their
parents and Miss Shepard and (most of all) Una, who now was
beginning to consider herself grown up. But they all liked the
affectionate little woman, with her quaint prattle, and in the end
even the younger children forgot to exchange smirks. When they
parted from her Miss Bremer kissed them all round, and for a
moment Hawthorne was afraid he too was going to be kissed
by one whom he afterward called a woman "worthy to be the
maiden aunt of the whole human race." She, for her part, told

Sophia of her husband, "Wonderful, wonderful eyes! They give, but receive not." When he was at Bowdoin an old gypsy woman had asked, "are you man or angel?" Seeing those eyes, and in England, one who had known Burns, said that only his eyes could match those of Hawthorne's.

When all was said and done, for Rose the chief wonders of Rome were her father and mother. Every evening the whole family would play cards, but she had her own little game that she played with her father on the Pincian Hill on Sunday afternoons. Together they sat on a bench and played cherry stones. It made her glow all over to have him as her courteous opponent, and when he threw a pebble upon one of the squares she had marked out with chalk she was enchanted. She remembered his hands as being large, broad, and generous without being coarse — with lines of refinement and childlike simplicity noticeable in the hands of charity. "At the base of the fingers," she went on, "where they spring from the palm, were the roundings-in which you will find in many prelates and in philanthropic natures." She loved to watch how he used his hands in the game: "When he took up a pebble and threw it he seemed to be really doing something." When the game was finished she trembled lest he would not wish to play another. But he would play with her for long stretches, in a brooding manner, yet with kind stateliness, seldom speaking but making amused sounds over the fortunes of the game — sounds that seemed to her like mellow wood-notes. The world of wealth and fashion drove by, but the famous author never raised his eyes except to the face of his happy little daughter. Writing nearly forty years afterward she could still remember it all, even to the scent of that cigar he smoked as deliberately as though smoking were a religious rite.

And her mother wrote: "March twentieth is memorable for a charming walk I took with little Rose to the Temple of Peace, the Coliseum, the Coelian Hill, and the Forum." Sophia was making sure that the prophecy came true that Sarah Clarke had made, years earlier, when any visit to Italy seemed an impossible dream, that her children would one day play in the Temple of Peace. They found it so full of rough boys, and so dirty, that they soon left. "Rose enjoyed, however," Sophia went on, "the magnificent arches — the richly sculptured capitals, the bases and architraves lying about upon the ground; and then we went on to the Coliseum, where the devout were kissing the black cross in the centre; and then to the Coelian, where I sat upon a marble seat, in view of the Palatine, while Rose gathered daisies on the lawn."

CHAPTER VII

Florence

It was the painter, Thompson, wise to the ways of the Romans, who engaged a *vetturino* to take the Hawthornes to Florence. There was no fixed scale, but under the prevailing rule a prince would expect to be charged a hundred and fifty scudi, though not a person like Signor Hawthorne "who was merely a good artist." For ninety-five scudi Gaetano, the man engaged, signed a written contract in which everything was set down, including just what food had to be provided for the passengers — all the expenses to be carried by Gaetano himself, who was to receive a tip of five crowns at the end of the journey.

On the day of leaving Rome the Hawthornes learned a new practice of its inhabitants. Lalla, the slatternly, but hitherto amiable, servant who had worked for them, turned up with her mother. Though Lalla had been given two weeks' notice, she demanded another week's pay, and her mother also had a bill to present for services they had, until then, never heard of. But Hawthorne refused to be imposed on, and Sophia also refused a baiocco more than was due. In fact they felt they should deduct from Lalla's pay a charge of six scudi they had had to pay for her breakage of crockery and glass. When the old woman and the young saw their demands were not going to be met, they took it out on the Hawthornes with those rich and lurid curses in which the Italians seem to specialize — all of course screamed at them in a mounting frenzy at the top of their voices. But Lalla and her mother had come to the wrong shop. Sophia looked sad but her face was set in determination, and the children saw that their father was smiling in the dangerous way he reserved for moments of stress. The family crowded into the carriage, Gaetano cracked his long whip, and the four horses rattled along the cobblestones with the shrill voices of the two women screaming behind them.

They could talk freely in English in the *vetturo*, sure that Gaetano would not understand what they were saying. Yet all they had to say of him was praise. For though the maledictory Lalla and her mother might represent one type of Italian, it was no more than just to take Gaetano as representative of another.

"But don't you think," asked Sophia, "that he really doesn't look like an Italian at all in color or expression?"

"What would you think he was, Sophia?" Hawthorne asked.

She saw the gleam in his eye and trilled with laughter. "You know very well what I think, and you're thinking the same. He's just like a good New England farmer with his placid and gentle face."

After the meals he provided — paying for everything himself, according to the contract — they had still more praise. For lunch he gave them an omelette, some stewed veal, and a desert of figs and grapes, besides two decanters of white wine. For dinner they had a vermicelli soup, two fricasseed chickens and a roast leg of lamb, with fritters, oranges and figs, and again two decanters of wine.

"Who would ask for more?" Hawthorne said.

And Sophia agreed. "Those who want very dainty and special dishes, and who will go to the trouble of explaining their wishes to the innkeepers, and are ready to pay three times as much as our *vetturino* can do things on — *they* may get something better. But what Gaetano gives us is quite satisfactory, who love art and scenery better than Lucullan banquets."

Gaetano even dealt with the beggars for them. He could get rid of them for a tithe of what an American "millionaire" would have been expected to pay. These came running beside the carriage, boys and girls, keeping up a low miserable murmur, like that of water rushing along a gutter. Hawthorne knew that most of them must be imposters, though he was more tender toward such people — as he always was — than he felt he ought to be. But he tried to justify them to Sophia by saying: "I imagine that begging is held to be rather an honorable profession in Italy, and that it has here some of the odor of sanctity that used to be attached to the life of the mendicant friars, when every saint lived upon Providence — and deemed it meritorious to do nothing for his support."

It was a wonderful journey along a road that was hung, all the way, like a picture gallery with the most romantic landscape. Sometimes going up the mountains two more horses had to be harnessed to their four; at other times they became more majestically picturesque with two milk-white steers helping to drag them along. At Città Castellana, where a precipice descended sheer hundreds of feet to the valley below, Hawthorne and Julian and Rose got out and walked by walls of rock in which ancient Etruscan tombs were hollowed out. A little further on was Soracte, coming suddenly into view. Before they left it behind them the bright Italian moon was washing the scene with silver. Even Hawthorne, master though he was of description, quite despaired of describing that beauty in his *Notebook*. What he did write down after reaching Florence was that "the journey from Rome has been one of the brightest and most carefree interludes of my life; we have all enjoyed it exceedingly and I am happy that our children have it to look back upon." It made up to him for the dull and uncongenial life in the consulate, "and before going back to my own hard and dusty New England."

In Florence they looked up Hiram Powers, the sculptor, whose statue, the Greek Slave, had been celebrated in one of Mrs. Browning's sonnets and which, when it had gone on exhibition in the United States, in 1857, had brought in a "gate" of twenty-three thousand five hundred dollars. He had just the thing for the Hawthornes, and took them to see it, being perfectly at ease in dressing gown and slippers. It was the Casa del Bello, a palace of three pianos, the topmost of which was occupied by Lady St. George. The Hawthornes took the ground floor, completely furnished even to silver and linen for fifty dollars a month, and decided that Florence was the paradise of cheapness of which they had been told but which they had not found in Rome.

Sophia went into raptures in her description. Their apartment opened at the back upon a broad terrace, leading down to a garden full of roses and jasmine and orange and lemon trees, with a fountain in the middle over which a large willow drooped. They had thirteen rooms, besides four basement kitchens. She considered it the very luxury of comfort and gave her husband for his study one of the three parlors. It was hung with crimson velvet and the very doors were draped. In that study there was an ormolu table, two couches, four stuffed easy chairs, candelabra, a chandelier, and a Turkish carpet — all a far cry from that bare room in Salem of which Hawthorne had written that it was there that fame had been won. There was no sound except that of the birds in the garden. Sophia thought it the ideal of a study, such as "an artist of the Beautiful" ought to have, but until then had never found.

Rose and Julian did not look at it in the same light.* The garden was no doubt full of gracefully drooping trees, but hardly a ray of sunshine came through and the children found it at once hot and damp — almost like a Turkish bath. Then Julian caught a bird in this Dantesque garden and kept it in a small closed room where it looked miserable and eventually died. When it did so, all Florence seemed intolerable to heartbroken little Rose. She and Julian started to eat the kernels of cherry and apricot stones,

---

* In a manuscript headed "Montaüto," parts of which were used in her *Memories of Hawthorne*, Rose writes: "altogether a place that should have filled me with kittenish glee, but I thought otherwise, as children sometimes will." This manuscript will be drawn upon further in this chapter.

having heard that these brought death. It was, however, less with suicidal intent than a curiosity to see what would happen. They were rather disappointed when there were no effects of any kind.

Hawthorne continued his conscientious, but not very successful, study of pictures. As in Rome, he preferred statuary and in his friend, Hiram Powers, he found a sculptor who, according to the artist's own estimate, was the only man fit to handle marble. This belief Powers was prepared to demonstrate, and before the whole Hawthorne family did so. He set up two casts of the Venus di Medici and then, leaning at ease against the pedestal of one, lectured. "Perhaps you'll think it's a bold thing to say that the sculptor of the Venus di Medici did not know his business." They did think so, but remained silent, and Powers remorselessly continued: "Look at that eye! Nature never made any eye like that." And indeed he showed them that, when examined closely, abstracted from the rest of the face, it did have a queer look — something like a half-worn buttonhole. "And now look at her ears — too low on the head, giving an artificial and monstrous height to everything above it!" Feature by feature Hiram Powers battered poor Venus all to pieces. Sophia felt there was some sophistry in all this, but when she timidly suggested that the sculptor had deliberately departed from actual nature in order to obtain a higher effect of beauty, Powers in his forceful way swept the objection aside.

"Not a bit of it, Mrs. Hawthorne! Depend upon it that he was trying to make a face as it really was. But he simply did not know *how*."

But they had to admit that this plain, simple, kindly man — so clearly honest and trustworthy — was a remarkable person. He was almost as proud of his inventive talents as of his artistic genius. He showed them an instrument he had made: by just pressing on a spike sixty thousand pounds' weight were concentrated on a thick piece of iron. "See," he cried, triumphantly, "one second and no effort and I've punched a hole through it!" He made these iron buttons or his Venuses with equal ease and quite indifferently.

Another Florence acquaintance was Seymour Kirkup, a mysterious old Englishman, who lived in what had been the monastery of the Knights Templars — a little shriveled-up person, with perfectly white and silky hair and beard and with wild, queer-looking eyes made all the queerer by eyebrows so arched that he seemed to be frozen in astonishment. He had been a friend of Trelawney's — the friend of Shelley and Byron — and it was he who had discovered the Giotto fresco portrait of Dante in the Bargello. The children were not told that the little girl, Imogen, whom Kirkup accepted as his daughter on the assurance of a young Florentine named Regina, whom he had patronized as a spiritualistic medium, was really the child of Regina's lover, an Italian peasant. But then nobody enlightened Mr. Kirkup himself on this point.

The children gazed astonished at the house of this ancient antiquarian and reputed necromancer. It was full of curiosities and very dirty and cobwebby. Hawthorne was to depict it and Mr. Kirkup in *Dr. Grimshawe's Secret* and also *The Dolliver Romance*. They all conversed with him in a kind of shuddering fascination, Sophia especially being impressed that little Imogen had inherited her mother's talents as a medium. Mr. Kirkup was conversing (so he assured his visitors) with the ancient Roman emperors; in this way he "discovers how they have been poisoned and otherwise ill-treated while on earth."

There was a good deal of spiritualistic dabbling going on at this time, largely because the Hawthornes encountered again, in Florence, the Brownings, whom they had previously met in London. Hawthorne disapproved of these séances as heartily as Browning did, but Sophia was more than half persuaded. Ada Shepard was discovered to have a medium's powers, and though she used them somewhat reluctantly, she delivered communications from the spirit world. Some of these came from Sophia's mother, but regarding them, Hawthorne sceptically wrote "I discern much of [Sophia's] beautiful fancy and many of her preconceived ideas, although thinner and weaker than at first hand. They are the echoes of her own voice returning out of the lovely chambers of her heart, and mistaken by her for the tones of her mother."

Much more extraordinary was the intrusion of a somewhat boisterous ghostly harridan, who, when she appeared, put all other spirits to flight. She gave her name as Mary Runnel.* She was identified as a young woman with whom Daniel Hathorne (our Hawthornes were the first to add the "W" to the spelling of their name) had been in love in 1755. Daniel gave her a copy of Sidney's *Arcadia* (perhaps in the hope of improving the peculiar grammar she afterward used in these séances), but if Hawthorne had ever seen that book, it must have been twenty years earlier. No doubt he would have explained the matter on the ground of buried memories rising unexpectedly to the surface of consciousness.

From none of these things were the children excluded, because their parents wanted them to be companions. But the spiritism seems to have done them no harm, for though Julian later in life dabbled in it, this was probably with tongue in cheek. Their father's cool scepticism was salutary, and their mother's enthusiasm was only evanescent. Dear Sophia was enthusiastic about everything, but her good sense could always be counted upon to restore her equilibrium.

Browning came to see them, as usual in the highest physical spirits, bouncing and bounding all over the place, and all the Hawthornes went frequently to Casa Guidi where they renewed their acquaintance with Mrs. Browning and met the famous little

---

* Julian in *Hawthorne and His Wife* (I, 31) gives it as "Mary Rondel." I have before me the copy Julian inscribed "To Rose and George with love," and in the margin Rose has written in pencil, "As I remember it — Runnell." The name was properly spelled with only one "l".

Penini. Somehow Rose got it fairly fixed in her mind that Galileo, though not on view, was a member of the Browning's family circle. She thought of him as holding the sun captive in his back yard, while he blinked down upon it from a prison of his own.

Mrs. Browning took Rose on her lap, but Rose — looking at her heavy, dark curls and white cheeks and great, dreamy eyes — wondered whether this wraithlike person was really alive. She was such a contrast to the torrential vitality of her husband. Later Rose was to speak of "her enormous thick-lipped mouth and her hand like a bird's claw. The most present personality was his; the most distant, even when near, was the personality he married." She and Julian looked at the most famous of women poets with the remorseless curiosity children so often show.

Penini was a monstrosity of another kind, and they gazed at him with some contempt. Of course Sophia was all in raptures when the little boy came drifting in with long, curly, brown hair and a buff silk tunic, embroidered with white — little Lord Fauntleroy born out of due time. She thought it wonderful that after having studied the piano for only fourteen months he played his sonata so well. Wistfully she thought of how Una had practiced hours on end, day after day, and for several years, without showing any talent. Hawthorne's verdict, though cautiously expressed, was much the same as the one his children passed on the pretty nine-year-old boy: "[He] seems at once less childlike and less manly than would befit that age. I should not quite like to be the father of such a boy. I wonder what is to become of him." There he was perfectly at ease, charmingly mannered, helping the guests to cake and strawberries, joining in the conversation when he had anything to say, at other times sitting apart and enjoying his own meditations. This was the child who used to tell people in Rome that he had to go out riding there, that it was expected of him, as he was one of the sights of the city! The little Hawthornes, much as they liked jolly Mr. Browning with the sweeping talk and the hearty laugh, could not abide his son.

Sophia records how sometimes she would take Rose to the Powerses and leave her there for the day. They had a little invalid daughter for whom Rose was a good playmate. Yet Rose's manuscript "Montaüto" speaks disparagingly of this play — always with wooden dolls, all six inches high — as a shocking and stultifying waste of time. She really enjoyed herself much more when Ada Shepard or her mother took her to the Boboli Gardens on the two days a week when they were open to the public. There with her doll Daisy in her chair and her jump rope and her fan she would amuse herself for hours. What was even better was the Boboli lake with its swans. Rose never wanted to move from it but would gaze, at the white majestic creatures, enchanted. Sophia was quite content with this. The gardens with their groves and avenues, statues and flowers, where impenetrable shades and sunny open spaces alternated, brought to her mind the "enormous bliss" of Milton's Paradise. In the lake of the swans was a rock upon which sat a marble Ariadne, stretching out her arms wildly and calling for help against a green dragon creeping toward her on one side, while a monstrous antediluvian frog was opening its jaws upon her from the other. In such scenes of nature and art, mother and child were equally content.

It was through the Brownings that the Hawthornes came to rent the villa of Montaüto, at Bellosguardo on a hill fifteen minutes' drive from the city. The young Count da Montaüto came to close the deal, and Rose wondered where the poor man was going to live, not knowing that he had a palace in Florence. His sweet, sad face made her feel that he was thinking, "Have I come to this, that debased from my rank I must live as a leaser of villas?" But despite the wound to his aristocratic pride he bargained very stiffly for an extra three dollars rent and received it. As for Signor del Bello, he demanded an extra fifty cents for broken crockery. There was, however, another side to that story. The Americans might be contemptuous of haggling Italian aristocrats, but it was rather extraordinary that the Americans should have made any

fuss; the rent of Montaüto, with its over forty rooms richly furnished, was forty scudi a month.

It was not only splendid, it was also romantic, and the Hawthornes believed that Savonarola had been imprisoned there,
though in fact it was some other monk. To the top of the stone
tower, where rested owls that knew, writes Rose, "every wrinkle
of despair and hoot-toot of pessimism," the whole family climbed
in the cool of the evening and looked out upon the throbbing
blue, gold, green, and lilac of Italian heaven and countryside.

Out of Una's bedroom there opened an oratory which figured
later in *The Marble Faun,* and it was supposed to be haunted.
Indeed, Una, in the overwrought condition they all were in as a
result of their spiritualistic experiments, brought herself to believe
that she had seen and heard the ghost. As for Rose — this too
comes out of the manuscript "Montaüto" — sitting alone one day
at the head of the winding staircase she said, to herself, "If I feel
three taps upon my shoulder, I will believe in spiritualism."

Immediately she did feel three deliberate taps, and "no cat,"
she added, "ever covered intervening space more rapidly than
I." That seems to have ended Rose's connection, such as it was,
with spiritualism.

Much better suited for a child were the grounds of the count's
villa, where his *contadini* brought the Americans grapes, figs,
pomegranates, and peaches, and though the Hawthornes knew
they were being cheated it was done, Italian style, with so much
affability, and in any event on so unimportant a scale, that they
felt such swindling was almost a pleasure. Behind the house were
fruit gardens and olive trees and on the dotted hillsides, vineyards.
In the evenings they used to sit on the lawn, and sometimes
entertained guests there, all under what Rose called "the sapphire
glory of an Italian night."

The picturesqueness of the place was excellent material for
the novel about Italy that was already forming in Hawthorne's
mind. He even put one of the servants into *The Marble Faun*

without changing her name. This was Stella, who was kind in spite of the rocky hardness of her features. Rose recalled her hair dressed in small, black, brilliant braids, the gold earrings dangling against an infinitude of wrinkles, and arms whose skin was like parchment of the color of autumn leaves. The wondering little girl sometimes caught her on her knees in her bedroom before a great black crucifix, as was occasionally the case with another servant, a girl of sixteen, when Stella drove her there. Rose, who had at this time little enough reverence, would whisper to the old woman at her prayers. Stella, perhaps by way of a bribe to be left alone, gave the little heretic a tiny bambino of wax, asleep amid flowers under a glass case — all of course in the very worst taste. But Rose, studying the face of the Child, came to feel that He loved her even in sleep. So she recorded nearly forty years later. If she really ever felt that at the time she must already have come some way toward the Catholic Church.

It could have been so, for her father and mother, in spite of all their anti-Catholic prejudices, were far more Catholic in spirit than they ever suspected. Sophia was showing at one and the same moment an almost rabid anticlericalism and feelings which were unmistakably Catholic in sympathy. Thus she was "always sensible of hollowness and emptiness in every ceremony" at which she was present and "especially the ennui and inward disgust of the priests themselves, who seem very anxious to get through the endlessly repeated task so as to go out and eat and drink and be merry." She charitably granted that there were no doubt genuinely devout men among them, but in general she found the appearance of the Florentine clergy "almost invariably repulsive and gross."

Yet almost on the next page she could describe with high approval the Catholic burial service of a child. "The coffin was covered with a white satin pall, embroidered with purple and gold.

The officiating priests were in robes of white satin and gold, and the altar was alight with candles . . . when the organ burst forth in a kind of tender rapture, rolling pearly waves of harmony along the large spaces, and filling the dome with the foam and spray of interlacing measures, it seemed as if angels were welcoming the young child to heaven." Rose's comment long afterward on her father and mother's attitude toward the Church was: "They did not really believe that Italy was under an 'incubus'; they felt the physical weight of Catholicity, or the cross, and half guessed its spiritual spring."

It was at this time that Rose Hawthorne obtained her patron saint, and strangely enough from Elizabeth Hoar. She had written to Sophia, "I saw dear little Rose's patron, St. Rosa, in the Staffa Gallery at Perugia."* On the way up Sophia had remembered to take Rose there and wrote in her journal: "We saw in the Staffa Palace a beautiful Santa Rosa, by Sasso Ferrato. She is a Peruvian saint, and in the Dominican habit I think." Rose was to become herself a Dominican tertiary, and the congregation she founded was that of St. Rose of Lima.

There were moments when Hawthorne was tempted to settle in Florence — a place where one could rent a palace furnished for thirty dollars a month. But though he found much of the material for *The Marble Faun* and wrote the first draft of that book there, he told Fields: "I find this Italian atmosphere not favourable to the close toil of composition, although it is very good air to dream in. I must breathe the fogs of old England or the east-winds of Massachusetts, in order to put me into working trim." But his real reason was that he wished his children to grow up as Americans. Much as he disliked giving up the delights of Europe,

---

* Sophia's book reads "Perujia" and "Perujian" — obvious misprints. She evidently did not read the proofs. Montaüto, which has been mentioned here, is down every time in *Notes in England and Italy* as "Montanto."

he looked upon it as a sacrifice to which duty called him. Accordingly on October 1, 1859, they left Florence.

First they took the train to Siena, three hours away, where the Storys were living. From there they intended to make the rest of the journey by *vetturo*, the mode of traveling they had already found so successful. The beauties of Siena had to be seen, and also the pleasant Storys.

The Storys found the Hawthornes lodgings and then drove them around the city in their carriage, Hawthorne deciding that Siena was more picturesque than any other town he had seen in Italy — except Perugia. Especially did they admire the cathedral where they attended Mass on Sunday. "The music," Sophia wrote, "was like the morning stars singing together." The cathedral itself seemed to soar and sing. Little Rose kept asking, "Mamma, what does it say?" At last Sophia found the right answer, "Darling, it praises the Lord."

And what good fun Mr. Story could be when he wished! Though probably an hour later he was plunged in the blackest melancholy, for that evening he gave rein to his exuberant fancies. One of the caricatures he drew for the entertainment of his visitors was of an imaginary presidential candidate, "evidently," noted Hawthorne, "a man of very malleable principles, and likely to succeed." Even droller was a series of drawings of Byron — "Byron as he really was" and "Byron as he might have been," a very pronounced Negro type. Then he made a portrait of Ada, the poet's daughter, writing under it the line, "Thy face was like thy mother's, my fair child!" and depicting a ludicrously leering face. The last sent the children into wild merriment; even little Rose, upon whom the point of much of Story's satirical comment was lost, understood that joke.

It was late when they all drove home — "too late for little Rosebud," Hawthorne noted, and in the darkness the streets of beautiful Siena had a grim look. The side streets, with a light burning dimly at the end, wore the aspect of caverns.

After their experience of Gaetano, and coming to know Constantino Bacci, the Hawthornes came to the conclusion that the best Italians were these superb coachmen. Sophia at once named Constantino the Emperor, and the name fitted him, for he was a man of sweet and shining disposition, noble and grand of bearing, massive, though not very tall, deliberate, and with great, dark, slow-moving eyes. His clothes were of the humblest, but Julian thought he wore them like imperial robes. Sophia said his smile was one of "stormy lightning."

He and little Rose became great friends. She was usually on the box with him, and when he was going up hill on foot — often with a couple of oxen added to his six horses — he would clasp the child's soft hand in his own great paw, while with his long whip he touched up the horses from time to time. But these he rather coaxed along with coos and grunts and groans, as though he were sympathizing with their efforts.

When he had Rose beside him he wrapped her carefully in shawls and put his own thick mantle behind for her to lean against, while he performed exploits of making his whip crack like musketry. Once when she gave him a little present of two grapes in a cup made of a chestnut shell, he accepted it most gracefully. Sophia called his manners as finished as a cavalier's. As for Rose, usually something of a handful, with him she was as meek as a lamb in her adoration. When at Viterbo they sketched a stupendous vase that had once been a fountain, the Emperor and Rosebud made their sketches sitting side by side. The Hawthornes could not conceive a more charming way of traveling, especially when they had such men as Gaetano and the Emperor as *vetturini*.

When they came within sight of the dome of St. Peter's Constantino took off his cap and said, "Roma!" And Sophia and her husband were asking themselves, "What then, is this Rome that *will* hold sway over mankind, whether or no, in past or present time? I have an idea, but it is folded up in a veil."

They proceeded up the Flaminian Way into the Porto del Popolo, and there they paused half an hour at the Dogano to gaze on the oldest obelisk in the world, one Moses might in his day have seen in Egypt and now standing in the middle of the piazza. But at last the Emperor drew up before their apartment at 68 Piazza Poli. When the Hawthornes parted from him he seemed more than content with the *buon mano* of five scudi he received above the stipulated price. But Rose wept a little at parting from her friend, and there were tears in the Emperor's eyes.

CHAPTER VIII

The Last of Rome

Hawthorne decided at once that all Rome did not contain a more comfortable house than the one they had taken for the rest of their stay in Italy. It was a small place compared with the palace they had had in Florence or the still grander Montaüto, but in both of these places there had been much unneeded space; the Piazza Poli was really vastly better suited to normal living, and it was very much at the center of all the things they most wished to see in Rome. But what Rose, and even Julian, counted its most wonderful feature was its miraculous door. When they descended from the *vetturo* and rang, the door swung inward but nobody appeared — as in one of those enchanted castles Rose had read about in the fairy tales. Not until they had mounted the stairs did they find the solution of the mystery — there the servant whom Mr. Thompson had engaged for them was waiting; upon hearing their ring, she had pulled a rope and this set in operation a complex contraption of wires that lifted the latch. Rose and Julian spent most of the next few days playing with this marvelous toy.

The Piazza del Popolo, the Forum, the Pincian, the Pantheon — all these were close at hand. And the front windows of the house looked out on a large oblong space — about a couple of acres in extent — of cobblestones, which gave all the clearer view of the intense blue of the Roman sky. At night, lying in bed, they could hear the musical splash of the Fountain of Trevi, and at the time of the carnival the roar of the merrymakers came to them from the Corso. If anything was needed to complete Hawthorne's satisfaction it came the day after their arrival when he took little Rosebud out for a walk to the Medici Gardens. On the way there they saw Lalla of the screaming curses sitting at her father's fruit stall. But Hawthorne, who remembered that grim story of an ancestor of his, a Salem Judge, who sentenced the witches to be hanged and who was most terribly cursed by one of them, thanked God that at least the curses of Lalla and her mother had not taken effect.

But Hawthorne himself uttered against the whole city of Rome what must be among the most bitter maledictions it has received. Writing to Fields he said: "I bitterly detest Rome, and shall rejoice to bid it farewell forever; and I fully acquiesce in all the mischief and ruin that has happened to it, from Nero's conflagration down. In fact, I wish the very site had been obliterated before I ever saw it." He was somewhat given to complain of the places in which he lived, but of none of them did he have the same cause for complaint as of Rome. It was during this visit that the treacherous climate all but killed Una; it was that that he could not forgive. Set beside this stroke against his child, Rome's glories of art were little.

Many things improved upon a second view. Such was the case with the Roman carnival. Partly it was that the weather was better than that of the previous year, for after all nobody liked to be hit with a flower that had fallen on a wet and dirty pavement. But partly also it was because the New England Puritan was willing to relax some of his former disdain. Writing to Ticknor about it he said, "We are now in the height of the carnival, and the young people find it great fun. To say the truth, so do I; but I suppose I should have enjoyed it better at twenty." Una got a special thrill this time. The young Prince of Wales from his balcony tossed a bouquet right in her lap as she rode in a carriage along the Corso. She did not know that the Prince was to spend a good deal of his life doing much the same thing. A few years later even the homely Louisa Alcott got a wink from his Royal Highness on Boston Common, though perhaps that was really meant for her prettier companion.

Mostly, however, Hawthorne's willingness to enter into the carnival represented his thankful relief that Una — who had been ill from November to February — had not died. There she was, a beautiful girl of fifteen, riding in a carriage along the Corso in the carnival procession. No wonder her father's heart could be glad! From the balcony of the historian John L. Motley — his friend and Bismarck's friend — he became a boy again pelting those below. In his *Notebook* he wrote that there could not be a more picturesque spectacle than that of the stately palatial avenue of the Corso, all hung with Gobelin tapestries and carpets, and with every window crowded with faces gazing at the fantastic figures in the street below. "If you merely look at it," he added on the third day, "it depresses you; if you take even the slightest share in it . . . you no longer wonder that the young people, at least, take such delight in plunging into this mad river of fun." Then remembering England and America he wrote: "It is worthy of remark, that all the jollity of the carnival is a genuine ebullition of spirit, without the aid of wine or strong drink."

Rome was at that time full of Americans — among them Motley and ex-President Pierce, Hawthorne's close friend since they were at Bowdoin College together. Though until now Hawthorne had had only a casual acquaintance with the historian, the two men became close friends during that Roman winter and spring. Motley was at that time about forty-five, somewhat younger than Hawthorne, handsome not only on account of his fine features, but because of the sensitiveness and vividness of expression he had, a scholar, a man of the world, an artist, and above all a warm-hearted fellow creature. He proved, thought Julian, that when New England wants to show what she can do the result is one hardly to be surpassed.

Other American friends were there — beautiful and brilliant Elizabeth Hoar, with an enthusiastic account of an interview she had had with Pio Nono; the Storys, now back from Siena; Charlotte Cushman and Miss Mitchell, the latter reveling in Rome "as though she were visiting a constellation," smiling all over her wrinkled, weather-beaten face; Harriet Hosmer — who would not admit them to her studio because just then she happened to be engaged in modeling Lady Mordaunt's nose. There, too, were Senator Sumner, Mrs. Samuel G. Ward and the Brownings. The great poet darted across the piazza to greet them, glowing with cordiality, tingling with exuberant life. But perhaps in the children's eyes the minor poet, Christopher Cranch, was to be preferred even to the jolly Mr. Browning. Mr. Cranch laid himself out to entertain the children with what they considered wonderful imitations of bees buzzing about his head and with other amenities.*

Closest to Hawthorne himself was Franklin Pierce, the ex-President, now on vacation after the cares of his exalted office. He and his wife were staying at the Hotel d'Angleterre, and there was constant visiting between there and the Piazza Poli.

Hawthorne noted that his friend had aged a good deal and that something seemed to have passed out of him. His voice at times sounded old and strange, and when the General remarked "why, what a stout boy Julian has grown!" Hawthorne detected a note of sadness. "Poor fellow!" he thought, "he has neither son nor daughter to keep his heart warm."

Later when the two men went sight-seeing together, Pierce seemed to become more of his former self again. Indeed, a few days later Hawthorne was able to write that he was getting him back, just as he had been in his youth. "This morning, his face, air, and smile were so wonderfully like himself of old, that at least thirty years are annihilated. . . . We hold just the same relation to each other as of yore, and we have passed all the turning-off places, and may hope to go on together still the same dear

* So Julian describes him in a letter to W. L. Reenan, the editor of Hawthorne's privately circulated diary of 1859.

friends as long as we live. I do not love him one whit the less for having been President, nor for having done me the greatest good in his power; a fact that speaks eloquently in his favor, and perhaps says a little for myself. If he had been merely a bene- factor, perhaps I might not have borne it so well; but each did his best for the other as friend for friend."

Hawthorne was still all but blind to the meaning of Catholicism. It is curious how most of his references to the Church in his *Notebook* continued to be highly critical. Nor was he any more complimentary in *The Marble Faun.* The question is not, however, as simple as it might appear to be, and Hawthorne's son-in-law in the early nineties used to lecture on Hawthorne's incipient Catholicism, concerning which Rose herself projected an article. A passage of this sort is typical: "I heartily wish the priests were better men, and that human nature, divinely in- fluenced, could be depended upon for a constant supply and succession of good and pure ministers, their religion has so many good points. And then it is a sad pity that this noble and beautiful cathedral should be a mere fossil shell, out of which the life has died long ago. But for many a year yet to come the tapers will burn before the high altar, the Host will be elevated, the incense diffuse its fragrance, the confessionals be open to receive the penitents."

To believe in Catholicism it is not necessary, of course, to have an exalted opinion of individual priests, and it is not uncommon to find people with a great liking and respect for priests who are without a particle of belief in the religion of which the priests are ministers. We can all share Hawthorne's wish that priests (and everybody else) were better men. But one may ask upon what he founded his implied opinion that they were, for the most part, of rather bad character. Nothing appears to support this except the undeniable fact that some priests are fat —

Hawthorne's main charge against them — though it is questionable whether statistical proof exists that their average weight is higher than that of the laity. He does introduce a venerable and admirable cleric into *The Marble Faun* — the only priest who can be called a "character" of that book, and one wonders whether this is not the Benedictine Father Smith, whom we run across in his small diary of 1859. He had met Father Smith, who was acting as temporary president of the American College at Rome, and who served as unofficial cicerone to most of the English-speaking visitors — especially those from the United States. So far as can be ascertained, this was the only Catholic priest Hawthorne ever actually encountered — and Hawthorne liked him. For the rest he glanced at those he passed in the streets and said to Sophia, "Gross! gross! gross!" Quite literally Hawthorne weighed people — and then gave judgment.

The way he and Sophia took Una's very dangerous illness was admirably Christian. One afternoon she and Miss Shepard lingered out a little too late sketching — and both came down with the insidious Roman fever, Ada Shepard first. Miss Shepard, however, soon recovered, but Una, when she followed, was ill for four months and never did fully get over the effects of her illness. This was a contributing factor to her father's own relatively early death.

Until this happened the household on the Piazza Poli had been a very happy one. The family did without any servants, except one old woman to keep the place in order, and had all their meals sent in — excellent meals they were too — in heated tin boxes from a restaurant around the corner. This set them all the more free to live as a family without domestic cares. Early in the morning — and nearly every evening — they settled down to playing whist or euchre or old maid. On these occasions Hawthorne was the life of the party because he was so delightful a partner — even, if possible, more charming in defeat than in victory. It was amazing how much boyishness there still was in this man in his middle fifties, and how perfectly content the celebrated writer was to be playing cards with his children.

Then came Una's illness. Her father was greatly worried, though he told himself at first that in the case of a vigorous girl of fifteen, there was no real cause for alarm. She was in the care of Doctor Franco, an English-speaking Maltese homeopathist, patronized by most of the Americans and English of his medical persuasions. At this time Sophia favored these, because she had been nearly dosed to death by the ordinary practitioners, and her husband acquiesced in her strongly held views.

But in spite of Doctor Franco, Una's illness would not depart, and by degrees her father and mother began to dread her death. At last there came a day when, after his visit to the sickroom, Doctor Franco told them to be prepared for the worst. It was that evening that the card playing ended.

Yet it began as usual, with Hawthorne in his chair at the head of the table. And the others were laughing merrily, to which he responded with smiles that he had to drag out on his face. One hand of whist was played, and then the grave-looking man laid down his cards. "We won't play any more," he said. Even before that he had ceased keeping any journal except the small — fortunately preserved — one in which he made mere factual notes to be expanded, with comments, in the larger *Notebook*. There a gap occurs between the dates November 2, 1858 and February 27, 1859 — and we have a note of explanation from Sophia made when she printed her edition of it in 1871.*

Doctor Franco found it somewhat hard to cope with the unauthorized ministrations of some of the Hawthornes' friends. "Who sent this broth?" he demanded one day. "Oh, that came from Mrs. Browning." "Tell Mrs. Browning to write poetry and not send any broth to my patient." The next day he wanted to

---

* The *American* and the *English Notebooks* have been recently printed in full (except for some passages that Sophia took care to make undecipherable). The full version of the *French and Italian Notebooks* is now in preparation.

know, "Whose jelly is this?" "Mrs. Story's." "Please tell Mrs. Story to help her husband model his statues; I'll not need her help."

But Mrs. Story — like Mrs. Thompson — did give help of a kind that even Doctor Franco would have approved of. They came themselves or sent their maids to help in the nursing.*

Sophia, however, did not accept much help and was no doubt near enough to the truth in writing: "No one shared my nursing, because Una wanted my touch and voice; and she was not obliged to tell me what she wanted. For days she only opened her eyes long enough to see if I was there. For thirty days and nights I did not go to bed, or sleep, except in a chair while Miss Shepard watched for an hour or so."

The stream of visitors meant to be kind but for the most part served to wear out what remained of Sophia's strength. The American minister, Mrs. Ward, Aubrey de Vere, Mrs. Pierce — all these came, as well as the Storys and Thompsons. Even Mrs. Browning — who hardly ever went anywhere, and nowhere where she had to climb stairs — went up to Una's room. Sophia saw her only a moment, but found the clasp of her hand electric and her voice one that penetrated the heart. Ex-President Pierce called to inquire several times a day, and Sophia felt that she owed almost the preservation of her husband's life to his strong and under-standing friendship. "He was," she wrote, "divinely tender, sweet, sympathetic, and helpful."

At last a crisis came. Una had been delirious for several days, muttering unintelligibly. And her father and mother had a new grief to bear: for if she were to die now it would be with no parting word. Sophia was alone in the room, while Hawthorne, fully dressed, was trying to get a little rest. Out into the night on the piazza Sophia gazed and saw that the sky was covered with clouds. This loss she was about to be called on to bear, she felt, was one she could not bear.

* So Hawthorne's small diary of 1859 records.

Suddenly her feelings changed. Her heart soared beyond the sullen, leaden sky overhead to God: "Why should I doubt His goodness!" she cried to herself. "If He sees it is best let Him take her. I give her to Him, I will not fight against Him any more."

With a mind more at peace she turned from the window toward the bed. She put her hand on Una's forehead; it was cool and moist. Her pulse was regular; she was in a gentle sleep. To her husband in the adjoining room Sophia went at once with the words, "She is going to live!"

But the Hawthornes were glad to leave Italy, glad more of the thought of returning to America after nearly a six year's absence. On their last evening — May 25th — they all went for a walk in the moonlight to the fantastic Fountain of Trevi near by. According to the Romans, all who did that would return to Rome. None of the Hawthornes ever did — unless we count that Rose's conversion to Catholicism was this. The next day all of them took from Cività Vecchia the steamer *Vatican* for Marseilles. As Una had been ill she traveled first class, and her mother with her; the others were content with second-class accommodations. They had enjoyed Europe but they had spent a good deal of money; now they had to think again of counterbalancing economies.

CHAPTER IX

The Last of England

As soon as Fields, Hawthorne's publisher, saw this new, grave, heavily mustached man, he found a name for him — Field Marshall Hawthorne. It is that handsome and striking face that is familiar to the world, whereas only a few remember the clean-shaven young man Hawthorne was before his Italian visit. But his new aspect not only made him all the more distinguished in appearance; it was also appropriate to one upon whom the melancholy from which Sophia had drawn him was to return with increasing weight until it pressed him to death.

The family had made various short excursions on the way from Marseilles to London, and these are described — a little per-functorily — in the *French and Italian Notebook*, as also in the small diary of 1859. Avignon, Lyons, Geneva, the Castle of Chillon, Lausanne — the significance of these side trips was merely that of sight-seeing. It was the last chance of looking at such places and a single glance sufficed. And after all, though Hawthorne was glad that he had seen Italy for himself, and had been able to take Sophia and the children there, he was also glad to leave. He never showed the slightest desire to return.

With England it was different. It was almost a home-coming for him, for was this not *Our Old Home?* To the end he was constantly dreaming about going back to England in which, for all his growling and grumbling, he had really been more happy than anywhere else in the world.

He intended to leave England at once — that same July — and would have done so except for being unable to book cabins.

As these were not immediately obtainable, Hawthorne sent instructions that they were to be secured in August. But as that very month Smith and Elder offered him six hundred pounds for the English rights on his new book, Hawthorne decided to stay in England and complete it there. He was rather glad of this excuse for deferring the return to Concord.

In London the Hawthornes took temporary quarters in Golden Square. And eager, boyish, affectionate Henry Bright shot down from Liverpool to see them. One beautiful July day — one of those very hot days that an English summer sometimes provides — he took them to Richmond Park. They had a one o'clock dinner at the Star and Garter high up on the hill overlooking the Thames, and then they walked under the great trees in the park, watching the tame deer roam on the grass and a few scattered merry-makers. Julian was the only one not with them; he was on a visit to Bennoch at Blackheath. At 8:30 that evening the rest of the Hawthorne family and Henry Bright took the train back to London.

To obtain quiet for the writing of what was to be called in America *The Marble Faun*, Hawthorne first took his family to a place near Whitby. And this, because of its association with the seventh century Abbess St. Hilda, supplied Hawthorne with the name of his heroine. But before long they were established at Redcar near by, also on the coast but a more secluded place.

There Hawthorne worked with dogged tenacity every day, until an hour or so after the one-thirty dinner — following which he spent the rest of the hours walking and meditating on the sands. The entries in the small diary for 1859 are quite regularly: "Wrote till three. After dinner walked with Julian and saw him bathe. After tea walked by myself."

During the mornings Sophia would usually take Rose down to the beach and there search for those seashells in which the east coast of England is so rich. Small, rose-tinted ones, and a few others, still more superlative but almost invisible, she and the little girl gathered, and these Sophia treasured a long time in her sewing box. Sometimes too they would hunt — Sophia "breathlessly calm" — for seaweeds. The Yankee elm, the English oak, the herbs of a kitchen garden, ferns and tresses, both dark and light — so they seemed — of women's hair; all these had their counterparts in the weeds Sophia and Rose gathered and tried to mount — Hawthorne himself assisting — in the evening.

Sometimes Sophia would take a book with her to the beach, Disraeli's *Sybil*, or *Oliver Twist*, or *The Romany Rye*, or the *Lives of the Last Four Popes*, or Carlyle's *French Revolution*; and at night, when Rose's father sat enthroned in his easy chair, "with his book resting on his right arm, and held the top by his hand,"* she was never afraid to interrupt him and run to him for sympathy about anything. "I knew," she wrote, "it would be sympathy so melodious that it would echo in my heart for a long time, but that it would be as brief as the single stroke of *one* from some cathedral tower."

Rose made friends with a little girl named Hannah. She describes her in the manuscript as "a good little girl, never hectoring me" — and patient under somewhat domineering treatment. Hannah's reward was that while Rose liked her she also despised her a little, looking upon her as something out of Mrs. Barbauld's hymns.

Everything about Hannah seemed despicable to the vivacious little American — her name, her homely neat clothes, her sweetness, and her silence. It was only in retrospect — after Rose had returned to America — that she discovered that she loved Hannah. Then she started a correspondence with her.

Rose had a pair of toy scales, and these naturally suggested the game of "shop" — at which she found that Hannah was "contemptibly skillful." Rose scorned herself for playing — as previously she had scorned herself for playing with the collection

---

* Again I go to R. H. L.'s manuscripts — this time to the one headed "Redcar" — the first draft of what was printed in the *Memories*.

of wooden dolls possessed by the Powers' daughter in Florence. Now on the beach at Redcar the two little girls pounded brick, piled up sugary looking sand, gathered minute pebbles, and set up their grocery — regularly ending, Rose confessed, in a one-sided dispute as to the honesty of their transactions — but when her picturesquely clad father appeared, she was filled with confusion. He would glance at the game, which Rose at once felt to be utter waste of time, a withering of her brains. But he said no word and somehow his little daughter delighted in what she supposed was his tacit reproach: "then loftier thoughts than those of the counter would refresh me for the rest of the day and I thankfully returned to the heights and lengths of wide nature, full of color and roaring waves."

She had indeed some reason for feeling a little ashamed of frittering away her time playing shop with Hannah, for she had an imagination which had a faculty for hearing splendid music or calling up before herself the gorgeous sights of an oriental bazaar. She was to write that "this pastime required a good deal of will power, a peculiar subtlety of condition, and could only be kept up for a few moments at a time." She thought this proved that, though she was "a very stupid child," she "moderately possessed artistic perceptions." In this surely, she claimed too little. It is apparent from the letters of this time that remain that she was an exceptionally intelligent child, and one who may even be credited with genius — at least in the bud — though her later life was to prove that it lay in living itself rather than in specifically artistic accomplishment.

The Marble Faun was completed at last on November 8th, at Leamington, the little town Hawthorne considered "unadulter-ated England" and to which he so often returned. It was there too that they spent their last Christmas in England, and the children learned how much could be done with very little money.

Their father and mother were now saving more strenuously than ever, and though a good deal of money still passed through their fingers they preferred it to go on charity rather than on expensive presents that were not really needed. But the admirable Fanny Wrigley was with them again — "Fanfan or Fancy" as Sophia often called her — and she was very clever in making charming little gifts out of unregarded odds and ends. The "great preparations" for that Christmas meant, Rose says, "that my sister made a few little handworked presents in greatest secrecy, and there was a breathless spending of sixpences." Una made a black penwiper for her father, embroidered in bright silks — something Papa was so kind as to declare "enchantingly beautiful."*

If the presents piled on the table were few, the children were nevertheless enraptured. Sophia, wrote Rose, threw over whatever she did "the magic which is akin to miracles; the simple twig in her hand budded, dewdrops were filled with all the colors of the rainbows, because with her the sun shone." But it is touching to record that the handsomest and most costly gifts the children received were from their nurse Fanny Wrigley. Her generosity was so great as to awe them; yet, they had to accept without question. What Rose got from her was a leather portfolio with "Rosebud" stamped on it in gold letters.

From 21 Bath Street, Leamington, Una wrote in October to Aunt Lizzie: "This note is to go with a photograph of Baby [Rose of course], taken from a picture of her by Mr. Thompson in Rome, and as it is an excellent likeness, and Baby is the least known to you of any of us, I fancy you will be glad of it." Before many months were passed Aunt Lizzie was to see them all again.

At Leamington too arrived a letter to Sophia from Mr. Fields, who had recently taken over the *Atlantic*, asking her to become one of its contributors. Of this Hawthorne definitely disapproved.

---

* Again there is a manuscript — this one headed "Leamington" — which is drawn upon here.

Like most authors he was quite strongly opposed to any of his children entering his own profession — of whose pangs he knew only too well — but he extended his protective opposition to include his wife. Sophia published nothing until after his death, and then only under the spur of economic necessity.

Transformation (the American *The Marble Faun*) though praised in England was also severely criticized in some quarters for its inconclusive ending. To satisfy these critics Hawthorne added, against his better judgment, a last chapter in which he was as flat-footed as his subtle nature would allow him to be. The book, however, is by some people rated as his masterpiece. And it certainly possesses, as fully as any, that "opaline" quality which Mr. Van Wyck Brooks sees in all Hawthorne's work. Motley wrote a magnificent letter which much more than made up for any British obtuseness, saying, "I like those shadowy, weird, fantastic, Hawthornesque shapes flitting through the golden gloom which is the atmosphere of the book." That letter, read out to the whole family, as was customary in that household where everything was so fully shared, was received with high approval.

The last days were spent in Bath at 13 Charles Street. From there Rose wrote on her birthday to her father: "This morning I awoke and saw the bright son beating on the houses opposite and thanked God it had come at last, these rainy days without any thunder or lightning . . . are very dull in deed. But now Papa cannot you come and stay with me today, its my birthday you know and I shouldn't have haf such a nice time if you don't. I shall be sure to have a doncky ride today as it is Saterday." She signs herself "your daughter Rose nine years old today."*

But before getting to Charles Street, Sophia had one last taste of grandeur, which she enjoyed all the more because she knew it must be the last. This was a stay at the York House, one of

* Letter in the Berg Collection, New York Public Library. First quotation of many drawn from this source.

the best Bath hotels. There they were given a sitting room so lordly and hung in such rich scarlet that the father and mother renamed themselves the Duke and Duchess of Maine — on account of some family claim to property there — while Julian was Lord Waldo, and Una, Lady Raymond; and of course there was also a little Lady Rose.

Sophia, always easily sent into tremors of excited enthusiasm, got eloquent upon the silverware and cut glass and the "Apician food, so delicately touched with fire." The waiters she named the Sublime and the Pensive; the Sublime had a shirt front of linen lilies in peculiarly wide bloom, while the Pensive was adorned rather with snowdrops. Whenever the Duchess left the room there was the Sublime at the door to open it for her, "bowing down with all his lilies." She almost felt the ducal coronet on her brow. And to make everything complete, when a cold day came there arrived with it a third attendant, whom she named the Soft. He was a boy who gently deposited the coal without raising the least dust and who poked the fire as tenderly as one would kiss a sleeping babe.

But the York House was much too expensive for people now set upon economy, though the children clamored to stay where they were. So drawn in a bath chair, with Fanny Wrigley to do the talking and Rose to look out for "To Let" signs, they set out in search of lodgings — which they found at 13 Charles Street.

But the return to the United States had long been determined upon, and only the English publication of *Transformation* had kept the family that extra year in England. All the same Hawthorne rather dreaded the thought of his return. Even when they were living in Southport, in 1857, he had told Ticknor, "I am in no great hurry to return to America. To say the truth, it looks like an infernally disagreeable country from this side of the water." And the abolitionist agitation made him add in a later letter, "I have no country, or only just enough of a one to be ashamed of." Still earlier he had written to Longfellow, "Our country looks very disagreeable and uncomfortable, morally, socially and climatically, from this side of the water. . . . I *love* America, but do not *like* it." America, he admitted, was a good country for young people, but not, he thought, for those past their prime. "For my part, I have no love for England nor Englishmen, and I do love my own country; but for all that, the honest truth is that I do not care whether I ever set eyes on it again." If such were Hawthorne's sentiments in the autumn of 1855, they were still more strongly ingrained in him by the spring of 1860. But he was thinking of his children; and he saw that if they did not leave England they would soon be completely English. And object though Hawthorne might to many features of American social and political life, he was very much of an American. He had written to Fields from Leamington in September, 1857: "We have forgotten what home is — at least the children have, poor things! I doubt whether they will ever feel inclined to live long in one place. The worst of it is, I have outgrown my house in Concord, and feel no inclination to return to it." Though in varying moods Hawthorne said different things, here is expressed his most constant feeling. But all this created further division in a mind already deeply fissured. By going back to his native land, so that his children might become attached to it, he increased in himself a malady of the spirit that was to prove mortal.

*

CHAPTER X

Golden Gloom

The Hawthornes arrived at Concord toward the close of June, on a day of the kind when the heat simmers and the air quivers. To Rose, who had long ago forgotten everything about the "Morica" she used to talk about, the very "un-English" landscape seemed ugly and depressing. And when they arrived at the Wayside in the station wagon and saw the dingy buff house that was their home, her spirits sank still further. Actually it was one of the pleasant places in the village and had been taken good care of in their absence by Nat Peabody, Sophia's brother. But after the splendors of Montaüto or even the placid prettiness of the Leamington villa, it looked almost squalid. To make matters (if anything) worse, they were accompanied from the station by little Benjie Mann. He was a brash youth, and seemed more than ever so to his Europeanized cousins. But the children would soon adjust themselves and forget Europe. Sophia, too, with her buoyant nature, could be counted upon to make the best possible terms with her fate. It was Hawthorne who gazed at familiar Concord with grim, though serene misgiving.

There outspread was the pleasant but undistinguished setting. The center of the town still seemed to be Stacy's general store, with its post office. Men were always there, around the cracker barrel; and, at the delivery of the mail, women and children gathered too. And Walcott and Holden's had their own unofficial town meeting. Hawthorne had noticed other landmarks, such as they were, the Middlesex Hotel, and Jonas Hastings' shoe store, and Mr. Moore's truck farm. Less than ever now did Hawthorne rejoice at his home-coming.

What Concordians noticed at once in him was that he was now a different man from the shy recluse they had known. He was by degrees to return to his earlier habits of seclusion, but he showed for a while the air of well-being he had acquired in Europe, and also the easy manners learned by his having been obliged to mix a good deal in society. He had mellowed with prosperity. He might be said now to have a certain polish were it not the fact that he had always been a man of refined and distinguished bearing.

This was vaguely resented in some quarters — not so much because of Hawthorne himself but because Sophia and Una were given to chattering about their European experiences. They were quite artless about this; they merely supposed that people would be interested. But there were those whose luck had not been so good as the Hawthornes' — Mrs. Alcott, for instance — who chose to think that Sophia was now giving herself airs. Poor Mrs. Alcott! Her lot was indeed hard. It would have been bad enough to be married to a poet, but to a poet *and* philosopher. . . ! As Louisa Alcott had confided to her journal three years earlier: "Philosophers are always poor, and too modest to pass round their own hats."

Upon the whole Mrs. Alcott put up with things very well, though there were times when she nagged her husband — upon which he just went on talking, as oblivious as any man can be on such occasions. And it must be admitted that she could rise nobly to the great occasion. While the Hawthornes were in America Alcott had made a western lecture tour which he hoped would replenish the family coffers. He came home one cold February night and Mrs. Alcott and the girls all gave him welcome but none dared ask the question uppermost in all their minds, until May at last ventured, "Well, did people pay you?" Then he opened his pocketbook and showed a single dollar, "Only that!"

he said with a smile that made their eyes fill. "My overcoat was stolen, and I had to buy a shawl. Many promises were not kept and traveling is costly; but I have opened the way, and another year shall do better." Then came Mrs. Alcott's grand response: "I call that doing *very well!*" It was her great moment. For that much can be forgiven a somewhat soured and suspicious disposition and a shrewish tongue. The time was to come, however, when Alcott went round, in great distress, to Hawthorne to ask if there was any misunderstanding between the two families. Though Hawthorne told him no, he added that it was not possible to live on amicable terms with Mrs. Alcott. "The old man," Hawthorne confided to Fields, "acknowledged the truth of all I said (indeed, who could know it better). . . . I clothed all this in velvet phrases, that it might not seem too hard for him to bear, but he took it all like a saint."

The situation is indicated in an undated letter of Sophia's to Elizabeth Peabody: "I think that Mrs. Alcott has a grand character. I used to think that she had a vast heart, full of tender humanity and generous help — so I was very glad when I heard she was to be our neighbor. She has that vast heart still, no doubt, if its sweetness had not become bitterness by a wrong point of view of her privations and calamities. . . . Since our return from Europe, she has always received my expressions of interest and regard with manifest distrust, as if I were telling lies. . . . She thinks that because she is poor, she is despised." Apparently even Louisa was not always kind in her remarks about Sophia, though she was civil when they met in the street.

Rose later found titles for the sage, those of "visionary plenipotentiary," and "a lamb in chains." Whenever his tall, black-clad figure, with a straw hat on its head was seen approaching the Wayside — as often happened because he lived in the next house — Hawthorne instantly would fall back for defense upon his reputation for having retiring habits. For much as he liked Alcott, one never knew when he would have a manuscript poem with him. From one that he had insisted on reading aloud to the Haw-thornes they never quite recovered.

Nor did Hawthorne think very much of Ellery Channing's poetry — "Sublimo-slipshod style" Thoreau called it — though at least he was not addicted to inflicting it on his friends. But he was a companionable man, and for young people better in the outdoors than Henry Thoreau himself. Ellery would often go to the woods with the girls, and when he and Mr. Sanborn were invited to Christmas dinner at the Hawthornes, Rose and Una and their father went with the poet to gather evergreens for the decorations. There was nobody in Concord more welcome than he, tenderhearted, whimsical, eccentric, and, as Rose thought, phosphorescent — a charming boy still, in his middle age. The greatest mark of favor he could show anyone was an invitation to climb some high point to look at the sunset. A Concord sunset, he fully believed, was the finest in the world. Rose was several times invited to accompany him.

That other nature lover, Henry Thoreau, was far more gifted but much less approachable. His famous hermit period by Walden Lake was long since past, and he was now almost an ordinary member of society, but Rose, whenever she walked in them, thought Walden Woods still rustled with his name. He was never a man to withdraw anything. But he did give the addendum: "We soon get through with Nature. She excites an expectation which she cannot satisfy. The merest child which has rambled into a copsewood dreams of a wilderness so wild and strange and in-exhaustible as Nature can never show him." He frightened Rose dreadfully at first, though, with those strange eyes of his and his long nose and his prickly manner, but when she got to know him better she caught an "April pensiveness" in his expression. But she would have agreed with Elizabeth Hoar, "I love Henry, I do not like him."

Then there was Judge Hoar and his beautiful sister Elizabeth. She wore, almost visibly, widow's weeds for Emerson's brother,

Charles, who had not lived to marry her. In 1842, when Sophia thought her the Rose of Sharon, she also decided that she could hardly be called an earthly inhabitant. Her presence in Concord cast a radiance over it.

But of course the very great man, the major star in that brilliant galaxy, as the world viewed him, was Emerson. They all saw a good deal of him, and though Hawthorne could not read his books, nor he Hawthorne's, they were sufficiently good friends. Emerson's great friend, however, was Una. Before the family had gone to Europe, when she was only eight years old, she had gone round to his house and had rung the bell and when Emerson appeared and said kindly, "I suppose you have come to see Mrs. Emerson," got the child's blunt answer, "No, I have come to see *you*." After that she used to go in and out of the Emersons' just as though it were her own home.

It was something like the girlish "crush" Louisa Alcott had had on him when she was fifteen and about which she told him later, greatly to his amusement. Louisa had been reading Goethe and thought that she would like to be Emerson's Bettine. So she wrote letters to him but did not send them, and sang Mignon's song under his window in bad German, and left wild flowers on his doorstep. Una was not so sentimental about the man, but she read him as devoutly as a gospel, and listened to his lectures, and if the ministers criticized him — as even Unitarian ministers did — Una undertook not only to defend him but to explain him and to show that there was no inconsistency between what he had said and what the ministers themselves believed.

But there was *one* lecture of Emerson's, when he alone could save himself. All Concord was there, as all Concord always did go to the Lyceum when Mr. Emerson was speaking. On this occasion he wore a pair of abominably squeaking boots. He could not move without that base accompaniment to his sublime thoughts. He could hardly take the boots off and continue in stockings. It was most edifying to witness how the philosopher accepted with meekness his distressing predicament. He lectured to the end — but nobody remembered anything afterward except his fortitude and the sound of his squeaking boots.

Sophia might have thought, eighteen years earlier, that Emerson's face "intruded no more than a sunset or a rich warble from a bird"; Rose could be almost cruelly detached in her comments. His smile, so she thought on first seeing him, and always finding him smiling, was an extra feature on his face. As he passed her, blandly benevolent, she realized that he was a great force and that she, after all, was a little girl. She was always waiting to discover what he was smiling *at*. Finally she concluded that he he had something to smile *for*, and she felt all the happier at witnessing his heroic cheerfulness. Even so, she considered that he ought to reserve a smile so striking and circumstantial for rare occasions, and thought his manner, in spite of its suavity, was patronizing.

But he could be warm and kind at the parties at his house, when Edith Emerson helped her mother, who looked like a Lady Abbess in winged lace headdress and black silk. Then the children would ride Edward Emerson's pony, as sometimes they would go bathing with the great man himself and his family in Walden Pond.

On one occasion, however, Sophia* had to make a vigorous protest against his having loaned Una Drayton's works. Sophia, looking the book over, had encountered a piece of Elizabethan frankness that shocked her. "I at once saw," she wrote, "why her father enjoined upon me never to put those old British poets into her hands. For when images are once presented, they may remain, and what is known cannot be unknown. . . . In this as in all other things concerning the children, I agree with my husband. . . . Your culture is so complete and rich that I value very much your

* I believe the undated and incomplete letter (at Hawthorne, N. Y.) is to Emerson, because of his close friendship with Una. It was written after Hawthorne's death.

advice to Una about her reading. But I do hope you will never be affronted when I do not entirely agree with you on some few small points."

Yes, Concord did have an astonishing collection of geniuses and scholars and interesting people. Yet in itself it was a rather dull little town, and though great books were written there, writers a little less than great found it somewhat lacking in stimulation. Louisa Alcott simply had to go off to Boston, and Hawthorne — though now it was probably not Concord's fault — never could get really going on any of his projects. It was gloom that settled upon him there, even if it was a golden gloom.

The children soon accommodated themselves to the new American life that was so strange at first. And though Rose, writing to Hannah from Bath, had boasted of all the wonderful things she was going to have in America — a large garden, and little and big girls to see her: "Never on earth shall I have such a nice time as when I am at home"* — yet in the middle of the first winter she sang a very different tune: "I am going out, after I have done my lessons, to have a good time — A very good time indeed, to be sure, for there was nothing but frozen ground, and I had to be doing something to keep myself warm. . . . I do not know how to keep myself warm. Happy are you who keep warm all the time in England."

When the spring arrived at last, Rose welcomed it not only for its own sake but because it reminded her of an England full of flowers. And her mother wrote: "Rose raised all the echoes of the county by screaming with joy over her blooming crocuses, which she had found in her garden. The spring intoxicates her with 'remembering wine.' She hugs and kisses me almost to a mummy, with her raptures. Little spots of green grass choke her with unutterable ecstasy."

There was a great deal of fixing up to be done before the

* Rose quotes this letter in her *Memories*, pp. 421 and 422, but must have edited it. For a long time after this her spelling was very eccentric.

Wayside could be made habitable, and though, after Montaüto, it would seem terribly poky, Montaüto had made Hawthorne feel that a tower was a necessity. Accordingly Mr. Weatherbee and Mr. Watts, the Concord carpenters, were called in and hammered and sawed away all day, greatly interesting Julian and Rose, but leaving shavings and sawdust and board ends all over the lawn, and making it impossible that Hawthorne should even think of doing any work until his tower had been completed. Hawthorne used to watch the men at work, his hands folded behind his back and his soft hat pulled over his forehead. He was, as Julian says, "humorously resigned," but Rose and Julian found it all fascinating. Sophia wrote to Mrs. Fields in January: "Ah me, we shall have order at some future date I dare to say. But now there is but one nook where we can take refuge from the Fury of Hubbab. This nook is a wee library, twelve by twelve!" But nearly two years after their return we find Sophia commissioning Mrs. Fields to buy house furnishings in Boston. The wallpaper was now going up; the garden had not yet been reduced to proper order. For that matter the Wayside never was made complete. The Hawthornes were continually tinkering with it, spending a good deal more money than they had expected and yet not making much of the place. It was, however, a house that would have satisfied anybody else in Concord. But the Hawthornes had been spoiled by Italian grandeur and English comfort. It is understandable why poor Mrs. Alcott, who never had a penny to bless herself with, should have interpreted her neighbors' efforts to improve their house a bit as meaning that they regarded themselves as superior to everybody else.*

---

* Ticknor, as usual, was Hawthorne's banker. And Hawthorne was still being generous to those in need — hiding his good deeds from Sophia — as this letter to Ticknor attests: "I have given B—— an order on you for fifty dollars. Pay it, and I promise not to trouble you again on his account. It is impossible not to assist an old acquaintance in distress — for once at least." The postscript is: "Do not write me about this; for I do not wish my wife to know how I throw away money."

Sophia's ingenuity and mild artistic gift had done a good deal with the furniture. Flaxman outlines of Greek mythological subjects were carefully painted on the furniture — some of them suggesting to Hawthorne those children's stories of his. The culture of Concord took very much to Flaxman, and it is still remembered in the little town how one winter's night a group of enthusiasts waded through deep snowdrifts merely to see a book of Flaxman's "attenuated outlines" that had just been received by one of their friends. Before her marriage Sophia had bought a set of bedroom furniture and, after painting it dull gold for a background, had outlined upon it classical figures. Later her children assisted her in these tasks. Some of the specimens of her skill are still in existence. At the Rose Hawthorne Lathrop home at Fall River is preserved a maple fiddleback chair decorated by her.

The children would have been content to gaze forever at Mr. Weatherbee and Mr. Watts. But with the arrival of fall, it was decided to send them to school — for the first time. Una escaped, as she was now over sixteen, except for taking special courses. We hear of George Bradford's tutoring her and of Elizabeth Hoar's giving her lessons in Dante. Mr. Sanborn, who had a coeducational school — something very novel in those days — would have liked to have had both Julian and Rose. But though he did get Julian, to prepare him for Harvard, Rose attended for a while the East Quarter Public School — the first of about four schools at which for brief periods she was enrolled. Sanborn's school was ruled out for the girls, in spite of the Horace Mann's coeducational ideas and a strong letter Ellery Channing wrote on September 3, 1860, saying: "If you were as intimate with Mr. Sanborn as I have the good fortune to be, I think nothing would give you so much satisfaction as to have such nice girls as yours to be directly under his charge." Hawthorne thought differently:

the only connection his "nice girls" had with Mr. Sanborn was to attend the school dances and picnics.

Rose spent relatively little time at any school, but continued for the most part to learn at home. In December, 1861, we have Una writing to Aunt Ebie — her father's sister, Elizabeth — saying that she is hearing Rose's lessons. Miss Phebe Ripley, who lived in the Old Manse, gave Una, and later Rose, lessons in music and was regarded as an exceptionally good teacher; while their mother taught the children various semiartistic things like painting vases and paper knives and baskets. A little later we find Sophia writing to tell Mrs. Fields: "Rose is going to make a book of the Life of Penelope from Flaxman — and I am to illuminate the cover for her." It has to be admitted, however, that the children's artistic aptitude was slight. According to her mother, Una for long periods practiced the piano for sixteen hours a day, and a similar fate overtook Rose. But neither girl reached proficiency. And though Rose painted earnestly until middle life, her work never amounted to very much. That they had the artistic temperament is true; what they did not have, to an adequate degree, was the power of translating their ability to enjoy the beautiful into the power of creating it. The fact that, in April, 1861, Una wrote to Aunt Lizzie Peabody, "I have begun to teach Julian and Baby music, and they show great readiness for it, and it is very pleasant to think they can acquire such a pleasant accomplishment without paying twenty-five dollars a quarter," suggests that the Hawthornes were practicing a strict economy. A little pathetically, Una adds: "I daresay I shall be able to teach them to play much better than myself."

But whatever regular schooling Rose had — and a letter from her dated April, 1863, tells Elizabeth Hawthorne: "A Miss Bailey is coming to teach a girls' private school here and I am going" — the teaching of spelling seems in Rose's case to have been more than usually ineffective. This fact is all the more striking because her handwriting is already very mature. But perhaps "eccentric" is not quite the word, "individualistic" might be better; for the letters of this period — written in a very flowing style for a child of her years — convey a vivid impression of a highly vivacious little person, scampering excitedly all over the Wayside and Concord, laughing, shouting, even (regrettable though it be to say) screaming and quarreling. High spirited, hot tempered, warmhearted, so she shows herself in her letters to her father, her aunts, Julian, and Mrs. Fields. We see her wild, red hair tossing as she dashes across the lawn or scampers up the hill behind the house. "Today," she writes to Julian on July 31, 1861: "as I was out in the woodshed a wasp came across me and I across him, and instead of running away, I ran right through him and then ran away and I screached so loud & so many times that both Joanna & Ann [these were the Hawthornes' servants] when I went for their assistance, were standing towards the door where the disaster happened with their hair on end & stood so for 3 or 4 seconds after I asked them if they saw the wasp round me." By some lucky accident that is spelled fairly normally, though she dates it "*Wensday*." And this bit of poetry, too, is better in its spelling than Rose's usually is:

> *Una & Julian have gorn away*
> *And I am left to wander about.*
> *Una & Julian don't like me*
> *And if they do, it you shall see.*
> *Unas a tirant*
> *And Julians a bore*
> *And thats the way forever more.*
> *The sun peeps through the trees at me*
> *And as to my sight it blindeth me.*
> *I'v got a kitten as black as soot*
> *And Benj'y my cusin says he'l her shoot*
> *The girls they are walking all round*
> *But as to the place theres not a sound.*

On July 28, 1861, writing to her father, she hopes he is not "perticular" about her letter "for you can see that I have done it wrong." And let us hope that the eminent educational authority made due allowances when she got letters from her "afectionate nice." The beautiful Una two years later got a letter from her romantic sister signed "Your silent adora."

A little later, when Julian had gone to Harvard, Rose wrote hoping that he had not had any "perolous adventures" — then hopefully asked, "have you?" She herself has nothing much to report except: "Mamma and Papa go to walk all most all the time, now. Yesterday they went to Walden, and saw the place where Mr. Thoreau's house used to stand." She adds that Una "is the great genious for finding things to say. Which I cannot do."

In all this we get a picture of a very happy and a very normal child, skating on Walden pond in winter and bathing there with the Emersons in summer, boating on the river, going to parties and being interested in the effect her clothes were likely to have on the girls (and also the boys), riding horses, and playing with dolls.

Though upon the whole she did have plenty of playmates, there is a letter she wrote to Mrs. Fields soon after the family returned to Concord in which she tells rather pathetically of her loneliness: "I have a very pritty doll," she writes, "though I never play with it, though I try to. I have a great many things to play with, but it seems so desolate to play alone that I never play with my play things now. . . . I never have anyone to play with me and I might as well play by myself if I could." To this Sophia adds a postscript saying: "it is true that Rose was quite lonely." She adds: "I intend to play with her myself this winter."*

It is rather evident, however, that Rose never cared a great deal for dolls or toys. Kittens meant much more to her and appear a great deal in her letters. She tells Mrs. Fields the following year:

---

* Rose's letters to Mrs. Fields are in the Boston Public Library. They seem to have been supervised by Sophia and are therefore at once better spelled and less lively than some of her other letters of this time.

"We have got some dear little black kittens with white stockings on that I love very much; but soon Sybil [the cat] will have some gray kittens and I shall give up the black ones with white stockings on." But, in 1863, Rose writes to Aunt Ebie: "Sybil Gray was drownd by Ben (who took great delight in it) the other day. She was getting so tiresome. And she was going to have some kittens too." The references to Ben Mann, which are frequent, indicate that he was not very popular with his cousins but that he made his presence felt. Of which of her pets the following is recorded, it is impossible to tell, but in an undated letter to Julian she tells him: "I think kitty smells as if she had been eating mice or rats I do not no wish. . . . Kitty has got up and hunched her back and stuck her tail up til it tuches her head."

In the summer of 1862 Rose tells Julian of having two affectionate little kittens in brown and white, with little black spots and stripes. And the year before Papa got a letter which told of a kitten "intirely blak." Rose goes on: "Its name is not quite desided but mamma sedgested Parygon." And the year of their return Rose wrote to "Dearest Julian": "I have told Kitty of thinking of you, and she gave a sort of groul (I am afriad I have put this rong)."

But even in 1862 (and later), Rose was still putting things "rong." She wrote to her father, who was visiting the Isle of Shoals with Pierce, that she was very "fritend" at the thought that he might be at the bottom of the "see." Her mother, it seems, had had "a bad influenzer." But by then she herself is having some fun. "Eddward" Emerson and Abby Alcott had been at a "celabration" party for Julian's vacation. "And a very nice time we had too. We had after tea some nuts and raisins and little cocoa nut cakes and lemonade." And in the morning Abby Alcott came to breakfast. And Abby was almost as amusing as her sister Louisa could be: "She went to here Mr. Agassi's last lecture on Ellefants. But she said that he lectured about all the animals instead of Elefants."

In March of 1862, we hear of a ball (presumably given at Sanborn's school), and about this there are three separate letters.* On March 17, 1862, Rose writes in her very best hand, but on faintly lined paper, to Mr. Fields to thank him for the dress he had got for her. She had worn it both at the masquerade and at a private dance which, because no masks were worn, she thought even "jollier." Una writing to Aunt Ebie on the 16th says: "Rose was Titania, had a very full short dress of white Tarlatan covered with silver spangles, and a pale blue and white sash going over her shoulder, crossing her bosom and tying under her arms, and a crown of silver damascened with gold and covered with pearls, with an emerald veil covered with spangles floated from it behind, and she carried in her hand a little gold and silver wand, tipped with flowers, and her hair was curled all round her head. She looked very lovely indeed and some people thought her the belle." But Sophia in her letter to Mrs. Fields says: "Rose, in her spangled Titania robe, hopped about on one foot like a stork on the evening of the party. Was not it a pity she could not dance on account of her sprain?" Perhaps it was as well for Mr. Sanborn's boys that so lovely a creature should have been under this handicap!

That seems to have been a big year for activities of all kinds. For Una had to tell Aunt Ebie of bathing in Walden with the Emersons, of Rose and herself blackberrying in Walden Woods with Abby Alcott, and of boating with Rose and Horace Mann. The Concord was not the best of rivers for sport. Hawthorne said he had had to swim across it a number of times before discovering in which direction it flowed. It was, he thought, like the earthworms he used to dig for bait when he was a boy: "The worm is sluggish, and so is the river — the river is muddy, and so is the worm. You hardly know whether either of them be alive or dead; but still, in the course of time, they both manage

* Those to the Fieldses are in the Boston Public Library. The other is at Hawthorne, N. Y.

to creep away." Sophia said of the river, more succinctly, that it was too lazy to keep itself clean. For lighthearted young people, however, it provided plenty of fun.

Other glimpses of Rose abound. In March, 1863, Sophia wrote triumphantly to Annie Fields how she had put the local allopathic practitioner, Doctor Bartlett, to rout when Rose had a fever, and he had declared her to be in serious danger. But Sophia prescribed the aconite in which she had such faith, and in six days when Doctor Bartlett found the patient completely recovered he stroked his snowy drift of beard and told Sophia: "Mrs. Hawthorne, I must take you into partnership. Drive round with me, and I will say what is the matter, and you shall — ." On the subject of homeopathy Sophia was disposed to be fanatical.

Then we meet Rose gardening — helping her mother in Sophia's letter, and in one of her own to Una telling how "Julian and I have made the cabbig bed beautiful hode and weeded and raked it and are doing the carrots now."

And in the same line of usefulness, performed with not too good a grace by the small Rose, are the references to visits paid by her and Una to a kind of Hawthorne pensioner, old Abigail Cook. Una writes to Aunt Ebie a little patronizingly about "the funney old woman." She says, "her principal desire in the world seems to be that we should take tea there. And we had a queer enough time — but it was satisfactory to give so much pleasure, though I shall not feel called upon to sacrifice myself again." It should be said in the girls' favor that they did so frequently, usually carrying some present, and that they had to endure the ordeal of eating some of Mrs. Cook's mince pie, strongly flavored, they fancied, with pepper and molasses.

Less edifying was Rose's attitude toward church services. She found worthy Mr. Frost at the First Parish — the Unitarian Church — then and afterward insufferably prosy and was candid in saying so. But Una, who was a Transcendentalist when in the neighborhood of the admired Mr. Emerson, was a somewhat primly pious young lady on all other occasions. Such bits as these are frequent in her letters. This one, dated February 19, 1865, says: "Monday I went to tea at the Emersons' and to the Bible class as usual. We are studying about Nehemiah and Esther; and Malachi, who is supposed to have helped Nehemiah in his work of regenerating the priesthood."

Rose was quite definitely not a pious child. Perhaps the explanation is that she was having much too good a time for that. Even the outbursts of temper of which we hear in the young child are no longer referred to, except very lightly and jocosely, as when Rose tells Julian: "I feel very lonely here, without any scobbles or fights with you, you dear creature." Everything that Cousin Benjy did, it is true, was turned to derision — even when he let his hair grow long and parted it in the middle, which he hoped made him look like an Indian — but even Benjy is let off lightly. No doubt Julian's description of Rose at this time, written after her death more than sixty years later, as "aggressive, quick-tempered, joyous, and confident" is accurate. But her high spirits were now more evident than the quick temper. Her father might be sinking deep into a golden gloom, but there was no gloom about her. Except for her complaint to Mrs. Fields, soon after coming back to Concord, of having nobody to play with, there are not to be found in her any of the little troubles that so often appear large to children. In her there was none of the melancholy that Una inherited.

What her father thought she might have inherited was something he would have regarded as even more of a calamity — a propensity to write. Sophia was given to encouraging her children in this matter, and even to boasting of their little efforts. Not so Rose's father. She had produced what she referred to in later life laughingly as a so-called novel of about a thousand words and to a little visitor one afternoon she was reading this masterpiece.

She did not notice that the window of the library was open, nor probably would she have imagined her father, the famous novelist, would be other than proud of his daughter's following in his footsteps. But as soon as Rose's visitor had gone her father came striding out. He seemed to be as angry as she had ever seen him as he said, "Never, never again let me hear of you writing stories!" Well, he never did *hear* of them again, but it became all the more delightful after that command to exercise her faculty of picturing people and scenes and of inventing conversation.

Between Rose and her father there was the closest and dearest affection. She was his favorite child and the one most like him. To her he wrote from Beverly Farms on August 5, 1861: "Dear Bab, I am very homesick, and have come to the conclusion that when a person has a comfortable home of his own, and a good little Bab of his own, and a great big Onion and a best Mama, he had better stay with them than roam abroad." Her letters to him are usually signed "Rose B B B Hawthorne" — the B B B meaning (as we see when she signs in full) Baby Bab Bad, as Una was still "Onion," though she was now getting so ladylike that she asked to have it in Persian. They are written in his own vein of humorous affection. On that last visit of his to Washington, in 1862, she tells him: "I was also glad to reseive a kiss though not so good as if from your own mouth instead of ink."

And on that last journey of his — except for the one on which he died — Sophia wrote to tell him on March 24, 1864, of how his letter was received: "Rose," she wrote, "was in such a trembling ecstasy when Julian gave her thy letter, that she could not open it, but begged me to take it and read it to her at once."

CHAPTER XI

The Fall of the Pillar

Looking back upon what happened later, Sophia was aware that she had divined from the start what was going to happen. Nobody, however, was ever able to say convincingly why it happened, though perhaps if all the reasons are added together their sum will come somewhere near to the right explanation, even if one continues to suspect that something has been left out. Hawthorne's feeling about the Civil War, his worry over Una's health — which was never fully restored after her illness of 1859 — probably the frustration he encountered in his literary work, all contributed. His son-in-law, George Parsons Lathrop (who presumably got his notions from Rose), suggests in his *Study of Hawthorne* that it was a longing for England. That Hawthorne did have this longing is true; but it could have been only a minor factor in his trouble. Sophia, writing to her husband on July 25, 1861, exclaimed: "Of all the trials, this is the heaviest to me — to see you so apathetic, so indifferent, so hopeless, so unstrung. Rome has no sin to answer for so unpardonable as this of wrenching off your wings and hanging lead upon your arrowy feet. Rome — and all Rome caused to you." Things must have come to a bad pass when Sophia could mention them so openly to him.

No doubt what Sophia meant by her accusation against Rome was that he, even less than Una, had recovered from her illness. But it is possible that Sophia glimpsed something deeper than that and was aware that his mind had been shaken by the powerful force of Catholicism, and that his resistance at this point had given him a serious wound. Rose was to say of his disease — whatever it was — "None of us analyzed [it] as fatal; though from his expression of face, if for no other reason, I judge he himself understood it perfectly." It was all the more disturbing because he had never been ill in his life before and even now, except for increasing lassitude and loss of weight, remained in very good health.

A change had come over him. There was no special need to worry, of course, that his thick locks had suddenly become white. What caused alarm was his languor and inability to work. The failing of his creative powers is to an artist even more than the effect of his malady, it is the malady itself. When a great writer can no longer write, he thinks that he might as well be dead. And very soon he is dead.

What they hoped would prove beneficial to him was his new occupation of dragging wood. The exercise in the open air was of a kind that permitted him to meditate upon the various books he tried to write during these last years. They could see him climbing the wooded hill behind the Wayside and then walking back and forth up there deep in thought. He wore a path under the pines among the huckleberry bushes and the ferns, where in the spring pale blue violets also huddled. And Hawthorne's path may still be seen, for paths made by the steady passing of feet seem to remain forever.

About the Civil War he was very depressed. To his Bowdoin friend, Horatio Bridge, he wrote in the fall of 1861: "For my part I don't hope, nor indeed wish, to see the Union restored as it was." Earlier he had written to him. "Though I approve of the war as much as any man, I don't quite understand what we are fighting for, or what definite result can be expected. If we pummel the South ever so hard, they will love us none the better for it; and even if we subjugate them, our next step should be to cut them adrift." But lick 'em and kick 'em out was not, even to Hawthorne, a very satisfactory war policy. His state of mind seemed to be so causeless that he could almost believe that the witch's curse on that ancestor of his, the Salem judge, was now taking its strange and terrible effect.

Concord made its contribution to the war — even to the extent of a draft riot — but Hawthorne was glad that he was too old and Julian too young to shoulder a musket. From next door, Louisa Alcott went off to nurse the wounded soldiers in Washington, but herself became ill and had to be brought home by a father who, for once, roused himself to action. And though this letter from Sophia to her sister, Mary Mann, was written in the last stages of the war, it describes pretty much what the family had been doing all through it. "You cannot think," she writes, "how busy Una and Rose are from morn to eve. The studies, the housekeeping, sewing and [piano] exercises make a mosaic of every day and nothing exceptional can squeeze in. Rose knits for the soldiers while she studies her lessons. Rose is often like a tightly drawn harp string."

And Rose, writing to Una from Brattleborough, Massachusetts, in 1861, tells her: "I have seen a regiment, last night at 7 o'clock a regiment marched round town of eleven hundred men. And as they came along we all went out & we said good bye and they said good bye & Aunt Tyler said God bless you and one said 'thank you old lady' & they said that they would come back if they were not kild and a young man went away who was a genral."

During the war they had a long visit from Aunt Ebie, whom the children now got to know very well. Miss Hawthorne was a remarkable person — more gifted than himself, so her brother used to declare. Mrs. Fields has described her as being small, fine featured (though with a full round face), fresh looking even in old age, and with notably brilliant eyes. But Mrs. Fields also thought she saw "a deterioration because of too great solitude."

Her brother's solitude had fed his powers, but "utter solitude" —
and this she had at the farm at Montserrat, where she read all the
time, except when she took her lonely walks — "utter solitude
lames the native power of a woman even more than that of a
man, for her natural growth is through her sympathies." But
Elizabeth Hawthorne was not really living in an ivory tower.
She kept very much in touch with what was going on in the
world and commented upon it pungently. Her niece, Rose, saw
her as "a good deal unspiritual in everything; but all besides in
her was fine mind, wisdom and loving-kindness of a lazy artistic
sort. That is to say she was unregenerate, but excellent; and she
fascinated like a wood-creature seldom seen and observant, refined
and untrained."

She at once perceived that Rose herself was a miniature mystery
and took her out into the woods, the better to establish contact.
There she noticed everything from the note of a bird to the
leap of a squirrel. She had her brother's eloquence in silence and
loved moss and leaves as much as some people love souls. But
there was this difference, Rose saw: Aunt Ebie had chosen these
things as being the least dangerous objects of affection; whereas
her father, much as he loved nature, loved men more.

In the evenings, this strange woman, who had "sufficient
strength of character to upset a kingdom" and who wielded the
sword of her sarcasm so that heads fell on every side, sat under
the lamp in her light-brown mohair dress — she should have worn
dark silk, Rose felt, and flirted a fan. There she instructed her
niece in the mysteries of knitting, meanwhile herself "knitting
titanically." It was so that Rose first remembered seeing her — and
at first sight she was not romantic looking or mysterious, but
only rather intimidating with her large, shining needles and heavy,
blue socks. Rose was so afraid of her that she pretended she was
most anxious to be taught how to do the same. Before she really
got to know Aunt Ebie she had to go out with her into the
woods.

Then there were the other aunts, her mother's sisters. To them, much as she loved them, Sophia could be at times quite tart, for she resented even the slightest implication of her husband or children having any defects. "In speaking of the children to you, dear Elizabeth," she explained, "I am never making comparisons between them and any other children. . . . There was a time when I could outpour into your sympathetic ear any amount of praiseful happy talk about them without being misinterpreted. But since my return I find you suspicious of me, and of my expressed opinions, and that you are apt to think me arrogant and self conceited if I say with any emphasis that my soul is my own, or venture to differ from you and your authorities. . . . I never said to you in my life that my children were superior to all other children — for I do not know millions of children who may far outgo mine." As for her husband — so she had written from England: "No, Elizabeth, what I object to and cannot allow . . . is to anything saucy said about him — for (whether you may or may not recollect) you have been in the habit of saying caustic and disagreeable things in reference to him during my whole married life. . . . Mr. Hawthorne never reads any of your notes and I should never wish him to." That letter runs to 21 pages and for once Sophia gets really angry.

To Mary Mann, in an undated letter about this time, Sophia writes: "I lay awake all night and loved you. I think it is because we are not infallible that we are commanded to 'love one another' and not judge one another. *GOD* only is able to judge, I more and more believe. Whatever I thought too hasty and unkind I remember no more forever. An Angel has blotted everything but love which never ceased and never can. Perhaps it was my love that has blotted everything out. . . . I shall destroy every word of yours which is not loving, which I have not already destroyed."*

* This is probably why so many of the letters at Hawthorne, New York, are incomplete.

In the middle of the war — on May 6, 1862 — Thoreau died.
Though he was far from being a bosom friend, Hawthorne liked
and admired him. His death, coming at this time, struck hard
home. As his was the long wasting illness of tuberculosis, Sophia
found and returned that music box Henry had given them in the
early days of their marriage. She had often danced to its tiny
tune, to the great delight of her husband and of the Irish servant.
Then, when she was away for Mary Peabody's wedding, Hawthorne tried to comfort his loneliness by winding it up. But as
Sophia was not there, there seemed no soul in its mechanical
tinkle, and he often felt like throwing the box out of the window.
It had lain in the Hawthorne attic for years; now in his last illness
it played its little tunes to Henry Thoreau. A month later he
was dead.

The following year Hawthorne got out *Our Old Home*, the
last of the books he was to publish, first printing its chapters
in the *Atlantic* but, when sending them to the editor, expressing
his unmistakable conviction that all were good for nothing. But
it was not much more than the salvaging and rewriting of some
bits from the voluminous *Notebooks* he had kept in England. He
explained in the Preface: "The Present, the Immediate, the Actual,
has proved too potent for me. It takes away not only my scanty
faculty, but even my desire for imaginative composition, and
leaves me sadly content to scatter a thousand peaceful fantasies
upon the hurricane that is sweeping us all along with it, possibly
into a limbo where our nation and its policy may be as literally
the fragments of a shattered dream as my written romance."
The English, much to Hawthorne's surprise, were rather hurt
by some of the things he said of them. He thought this was
rather rich, coming from a people who had never spared Americans their criticism. He did, in fact, tone down his *Notebooks*,

but even so what he allowed to stand seemed a bit harsh at the time. An English lady could hardly be expected to relish this description of herself: "She has an awful ponderosity of frame, not pulpy, like the lower developement of our few fat women, but with solid beef and streaky tallow; so that though struggling manfully against the idea you inevitably think of her as made up of steaks and sirloins."

He showed himself very noble in the matter of dedication. Though thinking of giving it to Bennoch, he finally decided on Pierce, as he it was who had provided him with the opportunity for observing England and the English. But Pierce was then so unpopular that Fields advised Hawthorne not to do this, lest he seriously damage the sales of the book. On July 13, 1863, Hawthorne wrote to say that he had delayed his reply in order to think about it and to smoke cigars over it. He concluded that "it would be a piece of poltroonery in me to withdraw either the dedication or the dedicatory letter. If he is so exceedingly unpopular that his name is enough to sink the volume, there is so much the more need that an old friend should stand by him. . . . If the public of the North see fit to ostracise me for this, I can only say that I would gladly sacrifice a thousand or two of dollars rather than retain the good-will of such a herd of dolts and mean-spirited scoundrels." He needed money at that time very badly, yet he persisted in his resolve. Emerson and others cut out the page where Pierce's name was printed; to me it shines with gold because of Hawthorne's loyalty to his friend.

Hawthorne was on terms of intimate friendship with his publishers. Ticknor continued to manage his affairs for him. At the Houghton Mifflin Company they still exhibit Ticknor's desk with its two compartments — one holding a bag of gold and the other a bottle of bourbon, both of which came out the moment the star author crossed the threshold. If between Hawthorne and

Fields the friendship was a shade less close, this was more than made up by the intimacy between their wives. In that day of fancy names Mr. Fields became "Heartsease," and Mrs. Fields, "Mrs. Meadows," in her husband's playful references to her; while by Sophia she was addressed in letters as "Beloved Annie," "My Dear Moonlight," "My Western Peri," and the like. As for Rose's appreciation of Mr. "Feilds" it appears in a letter she wrote from Boston, in 1861, concluding, "Tell Julian that I had a dinner of everything that I wanted and I dare say that I shall have all I want all the time that I am here for Mr. Feilds is so nice he can coks Mamma to do anything."

It was to Hawthorne that Fields dedicated, in 1862, the Household Edition of Scott's Works, and one of Scott's novels was usually read aloud to the family in the evening, Hawthorne's voice rolling in what Sophia, many years before, had called "such sweet thunder." There they sat around the father, Julian with his half-dreamy, half-shrewd eyes, the two girls rapt in wonder, and the mother sewing while she listened.

Hawthorne made several attempts, all so much along the same lines as to be regarded as various versions of the same story — *Septimius Fulton*, *Dr. Grimshawe's Secret*, and the *Doliver Romance*. But only the last of these was printed during his lifetime and that was only begun as a serial in the *Atlantic*. From what he had told Fields about it, the publisher thought it would be his greatest work, but though a couple of installments had been serialized, Hawthorne had in the end to tell Fields that it was no use, he simply was unable to finish the projected task. He had said at the outset: "There is something preternatural in my reluctance to begin. I linger on the threshold, and have a perception of very disagreeable phantoms to be encountered if I enter." At the end of February he gave up. It was then very near the end.

The following month, in the hope that a trip would restore his health and spirits, Ticknor took him on one. Pierce was to have gone too, but was unable to go, and Ticknor should not have gone, as was to be proved, but his doctor, whom he consulted about a cold on the chest, told him he was good for twenty years. From the Astor House, New York, Hawthorne wrote to Rose on April 3rd: "Dear Bab, as mamma does not condescend to write to me, I shall answer your good little letter . . . give my love to Onion." His postscript was: "I hope mamma will not worry herself about me any more; scold her if she does."

A week later Ticknor lay dying in the Continental Hotel in Philadelphia. He realized his condition and longed to see his family. Then suddenly his face lighted up: "Why, they are all here!" he exclaimed — "all standing about my bed." In the merciful hallucination of delirium he was consoled.

Hawthorne was stricken by the suddenness of it all. Over and over again he moaned that he should have died, not Ticknor. Some ghastly mistake had happened. It was more dead than alive that he reached Concord.

Sophia at once saw that something had to be done and Pierce was appealed to. He suggested taking Hawthorne as it was now spring — early May — in an open carriage for a leisurely trip through New Hampshire. In Boston, where he was to join Pierce, Fields arranged that Doctor Oliver Wendell Holmes should see him and Mrs. Fields recorded in her diary: "O.W.H. thinks the shark's tooth upon him, but would not have this known." There was no formal medical consultation, but the little doctor went round to the hotel and, there in the street, Hawthorne talked freely to him. He was obviously weary and ill, a mere shadow of what he had been. Nevertheless Holmes wrote, "there was nothing in Mr. Hawthorne's aspect that gave warning of so sudden an end as that which startled us all."

How solicitous, even in small ways, the ex-President was of his friend had been shown the previous December at the grave of Mrs. Pierce. Then the General, though he was overcome by grief, turned and drew up Hawthorne's coat collar to shield him from the cold. Now he had come forward again with his prompt friendship. As soon as he saw Hawthorne he realized that something was gravely amiss and attributed it to a disease of the brain or spine, or both.

A few days before this journey Julian came home from Harvard to ask his father something. He had only an hour to spare as he had to take the afternoon train back. He found Hawthorne sitting in his bedroom; Sophia and the two girls were there as well. They talked and Hawthorne did what Julian requested. As the young man got to the door he saw his father pale of face, but on it an expression of beautiful kindness — he was so glad that he had been able to give his son pleasure.

A few days later Hawthorne set out for Boston to join Pierce. Sophia went to the station with him, and Rose noticed how shrunken he looked, how full of suffering on the last day of farewell. Afterward she was sure he knew that he would not return. To Rose he seemed to be a snow image of an unbending but old, old man. Thus he stood and gazed at her a moment. Sophia was sobbing as she walked by his side to the waiting carriage.

At Plymouth, New Hampshire, reached by easy stages, the end came early in the morning of May nineteenth. The friends had adjoining rooms at the Pemigewasset House, and Pierce left the door open between them. He looked in every now and then to see how Hawthorne was. The last time he looked in, at four in the morning, he found his friend had died, evidently in his sleep.

It was the day before Rose's thirteenth birthday.

CHAPTER XII

Education Completed

In 1851, when her husband was absent from Lenox for a few days, Sophia had written in her notebook: "Was ever one so loved!" Now while his body was waiting burial Sophia wrote Mrs. Fields an extraordinary letter. It began: "I wish to speak to you, Annie," and continued with such things as, "To me — himself — even to me who was himself in unity — he was to the last the holy of holies behind the cherubim," and "When he awoke that early dawn and found himself unawares standing among the 'Shining Ones' do you think that they did not suppose he had always been with them — one of themselves?"*

Immediately after the funeral — "that festival of life" — Mrs. Fields got another long letter with passages of the same sort, and this Mr. Randall Stewart has recently printed. "Annie," Sophia wrote, "from a child I have truly believed that GOD was all good and all wise and felt assured that no event could shake my belief. Today I *know* it.

"This is the Whole. No more can be asked of GOD. There can be no Death nor loss for me forevermore. I stand so far within the veil that the Light from GOD's countenance can never be hidden from me for one moment of the ETERNAL DAY — now nor then."

But to her sister Elizabeth Sophia wrote an account of the funeral never before published. In part it reads: "The beauty,

---

* That is printed in *Memories of a Hostess*. What is not given there is Rose's drawing of an angel that accompanied it and that, together with the letter, is in the Boston Public Library.

the fragrance of the thousands of white flowers through which loving hands crowded to do him tender reverence and symbolize his unsullied soul, helped lift me out of the sense of Loss and more than the flowers was the mighty power of human love and sympathy around us to raise me to the serene height where he stood beyond the utmost scope and vision of calamity.

"My darling held the veil a little lifted that I might gaze along his shining way into the hitherto undiscovered country . . . so that my yearning heart did not break when I saw that the sacred and noble temple of the living GOD was shut from my mortal eyes. . . .

"The love was dearer to me than the reverence.

"How they loved him!

". . . I was in a rapture of gratitude. GOD gave me no moment for lament. . . . Mr. Longfellow — made so grand with his former sorrow — his long white hair blowing in the fresh air — on one side heading the illustrious line — closed on that side by Mr. Fields holding the unfinished manuscript. . . .*

"Mr. Emerson on the other! . . . Judge Hoar at the close of the left line— so near me — I could have said to him GOD bless you. . . .

"Slowly we returned at the slowest pace through the blooming trees, the birds in incessant warble, the winds in choir. . . .

"My whole being responded. Julian kept fast hold of my hand to guard me. His hand was *ice*. He feared it would be too much for me. But my hand was warm — and I seemed glowing with lambent flame. . . .

"Shall I not soon see then that Presence of uniform majesty whose sweetness casts out fear? Yes, it is here always. I can never escape from it. But the voice! Well, it was always in him very inward. It is now within me wholly — within my central music. . . .

* This was the manuscript of *The Dolliver Romance*. It was buried with Hawthorne.

"I can never tell you all the children are to me. Their foreheads are sealed with the white stone. GOD has given them the morning star. . . . I think I *had* better be alone now."

What is worth noting here is that Sophia, though Elizabeth Barrett Browning had deeply interested her in spiritism, and Ada Shepard had impressed her by her reluctant mediumship, never attempted anything like spiritualistic contact with her husband. She had what she believed to be the real thing, the séance would now have seemed only its profanation. To Horatio Bridge she wrote in a somewhat different strain, telling how she was finding her husband in his books: "I seem to be with him in all his walks and observations. Such faithful, loving notes of all he saw were never put on paper before. . . . No bird, nor leaf, nor tint of earth or sky is left unnoticed."

Sophia soon found that she was in rather straitened circumstances. Hawthorne's estate (which included the Wayside) was appraised at twenty-six thousand dollars and there were royalties to be expected, though their amount was incalculable. The provision made for her and the children was not bad, even though it was less than Hawthorne had hoped, and it would have sufficed had it not been that the Civil War had sent living costs up and the failure of a bank in which most of their money was deposited, knocked the bottom out of Sophia's budgeting.

Ex-President Pierce came forward with an offer to pay for Julian at Harvard, but from the letters Sophia sent to Fields, it is clear that she became more and more desperate. Her husband had attended to the financial affairs of the family and now she felt quite bewildered by them. After the bank failure she wrote to tell Fields that she did not have money — and it was then midwinter — to buy coal. Bills were being left unpaid and bankruptcy threatened. Una was going to teach gymnastics at a school.

Mr. Randall Stewart, who has published these letters written by Sophia to the publisher, thinks that some of her appeals for sympathy will strike the readers as surprisingly "indelicate," though he goes on to admit that "had it not been for Mrs. Hawthorne's editorial labors, there would have been scarcely enough money for the bare necessities of living." But a mother who has three children to support may surely be pardoned for being frank to a friend of her husband's who had been making protestations of his desire to be of service. And, as will appear soon, the idea was gaining ground in Sophia's mind, that Fields was taking advantage of her inexperience in business in the matter of the payment of royalties due her.

The necessity for what she calls "ferocious economy" is set forth in a hitherto unpublished letter she wrote on October 13, 1867, to Elizabeth Peabody: "After being away for five weeks, the house shut up to save expense, we three returned. I had already sent word to Rosy Burns to find a new place, as I was to keep but one servant now, and Ann was to stay by me. Una and Rose were to become housemaids and Ann was to wash and iron. . . . Una takes the west end of the house and Rose the east. . . . I claim to take care of my own chamber and to wash tea and breakfast cups. We get along beautifully. My two fairies sparkle and glow at this morning work. . . . They both think they gain a good deal for the exercise. . . . Rose has given up her music lessons and school. . . . Miss Ripley thinks it good for Rose to practice for a time what she has already taken from her, without more new things. And so Rose practices bravely alone. As she has to do all her own sewing now, she has been very busy at her wardrobe since our return. They have both turned inside out and upside down all their dresses, so as to buy no more, and they will look very nice and pretty after all. Rose also has painted things which Childs and Jenks sell for her, and she has bought materials for a bonnet and made it herself. She will study this winter with me and Una. She is reading Dante with E. Hoar critically, and enjoys it very much. Julian takes a father's place to his sisters with such a fine conscience. The beautiful spirit of that father surrounds us with almost a visible glory. Rose said when she got home, that if Julian went on so fast in the heavenly way, we should see an actual halo around his brows like that of the saints." Sophia concludes by telling her sister that there had been a slump in the book trade and that she now lacked the twelve hundred dollars the *Atlantic* had paid her for the serialization of the *American Notebook*. But she counted upon the publication of the *Notebooks* in book form to be her "Golconda mine."

Sophia, writing to Horatio Bridge the month before her husband's death says of Rose: "Rosebud is blooming out vastly. She is nearly a head above mamma, and will be very tall. She is now discoursing music on the piano, for which she has a good faculty; and she goes to school, and has a talent for drawing figures." The talent, however, was not very great, as the angel she drew for Mrs. Fields shows. Though she painted by fits and starts well into her forties, she clearly never mastered even the elements of drawing. She had feeling but only slight technical capacity in this field.

Sophia on the subject of the superlative qualities of her children should be taken with some reserve. But this is what she told Elizabeth Peabody on June 26, 1864: "The children join hearts and ring me round with a halo like the glory round the heads of saints. I must become a saint to merit so sweet a halo. They all seem to feel as if their father had silently bequeathed me to them to watch and ward — just as I feel as if he had left me them to cherish. They each start up like the cherubim in Eden, with a flaming sword to defend me from any possible harm. They observed in him such a sleepless care of me — such an all surrounding protection! Their prayer seemed to be that I might take his place — their fears that they could not — and that I must be desolate." And again to Elizabeth, at the end of the same year, Sophia writes: "The children have taught me rather better than I can teach them, because they are pure mediums of truth and goodness — nothing worldly having stepped between them and GOD. . . . You do not live with them and therefore cannot know all the little but pathetic, sublime and sweet amenities of daily life — the little sacrifices to pure duty — the magnanimities so difficult to practice." And much more in the same strain.

It is, however, something of a relief to turn from Sophia's too intense nature, to some of Rose's own letters of this period. Even when thanking Aunt Ebie for a lock of her father's hair she says merely, "I wonder if you meant to send it to me." Rose was far from being without fire, but one is glad she did not inherit Sophia's tendency to high-flown sentiment.

Yet she had her full share of the sense of the gravity of life that descends, for instants, upon a thirteen year old. To Una she confides: "I know that I am only a girl yet, but I have come to feel the responscibility of my own life — not mine, but given me in trust. . . . How beautiful experience is — I dispice innocent ignorance!"* Yet she was to remain "Bab" — only a few inches away from "Baby" — to the family for some time still.

Two years later the unutterable woes of adolescence press heavy upon her, though to be sure the clouds do lift. On January 13, 1866, she writes to Una: "You cannot imagine how I long for you. For I am just finding that everybody is *false*, somehow, and I need somebody substantial. . . . I love you with the whole of my heart. I think you are the only true person in the world. I only wish that it had been best for me not to be born. . . . For though I know what is good, and love God, yet I am very good-

* This letter is undated, but was probably written in 1864. Like those that immediately follow, it comes from the Berg Collection at the New York Public Library.

for-nothing. Oh dear me! I think Julian is the highest man; but he does not come up to my idea. In short I hate men as cordially as I love you. As much as they scorn us, I think however much they love us, they think us inferior and that shows a low homely mind. . . . I suppose I am in a morbid state. As mama is pleased to remark once and a while." She signs herself "Your most sincere friend."

Much more cheerful is the letter to Una dated the following May fourth. She and the children of the Bull family next door — Ephraim Bull was the producer of the famous Concord grape — had been hanging May baskets. But Rose and Edie Bull had got angry with one another, and so Rose continues with, "Johnie," for whom she hung "a great one full of sugared almonds and chocolate creams. . . . Then Johnie caught me, and hung me a lot of splendid rhubarb, with which I made a tart." From which it appears that even then she was practical in disposition.

On July 15, writing to Una, she is down in the dumps again: "One might just as well keep silent as pray, seems to me," she complains, "for heaven never gives anything unless it wishes to, after all. I don't see as a person need thank heaven for living, since it is nothing but a torment. I never shall have the rare pleasure of being loved infinitely, that is what makes a person the noblest and highest they can dream of. . . . Just because heaven does not choose that I should be a genious, I am miserable and sour. . . . A person needs another's help. Does anyone help me? I see how good mama is; but it don't make me good. The minute I have a chance I am naughty." But in December her mood has changed to flaring annoyance with Mr. Wild, one of the teachers at Dr. Dio Lewis's School she was then attending: "Mr. Wild told Bessie,"* she writes, "they must make me more demonstrative. If he pricks me anymore, he will be unpleasantly surprised for I will nock him over. He regards me with sublime pity."

Several exercises of masculine condescension had irritated her.

* This was presumably Bessie Whitwell, her roommate.

Julian was toplofty toward her. Moreover Julian had a new girl every few months, and though Rose admits framing his picture, she says, "I hate anyone tending to the other sex. It is not comfortable to love what one hates, I beleive."

So comprehensive a disapproval passed quickly enough, and Rose, in fact, was now and then herself slightly "tending to the other sex." Professions of animosity against it appear to have been considered the proper thing at that time in the case of well-brought-up young ladies, and, for all I know, may still be such. They obviously need not be taken too seriously, or regarded as specially "revealing." So Rose, writing to Una on October 17, 1867, admits a severe attack of nausea "when a certain Mr. Longworth appeared around these premises." She continues, "I thank you 1000 times for your kind inquiry as to when *our* engagement is to come out; and can only answer — not untill he 'pops' and I *accept!* . . . I am a scary fool . . . never to be able to make the best of my oppertunities . . . and so I couldn't 'flirt' with Longworth, plague take me!" She writes of young Emerson with admiration: "Edward goes about (on horseback) great yellow gauntletts, high leather leggins. . . . He personates the Cavelier. Looking the reflection of Benevolence, acting the example of Virtue, I have no doubt." The last she adds a little tartly, so as to guard the man-hating reputation she would enjoy. And Una writes to Aunt Ebie, on January 30, 1865, that Sam Hoar had given a lecture at the Lyceum, and though he was only twenty his story of the war was told so well as to turn the laughter with which he was greeted into applause. "Rose was delighted," Una says, "as she admires Sam Hoar very much." And Rose in an undated letter to Julian writes, "Sam Hoar is a perfectly jolly fellow. I wish that I knew him very well. How can I?"

The same letter touches, as so many do, on Cousin Ben Mann. "Ben," Rose tells Julian, "acts like a goose, he overlooks me at times and then is sweet. But he'll find that I'm not so easy to manage." In another undated letter to Julian — probably an earlier one — she tells him: "Ben is to have a tin rattle on Christmas from me. With 'For a good child' on it . . . won't he be *mad?*" And to Una she writes on December 13, 1865: "Ben said the girls would cry for him after he'd gone away. Do tell him that I saw Anna Folsom grinning away, as usual. So his beloved Folsom can smile." Yet two years later (January 16, 1868), when Rose was at school at Salem, Sophia advised her not to go to see Ben again or pay him any particular attention. "You must," she elaborates, "be very indifferent in your manner to young men, and as you often laugh at Ben and express distaste for him, I do not wish you to show unusual consideration. He would deceive both him [self] and Aunt Mary as to the nature of your feelings — and I think he is already too much inclined to admire you." Rose had spent seventy cents on flowers for him at a time when he was sick, and Sophia considered this attention quite enough, even from a cousin.

On December 27, 1864, Rose told Julian that when a certain G. W. J. was mentioned, she believed she had behaved in such a way that she was afraid people might think she was in love with him. (As she was now thirteen and a half that of course was just what they *would* be likely to suspect.) In the same letter Eliot Clarke (who appears to have been a cousin) also looms as a romantic possibility. And in the following September he and his sister Lilian were at Newport.* "Last evening," she tells Una, "there was a beautiful full moon and Eliot took us all . . . out on the bay in front of the house. . . . So away we went on the perfectly smooth water under the bright moonlight swaying about and feeling perfectly happy. At last we heard singing in the distance. . . .

"This morning Lilian and I went bathing on the beach in the great waves. We staid in ever so long and completed our idea of sea bathing. . . . In the afternoon sailing with a large party,

* In the following generation there were minor writers of these names — possibly Rose's friends of this time.

Furness and two other Collegians beside Eliot included to return by moonlight." In all of which appears the great good fortune of perfect normality marked only by an even greater degree of happiness common to this happy time of life.

The education of the children continued, though Rose's appears to have been more informal than that of her brother and sister. The children of famous people are often overwhelmed by their parents, and both father and mother in this case were remarkable. Julian, who was probably the least gifted of the family — for accomplished as he was, he lacked genius — was the most thoroughly trained, getting a Harvard education. As to Una it is difficult to pass any very secure opinion, as she died young; but perhaps it is sufficient to say that her friend, Colonel T. W. Higginson — who was also Emily Dickinson's friend — was sure as to her genius. Julian recognized the true state of affairs when he, a middle-aged man and apparently a successful one, wrote to his sister, who had so far accomplished little enough, to say that if in any of Hawthorne's children the entrails of his genius were to be found, then that one was Rose.

There were several schools Rose attended, though the most notable of these was the Dio Lewis School at Lexington. There she roomed with Bessie Whitwell of Concord, and was, for the short time she was there, sufficiently happy. I also find several letters from her written at a school at Lee, Massachusetts, brief though her sojourn there seems to have been, and not very happy. On November 4, 1866, she writes to "Darling Mama": "I don't believe you will be able to keep me here, for if I stay I must have ever so many things that I can't have. You can't do anything without money, and I can't get any good, feeling that I am using up everything." For that matter, as we learn from a letter to Fields on March 28, 1867, Sophia had not at that date paid Doctor Lewis a penny for Rose's teaching and board — and in the first of June her term is over and she leaves. The Lewis school was reputed to be good and was along rather advanced lines for those days, because of the emphasis laid there upon athletics. Sophia, however, wrote to Miss Peabody: "I do wish the Doctor was a refined man. He says hideous things in his lectures — and the other night told them they were all alive under their skins with vermin! ! ! and that when they had pimples a living creature was in each one! ! ! ! !" The learned doctor certainly might have spared his girls these pieces of scientific information.

After that Rose went for a time to a school kept by Miss Jane P. Phillips and her sister at 17 Chestnut Street, Salem. It was continued into the eighteen nineties and we are told that the pupils were noted "for their cultural tastes, fine writing, and excellent deportment." That she was able to do this was due to the generosity of Mrs. George B. Loring, referred to by Sophia as Cousin Mary, with whom Rose lived at 328 Essex Street and who paid the tuition.

One gathers that Rose did not greatly take to Cousin Mary from the way Sophia felt obliged to sing her praise when writing on January 16, 1868. "Dear Cousin Mary," she explains, "is without pretensions, which are not in her style, but effectually, has done you this immense service . . . when I had no money to send you to school with. . . . Her rectitude and veracity are as steadfast as the hills, and she would do her duty through all obstacles, though in a very silent way. With your fire and glow of nature, you would inevitably overlook the delicate points in her character at first. You might think her cold, when she is only self-contained and self-poised. . . . Her affections are constant and loyal, and far warmer than appears in her usual serene aspect." On April 16, Sophia wrote to her sister Elizabeth that at this "very superior school of twelve" Rose was very happy. So perhaps the following letter — undated as so many of these letters are, and also incomplete — may have been written at Miss Phillips's: "I am having a delightful time. . . . At least as delightful as a school can be. I intend now to *learn*. My ambition is to be accomplished. I have neither beauty nor fascination to atract my friends — I do not mean to atract young gentlemen. But I hope that I shall be able to sing, music, drawing and painting. . . . I wish very much to be able to read a great deal. And I want to be learned. I have great ambitions, Aunt Ebie, none, hardly, that can be fulfilled. I love Tennyson. He is the greatest poet. The Idylls, I have died often enough over the last one. I feel in reading all of them, as if I was in a dream. I feel as if I was not . . . and wish I was in heaven, where such noble things happen all the time."

Rose must have written to her mother to say that she felt vain, for Sophia in reply (perhaps in April, 1868) points out that the simple reflection that all our gifts come from our heavenly Father should destroy all vanity. But Rose is further advised: "Read a sentence of Thomas à Kempis every morning — for he has the very soul of humility with the utmost humility also." And as there must have been some hint of Rose's prickly disposition, she was told: "My Darling, Sweet briar Rose — I suppose you know that though the sweet briar rose has the most thorns of any rose, it is also the sweetest of all Roses. And so I think with you it will prove that the thorns will only defend you from harm and finally will not wound any one."

But Rose could herself be hurt easily enough. And on February 3, 1867 — when she was at Dio Lewis's school — Sophia had had to write: "You will have to learn, beloved, *not to speak of the affairs of others*, and I am sure that your late experience has taught you prudence, as well as to make no swift judgments. When you *must* speak, you must run to the cars and come home and relieve your mind. But do not deposit secrets in young girls' keeping, because they are imprudent and many love to tattle without malice or falsehood."

Rose had been taking music lessons from Miss Phebe Ripley of the Old Manse for some time, and apparently she continued to do so even after going to Salem, for on May 19, 1868, Sophia writes: "It is particularly desirable that you should faithfully improve this chance Cousin Mary is giving you. I rejoice unspeakably at Miss Ripley's thinking you improve so much in your music. But it will be more difficult to find another Miss Phillips than another superior music teacher. And besides Miss Ripley will still be there." This may have meant, however, that music was discontinued for the time being. It is sufficiently evident that at music Rose, though arduous, was not very talented. She dismisses her practicing, when writing to Aunt Ebie, as being as hard as playing a piece smoothly. But as for reading, that's a different matter, though she is ashamed when she thinks of her Aunt Ebie, who "must have exhausted all the authors." "I really despair," she goes on, "of ever accomplishing any reading, for the moment I think I will read, 'Tennyson' pops up and I grab it and read it until I have to stop." Not such a bad way, after all.

With church attendance she was frankly bored and got out of it whenever she could. At the school at Lee she wrote: "The preaching is so vile here, that I cannot go possibly [to church]; but if there comes a good preacher I will go." But it was the same wherever she was, in spite of her mother's urgings. At Concord, when Mr. Grindale Reynolds had succeeded Mr. Frost as Unitarian minister in 1858, she could note: "I do not often go to this uninstructive church here, but Una reads out of the bible and sermons to me on Sunday. But I wish I could hear a Weiss or Clarke."

That same letter, dated February 1, 1868, indicates that she is discovering her father as a writer now: "The beauties I passed over," she says, "without fully recognizing [them] a few years ago. It brings me very close to Papa, and I never knew him while he lived, but now I remember every look and tone of his voice, and his books make me understand his nature (according to my ability which increases with my life) and his ways on earth, which I remember better every day. It seems as if I felt his presence nearer to me the older I grow, and so deeply do I love him that I must always be guided by him, I think, as if he were to speak to me and I were to see his face."

It must have been about this time that Rose writes to Julian* — "Dearest Herculian boy" — telling him: "I dreamed of a little niggar girl that was very fond of me and that Aunt Mary wanted me to buy. But she had such horrid hands that it was 'imposs' — She was awfully ugly too. She kept taking hold of my hand and making me perfectly miserable. She had 2 too many fingers on one hand and they were no bigger than knitting needles and no bone in them. I guesse I dreamed it because I saw a boy at Dancing School who had two fingers off." The fact that she had been reading again the chapter on English Poverty in *Our Old Home* may also have had something to do with inducing that dream.

Meanwhile Sophia's frame of mind remained the same. She was harassed by financial anxiety, yet lived in what some people would call a golden dream, but which she believed to be an increasingly close contact with the most real of Realities. To Elizabeth Peabody she wrote on January 20, 1867: "Sometimes outward life oppresses me, and I think of the 'Nunc dimittis' with rapture. Yet not before the children are all settled in life. . . . While I can aid or comfort them I would gladly stay. But *affairs* disturb me. . . . So often GOD allows me to walk with my husband!" A sickness that came on her now provided an opportunity for her to withdraw into contemplation; then she read again Bacon, Shakespeare, Plato, and the *Bhagavad Gita*. "Silence holds all," she wrote, "and each one must have his own revelation, and no one can tell another the 'secret of the Lord.' . . . I should be very much harassed by having any more outward events in

---

* The curator of the Berg Collection, from which this letter comes, gives its approximate date as 1864–1865; to me it seems obviously a year or two later.

my life. Now only I yearn for chances to *go in*, and not to *go out*." She adds that she sees her friends now and then and her "pious old women." And the children have their "bright young friends come to see them for a day or two pretty often, and their joy is my joy of course." A year later (on January 7th) she writes again to Elizabeth: "The golden circle surrounds my earthly Dark always, and I am very safe within its eternal round. My soul never loses him for a moment. Even the background of dark is pure gold . . . and it seems merely finiteness that the black represents — not open vision, but very near it. And the central part of even the dark is light."

Alas, Sophia was often obliged to turn from her mystic contemplations to very mundane matters. Thus she wrote to Rose (at Salem) on April 22, 1868: "I cannot send money for the new jacket but you must send me the bill for it, and by that time I can send it immediately. . . . But I send you five dollars to be most religiously spent for absolute necessities and to get a hat. You need not be reluctant to ask Cousin Mary to lend you money for an immediate need, because I will repay *at once*, — and I cannot send money indefinitely now I am so short." Then the following June 10th, she tells Rose (who must have been apologetic over what she was costing): "No, you are not a great expense. You have been as careful as you could possibly be." But it is evident that Mrs. Hawthorne was pinched for money, and it is touching to see how often in the course of writing a letter she works herself up into sending more money than (at the beginning of the letter) she said she could afford. And as Rose had been talking of taking some sort of job, her mother tells her: "Do not think yet of earning. Banish that idea wholly at present. . . . [Mr. Fields] is now printing the American Journal of Papa, and that will give us quite an income when it is published. We shall get along very well soon."

Hawthorne's *Notebooks* did prove to be the financial salvation of the family. Fields wrote to Sophia (a letter now at Hawthorne, New York) upon seeing the *American Notebooks*, suggesting that Lowell edit them — and also that Lowell should write a life. Sophia's alarmed reply (preserved at the Boston Public Library) was: "I do not wish him to read it. I would even say, *especially* not Mr. Lowell."

Her own editing of these Journals has been subjected to rather severe criticism by Mr. Randall Stewart in his admirable "restored" editions of the first two. What Sophia published was prettified and emasculated, and she not only changed and omitted but, in some cases, obliterated passages beyond all hope of their ever being read. Yet after all, the excessively squeamish standards of the time were not of Sophia's making and by these a woman was bound even more strictly than a man. No doubt Sophia was more worried and fussy in her conscientiousness than she should have been, but one cannot reasonably expect any other attitude from her. Hawthorne himself, had he published his *Notebooks*, would have toned down their raciness. In fact, he did so when making *Our Old Home*. No doubt he would have recognized that his pungencies made for better writing than the "genteelisms" he had to adopt, but he would not have denied the necessity of adopting them.

This is of course not an attempt on my part to refute Mr. Stewart's thesis, for I have been in correspondence with him and we agree in our views. But though admitting that Fields had something to do with the matter,* he had not seen an undated letter now at Hawthorne, New York, that Sophia wrote to Miss Peabody in which she says that, as she finds that omissions have

---

* In his article in *More Books* for Sept., 1945, Mr. Stewart writes (pp. 314–315): "When I pointed out in my editions of the *American* and *English Notebooks* the discrepancies between Mrs. Hawthorne's text and the original manuscripts, I assumed that the responsibility was entirely hers. It now appears that Fields exerted an important influence upon her editorial work."

been made from her husband's journal, she thinks of reinserting them in an appendix to the second edition. "Now what am I to do," she asks, "about correcting the proof sheets of the English Journal here? So many absurd mistakes and misapprehensions occurred in the American Notes — that the Fields people cannot be trusted at all. They combatted the *niceties* of Mr. Hawthorne's style, and the ignorant grammar — suggesting quite wrong emendations. They do not know enough — they are not cultivated enough to know what perfect English is — nor what perfect grammar is. So it seems as if I *must* correct the proofs."

The unhappy breach between Sophia and Fields was due, however, to other reasons, and the one most responsible was Mary Abigail Dodge (now about thirty-five years old) who wrote under the name of Gail Hamilton. Hawthorne — who had a phobia against ink-stained women — made an exception of her and said she was "just as healthy-minded as if she had never touched a pen." The Hawthornes all liked her, and Rose spoke for the family when she wrote to Aunt Ebie on May 6, 1866: "We expect Miss Dodge up here in a few days. Is she not a splendid author? She is a gay, dear woman."

No doubt she could justly be called all that. But she was also a mischief-maker, and many years later (November 24, 1884) T. B. Aldrich, writing to T. W. Higginson, spoke the truth when he called her "the pestiferous Gail Hamilton." For when Sophia, worried by her financial difficulties and not understanding the publisher's statements, appealed to Miss Dodge (who was a very knowledgeable person), Miss Dodge, who had already accused Fields, Osgood and Company of defrauding her — and who brought legal suit against them, which was eventually settled in her favor by arbitration — told Sophia that she too was being swindled. Mr. Stewart has set these matters out in an article, but of course he did not have Gail Hamilton's letter to Sophia dated

September 2, 1868, as this is at Hawthorne, New York. In part it reads: "They [the publishers] are — either from dishonesty or mismanagement, utterly untrustworthy. I cannot say it is the former — indeed I cannot believe that they are so bad as their manner seems to indicate — but the results to us may be just as fatal — and certainly their reckoning is the most remarkable I ever heard of in Business."*

Whatever the merits of the question at issue, the quarrel was very unfortunate, especially as it was inherited by Julian and Rose Hawthorne. And it was all the more painful because of Fields' promise to Sophia early in her widowhood: "I write a line this early to say (what you already fully know) that I stand ready to serve you and the children in all business as well as in other matters. . . . Always count on me as ready and more than willing to do all in my power for the interest of your household. If Mr. Ticknor were with me he would feel as I do. This you know. We both loved that dear spirit who never came to us without a hearty welcome. His presence was a benediction, and his voice made the air sweet and musical about the old corners. But as I write I still feel that he is not far off and might speak to me at any moment."

It was in this pitiful and painful way that the Hawthornes severed themselves from Fields who, taking away with him from Salem — almost by force — the first draft of *The Scarlet Letter* in 1849, saw at a glance that here was a masterpiece, and who set Nathaniel Hawthorne on the road to perhaps modest enough fortune but enormous fame.

* Another letter of Gail Hamilton's to Sophia regarding royalties is dated August 24, 1868.

CHAPTER XIII

Dresden and London

There were several reasons why the Hawthornes wanted to return to Europe. One was that they looked back to their previous years there as a kind of golden age. Another was that they believed they could live less expensively in Germany than in Concord, and have cultural advantages lacking in America at that time. But probably a further reason, though this was one that was never explicitly mentioned, was that both Julian and Una were recovering from the effects of unlucky love affairs. Sophia no doubt saw that a change of scene and air would do them good.

Julian, as is common enough with young fellows, had been more or less in love a number of times. But in 1867, as we learn from a letter his mother wrote on March 24th, he had been jilted. And though this relieved Sophia, she was no doubt also anxious about her son. She said, it is true: "His letter written to tell me and Una after he arrived in Boston is beyond all words in its divine tone of charity, pity, patience and calmness." Una said: "What a magnificent creature. He is not earthly! He certainly is the flower of ideal chivalry and trust." But after the characteristic Hawthornesque outburst of family adulation, Sophia may well have felt it desirable to get Julian away.

Still worse was Una's case. She was engaged for a short while to Storrow Higginson, and apparently both families were disturbed on Una's account. Writing to Miss Peabody on April 16, 1868, Sophia told her that Storrow's mother and aunts had all confided that Una was far above him; they hoped, therefore, for her own sake that she would not marry him, though for his sake they hoped she would. And when mothers and aunts talk like that . . . !

Further, Sophia says, Elizabeth Hoar lamented the engagement, and so did Emerson. As for Ned Bartlett, who previously had told Una that he could not congratulate her, now did congratulate her — that the engagement had been broken. Though Julian, already a veteran in such matters, could be counted upon to survive his disappointment and to heal his heart by falling in love again, the high-strung, sensitive, and moody Una really did need to get away.

That the jilting of Julian seems, however, to have been a secondary motive appears from the coincident date of March 3, 1867, when Sophia wrote to her sister, Elizabeth: "Julian wants me and Una and Rose to go and live with him at Heidelburg. . . . Everyone says it is cheap to live there if you are once there. Maids ask nothing scarcely for service, are very strong, very amiable, eat nothing, and sleep nowhere, says Mr. Bradford. You take tea in Edens, by the music of angels and pay six cents for that, and a few pennies for your supper. The climate is delightful, the grapes abound, and nothing costs anything." It was all wonderful, in short — but with one catch — though it cost nothing to live, once you were there, it cost a great deal to get there in the first instance. Before long, in an undated letter to Elizabeth, Sophia was writing: "All our European plans have fallen to the ground for want of money. We do not have a penny to go with, not even to send Julian. It was a terrible disappointment to him. . . . Seeing that he must make some money he will study civil engineering and be able to enter the Scientific School here this month. Oh how I wish it could be the Technology School in Dresden — so splendid and free of cost too. But he must burrow down where he is. . . . There never was anything more divine than the way he feels and behaves. . . . When he has mastered his profession and made some money, he says he shall go to Europe with us."

In the end this became a thing that simply had to be done,

somehow or other. The Wayside was sold in the fall of 1868, and as the *English Notebooks* was on the way and the publication of the *French and Italian Notebooks* arranged for, and as, moreover, Sophia was about to bring out a book of her own, she counted upon these — together with royalties from her husband's earlier works — to provide an income quite sufficient for Dresden, the place on which they had decided. On October 20th the family sailed.

An indication of the seriousness of the breach between Sophia and her husband's publisher comes out in the fact that her *Notes on England and Italy* was issued not by Fields but by Putnam. And though Sophia was too ladylike to make acrimonious accusations, she was not quite above indicating to Elizabeth Peabody that, on the word of Gail Hamilton and George Putnam, she believed Fields to have been guilty of dishonesty.

To anybody writing of the Hawthornes, her book gives not only factual information but the "feel" of the family. There, rather than in her description of places or her comments on pictures, does the value of the book reside. But then, Sophia could hardly make out a shopping-list without conveying at least a hint of her own charm. It is, however, evident from letters of hers on Fields's tampering with the *American Notebooks* that she detested proofreading — perhaps all the more because, not being a professional author, she did not see why she should have the drudgery of authorship. Had she read her own book in proof she could not but have instantly noticed some of its mistakes in the matter of proper names. "Montaüto," for instance, appears throughout as "Montanto."

Una described the Dresden life not very enthusiastically. Writing on January 28, 1870, to Miss Higginson she says: "All the galleries and music of Europe can't make up for one's friends. Indeed, I don't believe I am very artistic at all. Of course I always knew I had no talent to accomplish anything, but I did think I had latent seeds of appreciation, and perhaps they would come to something if I was not among these stolid, dirty Germans, who disenchant one of all ideas of beauty, and make one doubt if there is such a thing as spirit." As for the language, she was quite content with English, and said, "My little jaws were never made to tear themselves to pieces with German monstrosities — I should never learn to talk it fluently if I lived a thousand years." Though in another letter she had said that European life was delightful, she could not have meant life in Saxony. She noticed that the woman there was a dull and ponderous specimen, whom the man holds not even "better than his horse" — for even on the slightest slope the men spare "their miserable old horses" by putting drags on the wheels, "whereas they expected the women to push the cart when it went up hill." It is clear that Una definitely did not like Germany or the Germans.

Nor could Rose have liked it much better. From an undated letter written early in 1870 to her mother, who had left her in a kind of pension school, one gathers that the Miss Runtze who ran the place was none too amiable. "Miss Runtze," Rose says, "was not atall pleased with having you write, but hardly spoke to me atall & this morning said she would rather I would speak myself about such little things and if they could not be done for me, she would tell me so, and not have the fuss of speaking to you. But I told her I preferred to tell you about anything I might wish for, because you might wish me to do without it. She said she was not atall offended. Why on earth should she be? But she was for all that." Aunt Mary also got a long letter about this time — hers was dated February 8, 1870 — telling of a terrific upheaval caused by a lost French grammar. But this could have been only the accidental cause for bringing the irritation on both sides to a head. Rose philosophically concluded: "I am notable for getting on the wrong side of people, and stroking them the wrong way"; and indeed it would seem, from her own version of the incident, that her quick temper was at fault, though she indicates she was unpopular among the girls on account of her privileges. She had a fire in her room, and could leave the place whenever she chose for drawing lessons. The life of a not too tactful foreigner can be made very miserable in such circumstances.

The important thing to notice here is that Rose was not only hot tempered but repentant on account of her failing. "No one," she writes Aunt Mary, "can tell how often and severe my struggles are to be good, any more than they could ever believe how sincere and great my hope is, that I shall sometime overcome myself, and be charitable, humble, and altogether righteous. Since I have been here, I have gone through the despair of not knowing whether to believe God would hear my prayers or not, I think you know, and now it is the glory upon which I found my hope, that I believe He does. I don't think I can ever lose that faith again, as I often used to and as long as I am religious with my whole heart and soul, I must grow better and better. I thank you so much that you will write me such loving words as your last were, for they show me you *have* forgiven unworthy words to you. Do always think me a good girl, till at last I *am* a good woman without a narrow mind and heart. A great deal seems possible to me when I think of the teaching my mother's and father's examples give me, besides other examples."

Another glimpse of Rose in Dresden comes from a letter Elizabeth Hawthorne wrote on June 30, 1871, to her cousin, Robert Manning. "[Julian] says she does not put herself forward as she ought, and she does not choose the right kind of friends; going, he says, to drink tea with elderly women who are quite insignificant in social position, and once, he said, in Dresden he introduced her at a party, and as she was looking very pretty, he hoped she might effect something; but she held down her

head, and only said 'yes' and 'no' and the nice young man*
(Herbert Browning, a son of the poet) after trying hard to draw
her out, withdrew, thinking, probably, that she had not an idea
in her head. Julian thinks she has a great many, and judging from
her letters, that is my opinion." In the article he wrote for the
Atlantic nearly sixty years later Julian says much the same thing
again: "She had no girl confidants; and in spite of her beauty
and charm, she disturbed rather than won her male acquaintance.
. . . One might almost say that she never really met people at all,
for all her impersonal cordiality and resource."

Sophia soon seems to have exhausted the possibilities of Dresden,
and so, leaving Rose to study there, she and Una went off to
England, from where she wrote to Rose every day or two, religiously covering all four pages in her small, faint, sloping writing.
On June 11, 1870, she writes from Union Villa, New Ferry
Park, Birkenhead, Cheshire: "Love you? darling, I am all love
for you and you deserve all I can give because your will is all
right and you have a noble nature and great gifts. And GOD gives
mothers to children that children may be loved infinitely, beyond
all exact measure — just as our Heavenly Father loves His children
beyond all their deserts." In January, that same year, Sophia had
been reading Louisa Alcott's *Little Women* and, like all the rest
of the world, found it very good indeed. Louisa had at last proved
the truth of one of the "naughty remarks" she reported, in 1860,
her mother having made — "Cast your bread upon the waters,
and after many days it will return to you buttered." It was about
time that the Alcotts should get something back.

In June, Sophia was at Great Malvern, "and there were Una
and Annie Bright [Henry Bright's sister], shining with welcome
on the platform." But a visit to the former Fanny Channing, now

* Some mistake here on Aunt Ebie's part. This could have been our little
sissified friend Penini.

married to Edwin Arnold, was a good deal less of a success than
Sophia had hoped. At first, she was full of enthusiasm for the
learning and accomplishments of Mr. Arnold. He understood
Sanskrit and everything else, and had been head of a college in
India — a stupendous fellow and cultured to the tips of his finger-
nails, "his conversation is fascinating, and poetry bubbles out of
his lips like Chian wine, as rich and sweet." He and his wife lived
on so lavish a scale that Sophia supposed he must be immensely
rich, but it turned out that his whole income was a thousand
pounds a year, earned as writer of the leading articles for the
London *Telegraph*. He had given her one of his books called
The Poets of Greece, "of which," Sophia cheerfully confesses,
"I have not yet read a word."

But Fanny Arnold was quite a shock to Sophia. "Fanny," she
tells Rose, "talked of herself every minute — of her pains and
her anxieties — till Una was perfectly distracted. Fanny really
thinks of nothing but herself. It is perfectly incredible, and I
should think she must wear out her husband's love. . . . She con-
tradicts herself every ten minutes, not seeming to have any law,
order or truth in her. I never knew anybody like her in my life,
and she really seems to have no heart at all. I hoped I should find
her improved by wifehood and motherhood, but really she is
more self-absorbed than ever."

Sometimes Sophia, instead of imparting news, would simply
give rein to her fancy. One letter, dated December 28, 1869, runs
almost entirely like this: "I was taken care of (this evening) by
a dear old fly, and it was perfectly delightful. He made a small
burr with his wings, and kept alighting where I could see him,
but not once touched me, except to walk along my shoulder in a
loving harmless way. He was not in the least hungry, but only
sociable, and desirous of reminding me of summer. He has evidently put away his annoying powers for the winter in some
india rubber bag to keep them from the moths. . . . Finding the
young ladies absent, he endeavored to be a pleasant companion

to me. And not hearing Miss Rose's sweet voice in the room singing, and no sound of the piano, he did what he could in the way of burring, so as to have some sort of sound to relieve the silence." At last Sophia killed it because, she said, Rose had told her that flies might be dangerous, but "I believe I should be haunted by its ghost — Immediately the ghost appeared, looking very much like a reality. It seemed to have a special errand to do, and was hastening on in high spirits. Is there no end to these minute creatures? . . . You see the blame must rest upon you, if there is any blame. Mershy! Mershy! There is the ghost again. . . . But it is a ghost now, at all event. Why Baby Hawthorne, why have you obliged me to take so many lives?"

Far off in Dresden, Rose was working steadily at the piano and the easel. But as in the case of Una, who at Rock Ferry, according to her mother, needed to hammer away at her music for sixteen hours a day — how fortunate for Sophia that no domestic noises, except that of children quarreling ever disturbed her! — Rose was assiduous to a very small purpose. In a letter to Miss Clapp,* dated November 28, 1869, Rose writes: "I have been studying German diligently for a month or two, so that I can talk a little better than formerly and now quite comfortably. But it is wonderful how little I have managed to learn in these twelve months. . . . The piano is somewhat of a trial to me, and certainly a great one to my family. I practice till the tips of my two little fingers wear off, and make a terrible hullabullo in our etage, I murder Beethoven's Sonnata [sic] or whatever I have in hand most cruelly, yet my teacher has a longer face each lesson. I love music heartily, but music don't love me, and the piano groans inharmoniously beneath my touch."

* I find in a postscript of a letter from Sophia to Mary Mann, dated December 11, 1864, a reference to Miss Clapp, but Miss Bartlett of the Concord Public Library, who has informed me on several points of this sort, is unable to identify her.

In the matter of drawing and painting, however, Rose, who seems to have quite despaired of ever getting anywhere with music, was now more hopeful. And again she worked. As she was to tell a lady who wrote an article on her, in 1893, in *The Ladies Home Journal* — she drew and painted in the studio of Herr Wagner at Dresden, unwilling to stop even for a mouthful of food, and indifferent to fatigue, for six hours a day, every day. In her letter to Miss Clapp she says that she is sure that her master is just the one she needs, "and he encourages me to think I have a right to use a great deal of my time in drawing" — which was a nice way for Herr Wagner to put it.

Yet Rose often became despondent and then Sophia had to be on hand with the encouragement. From Blackheath there came a letter dated May 30, 1870: "The fruit pictures will be precious, my pet, but you are pretty ambitious daring to paint grapes from memory! You have a good memory, however, and I doubt not they will be *vraisonable*."

About this time, too, Sophia — who had learned painting in Doughty's studio (though without receiving formal instruction), and whose work had been praised by Washington Allston — copied out a passage from *The Marble Faun* to restore Rose's confidence, adding: "You must not let yourself be too much disheartened by the decay of your faith in what you produce. I heard a great poet express similar distaste for his most exquisite poems, and I am afraid that this final despair, and sense of short-coming, must always be the reward and punishment of those who try to grapple with a great or beautiful idea. It only proves that you have been able to imagine things too high for mortal faculties to execute. The idea leaves you an imperfect image of itself, which you at first mistake for the ethereal reality, but soon find that the latter has escaped out of your closest embrace.

"And the only conclusion is that the blurred and imperfect image may still make a very respectable appearance in the eyes of those who have not seen the original. . . . Nobody, I think, ought to read poetry, or look at pictures or statues, who cannot find a great deal more in them than the poet or artist has actually expressed." Sophia ends her argument with, "Now, darling, have I not tried to encourage this way? Papa does it more completely."

There were times, however, when Rose managed to whip up a little belief in herself. By now she knew she would never do anything with music, but she still hoped to be able to paint. Some kind of artistic power seemed to her to be the only thing that made life worth living. So to Miss Clapp, in the letter from which quotations have already been made, she says: "I am happy, and if I don't come to a standstill, shall bless my lot all the rest of my days in preference to any other, and I certainly feel something within me rousing itself, that music never stirred — so that I hope my chance of success is not out of the question. To feel that one has, or at some future time may have, an excuse for being in the world, is to me the ideal sensation of all others, and I trust to realise it by and by, if I draw anything to send a thrill of pleasure through anyone. Can there be anything in me worth producing? — it will be something far higher than my best self that works through my hand, if it is the case, I know. Dear Miss Clapp, you have a piece of my heart now, and I should beg your pardon that I have inserted it in this letter."

That passage is most touching. It is also more revealing than perhaps Rose realized, and is, in fact, the clue to her whole life. The born artist never needs to write like that. He will know that he has much to learn; he will also know, for an absolute certainty, that he has that creative force within him without which all the training in the world is of no use. Rose did, in fact, have genius; and this her family perceived. But she and the whole family were wrong in supposing that, with her, it would come out through one of the ordinary modes of artistic expression.

Her brother, Julian, writing in 1928 in the *Atlantic*, still did not quite "get" the point in saying: "Rose inherited creative ardor, but lacked the ability to give her aspirations satisfactory projection. She painted, she wrote, she played the piano and sang; but the restraint of rules was irksome to her in all things. . . . In all her girlish products there were an impassioned surge and exaltation, the purpose flagrant, but the rendering obscure." What Julian says is true enough, but like so much that he says is too facile and allows a great deal to escape. Even with his sister's whole career before him, he still failed perfectly to understand it.

Julian was nearer the mark in what we hear of his having told Aunt Ebie. Writing on June 30, 1871, to her cousin, Robert Manning, she tells him: "Julian says that Rose is the only one who has any constructive genius, and I believe her father thought so too. But Julian also says that he does not think she will ever accomplish much, and there I hope he was mistaken." In an earlier letter to Rebecca Manning (February 23, 1869) Aunt Ebie says of Rose: "I hope she will become a distinguished artist. Her father used to say that she was the only one of his children who had any special talent for painting; the others could copy, but had no original genius." The point is that the whole family (including Rose herself) were at once right and wrong. They saw that she had genius. None of them had the faintest inkling as to how that genius was to be manifested. Perhaps it could flower only after she had tried in succession all the arts she could think of, and had failed in each.

Rose's letter to Miss Clapp tells of other plans. The next summer she hoped to travel the Rhine valley and after a visit to Switzerland, establish a permanent home in England — bringing all the family possessions over from America — and then spend three months every year in Rome and Florence. In spite of Sophia's previous experience with the English climate, it was in England that she wished to settle. "Certainly," Rose comments, "the Dresden climate is horrible."

That plan was never carried out for a number of reasons. The chief of these was that the Hawthornes had got to know a Mrs. Lathrop, an American, who had taken a house in Dresden and who had two interesting young sons. The elder of the two, Francis, was a painter, and already was showing such promise that he received an invitation from the great Whistler to go and work in his London studio. The younger Lathrop, George, only nineteen, was an alert, good-looking, aggressive young man, very sure of himself and with a gift for conversation that he regarded as brilliant and that was undoubtedly very smart. Both girls were fascinated.

Though reports were circulated in later years that he had first turned his attention to Una, and had in fact been engaged to her — reports that George Lathrop took some rather ungraceful pains to deny publicly — the truth appears to be that Una believed that he was in love with her, but that any indications she gave as to her availability were ignored.* Una, one gathers from hints that had appeared now and then in the family letters, had been left so affected by her Roman illness that there were those who used the word "insanity" in connection with her. In fact the talk about Una so distressed her father that it was a contributing factor to his own decline. It would be safe to say that Una was given at times to rather strange actions, though it would be very unsafe to say more. Hers was a beautiful spirit in a beautiful body, but there was a cloud that descended upon her every now and then. She may have got it into her head that George Lathrop was aiming at her, and though it is common enough an occurrence for a youth of nineteen to be violently infatuated with a woman of twenty-six, there is no reason to suppose that that occurred this time. What did happen is that George was strongly attracted to Rose.

But they were both under twenty and there the matter rested for the time being. Probably neither Mrs. Hawthorne nor Mrs.

* See the New York *Tribune* for June 25, 1879. The passage is quoted in my text later on.

Lathrop took the boy-and-girl affair very seriously, but no objection was raised. The Hawthorne's standing was glorious and Doctor Lathrop, George's father, was the United States Consul at Honolulu — a grandson of Samuel Holden Parsons and related distantly to John Lathrop Motley and Oliver Wendell Holmes. Neither side could have been much better vouched for. George and Rösl — as he was pleased to call her after the little German they had both learned — saw a good deal of one another in London, as they had in Dresden. Rose was now living there with Una and her mother; George was writing poems and stories and reporting on art topics for the New York *Independent*. The contact was all the more amusing because of the tales his brother, Francis, had to relate of the sinister and sardonic Whistler's eccentricities and elaborate arrogance. He could be almost equally entertaining on the subject of the pre-Raphaelites, as he was now associated with Burne-Jones.

Rose meanwhile was pursuing art in London, where she had transferred herself from Dresden at the end of 1870. An undated letter of Sophia's written from 5 Shaftesbury Terrace says: "I have just returned from entering Rose at the Kensington [Art] School. . . . Rose's face was like the most radiant Rose of Sharon when I left her. The Lady Superintendent is perfectly charming, and took a prodigious fancy to Rose — and declared her name to be wonderfully appropriate."

That Rose was anxious to improve herself in every possible way is proved from the existence at Hawthorne, New York, of a notebook in which she has written out very fully and carefully from more hastily taken notes a good account of the lectures given at the South Kensington Museum during November and December, 1870, by the famous Thomas Henry Huxley.

A change came, as changes so often do, suddenly — with effects nobody could foresee. About the middle of February, 1871,

Sophia fell ill, and said to Una as though in premonition: "I have a sort of defenseless feeling, as if I had no refuge." It soon became apparent that she was very ill, that she was not, in fact, going to recover. Una and Rose nursed her, sometimes assisted by Mrs. Bennoch's maid, Ellen, and the Hawthorne's own servant, Louisa; and concerning all this wrote a long minutely particularized account drawn upon by Julian in his two-volume work on his father and mother. Unfortunately he was in America at the time. Sophia had typhoid pneumonia, the doctor said, and little could be done for her. Toward the end she said very slowly — "I am tired — too tired — I am — glad to go — I only — wanted to live — for you — and Rose." Another time she murmured something about flowers. Rose gave her a little yellow crocus, the first they had found that very early spring, and Sophia smiled when it was laid beside her on the bed. The church bells were ringing and Una said, "It is Sunday morning, Mamma — a lovely day." That noon Rose's crocus opened wide upon the quilt of the bed where she had laid it; it was like a little sun. Soon afterward Mrs. Bennoch came and knelt at the foot of the bed, and then the doctor. It was so that Sophia died. As soon as it was all over Rose and Una went upstairs together.

Letters went to Julian and when his answer arrived it was arranged that George Lathrop should escort the two girls back to New York. Instead, very much to the surprise of everybody, and to the decided disapproval of the Hawthorne family, George and Rose decided to get married, and Una to remain in England where she intended to do settlement work. Pious in her Unitarian days, she was now pious in a somewhat high Anglican style. In her case England did what Hawthorne always saw would happen to his children if he did not take them back to America — England made Una English.

Julian, who regarded himself now as the head of the Hawthorne clan and as such to have a special responsibility, took no pains to conceal his anger over the marriage; and indeed to the end of his life was bitter, calling it fifty-seven years later "an error, not to be repaired." Whether or not it was an error, or capable of repair, Julian's attitude undoubtedly made the situation for the young couple all the more difficult.

They were in truth both impulsive children — Rose just turned twenty, and George a few months younger. The marriage was by special license, so relatives were not given the chance of intervening. But on the marriage certificate, signed by Robert Demans, the Curate of St. Luke's Chelsea, on September 11, 1871, George is marked down as being married "with consent." Under the heading of "Rank or Profession," he gives his as that of author; he had written a few poems and articles and short stories. But he was supremely confident in himself. The witnesses who signed the marriage certificate were Francis Lathrop and Lucy Madox Brown. It is to be noted that Una was not present.* Apart from her personal feelings, she probably felt, after what she had heard from America, that it would not do for her even to seem to countenance so rashly impulsive a marriage. But in case her character be misjudged by this circumstance, it should be recorded that Elizabeth Hawthorne, a very canny recluse, wrote to her cousin on June 30th of this year: "I think [Una] is the best person of the name — born to the name I mean [by which she clearly means to exclude Sophia from her judgment] that I ever knew; for I cannot claim the merit of much amiability for the Hawthornes as a race." As for Una's argument that the English doctors had told her she could not live in New England, Aunt Ebie was emphatically New England in her manner of speech: "My private opinion is that whoever cannot do that need not live at all."

The young bride and her husband crossed the Atlantic in De-

---

* The cause seems to have been illness, but may have been an illness brought on by the event itself. A letter from Elizabeth Peabody (of which the first page is missing) alluded to "Una's calamity," and on November 4, 1871, George wrote to Miss Peabody in terms that suggest that Una was suffering from a nervous breakdown.

cember on the *Oceanic*. They encountered delaying storms, and witnessed the saving of seven men from a shipwreck; "to feel the quivering of the ship . . . was enough to make me cling to George and scream idiotically," Rose wrote to Una. And when the bells and sirens rang suddenly one midnight, Rose woke George in terror that the ship was sinking; they were dressing hurriedly when "suddenly George dropped his arms in sleepy disgust and exclaimed 'New Years!'" As is frequently the case with newly married women, one catches a hint in Rose's letter of a certain parading of her status. There on her finger were an engagement ring and a wedding ring. These may now be seen on the hand of the Child Jesus of Prague at her cancer home at Hawthorne, New York.

Part Two: Mrs. Lathrop

CHAPTER I

The Young Couple

"As a general rule," Goethe has written, "the most significant period in the life of an individual is that of his development. Later we have his conflict with the world, and that is interesting only in so far as it produces results." The period of Rose Hawthorne Lathrop's struggle with the world, if it is to be judged by the production of results, came later, when most people would say she had seemingly withdrawn from the world and when she had incontestably withdrawn from any form of worldliness. But the twenty years in between, though summarily to be disposed of here, as being the least important and fruitful phase of her career, are far from being without significance. Nor is her married life characterized quite adequately by her brother Julian when he calls it an error not to be repaired. He himself nears error when he elaborates: "It obliterated whatever dreams of a happy married state Rose might have had (based upon the flawless felicity of her father's and mother's union), awakening her, instead, to the role of endurance, difficult for her temperament of buoyant independence." Of course it goes without saying that an unhappy marriage to George Lathrop prevented the possible happy marriage that might have occurred. But had there been such a marriage, Rose Lathrop would be remembered, if at all, as a daughter of Nathaniel Hawthorne's who tried her hand, with no conspicuous success, but one might almost say with rather consistent failure, to several of the arts in succession. And I would not be writing this book about her. Moreover happiness — in

the sense of harmony and prosperity and placidity and content —
is not the sole criterion of the success of a marriage. There is
many a marriage which has been a wonderful experience and
yet has had upheavals and, along with an intensity of love, a
temperamental maladjustment that has made it painful to endure.
But Rose Hawthorne Lathrop's biographer is not called upon to
assess the precise degree of her felicity, or lack of it. What he
should do is to point out that the apparent failure was necessary
to her development. Though, when she published, in 1888, her
book of poems, she could have had no idea as to what she was
to do with her life in the end, she evidently already knew, when
writing "A Song Before Grief" that something very important
was happening.

Sorrow, my friend
I owe my soul to you.
And if my life with any glory end
Of tenderness for others, and the words are true,
Say, honoring when I'm dead —
Sorrow, to you, the mellow praise, the funeral wreath are due.

No, in this matter Rose's brother Julian is not the best of
authorities.

We must start with the fact that the young couple had, from
the outset, to contend with the disapproval of most of their
relatives. Elizabeth Hawthorne at first was willing to think of
George Lathrop favorably; but before long her opinion of him
was critical. And Elizabeth Peabody had written in such terms as
drew from George a reply, headed Dorking and dated September 26, 1871, fifteen days after the marriage, in which he tells
Miss Peabody politely but decisively to go to the devil. And a
letter Aunt Lizzie wrote to Rose (of which the first page is missing but which clearly belongs to this time) tells her niece that she
has been acting very impulsively. Then Aunt Lizzie with

twinkling irony signs herself: "Affectionately (& *respectfully*) Elizabeth P. Peabody."

What was Doctor Lathrop's opinion about the marriage of his son is not recorded. He may not have had any opinions other than those of his wife. And though it is only fair to say that between George's mother and her daughter-in-law a cordial good feeling came to exist — as is testified by a number of long letters from her before me — in the beginning she seems to have made trouble. At all events Rose wrote from Cambridge, Massachusetts, on April 18, 1874, to Una, who was en route to New York, to warn her sister that if she sees Mrs. Lathrop there, "& she is inclined to speak of past difficulties, abroad or here, we hope you will dissuade her immediately. She has a sad persistency in speaking of things which had best be forgotten, after eliminating the wisdom I have derived from them — and so I thought, & George was anxious — she would wish to enter into a conversation about London & Cambridge, so far as we are concerned. We hope the time will come when she will throw off dark thoughts & emotions, & see the good of life. We could have loved her truly and given her happiness if she had been ready for them. George says no matter whom he had married — if the woman had not had [a] fortune his mother would have been as she has been to us from the first. We cannot help her by ordinary means, we have found, & are watching and waiting for something to turn up, either in her nature or circumstances which will bring help by extraordinary means."

As she and George had lived with old Mrs. Lathrop at 29 Washington Square during the first six months of their return there must have been ample time for friction to develop. Old Mrs. Lathrop may well have felt that his trying to support a wife on the proceeds of scribbling poems and articles for the magazines was a very precarious mode of livelihood. Perhaps she had said some time or other that if he really meant to take up the insecure profession of letters he ought to have picked a wife with a little money. What is clear is that almost from the start the young couple were under a strain, and though no doubt each had a difficult temperament, they also had to contend with difficulties not of their own making.

In an undated letter to Una, which probably belongs to 1872, Rose tells her: "George and I have enjoyed life inexpressibly in these days, as we have so much, but more and more and more. No words can tell you how good and beautiful he is, or how much we love each other, or how he treats me every moment. We are such good friends as the angels meant we should be." Though in some of Rose's other protestations of her happiness a hint may be caught of subsiding storm, this letter hides nothing between the lines. The young couple should be allowed to enjoy the early days of their marriage without too many questions being asked.

Long before George had written for the second anniversary of his wedding the lines "A Lover to a Rose" — not, to be sure, at all a good poem and never published by him, but preserved by Rose for over fifty years — they had left the uncongenial house of old Mrs. Lathrop for Cambridge. George had accepted a position as staff critic — afterward assistant editor — of the *Atlantic Monthly* under William Dean Howells. They were to remain in Boston or its vicinity for the next ten years.

Two things should be set down at the outset, not as a thesis to be demonstrated — for there will be here only a presentation of the situation as it is known — but by way of clarification. One is that George Lathrop owed a good deal to having married into the Hawthorne family. He yet came — understandably enough — to resent it, especially as no doubt it was often supposed that *all* his advancement came from this cause and not sufficient credit was given to his own talents (which were considerable) or to his energy (which was prodigious). The second thing — connected very closely with the first — is that as time went on he felt, first a vague and then an acute resentment against Rose for the superiority of her gifts. Here it will not be argued that her gifts were superior to his, and those who choose to do so, are welcome to do as he did, and take his long list of novels and stories and poems and plays — all the fruits of an incontestable proficiency — as proof to the contrary. The trouble was that he had this proficiency, to which may be added brilliant conversational powers, notable in an era of good conversationalists, and an ability to organize and get things done, and aplomb on the lecture platform — a dozen or more tokens of an easy versatility. And Rose was not proficient in any one of these ways. She painted and played the piano, and her friends said she did it very nicely; but it was, after all, in a rather amateurish style. In writing she had, it is true, a small reputation, but it is questionable as to how far she placed her stories and poems strictly on their own merits and how far she did so aided by the name of Hawthorne. The public saw what was published; what George saw was the mass of unpublished (and indeed unpublishable) stuff she turned out. Indeed, so much of this was begun and left that the proficient George had grounds enough for expressing his scorn when he felt in a bad humor. Time after time her projects petered out feebly, whereas the highly competent George never began anything he was unable to complete, or completed anything he was not able to place. Here he had incontrovertible facts available for his own consolation — or, alas, even for the upbraiding of Rose, on account of her little amateur efforts — when he saw, as he must have seen from time to time, that his wife had something in her that he lacked. For him to have felt otherwise would have called for a degree of nobility for whose lack he can hardly be blamed. He was a well-intentioned, industrious, talented fellow; it was not his fault if God did not make him a genius or a great man.

This is the situation in which they both were to find themselves, and though the disapproval of relatives (on both sides of the fence) made difficulties worse, these would no doubt have arisen even if the Hawthorne and Peabody and Lathrop connections had consistently shown themselves kinder than they actually were. It is scarcely to be wondered at that Lathrop sought escape through the anodyne of alcohol, or used the bottle to prop up his stricken self-esteem.

All this of course did not come about save by degrees, though there are indications that even from the beginning things were not always well between himself and Rose. She with a fiery temper, which her flaming red hair showed to be smoldering in her even in her gayest moments, and he with the irritability which goes with the quick and nervous constitution — and of course increased for both by the circumstance that their work was of the kind that kept them at home in one another's society — they thus found themselves in a position in which clashes between their highly temperamental temperaments were almost inevitable.

When Una was on the way from England to visit them at Cambridge, in 1874, Rose took the occasion to let her know in advance how well things were going between her and George; but her letter also conveys sufficiently clearly that Una knew that there had been trouble between them. The indication of another "fresh start" clearly appears here: "George and I," Rose writes on April 18, 1874, "have tried to reveal ourselves each to the other so completely, the good and the bad, that we can help each other to develop all the time, and so to help others whom we can. God be with us always. We have learned to know each other so much better of late, that we feel as if we had entered a new world — the same more widely comprehended — in the spiritual as well as material sense. And I wanted to tell you about it before you came." It is then that she went on to warn Una not to pay too much attention to anything old Mrs. Lathrop might say should she be encountered in New York.

Yet apparently there was trouble again — and even the suggestion of a separation — during Una's visit, for Rose wrote in an undated letter to Mary Mann: "As you will doubtless understand, I *cannot* agree with you about the restrictions I have put upon myself about meeting Una in George's home, at any rate until matters change very, very much. It seems to me one cannot tamper with loyalty any more than with faith, and as, if one doubts at all faith flies from us — so if we do not remain true in everything to the husband we have chosen to honor, the spirit of loyalty is lost." Things were evidently coming to such a pass that we may safely surmise that only the expected birth of a child saved, for the time being, an impossible situation.

It was just over five years after their marriage that their son Francis was born. Writing to Aunt Ebie shortly before, Rose alludes to her expected baby, and thanks her aunt for some little shirts. "But," she goes on, "your severe criticism of my husband hung like chains about my hands, and I could not bring myself to write to you. Your sweet letter has made me feel more than ever how much happiness is lost by family dissensions." And Mrs. Lathrop, signing herself, as always, "Your devoted Mama," tells of some binders she has been making of soft Saxony wool for the expected infant, along with other purely feminine details about the layette she and other Lathrop relatives are adding to, and makes mention of an article of George's Rose had sent her. It was in refutation of Professor Huxley and Mama thinks it "incontrovertible."

The birth of a son on November 21, 1876, made a number of changes in the mode of the Lathrop's life. Rose, except for the Wayside years, had never really had a home, and though the European wanderings, first in 1853–1860 and then in 1869–1871, had been delightful, they gave her nomadic habits. She was to revert to these later, until the need she discovered of providing a home for the destitute poor whom she was to make her guests kept her, for the last period of her life, safely tethered. Since her marriage she and George had more or less camped out, a convenience for a woman whose writing made housekeeping a nuisance. But as the child began to run about, his father and mother felt a need to give him something better than lodgings or a city apartment.

This, however, was not solely for the child's sake; Rose came to see that her husband needed a settled home. For a letter which can be dated 1878 — as that was the year "Saturday, December 21st" fell — Rose speaks of how worn out George was by his editorial work. "He was not well enough," she tells Aunt Lizzie, "to undertake it when he began, and he will not live long unless he has some quiet now after all his sufferings and labors and struggles of the last seven years. So we must go somewhere where we can live on very little, and pay up our debts, and give him a sense of peace and freedom again. . . . I am very, very anxious about my beloved husband; but I think if all can be arranged simply, that he will begin to gather strength again, and will write what is congenial to him, and success will come only a little later. We are thinking of a little cottage . . . in Cambridgeport; but I write to you in case that falls through. Pray send me word as soon as you can about the possibility of accommodation for George, myself and baby in Concord, and do not write to George, for he is not able to read a line that can be spared him. . . . I must borrow a few hundred dollars from someone. . . . There are some tradesmen in Cambridge who must be paid, and then the rest of our debts will diminish when we get to living so very cheaply." Only a person who has had any experience of this kind of existence can have any notion of how wearing it can be. If the Lathrop's marriage was broken by storms, here undoubtedly is one of the main reasons.

That the search for a home had been on for some time is indicated by a letter George wrote on September 8, 1877, to H. E. Scudder, who held his former position on the *Atlantic* and who was to become its editor: "You were very good and considerate to write me that long letter in reply to my little mercenary house-renting note. Was it only two weeks ago? Aug 23rd, it is dated and I seem to have lived months since then. At any rate, I have lived long enough since to decide that I shall not buy the Nantucket cottage this year. Your suggestion about Grantville is more like a dream than anything else. Is there a place where it is at all likely that somebody will build a permanent home for me, and let me have it at a moderate rent? It is a pleasant thing to have you suggest it, but I must warn you that we are becoming so disheartened about having any kind of housekeeping, as to feel strongly inclined — when we once get away from our Cambridge house — to room in Boston during the winters, and drift to one place and another in the summers. . . . I have been on the point of cutting thro' the whole situation with a sword two or three times. For the present the agitation has subsided in the necessity of going back to Cambridge without the interruptions of a break-up, for several reasons, one of which is that I am writing a couple of books under arrangements with publishers that demand steady and somewhat swift work."

The solution — no doubt the happiest — was the purchase of the Wayside, so full of memories of Rose's father and mother and of her adolescence. Yet Rose had so little taste for domesticities that a cousin of George's — a girl of twenty — went with them as housekeeper. However, Rose could write to Aunt Mary on December 29 (1878): "I feel as if this move was to bring peace and rest to us both, and that it will be the normal beginning of a more even life, for I think we shall find both health and time in Concord. But we shall be very poor for at least a year. . . . I shall not be able to use a dollar for car fare very often." One even gathers from another letter about this time that Aunt Mary was going to give Rose three dollars a week. Thanking her for it, Rose says it was "very much like a song." But we still usually find the Lathrops in Cambridge for the winter. A house was useful only when the weather let Francis play in the garden.

Just before this George Lathrop suddenly lost his position as assistant editor on the *Atlantic Monthly*. On August 29th, he wrote a long letter to William Dean Howells* replying to a note Howells had written him the previous day accepting his resignation as from September 1st. There had been correspondence since July between the two men on the way Howells had (so George maintained, unjustifiably) edited his contributions. Howells, while expressing high regard for Lathrop's literary ability, had remarked — Lathrop considered rather unkindly — that in his contributions to the *Atlantic* the advantage had been so vastly on the side of the writer as really to be "wholly" his. And the usually mild Howells added that if Lathrop never wrote another word in the magazine its fortunes would not be affected in any degree.

If that sounds a bit harsh, George's letter of July 4th was of so pompous a kind as would make even the gentlest of men disgusted. He had told his editor: "You know me well enough to understand that I speak without vanity when I add that more or less my qualities have been felt by the public in a favorable way, and a good deal of my editorial writing has been selected for praise when the author was not known. So far as I can judge, I have proved that I have a definite value." Obviously George expected Howells to promise not to edit his work again. And even when he resorted to playing the card of resignation, one cannot but feel that he hoped — as people so often do hope in a case like this — that he would be asked to withdraw it. Instead he was surprised by the promptness with which Howells let him depart. To any man this would have been a bad blow, but to a man of the vanity that George Lathrop displays one would suppose it to have been crushing.

He was not crushed at all, though of course he was hurt. When he wrote to Scudder on September 8th — that is, ten days later — it was to tell him: "In the matter of drudgery I . . . agree with you, and I should never have given up my *Atlantic* connection

---

* This, like the preceding letters and others in this chapter, is in the Houghton Library of Harvard University.

because of routine work alone. There were other strong reasons which made it desirable not to be bound to any relation with the magazine. . . . I am quite sure that my writing will greatly benefit by the change I have made; the repressive influence of the *Atlantic* has often made me feel like a man trying to speak in a nightmare and had stifled and almost frozen springs of life and thought that now burst forth with great energy."

It would probably be enough to let such letters speak for themselves. But I cannot refrain from the comment that if Rose had to listen to George discoursing upon himself at home in the same lofty fashion, I am amazed that a woman of her make-up could have endured it a week.

In the year following Francis' birth — in the month after George's resignation from the *Atlantic* — Una Hawthorne died. During her visit to America she had met at Rose's home a young writer named Albert Webster. He was a consumptive, and in the fall of 1876 he set out for the Hawaiian Islands in the hope of regaining his health. About this old Mrs. Lathrop wrote to Rose on November 1st: "I received a letter from Webster today. He sails for Honolulu on the 8th of this month — not a syllable in reference to an engagement either direct or remote! Strange — passing strange."

Probably poor Webster knew he was doomed, and he did, in fact, die at sea on that voyage. The news reached Una when she was with her brother Julian. She did no more than glance at the letter, saying, "Ah — yes!" slowly with a deep sigh. But after that her hair suddenly grew quite gray, and she seemed to relinquish her hold on life. While staying at an Anglican convent near Windsor, which she was thinking of entering, she died so suddenly that, though Julian was telegraphed for, he arrived too late. She was buried in Kensal Green near her mother.

Rose wrote to tell Aunt Ebie about it. The doctor had said

the cause of her death was pyrosis and exhaustion. "It is strange," she adds, "that according to Doctor Holmes, papa's death was caused by the same. . . . I have written to Miss Mary Ashpital, the Sister Superior."

Colonel Higginson, the friend of this woman — who as a child sat for the portrait of Pearl in *The Scarlet Letter* — called her "one of the rarest persons" he had ever known; and he and his sister were sure of her genius though they admitted Una had never written anything that proved it. Higginson's sister summed her up: "She was not transparent, though very confiding. . . . sometimes she seemed beautiful, then entirely the reverse. . . . It was impossible she should ever be happy." Be that as it may — and undoubtedly the poor girl did inherit Hawthorne's melancholy without much of the compensating Hawthorne gaiety or creative power — that she had a brother-in-law who could write as George did in the New York *Daily Tribune* for June 25, 1879, could hardly have contributed much to her peace of mind. There he corrected what he was pleased to call "some romantic flights of imagination lately published concerning the Hawthornes." He said he had never been engaged to Una, though he had a high regard for her. On the contrary, while visiting his wife, she had met Albert Webster, a friend of his, and it was to Webster that she became engaged. If young Webster died on his way to the Hawaiian Islands, he was going there partly at George's insistence and was to stay at the plantation of George's uncle and receive the medical treatment of George's father. He declares that the origin of the difficulties between Julian Hawthorne and himself are untrue. "Finally Miss Una Hawthorne did have an attack of insanity in London, having also had one ten years before." To which I can merely say that I can find no evidence for anything that can be called insanity — unless Una's early infatuation with George is to bear that name. It is a great pity that after Una's unhappy life, George should have written things which were so patently unmanly and disingenuous.

Writing to Scudder on September 8, 1877, George told him: "I can't say certainly that I shall do as well pecuniarily this year, as last, but at present the prospects are good. My relations with other publishers are strangely better than those with H. O. H. & Co. [H. O. Houghton & Co.] were." As a matter of fact, he was glad, in spite of all his high-flown talk about the repressive effect of the *Atlantic*, to take a position that paid a regular salary, and so became editor of the Boston *Sunday Courier*. The previous year he had published his first notable book, the *Study of Hawthorne*, and it had been upon the whole well received, as it deserved to be, though in a letter to Scudder, dated April 23, 1877, he mentions accepting the praise that Stedman had written to Howells "as compensation for the bitterness which was the last summer's fruit of the book."

The *Study* was rather shabbily produced by Osgood, which is surprising in view of its own importance and Hawthorne's literary standing. The book is a very competent and mature piece of work, all the more remarkable when we remember that it was produced by a man of twenty-five. Already Lathrop had a good reputation as a writer of the long serious critical reviews in vogue at the time, but in his *Study* he showed what he could do on a large scale; and it was very impressive.

It was, unfortunately, also a bit spiteful. Fields is mentioned only in connection with a "mistake" he had made, for George, now having married a Hawthorne, had accepted their view of Fields' dishonesty. But then Julian, in his much larger work never mentioned Fields at all, though he did in his *Hawthorne and His Circle*, and though Rose also did in her *Memories of Hawthorne*. It is a pity that private — and almost certainly, rather ill-based — grudges should have appeared. In spite of these the *Study* was a highly competent performance.

It was, however, very irritating to Julian, who had projected his two more or less definitive volumes. Understandably enough he regarded his young brother-in-law (of whom he had always disapproved) as an intruder into preserves that obviously belonged to himself by every possible title. And when this writing of the *Study* made George *the* Hawthorne authority and secured for him the editing of the Riverside edition of Hawthorne's Collected Works, again it is very understandable that Julian should have felt aggrieved. When his turn came he got a rather petty revenge by mentioning that Una had met Albert Webster at the home of "his married sister," at which moment Rose, who had been named freely before, was relegated to quasi-anonymity. The point must be mentioned here because it was another phase of a feud that went on for a number of years between Julian and George and had a culmination to be shown later.

George had ambitions to be a creative writer as well as a critic. On October 21, 1874, he availed himself of the excuse that Lowell had spoken kindly of his long, critical articles to send him — not giving him the chance to refuse — a pastoral in blank verse along with some shorter pieces. A year later Lowell again had to give his opinion — this time on a poem on Stonewall Jackson. George had shown it to Howells, he said, and "we couldn't make up our minds about it, his opinion being rather unfavorable, I being very diffident in defense of the piece." It was difficult, it would seem, for an amiable man like Lowell to shake George Lathrop off. But Lowell's good opinion was worth receiving and appears to have grown in the persistent George's favor, for on August 9, 1876, the confidence is made to him regarding the *Study of Hawthorne:* "I was obliged, at last, to write the book in so short a space of time, that its incompleteness and the defects in its style were able to attain mortifyingly large proportions; and my conscience has been wincing under self-inflicted chastisement, ever since my 'Study' was published. Then when the attack upon it came, as a violation of trust, the horrible notoriety of that needless quarrel almost sickened me."

Once George gets going in imparting confidences there is no

stopping him. He goes on to write of "The false position in which I was placed at the time of my marriage (partly through Julian's agency, too),"* and of "the agony of standing quite alone with one other soul against the world." He had had to make himself independent of all opinions, he declared, and to fight for it; "But," he added, "a bitter independence is not good for anyone."

But this is not all. Surprisingly he tells Lowell: "I need a vast deal of encouragement to overcome my self-distrust." (That assured manner of his *was* mainly defensive.) He offered to explain to Lowell some time "the origin of Julian's wrath" and said then that "in the face of singularly intolerable treatment I strove a long time to prevent the breach which has now widened into publicity. Julian was my great admiration, before my marriage, and when he utterly disappointed my conception of his character, it did not rouse hostility in me. . . . But the other party has apparently cared not a fig for the idol [of friendship], . . . or for me, or for anything but his own powerful temper."

Rose, too, did some writing — short stories and poems — and at this time made one of her many incompleted attempts to produce a novel. More will be said on this subject later; it is sufficient to record at this point that Mr. T. Niles of Roberts Brothers, the Boston publishers, reported to her on December 28, 1877, rather noncommittally upon seven chapters of a novel she had submitted to him. Even with a baby to look after she still found time to write. Her literary work, however, may well have sprung from the same root as George's industry — economic necessity. On July 29, 1878, Aunt Ebie writes from Montserrat reminding Rose that the five dollars she was to have received four times a year had not been paid in the last two installments. She does not like mentioning this, as she knows that Rose is herself short of money, but now that Una has died and her share of

* What this means I don't know. Perhaps merely that Julian had been friendly to George at Dresden, in 1869, at which time he could have hardly expected the marriage.

the legacy has come to Julian and herself, perhaps they will take care of her.

Rose was not so engrossed by working as to be unable to enjoy her motherhood, and it is probably safe to suppose that the verses headed "The Baby" in her collection of poems were meant for Francie.

> *Pray, have you heard the news?*
> *Sturdy in lungs and thews,*
>   *That's a fine baby!*
> *Ring bells of crystal lip,*
> *Wave boughs with blossoming tip;*
>   *Think what he may be.*

We can see from his later photos — one is marked by her, "This is the best position," another, "This, I think, gives the nearest approximation to expression. All are inadequate," and still another, "The expression here, a little strained, but gives faint suggestion of his smiling roguish look" — that he was a good-looking, well-fed youngster, with a strong resemblance to his mother, whose red hair he had. This hair is in a water-color sketch — probably made by Rose herself — of the child lying asleep, fully dressed.

On February 5, 1878, George wrote to Stoddard from Cambridge: "Rose and the boy-bud are well. They do tempt one to write poems; but I never feel I can quite do them justice, so I just go on loving them in prose." But on August 8, 1879, George writes to Scudder from Concord: "I lead a life of drudgery, violently severed from all that I like best." And on November 2, 1880, Rose writes to Mrs. Aldrich: "Sitting here, so much alone in this old house, the Wayside, as I have done of late, I seem to see things between slumber and waking, a bright queer time for insights, though they are always sad ones; and I wonder if all the saints about us avert anything except from themselves. Amelioration is quite another thing and I sometimes detest it." Rose had a queer way of writing at times. She herself terms the above "unwarrantable remarks."

Certainly neither she nor George sound particularly happy. It probably was because of this that she was exhibiting a piety never seen in her before. She now was teaching a class of boys — who were, so Rose told Aunt Ebie, charming — in the Unitarian Sunday School, and presumably was herself attending the services about which she had formerly spoken so scornfully. It was the same Mr. Reynolds who was still there as minister.

Suddenly tragedy descended upon them. On February 6, 1881, after a brief illness, Francie died of diphtheria. That same day George wrote to Aunt Lizzie to tell her that the lad had died at ten minutes past six that morning. They buried his little body beside that of his famous grandfather in the Sleepy Hollow cemetery. Writing to her Manning cousins, Miss Hawthorne told them: "To [Rose] he was the sweetest of companions. He would sit a long time singing, and did not speak when she was writing. He was always merry and roguish, and never bashful." Before another year had passed Aunt Ebie herself died, and Rose, with her at the end, reached another great turning point in life.

Rose never had another child. But to her dying day she carefully preserved such things as "an oak leaf from Francie's grave" — so the envelope in which it is kept is marked in her hand. There is another envelope "Rosebud from my Francie's hand after death. R. H. L." We have his hair at sixteen and again at nineteen months — the color a rich, tawny brown. Another envelope contains his meaningless scribblings; to his mother they had a meaning. On one scrap of paper Rose had written: "Francie drew this, and came to me saying it was an owl, which I think it is. F. just 4 yrs old." Under another figure of a bird — one she seems to have held him to copying till he got it done — she wrote in red pencil, "The iron will of a gentle woman."

CHAPTER 11

The Busy Writers

The death of Francie made Rose and George revert to their old nomadic existence. There are hints that George did not like it, but Rose's childhood — spent in moving about from place to place — confirmed her in a tendency which probably was native to her disposition. Only happy marriage and motherhood could have tethered her. Now that Francie was gone, she had to be gone too.

Not of course that this was from the outset a careful plan. It was merely that at that moment the Wayside had become intolerable. The recollections of her father and mother and Una — which had seemed a benediction so long as she could hear Francie at his play — now merely added to the pain she felt. She had to get away. Before long she sold the Wayside, realizing that she could never bring herself to live there again; but for the moment she just shut it up and fled. Anywhere, anywhere — so long as she could escape.

Francie's death seemed to her to snap the tenuous bond that had been holding her to George. From Morrisania — this seems to be a part of the present Bronx — where Julian lived — she wrote in an undated letter to her Aunt Mary Mann to say: "I have removed all my things from the Wayside, and there would be nothing for Julian to go on about. Aunt Lizzie's things I shall see to when I go back to Boston. I meant to go to Concord when I was last in Boston, but as George was to be there more or less, I found it best to put off going until he should return to New York. I of course dread a meeting with him. My outlook and my present situation are too sad to give me any courage for additional stresses of feeling. I have already begun to lose the bitterness of feeling which carried me through the first throes of my decision to leave George, and although my conviction about the separation will remain the same, I shall not care to keep alive the intense reproach which was the result of his attitude towards me." And later, even when an actual separation was not threatened, it could not have been indicative of domestic harmony that George could write to his confidant Aldrich from 39 West Ninth Street, New York City, on April 11, 1883: "Two or three days since, Mrs. Lathrop — by way of a little breakfast surprise — announced that she had decided to go to Europe for the Summer."* On the same date Rose herself writes to Mr. Aldrich saying that she was going with Emma Lazarus.

This, however, is anticipating a little. In 1881 there was a trip to Europe, when George went to Spain to write a book. We know from an undated letter to Mrs. Mann that Rose and George traveled there together on the *Nevada*. "George is full of cheer about the voyage," she says. But there is an ominous note in the last phrase of the next sentence: "We have a stateroom together which is one thing gained towards *respite*." Rose's intention was to visit Julian in London and from there go on to Paris to study art, while George went to Spain with Charles S. Reinhart, who was to illustrate the book Harper's had commissioned him to write. This was a means for giving both Rose and George something to do that would prevent their brooding over Francie's death. To brooding she knew herself to be somewhat addicted. This change would be good for them.

Though Rose, writing from London, on August 28th, to Aunt Lizzie, says: "George came home from Spain in much satisfaction with his trip," George himself later grumbled to Aldrich that his trip was a "failure." He did not see the Escorial, he says, but adds: "Still I found more than I could even begin to comprehend fully in what I did see." Not a very satisfactory basis for a book.

* It does not appear that she did go, however.

At that time Rose wrote to tell her Aunt Mary: "In the autumn I hope to be at the Wayside, for it is so lovely then, and I must be there for awhile, even if it breaks my heart anew, for I would rather suffer so much more than be too much away from those precious associations with Francie, and the sad quiet and rare rest of the Wayside. I do not think, dear, that George and I can ever sell the place now, I would rather, seems to me, be poor all my life, than not own the home Francie loved, and made so sunny with his smiles and golden hair." And on July 24th, when she was momentarily expecting George to join her in London after his visit to Spain, she tells Mary Mann she meant to talk to him about the sale of the Wayside, but had not been able to write to him about it. "I was afraid," she says, "that through a letter he might not understand how little I would wish to influence him in the matter, and yet how lothe I should be to have the house sold. If he thought I did *not care*, he might be discouraged about keeping it, although I know he loves it so much, and wants to, and if I expressed my real longing (as I have often done) always to keep it, he might not wish to dispose of it."

Spanish Vistas was a handsomely got out volume, but it is just one more travel (or rather, vacation) book. It is competently written though, as usual with George, in a somewhat swollen style, and in view of his conversion to Catholicism, the tone of his scattered remarks about Catholics is slightly surprising. His description of priests on page 54 seems almost to be an echo of Hawthorne, for he speaks of "a dreary succession of bloated bodies and brutish faces." But it is not necessary to Catholicism to admire priests as men, and poor George is only indulging in a bit of toploftiness when, writing of a forty days' indulgence, he "computed that a good Catholic could by a half-hour's industry secure immunity for two hundred and thirty days." Before long he was to discover that a *plenary* indulgence can sometimes be gained in a minute. The general impression he derived was that "Christianity in Spain meant barbarism." The best thing in the book was what he quoted in his Preface as from a Spaniard telling him of his country's political parties. "Party!" this man had exclaimed. "Listen! in Spain there is a separate political party for every man." Then the Spaniard had paused slightly before adding bitterly, "Sometimes two!" When it came out the book was inscribed by George, "To Rösl, a birthday gift from her husband, May 20, 1883."

A letter written by Alice Wheeler,* a painter and a very old friend, undated but bearing the Turnham Green postmark as having been received on August 5, 1881, shows that Rose was staying with Julian at the pleasant artists' colony of Bedford Park at that time. Miss Wheeler gushed from Geneva about the beauties of Heidelburg and how the waltzes of "Strausse" filled the air. But the letter gives us this much to the purpose. Alice said, "I am distressed to know of your having been weak and depressed." She did not like to think of Rose's going to Paris until the weather improved — when she did she was to be sure to see St. Cloud and Versailles — and she strongly advised Rose to get some lessons from Alma Tadema. Despite that confession of not very good taste, we learn that Alice's (like Rose's) favorite painters are Raphael and Perugino.

Rose, however, did nothing except visit London. Regarding this there is a long letter of Rose's to her "darling Aunt Lizzie" written from 39 Pelham Street, S. Kensington, on August 28th. She is at this address because George had returned from Spain and at Julian's house at Bedford Park there was no double bedroom to spare; besides, George had to have a room in which to

---

* From Miss Ellen Ware Fiske, of Wellesley Hills, I learn that Alice Wheeler was tall, thin, and angular. Miss Fiske also says her disposition was friendly and cheerful, but that she had definite opinions, regarding which she was very outspoken. She strikes me in her letters as a little fluttery and foolish, obviously goodhearted but not of the intellectual type. She lived with Mrs. Souther, her aunt, and Mr. Souther in a small brown house on Worcester Street, Wellesley Hills. With the Southers also lived Emily Shore Foreman, a lecturer on Browning. Afterward the Southers moved to Chapel Place.

write. He was working away hard on his Spanish articles and Rose is also writing for money. The museum is a great attraction where they are, and her mother-in-law and Frank Lathrop are in London.* "As for Julian," she says, "You may be sure my gratitude for the reunion with him is great. . . . He is lovely to George and the Lathrops, and is in fact the dearest brother!"

Mr. Lowell had called to see her, and "this morning — a most beautiful one — we went to see him, and a portrait Frank is making of him." The great man had walked with them in the Park and Kensington Gardens, "and I assure you it made the day twice as charming. What a wonderful thing genius and perception is!" But her "heart aches," she says, "for the dear boy," Frank Lathrop, "and I fear more than I dare say for him. He is just one of those noble, beautiful natures that live so much in the spirit as to leave us early."

She tells Aunt Lizzie that she does not mean to live away from the Wayside altogether: "We cannot bear to sell the house." At the end of the letter she writes: "All you say about our Francie's influence and revelation of heaven, darling, I feel to be true indeed, and it is a glorious thing to have brought a child into the world who has given you so much. . . . I feel the wonderful goodness of God in giving me my splendid and celestial child, as deeply as you know I ought to."

Yet for a while afterward she had no settled place of abode. We find her in Philadelphia, in January, 1882, where she was living alone at the Colonnade Hotel** (so Aunt Ebie says); but it

* On July 10th Rose mentioned to Aunt Mary that "Nothing could be sweeter and simpler and more engaging than [Mrs. Lathrop's] mood, and she does not seem to be any more the victim of depression and ill turns." In the same letter she says that George liked the illustrator of his book, Reinhart, and that she planned to meet him on August 1st in Paris and to stay there with him for about three weeks. Instead George joined her in London.

** The postscript of a letter to Aunt Mary, dated April 16th, suggests that this visit to Philadelphia was made in order that she might be under the famous Doctor Weir Mitchell's care.

is clear from letters from Alice Wheeler (who was invited there) that George was at least sometimes staying there too, and that both were "working like Trojans." This was for good reason, as some letters indicate that funds were low. "What a mission," Alice says in one letter, "what a mission you have to convert your luxuriant George to a thoroughgoing bohemian!" — which perhaps means that George would have preferred the comforts of a home, and that Rose could not be bothered with domesticities.

What the domestic arrangements of the Lathrops were at this time comes out in the letter written from 39 West 9th St., New York, on April 16 [1882], to Aunt Mary. Rose tells her: "It was not possible to find a room for George and myself, and so I kept the little attic room and he has a room at low rate but very nice nearby for sleeping and writing room. He is pleased with the inexpensiveness of the living, and I am much satisfied to have my nights begin so early and last so long as I need to have them. My sleep is so sound and refreshing that but a few days have made me feel quite differently. But I would not explain my arrangements to any one but *you people* at 75 Hancock Street. . . . We are taking our meals together all of us [including old Mrs. Lathrop and Frank, presumably]; but when I begin to go to my room over the Vienna Bakery I shall take my dinners there at noon, as they have a late dinner here." George, from the same address, wrote to Miss Peabody: "Rose has taken a studio on Broadway, for a month, and seems rather stronger the last day or two than for some time previous. I see almost nothing of her, however." The studio, as appears from an envelope addressed by Alice Wheeler, was Room 29, the Vienna Restaurant, Broadway, near Tenth Street.

In October, Rose turns up at Concord again, writing to Houghton Mifflin on the 2nd from the Wayside. The next month, though she is still at the Wayside, she gives her "winter address" as 8 Chestnut Street, Boston. In 1883, the old home at Concord was sold by her to a Mr. and Mrs. Lothrop. He was a publisher and she an author of children's books.*

In what follows it should be remembered that there was an old quarrel between George and Julian, and that this was acerbated by the fact that George — with Rose behind him, otherwise he would hardly have obtained the commission — was in charge of the Riverside edition of Hawthorne's works. Julian felt that a march had been stolen upon him, as he had also felt in the case of Lathrop's *Study of Hawthorne*, and was not at all well disposed toward his brother-in-law or (for that matter) his sister.

Now it was Julian's turn to do something that aroused their wrath; he announced — in the papers — that a posthumous Hawthorne novel had been discovered and that he was going to publish it — of course quite independently of the Lathrop project of the Riverside edition.

Rose was aware that, in the last years of his life, her father had started a novel which he had never finished, the manuscript of which (*The Dolliver Romance*) was buried with him. She also knew that Una, assisted by Robert Browning, had deciphered the manuscript of *Septimius Felton*, which was then published in the *Atlantic Monthly* and afterward in book form. But she did not know that her mother had begun the transcription of another posthumous work by her husband. Therefore when Julian announced it for publication she and George both publicly charged Julian with fabrication. It came to that, definitely enough, in her letter that was published in the New York *Daily Tribune* in its issue for August 16, 1882 (page 5). The letter was written at the Wayside three days earlier and runs in part: "As it has been announced that a new and complete romance by Nathaniel Haw-

* Regarding this there is a postscript in a letter dated January 28, 1884. George wrote to Aldrich: "I ought to tell you that I gave her one thousand dollars at the time of the sale of the Wayside, tho' her lawyers admitted her dower right was worth nothing."

thorne, entitled 'Dr. Grimshawe's Secret' has been found and will soon be published, will you do me the favor to correct the error? No such unprinted work has been in existence. A fragmentary and unfinished sketch, vaguely introducing some of the features assigned to the promised publication, has perhaps furnished the basis of the rumor. This sketch, which was preliminary to 'Septimus [sic] Felton' has been described by Mr. Lathrop in an article printed in *The Atlantic Monthly* for October, 1872. (Volume 30, page 452.)

"All Mr. Hawthorne's manuscripts were kept together until 1872. There were very few of them and nothing was overlooked. They were first examined by Mrs. Hawthorne, and after her decease again examined by Miss Una Hawthorne and myself. Still later, Mr. Lathrop and myself carefully read them all; and the sketch above-mentioned is the only one resembling the story now announced as 'practically finished.' It cannot be truthfully published as anything more than an experimental fragment."

George was undoubtedly very incensed with Julian, and Rose had a woman's partisanship. Also she was impulsive and hot tempered. And the way Julian sprang his announcement on the world made them sure that, if there was a manuscript at all, Julian had had to doctor it a good deal.

The charge brought against Julian should not be isolated from the ill will which, at this time, existed between the brothers-in-law. And such ill will is to be regretted. Still more to be regretted is the breach that occurred between brother and sister. But things of this sort are of everyday occurrence. Rose certainly was now in the mood to judge her brother harshly. "Julian's shocking notice in the papers," she writes in an undated letter to Miss Hawthorne, "has been a great grief to me. His dishonesty has been a heavier blow than mere cruelty would have been, especially as I could hardly expect anything but the latter after his conduct towards us."

The two men did afterward become reconciled and even collaborated on a novel published serially in *Collier's* though not in book form. But Julian's bitterness against George persisted even after a reconciliation had been effected with Rose, for on October 16, 1883, he wrote to her: "I have heard nothing of George, good or bad, for some months past; and I cannot help hoping that you have not." From that one incidentally catches a hint, as one does from other letters, that brief separations between husband and wife had already occurred now and then.

It is only fair to Julian to say that he took the lead in the reconciliation. Indeed, on March 15, 1881, before the *Dr. Grimshawe* affair had broken, he wrote Rose a long letter of condolence about Francie. In it he said: "I remember how you and I used to be children together here in England, five and twenty years ago; we had our childish quarrels then, and made them up before nightfall. Is there any quarrel so just that it may not be made up before the last nightfall of all? . . . I have never lost the feeling that you were my sister, or the wish to be to you all that a brother could be. You and I are all that is left of us now; and it is strange that we should stand apart." For good measure Julian offers George any service he might wish performed in England. "I say that," he assures Rose, "in no conventional sense, but with all my heart. It is a favor which I ask, not offer."

As a result of that appeal Rose and Julian were reconciled in London. But hardly had she returned when she got the shock of the announcement about *Dr. Grimshawe's Secret.* So again on August 28, 1882, Julian writes her: "Now, my dear Sister," he said, "you know the reason why I have hitherto refrained from making any defense or answer to the direct charge of forgery which has been again and again brought against me, always on the authority of your statements. With the proof literally in my hands — ninety thousand words of this story in my father's handwriting — I sit here day after day and wait for you to speak. . . . Yesterday Louisa Alcott called here, and was shown the *Mss;* and it was evident that she considered your action in having denied its existence, inconceivably rash, at the least. Others will not be so lenient as she, because they will not know you personally."

The suggestion made by Julian in that letter, that Rose withdraw her charges in the same paper in which they were made, was not accepted — possibly because Julian, using the blandest language in the world, hinted at legal proceedings. One can imagine Rose tossing her red head at that. But he did succeed in convincing her in the end that she was completely mistaken; and when she published her *Memories of Hawthorne* she went out of her way to indicate, by references to *Dr. Grimshawe's Secret* — which were a bit dragged in — that she fully accepted its authenticity. On pages 442–443 of the *Memories* she also lets it be known that she had seen the manuscript itself. If anything was needed to close the controversy, there it was. But before 1883 was out the quarrel between brother and sister was over, and for the remainder of their lives they remained on the best of terms. Previously when Julian's two volumes *Nathaniel Hawthorne and His Wife* appeared, in 1880, he had seen to it that George Parsons Lathrop was not so much as mentioned.

That the whole Hawthorne and Peabody group must bear at least some part of the blame for the lack of harmony between George and Rose Lathrop appears in a number of places. Among these is a letter, dated November 3rd,* and written from 78 East 55th Street, New York, in which Rose tells her aunts: "If George is yet too sensitive about the concerns of last year, I know very well that the blame of it all lies with me, and I cannot but hope that he will feel cheerfully and happily toward you again." Which is certainly an adroit way of fixing the blame on them while taking it on herself.

Julian Hawthorne at this time was an amazingly prolific author. His father turned out work — and work of the highest quality — with remarkable speed, considering that he did it all with the

---

* We can fix the year as 1884 from its allusion to the Cleveland–Blaine campaign.

pen, though he did not of course begin to approach Scott's or Trollope's prodigies. But we hear of Julian, from Aunt Ebie's letters, having an establishment at Sag Harbor with four or five servants and a nurse and "about eight children" — Great-Aunt Ebie may be pardoned for being a little vague — and of actually getting fifty dollars for a story! But of course he was living beyond his means and was deeply in debt. The result was that he had to produce an immense amount of copy, and this he did straight on the typewriter. Out of his letters I pick one, dated July 28, 1892, all in capitalized typescript, including the signature. On the 16th of that month he tells Rose: "I've set out to produce a fifty thousand word novel in two weeks" — child's play to him! On top of all this, and his lecturing and the business connections he formed, he found time to dabble — though probably not very seriously — in spiritualism. So that H. C. Bunner could write, on March 16, 1884, to Walter Learned: "Hawthorne is a psychic sharp, and has been lecturing on the Philosophy of magic. The manifestations, however, were meager."

George also worked very hard, harder than was good for him. And one fears that at least some of Rose's allusions to his not being very well are a charitable way of saying that he had been overindulging in alcohol. Drink had become a spur to activity when he was jaded; it was also at times what has been called a glass crutch. Beginning in 1876, when he published anonymously in the "No Name Series" his *Afterglow,* he produced during the next seventeen years about a dozen novels or collections of short stories. In addition to this, in 1885 he became the New York correspondent for the Kansas City *Times,* and his journalistic writing was syndicated by small newspapers all over the country.

This does not take into account some novels that were merely serialized, or short stories that never appeared in book form, or his articles and poems. Moreover, in 1886, he dramatized Julian's novel *Pauline* for Madame Modjeska, and though it was never produced — despite the contract — George's *Elaine,* which was based on Tennyson's poem, was staged in 1887, as was later the opera which he made of Hawthorne's *Scarlet Letter*, for which Walter Damrosch wrote the music.

Moreover he was beginning to be rather well paid. The *Century* gave him, in 1887, one hundred and fifty dollars for the 230 lines of his "Casket of Opals" and one hundred dollars, in 1890, for another poem, "Marthy Virginia's Hand." So assured was he of his position — but also of course of the friendship of Richard Watson Gilder — that in sending his story — "The Man Who Told the Truth" to the *Century*, he could say jocosely: "As a beginner in literature, I understand that large prices are paid for acceptable short stories. If you like this story, you can send me the largest amount you think it worth, without any danger of startling me."

A consideration of George Parsons Lathrop as a writer does not belong here, except in its relation to his wife, the subject of this book. It is, however, necessary to point out that he was a brisk and sufficiently successful writer, immensely competent and versatile and with a reputation for supplying editors and publishers with just what they needed. His best work was done in the field of criticism, and though it is probable that he obtained his position on the *Atlantic Monthly* because of being Hawthorne's son-in-law, and established himself by means of that position, this gave him the opportunity for making his mark rapidly but not his talent itself. It may be safe to surmise that one so proficient as he was, and who turned out satisfactory copy with profuse ease, and who finally was given to pompous self-esteem, was often rather contemptuous about Rose's little literary efforts, which so lamentably failed to come off. The efficient person as a rule has scant patience with the inefficient. And Rose Hawthorne Lathrop's writing, though produced in some quantity, was not very seriously regarded by her and was somewhat diffidently offered by her to editors.

Furthermore, she must have known — if she did not, George

would have informed her — that she had a definite advantage in being the famous Hawthorne's daughter, and also in having such editors as William Dean Howells and Horace Scudder and T. B. Aldrich of the *Atlantic* and Richard Watson Gilder of the *Century* as personal friends. Had it not been for these circumstances she probably would not have placed as much of her work as she did.

Perhaps Julian's opinions expressed to her were unduly partial, as he was her brother, but they might be quoted, before I proceed to my own. "You have," he tells her on October 16, 1883, "great power and originality, but you do too much of your thinking behind the scenes, and this sometimes leads to obscurity. What faults there are, however, are of the kind that become virtue when a little modified. If you keep on writing, you will become the most memorable of the women novelists of this country. But do not, on that account forego your lyrical poetry. You can hardly do anything more valuable to literature than that, though of course it is anything but remunerative to you."

On December 12th of that same year he wrote to her again: "I saw in some paper that Hawthorne's mantle, which had slipped from the shoulders of his son, was appearing on those of his daughter, — in reference, I believe to some of your poetry — the kind you send to Gilder, and he says is not quite good enough for that bloated magazine of his. But I think you should get out more and more stories, until you find just the kind of thing you can do with most enjoyment, and with the most general employment of your faculties and resources; and then sail in and write a long novel on these lines, whatever they may be. You really have in you the entrails of Hawthorne's genius, if they are anywhere."

It seems to me likely enough that Julian was saying rather more than he really believed — especially as he wrote this to her after the fortunate ending of the *Dr. Grimshawe* affair, when he naturally wished to please her. But though as an estimate of her

actual accomplishments, what he wrote sounds rather foolish, it
was penetrating if it be considered as Julian's perception that
potentially she was very remarkable — a far more remarkable
person than himself. After her death, in his article on her in the
Atlantic, he rounded his criticism out — and there he truly said:
"The gift of expression in art, much as she could appreciate it
in others, was beyond her control. Something else was needed to
satisfy her soul and release her energies. She was to be a woman
grown before the solution to her riddle appeared."

She was diffident — though perhaps in the bit that immediately
follows there is also a touch of mild scorn. She tells Robert
Underwood Johnson at the *Century*, "Mr. Lathrop objects very
much to the word 'fondle' and so I have changed it." But she
really was shy in offering editors her poems. From New London
she writes to Scudder of the *Atlantic*, "I do not know how long
you will endure my shower of verses!" and adds in a postscript:
"When any writing of mine is returned, I always find cause to be
glad although it is just a little more fortunate to have it accepted!
But I do so often make fiascos." Aldrich similarly hears about
1882: "I send you a poem which I much wish were worthy of
the *Atlantic* pages, and I *fancy* that it is so." Later in the letter
she says, "The price I set upon the poem is twenty-five dollars."
A little later to another editor she writes: "Would you like the
enclosed verses for *The Independent?* And will you give me
fifteen dollars for them?" Aldrich again is told: "If I greet you
with a bad essay at poetry, will you forgive me, and believe if
I could know the real worth of what I write, I should not ask
you to help me with your verdict?" And again Aldrich hears: "I
am proud to have your approval of the lyric, and very glad to
have you 'place' the verses I sent in their right domain, for I shall
put them where they will do me the least harm — in the waste
paper basket. If I write anything that sings again, I shall send it
to you to test."

All that is charmingly modest. Who was she to put herself up

beside the efficient George? And though it can hardly be but
that she recognized that such an elaborate performance as his
"Gettysburg" was not real poetry, at least she could be reasonably
proud of him as a good man at his job. Clearly he thought so too
when, on July 3, 1888, the twenty-fifth anniversary of the battle,
he rolled out the empty and orotund ode. It would be undiscern-
ing to sweep such a poem aside as would most modern critics as
of no merit whatever. What is true is that it was very good of its
kind — a piece of versified oratory — something that "comes off"
hardly once in five hundred times, so difficult is it to make
such a thing the magically exalted poetry which alone is tolerable.
Yet, Rose was justified in keeping the letter George's mother
wrote her, on July 2nd, the day before the reading of the ode,
and on the envelope her own notation, "Mama's letter about the
Gettysburg poem." Old Mrs. Lathrop tells Rose: "I cannot express what I feel about this great poem, but I cannot read it without tears, and joy mingled, — joy that a man and a poet to whom
I have given life, should give to the world such great, noble,
tender, sad, beautiful thoughts." Whether George's wife altogether agreed with George's mother, she shared her pride in
accomplishment.

Her own poems at least are simple and unpretentious and, if
not better, are certainly less offensive than so much of the graceful nullity produced in an age when Richard Watson Gilder was
at once the leading poet and the arbiter of poetic taste. Rose's
poetry is merely not very "accomplished," and verse which
was not obviously accomplished was as little esteemed in those
days as accomplished verse is in these. But sometimes her poems
have more in them than that, though honesty obliges me to admit
that I can find no single poem in her one collection, *Along the
Shore*, which is satisfactory all the way through. But in her lines
on Francie, her dead son, in spite of obvious efforts to conform
to the accepted standards under the conventions of the day, real
feeling is to be found:

Upon the shore of darkness
His drifted body lies.
He is dead, and I stand beside him,
With his beauty in my eyes.

So also with many other bits; they remain bits, and Rose Hawthorne Lathrop a potential rather than a fully effective poet.

When I turn to her stories, I confess to feeling dismay. At
Hawthorne, New York, there are stacks of her stories printed
in such magazines as the *Atlantic, Century, St. Nicholas, Harper's
Bazaar, Harper's Weekly, Scribner's, Rambler, Sunday School
Times, Appleton's Journal,* and *Commercial Advertiser.* So it will
be seen that she placed her stuff with the leading magazines and
was also content to have it published by those of the humbler
sort. If anybody wants to go and look these things up, let him
do so at his own risk. They are not bad, neither are they good.
I conscientiously read them and made my voluminous notes, but
I cannot bring myself to copy them out here. The reader would
be well advised to take my word for it that nothing of great
importance is involved.

What is to my mind far more revealing is the fact that there
are also bundles of unprinted or unfinished work — including
several novels and a play. In her sprawling penciled script she
would dash off from twenty to sixty pages at top speed, and then
lose interest. Had she been prepared to endure the pangs necessary to artistic creation, she could have done something. But it is
patent on almost every one of these pathetic pages that Rose was
not prepared to pay the price. Writing failed to engage her faculties to the full, just as music and painting had failed to do so. But
Julian was right; she did have genius. What she had not yet
found was its proper outlet.

If she provided a good deal of "igleaf," presumably that was
because the editors knew their readers liked "igleaf." But sometimes its effect on the modern reader is a bit comical, as in a
story in *Harper's Bazaar* for July 30, 1892, where we are shown

Lord Arthur Floray and Nicholas Damon taking together, as a final snack at night at the Fifth Avenue Hotel, welsh rabbit and champagne. But I am informed that this awesome combination was, in those days, regarded as almost the last refinement of luxury.

One of the funniest things is a scenario for a novel, made — so I would guess — in England just about the time of her marriage. There is to be an Earl of Carmairn who comes to America incognito, and when things begin to point to his being an Earl, people suspect him of being bogus. When the plot requires his being challenged he is to say dramatically, "Because I *am* Carmairn!" To him there is a duke as foil — the Duke of Mosshaven. "Dainty Devon might be the name of the girl." Her real name, however, is Teresa. She has a sister whose name is Allegra — or perhaps Nancy — and as Una is to sit for that portrait, Dainty Devon is presumably Rose herself. There are two specimens of bogus nobility, young Englishmen of bad character. The hero is to be Harry Sweepstakes, or Jack, or Alexander — called Lexis, perhaps. Vulgar American from Chicago, Damon Wopping. (This name of "Damon" was her King Charles's Head.) There is to be a nice American named Harry Wakely, "doing fine nice things for the plot" — though what they were she hadn't quite decided. Whistler is to be a character — which is what makes me date the scenario 1871 — and he is to appear as Mr. Mistler, or Sketchleigh, or Goldmist Lightly, or Waverly Goldmist, or Thames Mistler — "not sure which." A young man who appears frightfully wicked but is really pure gold through it all. A Frenchman, a comic Irish woman. "Cannot think what plot is to run through the general complications and love scenes. Something unique." Hopefully she jots down the idea: "There can be a moment of great courage on the part of Teresa which wins his heart, along with unaffectedly lovely nature. Perhaps she can save his life in some jolly excursion on land or water."

A letter of hers to Stoddard, undated but evidently belonging to about 1881, perhaps sufficiently expresses her attitude toward her own work. "I never could feel," she confesses, "that I did my relation to my father intellectual justice, but I do not expect to be a fine writer, though I *mean* to be. — Now if you think there's anything conceited in that word underscored, most truly never was anyone less confident of the efficacy of all but hard labor, than I am." About the same time it would seem, from an undated letter to T. B. Aldrich, that Mr. Houghton had approached her, with what she thought an insufficiently good offer for the book that eventuated as *Memories of Hawthorne*. Of that she says, "I should have preferred the ms printed many years later, after my death at any rate, as its nature is so fragmentary, but since my brother had other views in regard to *his* ms I find the time has come for this also to appear."

It was not published, however, until 1897 and has clearly been worked over several times. Even the early drafts of chapters of the *Memories*, in which I find useful details omitted from the book, bear every evidence of intense labor — something she never found it worth while giving to any other piece of her writing. It is true that of the article on the Hawthornes, at Lenox, contributed to the *Century*, in 1894, she wrote to Gilder: "The extracts I sent you I had not had time to ponder over much, and I know that the life in them must not be wrung out." But on the book, as a whole, she toiled as over nothing she had ever done. The result is that it is a masterpiece — or very near to being one — and, in my estimation, quite the best portrait ever drawn of Nathaniel Hawthorne.

CHAPTER III

New York and New London

In the two or three years that followed Francie's death Rose and George lived a rather unsettled and nomadic life. It is not perhaps very important to follow all their movements — some of which were only brief excursions for the gathering of literary material — but there is significance in the Lathrops' restless and unsettled state. One finds a number of addresses on the envelopes of the letters they received, the most frequent being that of 39 West Ninth Street, New York.

Apart from their feeling that Boston — and of course still more Concord — had for them memories too painful to endure, that New England city and village were no longer the literary centers of America. Its center was now New York. For people who had to keep in close touch with editors and publishers New York was the place to be. The contacts the Lathrops needed in Boston — those with the *Atlantic Monthly* and Houghton, Mifflin & Company — were so well established that there was no need for either George or Rose to be at hand to take advantage of them. New York, was, they found, at once profitable to them and lively. Even when they moved to New London, which gave them an easier and more settled mode of existence, New York remained the hub of their affairs, and there was much traveling back and forth for them, especially after the fall of 1886 when George became the literary editor of the New York *Sunday Star*.

In addition to professional engagements that took them to New York during the next ten or twelve years, there was a great deal of social activity, much of which had a professional character.

In all this it would seem that Rose was detached in heart while keeping at least one foot within New York's literary circles. This was of course very much the case as regards George's friends — though they largely went in for convivialities in which women were not wanted. But even in the case of the decorous Gilders, those frequenting their salon felt sometimes — and it gave Rose an added charm in their eyes — that she remained vaguely aloof, with her heart set on some far horizon at which they could only dimly guess.

The most interesting — and also the most valuable — of their contacts was that with the Gilders' circle. For Richard Watson Gilder was not only extremely influential as the editor of the *Century* magazine, he was also a delightful human being. He looked, with his large arched eyebrows and drooping mustache, a sort of melancholy Robert Louis Stevenson, thin, ascetic, distinguished; but he was really the best of company, and he and his wife, Helena de Kay, a warmhearted, as well as brilliant, woman, made a wonderful team. It is sometimes said, not quite accurately, that their house at 55 Clinton Place (afterward renamed and renumbered 13 East 8th Street) to which they had recently moved from their studio on 103 East 15th Street, was the only salon New York has ever known. What is true is that all the amusing people of the literary, dramatic, musical, and artistic world gathered there.

But the Gilders did not merely collect celebrities, even though a great many celebrities were present at what seemed to be a never ending party. Mrs. Gilder, who managed to look after her five children and to be active in many philanthropic organizations, brought along her social workers and millionaires. Sometimes a "visiting potentate," as they called him, would come, but there would always be a new poet, too, with his latest poem or a young musician finding his first audience. Now and then there was a special attraction, announced in advance; more often (and often more happily) the entertainment would seem to happen by lucky accident. In any event there was always good conversation, and, as Rosamond Gilder has said: "Casual geniuses, relying on my father's reputation for never sleeping, would stroll in for a social cup of tea at any hour of the night." Her mother, while running her household and her charitable schemes, remembered that her chief function was to keep alive "that firebrand of energy and emotion [her husband] who, without her support, could never have survived the struggle on this 'metropolitan battlefield.' " His relaxation, and hers — a very strenuous one — was in their friendly house where gathered such people as LaFarge and Saint Gaudens, Will Low, Stanford White — who made a wonderful peacock decoration in tiles for the outside of their studio — Madame Modjeska, Whitman, Paderewski, Kipling, and Duse.

Maurice Francis Egan, then a very young man, has left an entertaining account of the salon, in which anyone who knew Mr. Egan can be sure he played, even at that date with gay aplomb, his own entertaining part. "Some of the old New Yorkers," he writes, "and a sprinkling of New England Brahmins were generally found at the Gilders on Friday nights. . . . These evenings were the most delightful gatherings I have ever known. Mrs. Gilder brought in her knitting. She had lived in Dresden or Munich and she had something of the simplicity of the German life. . . . At a certain time chocolate and biscuits were served and everybody stayed until the last moment." In that period there was little lavish entertainment in New York, except at formal dinners. These, however, were sometimes formidable, and in literary and artistic circles there was, among the men, a good deal of conviviality.

Old Mrs. de Kay — but her daughter as well — took frequent digs at young Maurice Francis Egan's Catholicism, which they disliked or pretended to dislike. One day Mrs. de Kay's daughter, Julia, came in with two or three miniature Buddhas. This gave the mischievous old lady her chance.

"I know what you're going to say, Julia," Mrs. de Kay whispered to her in a tone intended to be heard by the Catholic Egan. "You're going to mention idols, but I warn you not to, because Mr. Egan will have no frivolity with them — as every one knows, they are part of his religion."

As Egan had no witticism handy, and it would have taken too long to explain seriously, he pretended not to hear. The old lady's chuckle told him of her satisfaction at having scored, as she believed, on the Catholic.

In such a circle the daughter of Hawthorne was always welcome, and indeed she and George, who when he chose could be very lively and entertaining, were welcomed for their own sakes. But the Hawthorne name and fame made Rose valued more, even when she came — as she always did come — to be valued for something in her that the more discerning perceived to be much more important than the immediate cachet she possessed. She did not much resemble either of her parents, but those who looked at the rich ruddy gold of her hair and her soft strawberry and cream skin, thought at once, if they had known Nathaniel Hawthorne and his wife, of a resemblance. It was so at that dinner she told about given on ladies' night at the Papyrus Club in Boston. She found herself sitting beside a little old gentleman with wrinkled ugly face and dancing eyes and white hair — nobody needed to tell her that this was Doctor Oliver Wendell Holmes — who passed his place card over her goblet.

"That's the simplest way, isn't it?" he asked.

"I was just about to introduce myself," Rose said, and at that moment Mrs. Stoddard sat down beside her, and she turned to speak to this friend.

Doctor Holmes was now looking at her card: "Now let me see!" said he.

"And you don't know who I am yet?"

He smiled quizzically, looked at the card through his eyeglasses and then at her. He had learned that this was Mrs. Lathrop.

"And what *was* your name?"

"Rose Hawthorne."

He started and beamed at her. "There, I *thought* — but you understand how — if I had made a mistake — could anything have been worse if you had *not* been you? I was looking, you know, for the resemblance. I thought I noticed something."

In every room into which she carried her striking presence people turned to look at her. There was a further excited little whisper that this was Hawthorne's daughter. And then, as she sat, talking in her simple unaffected way, radiant in cheerfulness, from this gently passing into a still more charming brooding silence, her mother and her father were seen to appear in turns in their daughter.

She became very intimate with both the Gilders, who were only a few years older than herself and George, and before long Mr. Gilder became "Richard" to her. Mrs. Gilder was of course "Helena" a long time before that. "My dear Rose," Helena wrote early in 1886,* "can you take my place as chaperone of the theatre-party: Mr. Gilder, Mr. Tompkins and Miss von Stosch to see Madame Modjeska in Mary Stuart Thursday night? Don't say no. I am so delighted that you are going to be here on the 14th. . . . I want you to go with us to Chase's studio to hear Mrs. Wiggins read — if this will not bore you. There will be music too. It will be a lot of people whom you know." Rose could be put up at 55 Clinton Place at any or all of the three nights. "You will have Dorothea's little room. I have no spare room this year — I am sorry to say."

It was a brilliant circle and happy family that George and Rose saw much of in those days. As to the happiness, Stedman, from time to time, used to express his opinion privately that Gilder might well have been a better poet if not so happily matched

---

* I can date this letter because George C. D. Odell's *Annals of the New York Stage* gives January 5 and 8, 1886, for the first times Modjeska appeared in *Mary Stuart* with repeat performances on the 12th and 13th.

with his Helena. But a man cannot have everything, and Gilder looked like a poet and wrote undeniably graceful verses, and was prosperous and had delightful friends: only the very greatest kind of poet could have overcome such handicaps. And if he had been that, what would poor Helena and the five children have done?

The Gilders were a focal point for almost everything going on in literary and artistic New York. But though Rose was liked by everybody there, they noticed in her a kind of aloofness — something else that marked her as Hawthorne's daughter. The only one of that circle — apart from the Gilders themselves — with whom she became intimate was Emma Lazarus, the younger daughter of a wealthy and highly cultivated Jewish Sephardic family. She was already greatly interesting herself in the plight of her people, and when the Statue of Liberty was put up a year or two later, it was one of her sonnets that was placed upon its base:

> *"Send them, the homeless, tempest-tossed to me;*
> *I lift my lamp beside the golden door."*

She was now passionately conscious of her place as a champion of the poor of Israel; America she thought of as their home. It seemed strange when, before many years were passed, Rose's companion who had suffered so much spiritually already, should be brought to suffer at the end the most painful of all physical diseases.

George's friends — of whom he had a great many — were of a different sort. The "cause" that he was most interested in was that of the passing of a fair copyright law. It was an excellent cause, though George's enthusiasm was not entirely disinterested, as he would benefit along with all writers.

The first meeting of the American Copyright League, of which he became the secretary, was held in Brander Matthews' house in April, 1883, Henry James being the earliest of a dis-

tinguished company to arrive. Two years previously Gilder and
Edward Eggleston had planned a similar organization, but nothing
had come of it at the time. Now George pressed matters
energetically, and though the bill Dorsheimer introduced in the
House of Representatives was quite independent of the League,
the Hawley Bill, which followed it and was presented in the
Senate, was drawn up under George Lathrop's supervision. Both
bills failed to pass and the reason, so it was discovered, was that
no provision had been made for printing foreign books in this
country. A printers' and paper manufacturers' lobby had worked
against the proposed law.

At a meeting of George's committee in May, 1885, the amendment of this clause was suggested by Allen Thorndike Rice, the
editor of the *North American Review*, with R. H. Stoddard, E. L.
Youmans, and Lathrop supporting Rice's suggestion. But politics
within the League prevented its passage, with the result that
Lathrop, together with Rice and Stoddard, resigned from the
committee. But during George's secretaryship the League had
grown from thirty to over seven hundred members. For this
work, which included a series of readings held at the Madison
Square Theatre on April 28 and 29, 1885 — with Mark Twain,
Stedman, Warner, Eggleston, and Howells on the program — and
which brought in two thousand dollars, he received no salary,
though he was given a present of two hundred dollars upon
resigning. Edgar Fawcett wrote to Rideing that he had been at
these readings and afterward went to a dinner party at Courtlandt
Palmer's where he met Julian Hawthorne and George and Rose.
"At the dinner we all agreed that the Readings had been a great
success. Howells was admirable." When at last an equitable copyright law was passed, it was substantially what had been drawn
up, in 1883, by George Parsons Lathrop.

But if there was no salary attached to much hard work, there
was a good deal of fun. In some sort of connection with the
Authors' Club there was the Fencing Association, in which

Charles deKay was the moving spirit. Henry James, William Dean Howells, Brander Matthews, and Gilder were among those who went most frequently, and toward midnight the fencing master served claret cup and sandwiches, much to the approval of everybody. Here, as at the Players' Club at Gramercy Park, George was of course in a man's world, safe from feminine profanation. And Egan forty years later recalls George as one of the most brilliant of the talkers when in the mood. That was high praise for anybody when Bunner was at the height of his fame as a conversationalist and wit.

Among George's closest friends and boon companions during this period were Lawrence Hutton and Edgar Fawcett and William H. Rideing — none of them remembered very much as authors now but all with a contemporary vogue and all convivial souls with whom the convivial George was in his element.

Edgar Fawcett had a slight enough talent, largely devoted to satirizing New York society and attacking religion. In neither case did the assault have much weight behind it, and it was reiterated so wearisomely that Stoddard found the words that were in many people's minds "won't somebody please turn this Fawcett off?" But Rideing is fairer, if less witty, in saying that "[Fawcett] was the most prolific of us all. His industry and his versatility were amazing. . . . He never waited for a mood or allowed lassitude to excuse inaction." At the time George Lathrop knew him he was in his middle thirties and at his liveliest as a companion. Perhaps he was a little too lively, according to Rose's ideas. She would have been correct had she surmised that the morning often broke on a room littered with books and cigar butts and empty glasses, after all-night sessions with Maurice Barrymore, Frank Saltus, and George.

It was at Oscar's, opposite the Old Academy of Design, on Fourth Avenue, that sometimes they would gather, twenty strong, around the circular table — George and Bunner and Fawcett and William Henry Bishop and Saltus and the young poet, George

Edgar Montgomery, who liked to call himself "the poet of the future" until Saltus turned the title into "the poet of the middle of next week," — and Rideing himself, the distinguished looking Englishman, friend of all Bohemians, and very willing to be called the handy man of literature.

Equally appreciated by them was the restaurant du Grand Vatel in the French Quarter, where veau à la Marengo cost twelve cents; boeuf braisé aux oignons, ten cents; fromage Neufchâtel three cents. "We never," declared Rideing, "made fifty cents go further than at these repasts."

But if one of them had sold a story to *Harper's* or *Scribner's* or *Appleton's Journal* nothing less than Delmonico's or Seighortner's would do. There, as Rideing described it, was "old Seighortner himself, oiliest of hosts, hovering over us, smiling and rubbing his hands; while the solemn and unhurried waiter set before us the incomparable chicken gumbo, the pompano and English sole, and the bird so white and tender that it might have been nursed in the bosom of the same angel that has brushed us with her feathers." In that circle the "feathers" were the cheques that drifted, as though from the sky, upon them.

George's case in this company, so far as Rose might be concerned, was different from that of his father-in-law. Sophia, knowing how solitary her husband was inclined to be, may have been heartily glad when he went out for an occasional convivial evening. But Nathaniel Hawthorne had a head like iron, where George, made of softer metal, was all too easily overcome. These *Noctes Ambrosianae* are highly entertaining to read about, but when a husband comes in haggard and bedraggled with the milk a little too often, even the most indulgent of wives — those who best understand a man's need for masculine companionship — may be pardoned for believing that a good thing has been carried a little too far. This merry band, bold in a temporary freedom from domestic thralldom, would quote to one another Byron's

Man, being reasonable, must get drunk;
The best of life is but intoxication.

But even Byron's Contessa Guiccioli did not really agree with those sentiments. Neither did Rose. Probably George expressed his own views rather than hers when, on October 28, 1885, he wrote from 29 Washington Square to tell Aldrich: "Mrs. Lathrop and I like New York extremely and are very happy here; we are now installed in a charming apartment, which my brother has decorated." It was one occupied only temporarily during the absence of old Mrs. Lathrop.

Lawrence Hutton was a few years older than Fawcett, but still a couple of years younger than George. Having private means, he was not obliged to work, and somewhat ostentatiously took his ease — keeping his literary toils hidden like a secret vice. Nevertheless he managed to produce nearly fifty books in not a very long life — not bad for a professedly lazy man. He was a fellow member with George at the Players, and there found an outlet for social gifts that sometimes reminded his friends of how Samuel Rogers used to say that his idea of heaven was eating paté de fois gras to the sound of trumpets. He liked to be at once a literary man and a patron of literature. Writing was to him a hobby rather than a profession, and as such he enjoyed it, collecting rare books with one hand and rare birds — especially among authors and actors — with the other. He reveled in George's company, but perhaps his was not the best company for George.

Henry Cuyler Bunner — he carefully concealed the "Cuyler" under the initial, and even to his wife was simply "Bunner" — was a man of real talent. That he had prejudices and foibles and peculiarities all the more endeared him to his friends.

"I don't like Englishmen," he used to declare, for no reason that anybody could discover.

"Oh yes you do, Bunner," Hutton would tell him. "At any rate three kinds of Englishmen you — well, you tolerate."

"What three kinds, Lorenzo?"

Hutton had been waiting for that: "Let me see, Bunner: oh yes, the Irish, the Scotch and the dead."

He was a poet in the rather bric-a-bracish manner of the old French forms that had been revived about that time, a story writer whose *Short-Sixes* gave him further celebrity when it was published a few years later, a wit in a self-conscious style but nevertheless a real wit. (One of his contemporaries spoke of his mercilessly entertaining mind.) He not only edited *Puck*, but looked like Puck — a Puck in holy orders, one whose side whiskers marked him as of very low-church persuasions. His eyeglasses dangling on their black cord and his high, hard hat only heightened the Puckish effect.

George Lathrop, at a moment when he was finding New York too full of good fellows and distractions for a piece of work he had on hand, confided his need to Bunner.

Bunner thought a moment and answered: "I know, P. B." — in that circle George was usually called that because of a poem of his, *The Phoebe Bird*, they much admired — "I know exactly what you want. New London — nice quiet place. I have a friend there — man named Learned. Banker, but writes poems. You may have seen some of his things in *Puck*."

George nodded.

"Well, I'll write to Learned. He'll find you just what you want."

Accordingly on July 30, 1883, Bunner wrote: "George Lathrop, my friend, wants to find a place where he can stay in dead seclusion for two weeks or a month, while he finishes some very important and vexatious work. Can you, without trouble, find him a decent, *not expensive*, boarding house or small hotel, where he will have no distractions, save an occasional saline wash? . . . You will meet a nice fellow."

It was at New London that George's novel *Newport* was finished. When it appeared, in 1884, it made something of a hit.

The following month, George, having got rid of that job, turned at once to another: he and Bunner set to work on a play in collaboration. At the end of the month Bunner wrote to Learned, "Glad you caught on to Lathrop. If the man could only be given a sleeping draught, carried while under its influence, to the middle of the pathless wilderness, persuaded he was some one else, and given a good six months of fishing and woodchopping in which to get *unworried*, he would be ideal. . . . Poor fellow! he has enough to make him nervous." The following day (August 28th) Bunner wrote to Brander Matthews: "I don't know how I should have got through the season if it hadn't been for Lathrop." It is evident that George, whatever may have been his short-comings and weaknesses, was a likable sort of person.

Rose was by now glad of an opportunity to retire to some place where George would see a little less of those friends of his in New York who were only too likely to keep him up drinking and talking half — or even all — the night. George, too, was glad to retire to a place where he might get a little more work done, and where later a settled home could be established. And his short stay at New London made him think that it was just the place for them.

Rose, after she had seen it — staying with him at the Crocker House — thought so too. And it was near enough to New York for visits, or to be visited. Mr. Bunner with his sly, sometimes sprightly humor, was frequently down to see his friend Walter Learned and Learned's sister, Alice, whom, in 1887, he married and took off to live with him in suburban Nutley, New Jersey.

Learned was the intellectual, or rather literary, center of the town — banking, rather successfully, for a living, but really living for his books and his translations from Coppée's stories and Béranger's poems and his verses in the Locker-Lampson manner. Almost the first time Rose and George saw him together he showed them his latest triolet:

> *Out from the leaves of my Lucille*
> *Falls a faded violet.*
> *Swift and faint as its fragrance, steal*
> *Out from the leaves of my Lucille*
> *Tender memories, and I feel*
> *A sense of longing and regret.*
> *Out from the leaves of my Lucille*
> *Falls a faded violet.*

He was a strange person, gnarled and unhappy and sensitive, his wife being a very difficult woman and their one child, Molly, a hydrocephalic. Had it not been for her he would have gone to New York, where good offers were made him. But Molly's disabilities were less hampering in a small town.

He was a rather ugly man with a snub nose and a long upper lip. This he more or less hid behind a drooping mustache, and his height and dignified bearing made him upon the whole impressive. When people got to know him they discovered that he had charm; until then they were likely to be afraid of his cutting wit. He was respected in the town, but hardly popular there.

But George and Rose liked him, and Rose formed a close friendship for his sister Emilie — "Millie" as she was called. George even humorously invented a cousinship that did not exist when he discovered that there were Lathrops in the Learned family. To Learned the Lathrops were a godsend, but indeed whenever he could lay his hand on a literary man there was always a spare room for him at 63 Church Street. Then there would be great arguments. In fact it was said in the town that at any hour a person dropping into the Learneds' would find a hot discussion going on — even if it was as to whether in a shipwreck a man should save his wife or his mother.

One such argument was in full swing on the evening the Lathrops' old friend Gilder was staying with Walter for the night. They were there when he arrived — in a downpour of rain.

His shoes were soaking, and the kitchen fire was out, so Millie had an idea.

"Put Mr. Gilder's shoes to dry in the chafing-dish."

Not for an hour later did the argument lessen a moment — long enough for Millie to remember the shoes. By that time they were beautifully cooked and all ready to serve.

With a prosperous banker to give some degree of respectability to the *vie de Bohéme*, writers and painters were received with a greater degree of tolerance in that community than in most others. And certainly the Lathrops' departures from conventionality were sufficiently mild. Especially was this true of George, who became president of the local yacht club. His departures from the norm were only in the form of that conviviality that served to make him more popular with the members. Rose, however, was something of a puzzle. There was almost a local scandal when she painted the floor of one of the rooms in her house pink; and that she was utterly indifferent to criticism about it only made matters worse. That her favorite color was yellow was pardoned in her — or the men pardoned it — because her yellow dresses went so well with her tawny hair and gray eyes and her beautiful complexion.

After staying for a while at the Crocker House, they lived at 43 (and afterward 63) Federal Street, finally building a house at 27 Post Hill Place, the highest section in town, with the best view. Again Rose's ideas were unconventional — a square design, with the front door at the corner instead of at the middle. On the basement level — possibly because of a sharp drop behind the house — was a book-lined study for George, with stairs to the dining room. Though at first people called it a rather queer place, in the end they recognized that it stood out in its simplicity as much better looking than the verandah-fronted houses all around. It is still standing, has occupants, and is in excellent condition.

The building of the house called for a good deal of money,

as, for that matter, did the Lathrops' whole manner of life. For neither of them was at all good at controlling expenditures, and though there was no waste upon which anybody could lay a finger, the dollars did seem to evaporate. Both were generous, too, and even in those days Rose was often seen carrying a basket full of good things to some poor family — and with not too much thought that because they were poor they should not get something a little expensive.

But one catches now and then a hint that under pressure of this sort there were quarrels, each suggesting probably that really the other ought to be more economical. And once in awhile the wolf scratching at the door had to be kept off by a special expedient. I find letters to a Mr. Carey who was charged with the selling of Hawthorne manuscripts in Rose's possession, for which it is very doubtful whether she got a price anywhere near their true value. But Rose also could *give* a manuscript to a friend, and one such did go to George A. Armour of 120 Lake Shore Drive, Chicago — though he no doubt would have been willing to pay well for it. From an undated letter to Scudder of the *Atlantic*, written about 1898, we know that there were some of the *Notebooks* in their possession, and that the manuscript of "The Ancestral Footstep" had been sold for them by Scribner's.

Of the kind of detailed critical articles George did well, and of which he had written so many up to the time he left Concord, hardly any was produced now. Fiction was more profitable, and George and Rose needed the money. Following *Newport*, which was published in 1884, he turned out a novel or a collection of short stories nearly every year, on an average. In addition there was his volume of poems, *Dreams and Days*, which came out in 1892, his plays, and at the end, a book written in collaboration with Rose.

But it was in 1890 that George struck what he believed was going to prove pay-dirt on a large scale. His brother Francis had painted a portrait of Edison, and he and Rose got to know the

Electrical Wizard, after going to stay with his secretary of that time, Alfred Tate, at Hillside Cottage in Llewellyn Park, and seeing a good deal of Edison himself both in his West Orange laboratories and at that grand house "Glenmont." It had been built for one hundred thousand dollars by an embezzler named Pedder, who spent four hundred thousand dollars upon it in one way and another. When Pedder fled for refuge to Spain, Edison picked it up for a beggarly fifty thousand dollars. And there, simple (but also cocky) amid his grandeur, he talked very freely.

It was a little easier though for George and Rose to talk on an equal footing with Tate.

"You know, Tate," George would say, in confidential moments, while Rose sat there smiling and deprecating some of the things he said, "I'm really a journalist — a critic if you like. But I think I could be a biographer."

"Why don't you write the old man's life?" Tate put in.

George jumped up excitedly: "That's just what I am going to do! I was talking about it only today. We're going over to see his kinetograph."

"You'll see something there, Lathrop."

"I know it. But what I was going to say was that I have a facile pen, I don't really have much of the inventive faculty. Now Mrs. Lathrop here has any amount of it."

"Oh, George. . . !" Rose put in smiling. "You know I never finish any of my writings."

"Yes, but you help me. What do I do? I write Tennyson's *Elaine* as a play. I'm going to do the same thing with Mr. Hawthorne's *Scarlet Letter;* that's to be an opera, and I do turn out a lot of fiction. But I don't believe I could do any of it if it wasn't for Mrs. Lathrop."

The night wore on, and Rose being tired went up to bed, leaving the two men with their drinks. They soon had the effect of making George more confidential. Dreams of glory — frustrated glory — swam before his eyes.

"I firmly believe, Tate," he was saying, "that I might be a good novelist did I not have weighing upon me the enormous Hawthorne prestige. How am I to live up to *that* standard? It gets me all paralyzed. Everybody says, 'George Lathrop — oh yes, Hawthorne's son-in-law.' I recognize that it has done me good, but it also crushes me. What could I *not* have been except for that?"

Shrewd Mr. Tate, puffing thoughtfully at his cigar while George orated, was more inclined to believe in what his guest had said earlier in the evening than what he confided after the whiskey had done its work.

The next morning George and Rose went on to the laboratories. Edison had spent most of the night there, and his breakfast had been brought to him and eaten from a bench littered with the parts of machines. Yet he seemed as fresh as a daisy.

"Work doesn't seem to hurt you, Mr. Edison," Rose remarked.

"No, it would hurt me much more to stop working when the mood is on me. And I'll show you what I do to revive myself."

He dashed into an adjoining room and with ferocious vigor played a couple of simple tunes upon an organ.

"There," he said coming back smiling, "now some people would take a shot of liquor. That's *my* liquor."

"But when things get too much of a strain, Edison," said George, "you let off steam with picturesque profanity, Tate says."

Edison grinned. "Tate said that, did he? Well perhaps I do, perhaps I do."

He now showed them the marvels of the kinetograph — a machine that showed pictures actually moving and also a device by which sound effects could be synchronized with them.

"But how wonderful, Mr. Edison!" Rose exclaimed. "Wouldn't children be delighted?"

"*Children*, Mrs. Lathrop?" the Wizard said. "Then the whole world is full of children! You'll see; this is going to do more to mold the mind of humanity than all the scriptures of all the religions." He swung round on George. "I know what you're going to say, Lathrop: you'd like to write an article about this. Ask Tate. He'll give you all the dope and diagrams."

The Wizard mused a while in silence. Then he said slowly, "Lathrop, though I read a good deal I believe I've never read a novel in my life except Hugo's *Les Miserables* — not even Mr. Hawthorne's novels. But when I think of what we have here — all the possibilities of science of the electrical age just round the corner, I sometimes feel I'd like to write a novel myself. This is my novel, I suppose," and he pulled out a notebook, written in his beautiful script. "Ideas! Things that occur to me sometimes in sleep."

George and Rose looked at it, and Rose said, "It's just the sort of thing my father used to keep. George does much the same too. So that's *your* novel, Mr. Edison."

"The only one I'm ever likely to write." He turned to George. "That's not my field. But how about you, Lathrop? What would you say to writing a novel in collaboration with me?"

Just a little later — on October 20, 1890 — George was able to tell Scudder: "I have been staying out here near Edison, in order to get our collaborative scientific romance under way. Mrs. Lathrop has been with me." The following New Year's Day Julian wrote to Rose: "I am looking forward with great interest to George's and Edison's joint novel. I expect it will swamp the country. I think Edison would continue, now that he has begun, and collaborate a fresh story every year." And the Worcester *Spy* announced on May 4, 1891 — merely one of many such announcements: "The combination suggests the possibility of an American Jules Verne. A New York newspaper syndicate will publish it this year, and afterwards it will appear simultaneously in several European countries. It is said that Mr. Lathrop received a very large price for this story. It is intended to show the future perfection of humanity by the helps growing out of the marvelous development of electricity."

Some such novel did appear later, but on nothing like the scale

Edison had projected. Edison was able to deal out scientific facts, but it was beyond the power even of Rose's inventiveness to fit them into a framework of plot. It proved in the end a great disappointment to the smart young literary man who thought that he had discovered a gold mine. And from the beginning Rose had been less impressed than George. She would say after the discussions in the gorgeous drawing room at Glenmont, when she and Edison's young wife sat side by side in silence and listened to the two men: "George, Mr. Edison's view of the world leaves out so much. This electrical world of his — it may make people *better off* but how is it going to make them *better?* Only religion can do that."

George turned to her thoughtfully. "You may be right, Rösl. We'll see at dinner tonight what he thinks about religion."

When George spoke of it, Edison woke as though out of a deep dream.

"Lathrop," he said, "what a great thing it would be if a man could have all the atoms of himself under complete control, and detachable and adjustable at will. Then I could say to one particular atom — let's call it atom number 4320 — 'go and be part of a rose for a while.' All the atoms would be sent off on various missions — to become parts of minerals, animals, or other substances. Then I'd like to be able to push a little button and call them all together again, and ask what their experiences had been; and so have the benefit of all this knowledge."

Rose looked at his smoldering eyes and asked: "The poet does something like that, doesn't he, Mr. Edison? You don't think of matter as inert, I see."

"Inert? No, certainly not. I can't believe it is acted upon by an outside force. To me it seems that every atom is possessed by a certain amount of primitive intelligence. Look at the way thousands of atoms of hydrogen combine with those of other elements, forming the most diverse substances. Do you mean to say that they do this without intelligence?"

"But does it follow," asked Rose, "that *they* possess this intelligence?"

George asked another question, "Yes, Edison, even if they do possess some primitive form of intelligence, where does it come from?"

Edison thought a moment. "Of course there is only one possible answer. It comes from some power greater than ourselves."

"Do you, then, believe in an intelligent Creator, a personal God?"

"How can I help believing in such an intelligence, Lathrop? The existence of God can, to my mind, almost be proved by chemistry."

CHAPTER IV

Conversion

The circumstances and incidents of the life led by Rose and George Lathrop during their New London years seem, as revealed in such letters as exist, to have been so happy and prosperous, that the final tragic outcome is a little puzzling. This becomes all the more of a mystery in view of the fact that it rather closely followed their coming into the Catholic Church together, an event one would have expected to establish harmony. Prior to that event one is often conscious — however vaguely — of tension. Afterward such a harmony did prevail — at least so far as appearances went — until the final and all but inexplicable catastrophe.

I for one conclude, not that appearances were fallacious, still less that a false façade was deliberately erected to hide the true state of affairs, but that in proportion as perfection drew near, so also did a perverse insistence upon too much; and that it was this insistence that ruined all. It is possible that the fact of Catholicism — as yet imperfectly understood — itself contributed to bring this about. Or if that is too much to say, it may have helped to precipitate the issue.

Newspaper reports are not always very reliable, but this account of the Lathrops in 1889 which appeared in the New York *World* is borne out by private letters. "Mrs. Lathrop," said the *World*, "is as vigorous a little woman as anyone would care to see. . . . She is short and plump, with grey eyes and a great shock of red-brown hair, and she and her husband spend their summers like two children on a picnic together, putting most of their time out on the beach . . . to which they carry their books and papers, their lunch and bathing suits. There they spend the whole day, frolicking in the water, lying on the sand, napping or reading, or else scribbling with a stylograph pen in the shadow of the bath house." They not only played together but collaborated that year on a novel entitled *The Last Millionaire* which was serialized in *Once a Week*.

As to Rose's similar mode of life the previous summer, her nice kittenish friend, Alice Wheeler, who several times visited her at New London, writes in a letter postmarked from Wellesley Hills, October 8, 1888: "I like to think of you as having spent so many ideal hours upon the beach last summer — making the husband proud of your feats in swimming — then appealing to him in another way with your wonderful draughts of coffee. You speak kindly of my coffee — but in comparison to yours, it is a mere shadow of a substance." One may suspect Alice of being a little addicted to gush, but one does not have to rely only on her — this time it is a letter postmarked November 27, 1885, and written by old Mrs. Lathrop — to know that Rose took by storm "everybody who meets you or has a visit with you in your gem of an abode." Seemingly she fascinated women even more than men. It was Emilie Learned who said that she walked like Ellen Terry.

As for George, Alice Wheeler, writing on October 16, 1887, says she is delighted to hear how well established her friend was and how interested "in the marvelous change in Mr. Lathrop's health and spirits." And though now and then Rose does write of George not being very well — which may have been an euphemism for something else — the general picture is a pleasant one. Newspaper and other accounts of him tell of his being strongly built, broad shouldered, agile, with quick, bright eyes in a somewhat swarthy face. His photographs show him to have been slightly, but not at all unpleasantly plump, and adding to his good looks when he grew a mustache, and then adding to them still more when he sported a little pointed beard. He did not look like a literary man, and had no wish to look like one.* He was prosperous and happy; and if (as in writing to Scudder on October 3, 1890) he shows a certain desire to do some of his former extended critical work — suggesting an article on John Boyle O'Reilly or of going down to the New York Customs House to unearth the (by now) totally neglected Herman Melville, and complaining "the magazine seems to have forgotten me as much as if I were at the other side of the globe" — this can perhaps be safely taken merely as one more instance of the human disinclination to leave well enough alone. He was getting along famously — just about to make (as he supposed) pots of money by collaborating on novels with Edison; yet he was hankering to do some work of the kind that he used to produce for the *Atlantic*.

They were both of them sufficiently busy, even apart from their writing. George was one of the active promoters of a local theater about which he wrote to Mr. Fiske on April 3, 1890. He tells him proudly, "Our theatre is remarkable for such a small city — and for almost any city." It had been built for sixty thousand dollars, in what George said was "exquisite artistic taste, with a fine façade encrusted with terra cotta relief in the best style." He did not believe there was a theater in the country that provided so well for the comfort and safety of the players. To top all this off he enclosed in his letter to Mr. Fiske the prologue he had written for the opening night the following week.

As for Rose we hear, in a letter written to her on September 10, 1891, of her attending some celebration of the battle of Groton Heights, fought a hundred and ten years earlier, and of her taking some part in this function. And the following June 16th she was called upon to respond to a toast at the twenty-fifth anniversary of the closing of Dr. Dio Lewis's school at Lexington. Mrs. Woodbury wrote to her about it from Boston, offering to put her up, and the former Lizette Hunt (now married to Mr. San-

---

* "[He] would be taken for a broker or a merchant rather than an author," said the New York *Independent* (May 29, 1891).

born's son) wrote saying that the Massachusetts House would be a delightful place for the reunion. Will Rose please get in touch with all the "old girls" she knows?

On both sides of the family things were now most cordial. From Francis Lathrop — or Frank, as they called him — came, on Christmas Eve of 1891, an admission that he and Mama "couldn't resist opening the parcel that had just arrived from New London," though they should have waited until morning. And during this period old Mrs. Lathrop writes to Rose to tell her quite frankly which she would prefer for a Christmas present — a Japanese quilted gown or a case of dessert knives in silver with pearl handles. The price of both is the same. And little Beatrix Hawthorne writes to her "Dear and lovely Aunt," to thank her for some gifts and adds, with a child's candor: "By the bye you can tell Uncle George that the oranges are very fine and sweet, except some, which are uneatable."

In the fall of 1892 Julian had one of his tremendous ideas about which his wife, Minne, wrote in a flutter of excitement, once on a letterhead, of "The Literary Argonauts." The whole family was going to sail to the South Pacific in a yacht, and live in Paradise for the rest of their lives. Julian was to write articles for a number of newspapers and magazines; he was to publish a book every Christmas, and also write pirate novels on the spot with all the local color. Even Minne and the children were going to turn out a monthly article for some family magazine. They had chosen no definite course but would sail as the fancy took them. A number of acquaintances were to go along, paying for the privilege to the tune of from sixteen hundred to five thousand dollars apiece. And the expedition had attracted so much attention in the press that they had offers of supplies that would keep them going for the next six months. They might follow the summer round the world until they had found the perfect island. Then the boat was to bring George and Rose out. "Picture a whole family, all ages and both sexes, among the South Sea

Isles," Minne exclaims. "O Typee! O Omoo!" Nothing remained
but to visit New London and Boston to pick out a yacht. And
by the end of the year even that was done. But perhaps for no
other reason than it was all too good to be true, to the intense
disappointment of the whole Hawthorne family — with enthusiastic Minne as crestfallen as any of her children — the scheme
had to be abandoned.

It was in such a happy and friendly atmosphere that the reception of Rose and George into the Catholic Faith occurred
early in 1891. So little was the public prepared for it — either by
the writings or the manner of life of the Lathrops — that some
of the newspapers made almost a grievance out of the event. The
News of Tacoma, Washington, writes: "Although it has been
rumored for some time that George Parsons Lathrop, the well
known writer, and his wife, daughter of Nathaniel Hawthorne,
had been converted to the Roman Catholic faith, there have been
many who have given no credence to these reports, chiefly because of the agnostic tendencies of both parties." Of course it was
quite ridiculous to talk about "agnostic tendencies," and the
New York *Independent*, a paper for which both George and
Rose wrote, was nearer the mark in its comment: "It was a matter
of common knowledge among Mr. Lathrop's friends that he was
not in active fellowship and sympathy with any church, whatever
may have been his attitude as a boy." This is an allusion to the
fact, evidently known to the *Independent*, that George had been
confirmed in the Episcopalian persuasion. But the Boston *Beacon*,
which should have known better, declared, "this is the third or
fourth [religious] change he has made."

George replied to the *Independent* editorial by writing a long
letter to that paper. In it he said: "The *Independent* implied that
Mrs. Lathrop and I before our conversion to Catholicity had
stood 'in the camp of unbelief.' Mrs. Lathrop was brought up as
a Unitarian; and Unitarianism, it is true, cannot be called strictly
Christian belief. But it should be remembered that the earlier

Unitarianism represented by her parents, Nathaniel Hawthorne and his wife, was yet full of a reverence for Christ, little differing in devoutness from that paid to Him as the Son of God, one with the Trinity. Their disposition was that of Channing . . . and retained much of the Trinitarian feeling, even while it tried to eliminate the Godhead of Jesus.* Their place was not so much in the camp of unbelief, but rather on the outskirts of belief. It becomes necessary to say here that Mrs. Lathrop never in any manner tended towards agnosticism; and, even while she was in a measure associated with Unitarianism, her inclination was to worship Christ as divine." He affirmed his own previous position sufficiently by pointing out his Episcopalian antecedents and declaring, "Never have I been an unbeliever."

This, however, is merely a rebuttal of the charge of previous unbelief; it does not explain the positive steps that led Rose and George into the Catholic Church. Nor can all those steps be traced with perfect definiteness and security — should anybody think that this is necessary.

But some part of the matter we already know: the Hawthornes' very genuine religious feeling; their attraction toward the Catholic Church (something much stronger than they ever realized); the memories of Catholic Europe and their effect on Rose's impressionable mind. Yet such things can be added up to an impressive total without anything happening. The world is full of people who have thought about becoming Catholics and have then forgotten the whole matter. There is hardly a person of education and intelligence who has not at some time felt the Faith's strong drawing force; and many a person of that kind has said, "I have no religion, but if I did have one, it would be Catholicism." More, much more, is needed than that. So we go back to see what can be found — even though its precise weight and significance may be hard to assess.

* It might be possible to say even more for Channing, whose "Unitarianism" was, in the main, a rejection of the Calvinist rigors.

The statement has appeared in print that the great Orestes Brownson gave George Lathrop his initial impulses toward the Church. It is however made perfectly clear in the article on Brownson that Lathrop wrote for the *Atlantic*, in 1896, that no such meeting ever occurred. This much may perhaps be safely said: in Boston, George became rather friendly with a Catholic of a different type — the journalist and poet, John Boyle O'Reilly, a genial and pious man with nothing of that ferocious intolerance Dr. Brownson carried into the Church from the Presbyterianism with which he began his strange career. Poor Brownson could never understand how it was that he hadn't succeeded in converting America with his unassailable logic; but John Boyle O'Reilly never tried to be an apostle or a philosopher, or set out to convert anybody. If the whole truth were known, the conversion of the Lathrops — at any rate of George Lathrop — probably was due to this friendship as much as to anything else.

The conversion, however, is usually attributed to Alfred Chappell, a New London neighbor — though in all likelihood Chappell did little more than give the Lathrops a push in the direction in which they were already tending. Yet as there are occasions, so they say, when a tower that is about to fall can be scattered by a butterfly's wing brushing against it, Chappell's influence need not be denied.

He was a short, bowlegged man with a pointed beard and a red face. In his manner was a faint touch of pomposity. A Congregationalist originally, he became an Episcopalian and studied for the ministry, thereby reading himself into the Catholic Church. He was a fine organist and could have been a leading professional (so his friends thought), but it was with him merely a hobby; for his living he ran a music store until he gave that up to go into the coal business with his brother.

In this business he was extremely successful, and with his wife, Adelaide — a Huntington, one of the town's leading families — entertained very lavishly, according to New London standards.

Addie, as her husband and friends called her, was a pretty little brunette, already inclining toward plumpness. She was not at all brainy but very pleasant. They had a large family — five that grew up and four that died young — and were among the most solid and popular of local citizens. Adelaide Chappell never became a Catholic, but she used to go to Mass with her husband. Both were purely New England in background and of unmixed English descent — just like the Lathrops and Hawthornes. The two families found much in common, though their friendship (until religion entered in) was no closer than the friendship between George and Rose and Walter Learned and his sister. The only actual letter bearing on this is one from A. H. Chappell, headed 38 Huntington Street, but undated, accepting an invitation and saying that he was sorry but he did not possess the Father Hecker books. Rose, probably remembering that Hecker had been at Brook Farm, had evidently tried to get them. Presumably she did obtain them elsewhere.

But a group of letters from a Nellie Sullivan, a former servant at the Lathrops' house, living at 4 Prospect Street, Willimantic, Connecticut, written during late 1891 to the fall of 1892, incline me to the belief that here was an influence not to be overlooked.

The Hawthornes had always employed Irish Catholic girls — the main source of domestic service in those days — and had clearly valued and respected them. They were given ample opportunities to practice their religion, and, though, until the Hawthornes went to Europe, they were perhaps disposed to share the prevailing New England view that Catholicism was more or less to be identified with the Irish — and the Irish were thought of as good for building railroads and working in kitchens — they could hardly have failed to notice how deeply religious these Irish girls were. And the Hawthornes were of a distinction so unassailable that anything like snobbery in connection with them was quite unthinkable.

So for that matter, to do George Lathrop justice, was he quite free of this failing — at all events in relation to Nellie Sullivan. For it is evident from Nellie's letters, which Rose kept until her death, that George treated her like a friend. To Rose she signed herself "Your true friend and servant" or "Yours with love and affection" or "Your affectionate servant" or "With fondest love your humble servant" and (in the last letter of the series): "So I will say good night and sweet dreams from your own Nellie."

Nellie Sullivan of course was not in the least intellectual and probably could not have expounded Catholicism very clearly. But though her spelling was not always very good, she was certainly a person superior in mind to most of those of her class, and she had qualities of heart that Rose (and George too) recognized. It was a spiritual friendship between mistress and maid, and though Nellie has no very striking thoughts about religion — but only pious gossip about the priests and the nuns and the devotions for the souls in Purgatory and the promise to make her dear Mrs. Lathrop a "novenia" any time she wants it — I confess to finding these letters very touching.

Yet Nellie is not devoid of intellectual interests. She attended some of the sessions of the Catholic summer school organized by the Lathrops in August, 1892, and greatly admired Mr. Lathrop's lectures. "But pardon me, my dear Mrs. Lathrop," she went on, "when I say that your voice was sweeter to me than all the rest when you read your sweet lovely poems."

The next letter from Nellie (one dated September 14, 1892) thanks Mrs. Lathrop for the gift of a gold dollar she had given her. "I am going to have a pin put on it," she says, "and keep it as long as I live in sweet remembrance of the giver as I know how dearly you must have prized it being given to you by your dear good mother."

There are several references to a Maggie — who will appear later: she was Maggie Biglin. "She says you was so lovely to her," Nellie writes, "she thinks you got the most patience and sweet disposition of any one she ever saw." The same letter — dated

September 14, 1892 — tells Rose that she was to be married the following month "if nothing happens that I don't know of now and I think it a very serious undertaking therefore I want your prayers and will be honored if you and Mr. Lathrop can come up."

The next letter, two and a half months later — and this is the last of them — makes no mention of a husband; but if "something had happened" Nellie gives no indication of it, and was clearly not brokenhearted. Perhaps she had merely settled down quietly into her new state in life by that time. The main importance of this last letter is its reference to the house the Lathrops were building on 27 Post Hill Place: "I am more than glad," Nellie tells Rose, "that you are going to have your own home. I hope you will live manny, manny years to enjoy it."

A further influence, whose force can hardly be measured, is the fact that, as Rose told Lillie Hamilton French when interviewed for the *Ladies' Home Journal*, the death of Francie made "the next world more real than this." That already disposed her to Catholicism, by giving her a better insight into the true nature of reality. In a case of this kind nobody can gauge the precise importance of the various factors, and probably these did not have the same weight with George as with Rose. The specific means were, though, in each case leading to the same end, and, were, after all, merely the channels through which God's grace operated. In an event of this sort, not even he who has experienced it can afterward give a completely satisfactory account of the developing process.

The New York *Press*, announcing the conversion, found something fitting that the daughter of Hawthorne "chose for her reception the only Catholic Church which is in any way connected with her father's life and association." That was the Church of the Paulist Fathers, founded by Isaac Hecker. This, however, is surely discovering "significance" where none exists. Hawthorne and young Hecker were not at Brook Farm at the same time, and though Hecker went afterward to Concord, to lodge with Thoreau's mother while studying Greek and Latin with George Bradford — at which time Hawthorne probably was aware that the earnest young man of papistical tendencies was in the village — they had no special contact. But the writer of the *Press* article was fanciful throughout, for he dug up the germ of Brook Farm and Fourierism in Sir Thomas More. He manages to work himself to the conclusion: "There is something almost touching in the daughter of the classic Hawthorne journeying from her present home at New London to be received in the church founded by her father's old comrade." A good deal to my surprise I learned that there are no letters from either of the Lathrops in the Paulist Archives, or any letters there to them from Father Alfred Young, the Paulist who received them. But there are before me several long letters of his to Rose, and one to Rose and George jointly. These show a personal affection for them, but as they are written after 1891, when he received them, they do not cast any light upon the motives for their action. We know Father Young to have been old and with a heroic beard that hung to his waist. And in his letters he talks a good deal about his invalidism and was never able to make the visit to New London he frequently promised.

The only real explanation ever given of the matter was in the form of a very long letter by George Lathrop to John Jeffrey Roche, the editor of the Boston *Pilot*. But this throughout is couched in terms so general as not to be particularly enlightening. "My attempt to inform myself about the Church," said George, in part, "began with the same impartiality, the same candor and receptiveness, that I should use toward any other subject upon which I honestly desired to form a just conclusion. Notwithstanding that education had surrounded me with prejudice, my mind was convinced as to the truth, the validity and the supremacy of the Roman Catholic Church by the clear and comprehensive reasoning upon which it is based. And while the reasoning of other religious organizations continually shifts and wavers, leaving their adherents — as we now see almost every day — to fall into rationalism and agnostic denial, the reasoning of the Church, I found, led to sublime and inspiring faith. This union of solid reasoning and luminous faith I cannot find elsewhere."

That letter was copied into a large number of newspapers and aroused much comment — some of it hostile. A common (and not unreasonable) objection raised to it in some papers was that its tone was so "official" as to tell nothing. The public had, in effect, been informed that the Lathrops had become Catholics because they believed Catholicism to be the true religion; the steps to the temple were not indicated.

The Boston *Beacon* objected for diametrically different reasons: "It is certainly contrary to the dictates of good taste," it editorialized, "to say nothing of common sense, that so much fuss should be made about so very simple a matter. Hundreds of people join a church every week, and none of them consider it necessary to proclaim the fact to the world. True religion invests its possessor with modesty and humility, and the absence of these traits, seems to indicate a desire for notoriety hardly in keeping with the precepts of sincere and honest men." Poor George! The answer to that was so patent that there was no need to make it: the newspapers gave publicity to the matter for no other reason than that this particular conversion was news.

Another paper, *The North-Western Christian Advocate*, took the more-in-sorrow-than-in-anger line, saying: "If these earnest people had turned their investigations upon Rome in its consummate perfection in Europe, they might have been content to remain Protestants for the same reasons more strongly urged." *That* is rather comical. The writer is evidently unaware that — at any rate in the case of Rose — it was seeing Catholicism in Europe that had first turned her face toward the Church. But then, probably the editor of the *North-Western Christian Advocate* had never crossed the Atlantic in his life.

Rose's conversion naturally brought her a good many private letters. But I can find only one from a Catholic — and that a stranger — a Louise Sanienska, writing from 242 West 46th Street. This has two points of interest: the writer had stayed at Newport at Julia Ward Howe's at a time when Miss Hawthorne was a fellow guest; it is this circumstance that enboldens her to write. Also she quotes a letter Father A. F. Hewit, the well-known Paulist, had written to her in which he had said: "I am very much pleased that Hawthorne's youngest daughter had become a Catholic." Miss Sanienska adds: "When he was here he often spoke to me of your father's work of whom [sic] he was a great admirer and is now. Both Mr. and Mrs. Howells are friends of mine."

Rose's Protestant relatives took her change of religion very well upon the whole, but it was too much not to expect some of them to bristle. Ellen Howe wrote from Concord on December 29, 1891: "If you and [George] grow to be more Catholic, I as surely grow to be more Unitarian or Protestant. When the Church and Government does its own legitimate work — or the Church does not interfere with the Government, there will be peace between the Catholics and Protestants — until that occurs there never will be." After more in the same strain, Cousin Ellen softens and says: "I am trying to follow Christ's law of love — no creed — He made none — and so are you — & if earth never sees us meet — we will meet on the other side where all distinctions of opinion dissolve themselves in the light of God's face and His Son's love."

Aunt Amelia (Mrs. Shotwell*) wrote from 239 Carroll Street, Brooklyn, on April 5, 1891, of her astonishment to read in the paper of Rose's "consecration" in the Roman Catholic Church. But she kindly adds: "I sincerely hope you will find that rest which your soul craves, in simple belief in Christ Jesus, as your Saviour and intercessor, in whom alone you have assurance of the

---

* This appears to have been one of the Lathrop relatives.

abundant comfort, and riches, of our Heavenly Father." She might well be a bit surprised at Rose's "consecration."

Cousin Lillian writes two weeks later: "I have known for a long while you did not feel the Unitarian Church sufficient for your religious nature and of course I consider the Catholic Church neared [sic] orthodox. I suppose the *beliefs* are orthodox but with many of the practices I cannot agree."

A Mary P. tells Rose: "[I am] a good deal taken aback at the news of your change of faith — not having a suspicion of there being a tendency in that direction." She confesses that she is unable to understand how Rose and George could have become convinced that Catholicism is the only true religion. Poor Mary P. — is greatly troubled at the thought of "the lower class of Romanists."

Most tenderly and lovingly, "Mattie"* writes to her "Darling Sister" from Dorchester: "I rejoice in your joy — the highest joy — Oh! Rose! how could I ever be sorry you have taken the step you have when it is so *much* to you? Surely I cannot! And tho' we do not see alike, in all points, we surely do see the one great Truth — *Our Lord Jesus Christ*. Oh! Rose! If you had gone, as so many dear to me do into speculation and doubting as to the dear Lord's nature, and had become one of the radical Free Thinkers, my heart would have ached, but how can I but rejoice when you have accepted Him as the 'Rock of everlasting strength.'"

Helena Gilder was surprised and a little regretful saying, "[change of faith] puts a line between friends as a rule, which is all the stronger for being ignored — but I respect honest conviction."

But in many ways the most interesting — and assuredly the most intelligent — of these letters were several long ones from

---

* This I take to be Martha Stearns, a close friend from girlhood alluded to several times in the letters. Her sister, Mrs. Holmes Hinkley of Cambridge, Mass., tells me that upon Martha's death all of Rose's letters to her were destroyed, according to instructions she left.

Julian. On March 27, 1891, he wrote to Rose: "The Catholic Church offers more substantial assistance than any other to the leading of a worthy life; and the beauty and grandeur of its ritual, and its venerable history, win the mind and solace the heart." He goes on to tell Rose that, even had she become a Mohammedan or a Mormon, "I should still rejoice that you have communed with your Creator."

The same letter tells her: "When I was in Hastings, living next door to Coventry Patmore, I used to spend two or three hours with him every day, and much of the time we spent in discussing the philosophy and essence of religion. Delightful talks they were. He gave me an insight into the esoteric teachings of the Church that was deeply interesting to me, and in many respects we were in cordial sympathy, though, in some fundamental views we were, of course, far asunder — further than he imagined. It is a singular fact, and fortunate for me, that I have never felt any religious doubts or uneasiness."

One gets just a little irritated at Julian's bland tolerance. The suspicion crosses the mind that he had no convictions, in spite of his telling his sister that he accepts the fundamental Christian doctrines. Earlier in this letter he had said: "I am glad . . . with all my heart that you and George have been led into the Catholic Faith. Una took practically the same step nearly twenty years ago, and, had she lived, would no doubt have definitely accepted the older creed." Julian's wife, signing herself "Your littel Minne" adds a postscript: "Dearest Rose, I send you my love & deepest sympathy & ask you to believe that Julian and I are at one in what he writes. How beautiful that George and you come together to the Lord."

The following May 20th Julian tells Rose: "I hope this first Catholic year of yours will be as happy as all the previous ones combined. . . . In my giddy youth I wrote a work on Catholicism (of course never published) and rang the changes on all sorts of arguments; but came to the conclusion that to believe is one thing, and to be convinced that you believe quite another." With which profound philosophical reflection Julian sums up his argument.

One must not generalize too much from particular instances. But from this set of letters two rather surprising facts emerge: one is that Rose seems to have had among her relatives and friends many with strong "evangelical" sentiments — to use the title they themselves like to claim. And these people, who might have been expected to be extremely antagonistic to her Catholicism are the very ones who show the most sympathy. On the other hand, the Unitarians, the people who profess such wide tolerance, are, as they appear here, decidedly "snooty." Their attitude is amusing; but the Catholic will be rather touched by seeing how the "evangelicals" do seem to consider an essential oneness with fundamental doctrines of Catholicism to exist on their part.

Not until after their reception did Rose and George have much to do with the local priest at St. Mary's, Father Thomas P. Joynt, with whom they had some social intercourse, as well as the benefit of his ministrations. He was a lean man with a face more attractive because of its inner light than because of the regularity of its features. He was beginning to get a bit affected by the arthritis that eventually crippled him, but he still got around and was popular with everybody, including the local Protestants. His public spirit, his cheerfulness, his industry, and his witty tongue all made him a notable person in the community.

But Rose's main religious guide remained Father Young, though the sound spiritual direction he gave had to be largely by mail. One or two interesting points come up here.

In the zeal of their conversion the Lathrops wished at once to do something for the Church. On January 3, 1891,* George writes

* So the letter is dated in the Century Collection. But this seems to be a case of a man who in the early days of the New Year, continues for a while to give the date of the old.

to Gilder suggesting an article on "The Position of Catholics."
He explains: "I think I am in a position, through my experience &
knowledge of Protestantism, & my conversion to & knowledge of
Catholicity to do a great deal of good. . . . Here, in a very great
matter, it seems that I might explain both from the inside &
outside." Though this article never appeared in the *Century*
George did write one along similar lines for the *North American*.

Rose also projected similar work. Among her manuscripts is
a slip of paper headed "*The Way as I Found It* — a book upon
my experience during and after conversion." And she wrote to
Scudder an undated letter — suggesting for the *Atlantic* "a paper
showing my father's interest in Catholicity." Scudder had evidently told her that he thought the idea good in itself but not
for the *Atlantic*, because Rose later in her letter says: "Probably
I should print the essay in a Catholic magazine, or possibly in the
North American." She assures Scudder: "I shall have the papers
subjected to the judgment of a Protestant critic of taste as well
as a Catholic one, before venturing on my own strengh."

One finds something bearing closely on this in Father Young's
letter to Rose of August 26, 1892. He tells her: "I take it that
by your next question you ask if you should use your pen in
writing upon subjects more or less religious, even tho' you should
receive but small remuneration compared with what you would
receive for writings on secular subjects.

"To which I reply that you should feel free to choose what
you know to be the more profitable, taking into account what
you call your 'debts' and the daily needs of your household."
Though he goes on to say that he hopes that some time she *will*
write something on a religious theme, he appears to detect a certain scrupulosity in her, and this he corrects with: "You seem to
fear that contemplation of nature — in treating of so-called secular
subjects — may render you materialistic and unspiritual. You must
not allow old Protestant error to cast its baleful shadow across
your views of nature. Nature, in itself, is neither defiled nor de-

praved, but all sweet & dear to its loving Creator whose very word it is, expressing His Divine Ideas. The *supernatural* is not the only truly and divinely spiritual, although it is true that by our divine faith we are able to attain a spiritual view of all things earthly & heavenly not to be gained without its aid. This view is supernatural, but not contradictory to Nature but rather built upon it — as says the theological maxim: *Gratia supponit naturam.*"

If he goes into the question at some length it is because he sees that it bears upon something else troubling Rose's mind at that time — a fancied opposition between her religious duties and her duties as a wife. Very emphatically Father Young assures her: "I can conceive of nothing which ought to be more agreeable to the heart of a true Christian wife than to cheerfully put aside any occupation even of devotion, if thereby her husband's happiness is subserved. And so, in like manner should a husband rejoice in making such personal sacrifices for his wife." In a previous letter, dated July 26, 1892, he shows that he has been asked to act as Rose's spiritual director, and had recommended her the seventeenth-century Benedictine Father Baker's *Sancta Sophia* as her guide in reading. The following January ninth he writes to Rose and George jointly, concluding: "God is good, divinely kind, to give me two such loving arms to lean upon as I enter the shadows of weariness that precede the Dawn of life and strength."

She was soon to discover, even though she did not immediately understand the full meaning of the lesson, that God, who gives grace to supernaturalize His children's gifts, can also turn the very faults in their character into something fine. Her impulsiveness and her hot temper — transmuted to heroism and abnegation — were to be the foundations of what she was soon about to do. Her failure with everything she had so far touched was to prove but the preparation for her greatest triumphs.

CHAPTER V

"For You, Mistake"

In several of Nellie Sullivan's letters to Rose there is mention of a "Maggie." On September 14, 1892, Nellie reports Maggie as having said that Rose was the most sweet and patient person in the world. But on September 1st, Nellie wrote to say that she had just heard that Maggie had left Rose. Therefore the date, 1892, added to the letter of Rose's to Maggie written from the Clarendon Hotel, New York, is a false conjecture. This is Maggie Biglin, who is described to me by her priest-brother "as a kind of secretary" to Rose. She was at all events left in charge of the house in New London when the Lathrops were away, with Mary McKinnon, as cook, under her. And the letters to her are signed "Your affectionate friend, Rose H. Lathrop."

One of these letters is worth quoting as showing Rose's solicitude for her husband. It is written on November 11, 1891, from the Glenham Hotel, New York, and like all of the other letters to Maggie is full of little domesticities. Perhaps one should draw a veil over the fact that Maggie is told that, when Mr. Lathrop leaves alone by the five o'clock train the following day, he will take the soiled linen with him. But the instructions that follow indicate that Rose was a wife who was trying to provide for George's creature comforts. "I hope you will get this letter in time to get some steak, & some of Mr. Smith's best *package* sausages, so that Mr. Lathrop can have some sausages for his breakfast, & the steak for his supper the evening he arrives. I think he will take the five o'clock train on Tuesday, & arrive home about ½ past eight, when he would need the steak at once. If

242

Mary begins to cook it at ½ past eight, it would be just right. Mary had better cook some rice to be served with it." Rose was evidently not so much of an *exaltée* in her recent conversion as to be unmindful of rather painfully mundane matters.

Moreover the Catholic activities of the Lathrops were of a very practical sort. It was they who took the lead in the founding of the Catholic Summer School, which developed to an un-dreamed of extent in its present magnificent location on the shores of Lake Champlain. It soon passed — it soon had to pass — out of the Lathrops' hands into those of a young Paulist, named Father Thomas McMillan. But it probably would never have begun at all had they not organized the lectures that were to be given at New London, and had not Rose taken the social ar-rangements in hand, helped by Mrs. Mosher.

They secured extremely good lectures — John Jeffrey Roche and Katherine Conway of the Boston *Pilot*, and Maurice Francis Egan, the brilliant young Notre Dame professor, a friend of the Gilders' salon days. Mrs. Egan wrote on July 28, 1892, from Notre Dame saying how much she regretted not being able to be Rose's guest, but explaining that she was getting the children ready for their summer vacation at Mackinac. Mr. Egan, however, was looking forward to being at New London by August 8th.

As for Katherine Conway, she noted that her reading — pre-sumably of her poems — was scheduled for August 2nd, but asked to have it delayed in order to allow Mr. Roche, the other *Pilot* editor, to attend the opening session. Both of them were looking forward to Mr. Lathrop's lecture on "The Pole Star of American Literature." It was pleasant for Rose to hear: "Last week I saw Cardinal Gibbons, during his brief stay here, and he had many lovely things to say about Mr. Lathrop." After her visit Miss Conway wrote on the 7th: "Dear, you don't know what a bright spot that week with you in New London has been! You were so sweetly thoughtful for me, with all that you had to think of besides, and gave me so much of the home feeling that

I was positively lonesome all the way to Boston." In a letter written after Rose's death, Father McMillan, then old and white bearded, said, "Her beautiful house was the brightest spot in New London."

The following year, when the summer school moved to Platts-burg under Father McMillan's direction, but with the beautiful, young Mrs. Mosher and her husband attending to practical de-tails, Rose went with George who gave a lecture on "The Mind of Hawthorne as Reflected in the Marble Faun."

Happy though these events were, it was soon after them that the Lathrops finally separated. As has been shown, there had already been several separations. Certainly the extant letters sug-gest that these had not been infrequent since the death of Francie in 1881, and perhaps even began before 1877, though it is possible (and indeed more than likely) that most of these were only pass-ing quarrels conducted with perhaps a little more than ordinary vigor; there is no doubt at all that, for a number of short periods, the Lathrops were apart from one another.

But as it is also true that Rose went about with her husband a great deal at the end of 1892, and later. Some of the letters that show this should be cited here. We find, for instance, that Rose and George were expected by a Mrs. Gaffney at Rochester where they were to arrive on November 28th, at 3:47 on the Empire Express when George was to speak at the Orphans' Fair. On December 10th (as a Jenny Mastern indicates) they were due at Syracuse, New York, where George was to open an exhibition of dolls in aid of the foundling hospital. And letters from Sister Mary of Mount Carmel, dated December 20th and 26th, show that Rose had recently visited the Loretto Convent at Niagara Falls. Presumably it was on this trip that a correspondent of mine heard George give his lecture "The Pole Star of American Litera-ture" at the Holy Angels Academy, Buffalo, New York — though all she could remember after fifty years was the subject of George's lecture and Rose's "glorious golden hair."

George, however, evidently — and one would suppose inescapably — did sometimes have to travel, unaccompanied by Rose, on his lecture trips. Thus John Boyle O'Reilly's widow writes to Rose on January 15, 1893, from 34 Winthrop Street, Charlestown, Massachusetts, about a lecture George had just given there. She had enjoyed him very much, "and I thought him looking particularly well and strong." It also appears that Rose was to give a reading that same May. "I hope you are going to agree to run away from home when that time comes." Perhaps it was on this visit that she received a letter from a Miss Schmidt to lecture at Wellesley gratis. As she was then staying at Wellesley Hills with Alice Wheeler (the year does not appear), she said she hoped it could be arranged. This probably, however, was at a later date. Rose says about her "little lectures," "[I] feel as if all that sort of effort was a thing of the past with me. But how little we can tell what we are going to do & feel!" The last dates I can fix with any certainty are December 17, 1893, when George writes to a Mrs. Palmer from "Overdale," Post Hill Place (the house they had built at New London) to say that Rose "has been ill two months, & we are . . . heavy with many things just now." On July 2, 1894, they are still together at the same address. Somewhere between that date and the spring of 1891 when they were received into the Catholic Church, there could have been a brief separation. But I find no proof of any during this period. The last pathetic touch was given when on Palm Sunday, 1895, George wrote the date on the palm he had received at Mass at New London and sent it to Rose with his love.

But here is what seems to me something of considerable significance. In her book of poems *Along the Shore*, published by Ticknor and Company, in 1888, there is a piece which could have been composed several years earlier entitled "The Roads That Meet." It is purely personal, though written with reserve. The

first group of lines is subtitled "Art" and ends, "For you, mistake!"
The second group of lines — these are headed "Love" — also ends
with "For you, mistake!" The last half of the poem — 24 lines —
is headed "Charity" and this section concludes:

> *If all we miss*
> *In the plans that shake*
> *The world, still God has need of this,* —
> *Even our mistake.*

It was written long before Rose was a Catholic, but already she
knew in what direction her heart was pointing. The music and
the painting had been failures, nor could the writing be called
a success, and for her, she already admitted, a marriage had been
a mistake. But already she also perceived that God can do something with our mistakes — and before her life ended she was to
find out what that was. Afterward she could learn that, seen in
the light of Providence, her marriage was not a mistake at all,
though Julian described it as an irreparable error. It was the
preparation for something else.

It may be true, as has been suggested, that the collaboration of
Rose and George in a book was tried as a means of holding them
together, though I can find no evidence to support this. Rather
it would seem that the Annals of the Georgetown Visitation
Convent they published, in 1894, under the title of *A Story of
Courage,* in order to be written by a man at all had to be written
by a man in conjunction with his wife. This is because the Visitation nuns are very strictly enclosed, and George would be admitted into the cloister only by special dispensation from Cardinal
Gibbons, and then only in company with Mrs. Lathrop.

Their book is not very good, nor is it hard to tell why. The
material is interesting enough, but had clearly been written by
one of the sisters in annal form and as such had proved unsatisfactory. The Lathrops, a competent literary couple, were brought

in to remold the whole. And had they done so thoroughly the result might have been excellent. But it is doubtful whether they really did much except a little rearranging and the writing of a few pages here and there.

A further account of the book is hardly needed here. It is enough to say that, though published by Houghton Mifflin and written by two well-known authors, it was reviewed only by Catholic papers. Those all praised the book, many finding in it charm. The Boston *Pilot* for some reason or other took this occasion to remark that, though Mr. Lathrop's works had all been notably "decent," they were "as far from religion as if there were no such thing in life." To him are attributed the *Story's* occasional "incisive comments," and Rose's feminine hand is thought "visible in many a delicate touch." The *American Catholic Quarterly Review*, in the usual pretentious style of so-called learned periodicals, is very severe regarding some of the authorities cited, and calls the index "a pretense." This last criticism is a little strange, as there is no index at all.

Though at last enough letters have come to light that reveal more clearly than before the Lathrops' marital infelicity from the beginning, it was clear enough that George's "official" version of the final separation — that his wife was immersing herself in charitable work with his full approval — was merely official. Those who can read between the lines of letters can see plainly enough that very early Rose was not happy in her marriage. And it would seem that a separation may have been impending when on July 19, 1892, a letter was sent by hand to Rose at 43 Federal Street, which though signed only J. R. T. can be identified as written by Juliette R. Thomas of Yonkers, another convert of Father Young's. It opens: "My dearest Mrs. Lathrop: I cannot bear to think that anything is troubling you or Mr. Lathrop — two people whom I trust you will allow me to think of, as among my dearest friends. You have both helped me more than you know, not only by example & letters, but by your disinterested prayers. I remembered you at Mass this morning."

Mrs. Thomas's other letters to Rose contain nothing except pleasant gossip and a few pious reflections — such as one might expect from one recent convert to another. But indeed so many of the letters Rose kept — and she was a great keeper of such things — show that, whatever domestic troubles may have occurred every now and then, she and George lived most of the time the kind of life that gave their friends no suspicion of any imminent disaster. Thus Mrs. Nelson of New Rochelle, whose husband was "President" of that village, wrote on March 22, 1891. Her eight pages of cheerful gossip show, as do many other letters, that the Lathrops were living a pleasant and normal social life. Mrs. Nelson wants Rose and George to meet Mr. Cunliffe Owen and his wife, "who is a French countess, and who married when she was fifteen an Austrian dragoon officer, of high social rank, and became lady in waiting to the Empress Elizabeth. She has nearly every accomplishment that a woman can have, and a few vices — such as smoking and swearing. She has the worst manners I ever saw, and is altogether the most interesting spectacle that has come within my horizon. She sings, plays, paints, *sculps*, writes (books and newspaper articles), composes music, shoots, rows, rides, speaks seven languages and makes her own bonnets. If there is anything I have omitted to mention that a woman can do, you may be sure she does it." For counterweight Rose is also offered Mrs. Hoyt, the daughter of Chief Justice Chase, and half sister of Kate Chase Sprague. The only suspicious thing is that now and then part of a letter is missing, suggesting that it was deliberately destroyed. It can hardly be that friends made no allusion to troubles had they known of them; and it is more than likely that Rose was so sensitive about this matter that she could not bear to keep anything that touched on so sore a spot.

If letters are not, in this respect, a source of very definite enlightenment, still more of course must caution be exercised in discovering biographical significance in any of Rose's writing. It could be, for instance, that in her story "Huff and Tiff" in *Harper's Weekly* for September 2, 1882, Rose was telling something about her own somewhat stormy married life. Here, though the incidents are humorously treated, it is clear that the people in the story, the Thwaites, found cause for contention in the improvidence of both parties; and I can imagine that that, though not the real root of the trouble between Rose and George, was often seized on by both as a pretext. But again, it is not safe to deduce too much.

A jotting in one of the small notebooks Rose kept may really tell us more. "In looking back," she writes, "married life loses none of its piquancy though memories of injustice & bitter sneers, which the woman hears with lowered eyes and quivering lips, while the bystanders give their hearts to ache for her. If she revolts all the picturesqueness flies — otherwise, she finds zest in reminiscence, which a perpetually devoted husband would render insipid. Of course it is necessary that there should have been love, and if the love returns and returns to the husband's heart, the woman is a fool to lose her courage."

As for what Rose wrote in her poetry, just this much must be said. Most of it is obviously quite personal, but in using his own experience the poet generally transforms it. Then too he knows that he can dare venture on a good deal in this medium — his poem will not be read, or if it is read, it will not be understood, or if it is understood, it will not be believed. So the poet can tell the truth with almost perfect impunity. Perhaps the second stanza of "Life's Burying-Ground" is a case in point:

> *I visit every day the shadowy grove,*
> *I bury there my outraged tender thoughts;*
> *I bring the insult for the love I sought,*
> *And my contempt, where I had tried to love.*

Some suggestions have already been made as to what caused
the final breakup, and what evidence there is has been produced.
One does not wish to dig too deeply into a painful subject, especially as there can be little certainty. But for George, it is safe
enough to say that though there are indications that he was a
spoiled boy, and therefore perhaps, in a sense, a drunkard even
before he began to drink (and the same thing is more or less
true of his brother, Francis, who never married), still his unhappiness in marriage was what drove him to the bottle, rather
than that it was the bottle that caused the unhappiness. Of course
his drinking — sought as a means of escape — did not prove one
at all but only greatly increased his unhappiness. Nevertheless it
is only fair to allow this to a talented, rather vain, personable
man, popular among his friends, and to his death (and beyond)
loved by Rose.

But there was a profound incompatibility between this couple,
and despite G. K. Chesterton's remark on incompatibility as a
cause for divorce in America — "then I wonder why *all* Americans
are not divorced, for men and women are, by their very nature
incompatible," — there is no getting away from the fact that incompatibility can pass far beyond what Chesterton has in mind
— the incompatibility that is not only endurable but that the two
sexes find upon the whole attractive — and reach a point where
it is simply unendurable. To put the whole matter in a sentence,
it was the irreconcilable incompatibility of both, rather than
George's drinking, that seems to have wrecked this marriage.

The truth would appear to be that, as Colonel Higginson's
sister said of Una Hawthorne, Rose could never have been
happy — not with any man. She found plenty of happiness later,
when she ceased looking for it. Her poem, "The Roads That
Meet," does not suggest that her marriage to this particular man,
George Lathrop, was a mistake, but that, for her, marriage itself
was a mistake. The little section headed "Love" runs:

One leads beneath high oaks, and birds
Choose there their joyous revelry;
The sunbeams glint in golden herd;
The river mirrors silently,
Under these trees
My heart would bound or break;
Tell me what goal, resonant breeze?
'For you, mistake!'

George's drinking, however, did precipitate the disaster which had been threatening ever since they married. He had, no doubt, over and over again vowed amendment, and probably had kept his weakness under control for a time, only to relapse once more. But there could be only one end to such a case, and there came a time when George grew so violent in his cups that it was no longer safe for Rose to be with him. She therefore applied to the bishop of the diocese for permission to leave her husband. This the bishop's vicar-general gave her in writing. Upon receipt of it, she left the pleasant house on Post Hill Place and never went back.

Part Three: Mother Alphonsa

CHAPTER I

The New Start

Rose Lathrop was invited, in 1894, to read at the New England
Women's Press Association* what was expected to be the usual
literary paper. The appearance of Hawthorne's daughter brought
out all the literary lights and intellectuals of Boston and Cambridge, together with a large general audience. As the subject
had been left to her, she rather startled those present by talking
on Catholic works of charity, largely illustrated by the career
of the famous Father Drumgoole. It was after this address that
she confided to the friend who asked her to give it: "A married
woman loving children as I do, and bereft of them, must, it
seems to me, fill the void in her life with works of charity."

About this time — certainly in October, though my informants
are not quite sure as to whether it was 1894 or 1895 — she attended
a retreat at the Academy of the Assumption, Wellesley Hills,
under the charge of one of the many branches (that of Halifax,
N. S.) of the American Sisters of Charity. Rose had often been
to Wellesley Hills, but until this time only to visit Alice Wheeler.

The retreat — a private one — was made under the direction of
Sister Mary Bernard Stuart. As Sister Bernard was at that time
at the academy resting, the superior, Sister Fidelis Eustace,
appointed her as Mrs. Lathrop's directress. She, finding that
Rose was deeply interested in charity, took the teaching and
work of St. Vincent de Paul as her main theme. It was no doubt

* "In 1894, I think," says the anonymous friend who wrote a valuable
article on her after her death. Though the clipping has been supplied me,
I am unable to identify the paper in which it appeared.

from this retreat that Rose bore away St. Vincent's motto, "I am for God and the poor," and also his idea — which she was often to suggest throughout her life — that charity should be organized on a parish basis. We may be sure that many issues, that had up till then been confused in Rose's mind, now became quite clear.

The nuns were charmed with her, and she loved the academy and its beautiful grounds. At that time one of the most picturesque features of the place was an old windmill which was at the end of a path between high hedges. They called it Lover's Lane — no doubt with all the greater sense of appropriateness because no lovers were allowed anywhere near. Sisters and pupils alike loved to watch from a distance Hawthorne's daughter, her red-gold hair gleaming in the sun, sitting on the steps of this ancient landmark, writing. They were sure it was poetry — and perhaps it was.

It is still a favorite story in that convent how once when, in the parlor, Sister Fidelis knelt to ask a priest's blessing as he was about to leave; then, after the Sisters had risen to their feet, Mrs. Lathrop, who was present, crossed the room and, kneeling before Sister Fidelis, said, "And now, it is *your* blessing that I wish." This was to the consternation of the superior and the amusement of everybody else. They all saw that Mrs. Lathrop was still rather newly a convert to the Catholic faith.

One evening Sister Bernard got an account of Rose's conversion. "Could you tell me how it happened, Mrs. Lathrop?" she asked.

"Oh, a lot of things were involved, Sister. But here is one. My husband and I were not at all happy about religion. We saw we had need of it, and one day I told him that I thought that some Presbyterian friends of ours seemed to derive benefit from their faith. George gave me a rather strange look and said, 'If I ever change, the only church I'll ever join is the Catholic Church.' "*

* But practically every educated and intelligent person I know — and some of them are brilliant and famous — has said much the same thing to me. Very few act upon it. This account is made up from the letters from one Sister who often did talk with Rose during this retreat and from

This only confirms the impression that it was he, rather than Rose, who led the way into the Catholic Church. It is something that deserves to be remembered to his credit.

Things had come to such a pass that it was impossible for Rose to remain with George any longer. Yet her departure — this time so quietly final — might have been to him a mortal blow had it not been so much a wound to his vanity. No doubt he suffered, but he was not a big enough man for tragedy. He did, however, go to pieces — more or less. Though his operatic version of *The Scarlet Letter* was not produced until 1896, it was written before the separation and published by Houghton Mifflin in 1894. After that date George produced nothing worth mentioning and one fears that his drinking was now of the sodden and solitary kind. As for Rose, she stayed most of the time now with Alice Wheeler at Wellesley Hills, and, the Sisters recall how Alice sometimes used to accompany her friend to the convent. They also noticed Rose's great fervor at Mass. For this she went to the convent chapel every morning.

There were a number of influences that shaped her new course. Her brother, Julian, was to write in the *Atlantic* in 1928: "No one familiar with her as a girl could have foreseen what her maturity was to be; the change was abrupt and strange." But he does add: "Conditions for the departure were no doubt present, but hidden — even perhaps from herself." Had Julian known much about the psychology of the saints, even he might have foreseen a good deal. The sunny graciousness that was so marked a characteristic of St. Francis de Sales, for instance, was not natural but acquired by an effort of will, and then made a habit. So with

another who got an account of it from Sister Bernard. Unfortunately, Rose's letters were destroyed.

Rose, the vehemence — if you like, the violence — of her disposition was necessary to the career of self-sacrifice she was about
to begin. Those who are to practice heroic virtue likely have
heroism — though but in its defective form — from the start.

There were, however, certain influences frequently acknowledged by her in later life. Very explicitly she did so in the little
magazine she edited for a few years.* "My own convictions about
human duties," she said there, "towards human suffering were
clearly formed in youth by countless passages read in the works
of Nathaniel Hawthorne." And then she proceeds to quote at
length the account he gave in *Our Old Home* of the workhouse
child. She concludes, "What this man could do, and taught me
that I should do, under the standard of Christ, must I do, or not?
That question returned repeatedly, and I met it trembling. If
occasion presented itself, I knew well that I must do a thing,
however difficult, which the fearless writer inculcated. In short,
we can never make a successful argument against the principles
of Christ." For herself she was to discover, as did St. Francis of
Assisi when he embraced the leper, as did St. Elizabeth of Hun-
gary when she put a leper in her own bed, that it was Christ to
whom this charity was shown.

And though, in her own case, lepers did not literally come
upon the scene, the disease she was to alleviate was as terrible as
leprosy, and far more common. It was the work of Father Damien,
far off on Molokai, that inspired hers. As to this she was to write:
"[We] would never have gone into action had it not been for
Father Damien."** And when she felt that her work needed the
man who had been Father Damien's assistant more than Molokai,
she appealed to him — though vainly — to join her in New York.
She was never a very great reader, but she had no doubt read
Robert Louis Stevenson's *Letter to Mr. Hyde*, and probably also
Charles Warren Stoddard's book.

* *Christ's Poor*, Vol. III, No. 3 (1904), pp. 6, 8, 9.
** *Christ's Poor*, Vol. III, No. 6 (1904), p. 14.

One of her acquaintances, knowing how fastidious was this daughter of the fastidious Hawthorne, had asked her "why she chose such a dirty occupation." This she explained at some length — * yet, it was all condensed in one phrase she used: her resolve had come "warm from the fires of compassion." To quote her further: "Any life that is worthy of respect is in some way consecrated to God." She was fond of citing the saying of John of Avila, St. Teresa's friend: "Those who give themselves to God must have a lion's heart."

Only five minutes, she used to declare, were needed for decision. And her theme may be said to have been — "*Now* is the acceptable time." In one of his letters to her, Father Young had assured her that, if one is going to give oneself at all, it is easier to give oneself wholly than in part. It was a complete sacrifice that she decided upon.

Further, as she put it later, she meant to be "untrammeled by common sense." She had been reading something that the Empress Frederick of Germany had said — something very kind and sensible but not for her because it was at bottom cautious and cold. The sociological style could not be hers. Whatever she did had to be headlong and reckless, without thrift, the breaking of the precious alabaster box. She had shown herself from girlhood to be eminently practical. Never was she more practical than now when she threw to the winds what mean men call prudence. The kind of practicality she insisted on after that was just steady, faithful diligence. Nobody ever went in for less of the pose of sanctity than she did: nobody was ever less of an aesthete than this unsuccessful artist who now became an artist in living.

That she took up her work for destitute sufferers from incurable cancer has been set down to the shock she received when

* This was in the article Maurice Francis Egan wrote for the **New York** *Times* book section.

her friend, Emma Lazarus, died in 1887. But though Rose never denied that Emma's death was one of the factors in the case, when, toward the end of her own life, an attempt was made to capitalize on her friendship with the brilliant young Jewess — as a good means of appealing for support to the charity of New York Jews — Rose simply put her foot down. Then in talking to Maurice Francis Egan she said: "Miss Lazarus and I sometimes walked and talked together [after meeting in the Gilders' salon]. And she had such sweet delicacy of spirit that she never gave the least sign that she did not find a very secure footing for her mental explorations while accompanying a person who knew little Latin and less Greek. On the contrary, she assured me that I was a paragon for 'stirring her up with suggestions.' I doubt if two more fundamentally disconsolate minds could have been found in the whole world than hers and mine." But when Emma was stricken with cancer, though Rose grieved, she also realized that Emma's had been, after all, a happy and fortunate life — not merely (or mainly) because of the wealth of her devoted family, or because of her friendship with Emerson, to whom she had dedicated her *Admetus and other Poems* in 1871, but because she had found for herself a great and ennobling cause — that of her persecuted people. After the Russian pogroms of 1879–1883 she became their champion, not only writing with the moral indignation of the prophets but organizing efforts for the relief of the Jewish refugees crowding into America. Though she suffered, she was also uplifted by joy — the joy that comes through suffering.

The real spring of action, as Rose often was to affirm, was the case of a poor seamstress. And whether it was about this or a similar case, Father Young wrote to her on June 2, 1894: "I cannot tell you how happy I would be to aid you in finding what you wish for the poor sufferer in whom you have taken so charitable an interest, but I am quite sure no New York hospital would receive a patient out of the city limits unless fully paid for. One cannot find fault with this, for as it is, their wards are literally crowded — overcrowded — by charity patients. I am often thinking affectionately of you both, and always praying for your happiness." This was at any rate the sort of case that roused Rose into action, not generalized reflection. Here was a young woman, refined but poor; and nothing could be done but to send her to Blackwell's Island which — odd as officially minded social workers thought it — the destitute sufferers looked upon as hell on earth. As nobody else was going to help such people, Rose decided then and there to help them herself.

Some years later she described the situation. As the hospitals had no beds for incurable diseases among the destitute — especially the cancerous — they were allowed to rot and die in damp basements or wherever else they could find a hole to crawl into. Either that, or they would be taken charge of by the apathetic authorities, and after being moved — about three times and not too gently, she found — arrived at last at the almshouse on the Island. She reports, with her blood boiling, how a high official in one of the so-called charities had told her, "No, Mrs. Lathrop; you distress yourself quite needlessly. Why, it's quite *difficult* to find a case of genuine destitution!"

"Yes," she flared back, "but I could take you and — but what's the use of talking? Another social worker in one of our largest American cities told me that two dollars a year is considered more than enough on an average for a family on relief."

He blandly put the tips of his fingers together. "Well, in New York we average a bit more than that, Mrs. Lathrop."

With eyes as blazing as her hair Rose turned and walked out of his comfortable office. She resolved that in *her* treatment of the poor she would be so gentle that even they could praise it. A lady who lived in Paris had written to tell her that the doctors there said that the best thing was that the cancerous poor should not be nursed at all but left to die as quickly as possible.

Not if wrathful Rose could help it!

Things of this sort served as topics for the pen in the magazine she edited — writing almost every issue from cover to cover. Though her object just then was not at all that of explaining herself or her career but simply the practical one of arousing enough public interest to secure public support for her work, she did in effect become, without in the least intending it, her own biographer and the historian of the organization she founded.

Not very long before she had decided how best to proceed, George's opera of *The Scarlet Letter* was performed for the first time in New York, at the Academy of Music, on the evening of March 6, 1896. It was written while she was still with him, and after that he had no heart for anything else. She was glad to hear of its success, for she was fond of this clever, vain, weak, boyish husband of hers. It was with a pang that she left him, and at least a year seems to have gone by before she found something definite to do with her life.

When at last she had reached her decision, she went, in order to prepare herself for her work, to serve as a nurse during the summer of 1896 at the cancer hospital at a Hundred-and-sixth Street and Eighth Avenue. It is what is now known as the Memorial Hospital. Three months was not a long period of training. But it sufficed for what she intended to do; it had to suffice, with so many waiting for her help.

The head nurse took her to the ward where the incurable women patients were and said, "This is where you will work." The large, circular room reminded her of a circus tent with its great shaft like a pole in the center. The patients were in beds pointing out from the walls.

In spite of all the suffering endured, there was — not constantly but more frequently than one would expect — a good deal of fun. One patient, of whom the new nurse soon got very fond, sometimes contrived to make it a circus. This was a Mrs. Watson, an old Irishwoman, but with arms as pretty as a dairy maid's and with hands as soft and smooth as a child's. She set the whole large room in an uproar of mirth when the prankish fit was on her. Deliberately she gathered together as the "costumes" necessary for her performance the most antiquated of undergarments. In the most monstrously betuckered petticoats — women still wore them, but not of the vintage *she* displayed — and billowing lacy drawers hanging below the knees — the more fantastic the better — she would clown around the ward, and dying women gazed at her comicalities and for a few minutes nearly died of laughing.

Mrs. Watson herself was one of the terrible "face cases." Her countenance was hidden in bandages held in position with adhesive tape; but the blue eyes twinkled with mischief, and she carried her head as only the Irish can. Though she was a grandmother, her wavy brown hair was quite untouched with silver. Even about her slippered feet there seemed to be something pert. She walked about with as much assurance as though she owned the place and visitors were admitted only with her permission.

Of course Rose found even before her first day in the hospital was over what hard and disagreeable work was involved. But she had come there expecting just that. What she had not thought to find was Mrs. Watson's gaiety and courage. Seeing it, she marveled, and herself took heart. Yet Mrs. Watson's face was so terrible when its bandages were removed that Rose shook from head to foot as though with ague the first time she had to dress it. The process was quite elaborate, so she got the very first morning a thorough initiation. Afterward she never flinched, whatever she was called upon to do.

One day Rose arrived to find that the chief ornament of the ward, the sprightly Mrs. Watson, was dressed to go out. Few of the patients were allowed to do that, and Rose had hardly supposed that this gruesome face case would be allowed to show itself on the streets of New York. But she had arrayed herself in the best clothes of those recently dead who had been in the adjoining beds.

It was the middle of the New York summer, hot and humid, but Mrs. Watson looked as round as a barrel with all the clothes she had put on, some of it winter's wear but chosen for its embroidery. On top of everything else, as the last touch of perfection, she was putting on a veil — actually a shoulder scarf, thus hideously enlarging a huge bonnet. This she wore, not because it fitted her or seemed becoming, but because she thought it looked expensive. Her clowning could be of a solemn, as well as a hilarious, sort. She stood there, somber and grotesque, waiting for the minute hand of the clock to tell her the moment she might leave.

Once a month — and the day had now arrived — she used to visit a grandson in the Catholic Protectory. She was never tired of talking about little Willie, that angelic child, with his beautiful, golden hair and a heart of gold — the veritable paragon of boys. She always looked forward to this visit and prepared for it by collecting all the dainties she could lay her hands upon, wheedling them out of visitors or the other patients. Nothing was too good for dear little Willie. But when Rose offered to add a piece of silver, she refused it; in making her collections, she maintained her own code. When the clock struck she put her arm through the basket handle, and, like a four-masted schooner, Rose thought, with all its canvas on, she sailed away.

At the time it did not seem very remarkable to Rose that little Willie's grandmother returned from these excursions looking battered and weary and all awry. Rose set this down to the New York heat. Mrs. Watson at all events returned less burdened than when she left. For then her basket was crammed to the top with goodies; now it contained nothing but a pig's ear. She explained that she had stopped at her sister's on the way back and they had had pig's head for supper. The ear was a dainty she had brought back for the sickest woman in the ward. Afterward Rose wondered whether pig's head had special restorative properties useful after a visit to an angelic, golden-haired grandson.

One day Mrs. Watson disappeared. Rose did not find out why at first, as she was then on night duty and did not know what had happened during the day. When she noticed Mrs. Watson's empty bed she wondered if there had not been a sudden hemorrhage and death. That had been expected for some time.

But the following day the new nurse heard what had happened. Mrs. Watson had been getting worse gradually, so that recently her cancer had to be dressed three times a day, with the doctors carefully watching her condition. Then they pronounced her case inoperable, and there was a fixed rule that when they were sure of this, they sent the patient away. Only of course a patient who was unable to pay, but Mrs. Watson was one of these. It was an epitome of the story of destitute cancer sufferers. She could go to Blackwell's Island if she chose; she could no longer remain at the hospital.

She refused Blackwell's Island. Yet where else *could* she go? The sister who gave her the supper of pig's head was almost as poor as herself, living as a housekeeper in a tenement, and she had two little grandchildren crowded in with her. As Rose was anxious about Mrs. Watson, wondering where she could have found lodgings, she wrote several times to an address that had once been given her. No reply came, so Rose wondered all the more what was the fate of this poor, fantastic creature, homeless in New York.

CHAPTER II

First Taste of the Slums

From the beginning Rose Hawthorne Lathrop saw that if she was to accomplish much for the destitute sufferers from cancer — at any rate with the all but nonexistent means at her disposal — she would have to go to them, not wait for them to come to her. Therefore she set out to find a base of operation on the lower East Side.

It is probable that she had never been in that locality before. There was nothing that would have led there a woman like herself whose interests had all been in the literary and artistic world. Her brother, Julian, about this time moved to 216 West 138th Street, but that was then hardly less out in the country than Sag Harbor where he lived in the summer. None of Rose's many New York addresses went farther North than 55th Street and none farther south than Washington Square. Between these points hers had been a very narrow terrain extending a couple of blocks on each side of Fifth Avenue. Where she now went was very much *terra incognita* to her.

Moreover, ugly and malodorous as much of the East Side is today, it is a paradise compared with the East Side of fifty years ago. And where Mrs. Lathrop located was not one of the better bits, though in all likelihood it was not one of the worst either. She got it more or less "by chance aided by inexperience."

So as to be able to start her work as soon as she had completed her short course at the cancer hospital, she did not wait for it to end but took a Sunday, her day off, to explore.* She was praying all the time to be given the intelligence to know where God willed her to settle. For the much-traveled Rose that trolley ride was the shortest journey she had made; it was also the longest — for it took her away from all she had ever known. The first visit merely made her see that the East Side was where she should be, as the most crowded and desperate of New York districts. That first day she had no time for anything else.

On the very next afternoon she had off, down she went again, this time trying to settle upon a street and the kind of house where she should locate. She felt lonely and frightened, but she was also quite determined. Then and there she made up her mind that she would throw her burden upon God, who knew her incapacity, and then act as He guided.

Yet she was really alarmed at the thought of living there. Not only was everything so squalid, but the faces of the men — and even of the women — made her feel that she would be robbed, if not murdered, if she settled among them. She was indeed heavy of heart. "I wonder," she began to say to herself, "does God really mean me to come here? Would I be feeling as I do if this was really the field I should work in? This may be His way of showing me that I have made a mistake."

Every time she mentioned nursing cancer patients people drew back in alarm. As she was at a loss what to do she went round to St. Mary's Rectory on Grand Street for advice.

The young priest she saw was very patronizing, and Rose felt he was trying to annihilate her by his manner.

"My dear Mrs. Lathrop, you are not needed in this locality," he said loftily. "Very little cancer here, I assure you. Besides the Catholics are moving further uptown, and the Jews are coming in." He glanced at her over his shoulder as he sat writing.

* The following account, and most of what immediately follows, is based upon a diary Rose Hawthorne Lathrop kept for a while. Some excerpts have already appeared in print, but this is the first time it has been made available as a whole.

"Father," Rose returned mildly, "cancer may be far more prev-
alent than you imagine. Often people have it and are not aware
of the fact, and when they *are* aware of it they don't always tell
everybody. But as for my patients, it doesn't make any difference
whether they are Catholics or Jews."

At that he became a little more interested. "In that event why
don't you look for a loft?" he asked.

"I had thought of that, Father. In a big loft I'd have space for
a dozen beds — and plenty of air."

She departed, glad to have had her ideas confirmed. And when,
after several hours' search along the waterfront, she did find a
loft, not too thickly surrounded by saloons, she was very greatly
excited and felt that her first and irrevocable step had been taken.

As a matter of fact she had as yet done nothing. Nor could she
do anything just then, as word came that she had to go to Boston
to see a friend who was critically ill. The question of renting the
loft was therefore left in abeyance. But she felt faint, as though
tearing herself up by the roots, on leaving already; she was so
deeply committed in will to this work.

By the time she got back, she realized that a loft was out of
the question. Her idea had been to start, singlehanded, a kind of
small hospital. Now she realized that it would be better to take a
few rooms and go out to her patients in their homes, except for
those who went to her for treatment. It sickened her to give
up her plan of taking bed patients under her care, but at the
Nurses' Settlement in Henry Street she had been advised to adopt
the visiting scheme, and she decided to follow that advice.

Upon her return a real-estate agent told her about an apartment
at 1 Scammel Street. She went to look at it, quite sure it would be
both too expensive and not what she wanted. She found every
window broken, the house apparently abandoned, and a defunct
liquor store on the ground floor. If only she had enough money

to repair it a little! Feeling very brave and making the sign of the cross, she went inside the dilapidated wooden fence — where she found an alley cat with one blue and one green eye, and set out to explore the place.

A family was living in it — good-natured Irish people. "Lucky you are, ma'am, that you didn't run across that dog first!"

But when Rose inquired about rooms to rent she was told: "This place is going to be pulled down for a school. We have to move in a week or two. No use coming here, ma'am. And it isn't fit for a lady like you."

Her "ladylike" qualities Rose considered could go into permanent storage, so up the dirty, dark, broken stairs she climbed in search of the apartment she feared would cost too much — two little empty cells entirely shut off from air and light by the blank wall only a foot from the windows. That settled her. It suited her ideas in every possible way: nothing could be more inconvenient or devoid of necessary comforts. Only a very poor person could have endured it. She wished to be not only among the poor but of the poor. She even was beginning to think that perhaps, after all, the neighborhood was not as dangerous as she had imagined. In fact by now she actually had the idea that there was no place really dangerous to those who went to it for the love of God. Even that her tenancy was insecure — this being a property condemned by the city and about to be pulled down — added to its attractiveness in her eyes. Was not insecurity one of the constant features of poverty?

That reflection made her natural spirits rise. The night she took possession of her floor she noticed a pleasant little square near by — so small she had not noticed it at first, and between the houses the moon made glorious scenes of light and cloud. She looked out on the sky from her window, and found she could smell a salt breeze blowing from the harbor. When she awoke in the morning the hideous, little, black bedrooms were gladdened by what positively seemed a miraculous sunbeam. Somehow it slid through a little window high up on the wall and shot its rays right into the second formerly dismal room.

But the frightful dirt! *That* the morning light made clearer. So down on her knees she went with pail and scrubbing brush. Then she painted her floor a marigold yellow. Something more than the pink of her New London floor was needed here. By the time she had finished the smells had gone, brightness had come; those crannies and corners that had seemed worst were now best, because on those she had given most attention.

A change — miraculous like the sunbeam — had come over the other tenants. There was an old Jewess on the ground floor, sour and disliked — called by everybody "that thing." Now she was shining with happy smiles because a fellow human being had been kind to her. To Rose she in turn was kind. It was the same with the woman overhead who had a battle royal with her husband every evening. Rose could not quite make it out, but stopping for a short rest, she reflected: "Well, my dear, you have set out to love everyone and to try to make them love each other. Of course you can do very little, and you are as stupid as you can be, still even this little effort seems to have its effect. How strange it is! The moment we set ourselves free from selfishness and sloth, everybody is refreshed. You may well tremble, Rose, to see this power — such a little bit of the right spirit. But it works wonders — just as though God had brushed you aside and said, 'I am here.'"

She could have had, even after her life as George's wife ended in apparent disaster, ease and dignity in a pretty little apartment in New York or Boston. She would have had the Hawthorne royalties to live on, and to these could have added her own literary earnings; and George no doubt would have been glad to contribute to her support. Yet here she was, choosing not only the slums but the filthiest of all diseases for her speciality — an abnegation that was absolute. Now that she had reached her decision and had made her start, she more than ever felt certain that what she was doing was right. At any moment she could have turned back and accepted instead a quiet life in which good deeds had a reasonable amount of time given to them. It was the heroic thing she had undertaken instead. Not for an instant did she regret it.

She had started in terror of the people upon whose faces she thought she saw expressions of the most satanic cruelty and selfishness. Before long her alarm disappeared. These people were no different from others, except that they were wretchedly poor. She found families of eight or ten with only one bed among them all; in such groups anyone with a disease like rheumatism or cancer slept in chairs or on the floor; and little children were deposited anywhere. Looking out on the squalid, but often animated, streets she told herself: "Rose, my dear, don't get it into your head that you're doing something grand in putting yourself upon the same plane as these people. Try to remember that there are no planes in people themselves but only in their circumstances, and that the circumstances of the poor, the ignorant, and the corrupt are a disgrace. God loves them better than He loves the more fortunate in circumstances — unless *they* love the poor."

She soon learned that the great problem for such people was that of finding the rent. Rose did not blame the landlords for insisting upon its payment. She was not sure that she even blamed them for the high rents they charged; she knew that they often failed to collect what was owing. Something or somebody was to blame — that much was clear; but she could not make up her mind where the blame belonged. But without trying to settle that problem, she did now and then, when she was in funds, pay the rent to prevent an eviction. How often she came to see that her patients, whatever else they received from her — clothing or food or fuel or medicine or a doctor's advice — remained in a state of miserable terror, wondering where the rent was coming from. A familiar sight was that of the van at a door, the furniture being hustled into it in haste, and a tearful woman with children clinging to her skirts standing by as the men brought out her few chattels. When Rose saw the poor woman's desperate look she felt somehow that here was a personal responsibility.

At first she supposed that the cancerous poor she visited would, after making a trial of her skill, send her packing. She was glad to discover that they were glad to have her, and their gratitude was so great that again she felt the Voice saying, "I am here!" Then she knew that a privilege was being conferred upon her that she was allowed to do this work. After being storm-tossed with dismay, she seemed to drift into a halcyon sea, like the peace of the mercy of God — circled with the unchanging horizon of heaven.

There were natural consolations, too. The first night she was there she had lain in bed quaking, quite expecting some drunken man to break the door down. Instead she heard the voices of children in the street till quite late at night right under her window. These reassured her, and later, when she did go out — sometimes for a breath of fresh air, but usually only when somebody sent for her — she saw along the water's edge pictures she thought quite Dutch, the shipping mounting and dipping over the trees of Corlaers Park. Brooklyn Bridge, seen from many different points and with differing effects at different hours, was always beautiful, especially in its majestic calm at sunset. "At this hour," in her enthusiasm she told a slightly bewildered policeman, "all the criss-cross streets of New York end in the west in orange gold."

The policeman scratched his head and agreed, "Yes, guess that's about right, ma'am."

"And the sunrise!" she went on, "the sunrise — why it's a pageant worth getting up to see! After a night of sad sounds it soothes the soul as instantly as dawn upon the Alps. Don't you think so?"

"That's so, ma'am. But I never saw the Alps."

"But you've seen *this*," she told him — "the moonlight and the cloud-rack are a harmonious, beneficent message from God at the end of the day — something with which sin and poverty never interfere."

She felt afterward that the policeman did not quite understand. "Probably," she told herself, "the poor do not always realize that they are being cheered by beauty. Yet probably, too, I do not think of half the things they do enjoy — the simple, homely, reasonable comforts, and catlike satisfactions and resigned cogitations, the fragments of primitive life they preserve."

What she did notice — and her father had noticed the same thing in his walks in the Liverpool slums — was that everybody lived as far as possible in the open air, from the grandparents down to the babies. Only to sleep did they go under roofs, or when the weather was too bad.

Also Rose noticed, as her father had done, how every little girl had a baby as a live doll; if her mother didn't have a baby, the child used to borrow one. The baby of the slums was the focus of fun, charm, surprise, and pathetic sweetness. The fresh air, she concluded, was the land of the poor. In the summer they slept in it, on the fire escapes, but in winter, though that was impossible, it had to be very savage weather that kept them indoors. In their dark, stifling rooms was nothing but the misery of dank, hungry, landlord-visited despair. In the winter the children of the poor, like the Chinese, provided against the cold by layer upon layer of habiliments — oddly assorted and ragged, but still warm.

Then, too, she saw that the poor really enjoyed noise. At first this was for her one of the hardest things to bear, for though between midnight and four there was something of a lull — broken only by the scream of a parrot or a wailing cat — at daybreak there clattered out from their stables the dray horses; then the East Side began to stir into another twenty hours of uproar. If by any chance during the day there was a moment's hush, the frolic of a hurdy-gurdy broke upon the stillness. At once out would come squads of dancing children, and the organ grinder would be the center of a wheel of graceful girls in pairs, advancing and retreating, performing with stately melancholy until the tune came to an end. Then they tumbled down as one, and jumped up dancing with glee.

She observed that the children of the poor had constant excitement. Her own childhood had been as happy as such a period could be, but it now seemed to her that its pleasures were sedate — in spite of occasional mischief and unruliness — compared with the frantic enjoyment of life known by these East Side children. Up until late at night, with full liberty to scream and shout at the top of their lungs — she watched a group of boys building a bonfire and another dragging along an old boiler helter-skelter — all this was part of the fun. No apple orchard in the country or school gymnasium could possibly vie in interest with climbing on back-shed roofs or walking a fence like a tightrope.

So too with the staid and elaborate pirouettes of the dancing school — how dull compared with the dancers around the barrel organ! She thought it one of the prettiest sights she had seen when, from her back windows, she watched little girls dressed in colored tissue paper, perform. She was astonished at their nice manners. More than ever was she convinced that the barriers between the children of the poor and a true refinement are slight and pliant. Obviously these children had a quick native sensibility to the beautiful and the gentle. When she made friends with the children of the neighborhood, their smiles and sweet voices and caressing hands seemed to do as much for her as the glorious skies.

One thing troubled her a good deal — no doubt all the more because of poor George's unfortunate weakness: this was the saloon. She recognized that beer and gambling did give pleasure to many people who did not strike her as particularly wicked. And even if there was too much beer and gambling, she did not understand why the prosperous and respectable should demand that the poor be saints, or take upon their shoulders the double burden of ill luck and self-conquest. After the worst had been said, she made up her mind that the semidepraved poor were an open book, and the semidepraved rich a decorously closed one.

These East Side saloons were so different from those beer gardens she had seen in Dresden, where music played and people talked as families over their steins. Here she supposed that the trouble was that the beer was "abominably impure" and decided that "the concoctors of unreal beer" should be electrocuted, a somewhat naïve solution of a problem which is, in large part, climactic. And as the future Bishop John Lancaster Spalding had recently discovered, life in the New York slums is endurable only if people did drink. But Rose did not do more than mildly propose the electric chair for brewers of bad beer. Though with every temptation to take up a rigidly Puritanical (and therefore un-Catholic) attitude of rigid condemnation of drink, she went no further than that.

She did not give much time for reflection. But she summed it all up for herself with: "Well, Rose, you've just got to revise all your ideas: what are needed are not so much missions to the poor, as missions to the rich, settlements for the learned, free lectures for the fledglings of wealth. Then perhaps we might get some social betterment."

All the same she was glad to find that something was being done in that deplorable district. It was like wine to her spirit to know that she was not alone — that the College Settlement was working there, along with the settlement of nurses and Miss Mc-Dowell's kindergarten, and Mrs. Van Rensselaer's beautiful parlor for a girl's club. She was one of a stalwart company.

She went to the board of health to ask if she would be permitted to nurse people without the constant supervision of a doctor.

At the word "cancer" the official to whom she spoke was struck silent, and his face whitened. After a while he said in a low, strained voice, "That's what my wife died of." How often

that happened in her experience — a sudden silence as the prelude
to revelations. These people all asked a tremulous question: "Have
you found that cancer can be cured?"

She was told at the board of health that no objection could
possibly be raised to what she wanted to do. That was a relief.
She wondered why she could ever have hesitated. She had
already discovered that helping the sufferer fired her with
enthusiasm, after the initial repulsion was overcome. Without her
this sufferer would have known no love, nor found relief —
horrible thought! Again she told herself, "Rose, those who wish
to keep the fire of charity from their hearts had better not come
near the agony of the poor!"

Cancer itself remained a mystery: it was that even in the case
of dear Emma who had died of it. But Emma had had every
possible comfort that her family's wealth could provide. Rose's
concern was with the plight of the destitute who were afflicted
with this terrible disease. The thought of their poverty roused
in her a hot indignation, and unless she had limited herself
strictly to the helping of the cancerous poor, she might have
become what is called a social reformer and perhaps turned
perforce, as so many social reformers do, into a rather cold and
bloodless analyzer of statistics.

Not so Rose Hawthorne Lathrop. She was indeed a champion
of the poor, one who threw her mantle round them. Time after
time her anger flared — not only against the oppressors of the
poor but the callousness of so much of what is called social
welfare work. Then her scorn could be scorching. But she had
not set herself to the solving of any economic problems — only to
the bringing of immediate relief to those who needed it, the few
cases she could deal with.

Though she had no illusions about the poor — she smiled
scornfully at one sentimentalist who told her that they were
"such dears" — over and over again she witnessed how, in the
very midst of the weedy confusion of grossness and dissipation

and cruelty, there would spring up a sudden and unexplained flower of perfect loveliness. How much God has given to human nature, she used to tell herself wonderingly, that He will never permit it to lose. It was no longer so inexplicable to her that Christ delighted to be with the sons of men. She began to believe that the obnoxious traits of the poor — the things one always saw first — were there in order that those who recognized their duty to the poor would have at the very outset a sacrifice to make, a demand made upon their generosity. She came, too, to learn that there were subsequent refinements of revulsion; but when these were disowned for the sake of human brotherhood, then one came to find oneself at last one with the poor. At that stage she saw she must herself accept as her own all that could be charged against the poor. They were what they were because of misfortune; the sins of the respectable were of a darker hue.

CHAPTER III

The First Patient

It did not take long for Rose to start work — only just so long as it took to get word out that she was in the neighborhood to bandage cancers or similar diseases. The first case actually treated was that of a little Jewish boy of seven named Louis, whose eye and neck were affected. Later she took him to the skin and cancer hospital for examination. There her treatment of him was commended.

Most of those first weeks were spent in getting ready, for though she knew that her tenancy of the Scammel Street tenement could only be brief, there were many preparations to be made for the patients she was expecting. By way of doing this she was daily at the six-thirty Mass at St. Rose of Lima's Church. It was rather curious that this should be her parish: she remembered how nearly forty years earlier, when she was just a little girl, dear, beautiful, brilliant Elizabeth Hoar, Emerson's friend, who had been engaged to Emerson's brother, had picked St. Rose of Lima for her as her patron saint.

Doctor Miller of Monroe Street heard what her purpose was and promised to give his services without fees, which he did for two years. And other doctors came forward with similar offers, touched by the heroism of this work but perhaps not altogether unaffected by the wild Titian hair and the creamy complexion of the woman who had come to work in the slums. Doctor Coyle of Henry Street was one of these. He was a young man, hearty and rosy cheeked, and Mrs. Lathrop was not only charmed by the way he swept aside any suggestion of being paid but by his bringing his little daughter into that dingy apartment. The first visit was toward dark one winter's afternoon, and he put the lovely two-year-old child on the tenement floor as though, wrote Rose, "he expected her to enjoy the scene. The tiny *débutante* was ready to be pleased with the world in any guise, as long as she was herself a dazzling success. 'Take off your mittens, my dear,' said the adoring father. Having done as she was told, little Miss Coyle peeped down over her furs with the intention of taking off her pigmy snowshoes. Her father laughed at her complete willingness to fraternize for a social hour with the dwellers in a corner of misery and disease. All the laborers for cancerous sick were devouring a picture such as their fatigued eyes had not seen for several years; and they appreciated the gentle act of the debonair young doctor, as one of the kindest of his noble, charity-filled life."

When Dr. Coyle moved to 35th Street he asked Doctor Shiels to help the work, though he continued to come once a week himself. And Doctor Shiels stayed with it, watching its growth until the day of his death. A little later young Doctor James J. Walsh, who was to be the first of Rose Hawthorne Lathrop's biographers, assisted in various ways.

But she saw that her work was never going to need doctors for much more than morale. Though it grew prodigiously, its scope became even more strictly defined with the passage of time. Early she settled, however, that she would receive only those cases diagnosed as incurable. She never permitted any use of the knife, or (after its discovery) of radium. She was to take poor people in and make them comfortable in the home she provided. And the doctor was useful as a kind of cheerful robin, scattering his words of encouragement. But there was really nothing else for him to do. Though she was always very grateful for this, a great friend of her work, Doctor H. R. Storer, of Newport, was to advise her to be careful to keep on good terms with the medical profession — especially with the cancer specialists. He saw a possible danger for her here. But her tact proved quite equal to the occasion. All the doctors she met she charmed. Never was she to have any difficulties with them.

Another lifelong friend made at this time was the distinguished lawyer, J. Warren Greene. His wife had died of cancer and in her memory he gave his legal services without charge in the business of subsequent years. Not only that; no month passed without his substantial donation. Others were benefactors on a larger scale; none was so constant in his gifts. And in later years, when the work had expanded and it was put into the hands of trustees, this Protestant friend was one of them. Without the support of such men as this, Rose Hawthorne Lathrop's enterprise would have soon withered away. But it was her firm conviction that the world was full of charitable people, and that these only had to be told how great the need was to come forward with their prompt help. With Doctor Geer, the Episcopalian minister of Trinity chapel, she had a close friendship, though from him there came nothing but moral support.

There were two women who went to live with Rose at 1 Scammel Street. One of these was a Mrs. Sheehan, of whom we know no more that that she was there. The first patient to be received into the house was Mrs. Watson, who is shown (along with her grandson) in the picture that forms the frontispiece of this book. Some other women, however, had already formed a contact close enough to be completed later by residence. And the story of one of these, Mrs. Dwyer, has been told at some length but a little vaguely in *Christ's Poor*. Mrs. Watson, however, is another matter. She was not only the first patient, but a friend made at the time Rose Hawthorne Lathrop was at the cancer hospital. And she had so much character — not to say eccentricity — that she deeply impressed herself upon the consciousness of all those who knew her.

About six weeks after Mrs. Watson's departure from the circular ward at the hospital, Rose had established herself in the slums. And as Rose was aware that her venture was news, and that the publicity would be useful to her, she took pains to see that notices appeared in the New York papers about her plans for establishing a charity for the cancerous poor. It should be noted that from the very outset she depended entirely upon what she called "the daily charity of the public"; and from that principle she never departed. This was one of the means by which she obtained money to maintain her work; but in this instance it served to bring an appeal from Mrs. Watson. She wrote frankly asking for a home — complete support.

It was on one of those soft early autumn mornings, with a high, sunny wind and clouds blowing across the sky, that her letter reached Scammel Street, and Rose's heart went among the clouds at the thought that now her life of usefulness to others had really begun. She was about to welcome her first guest into her tumble-down tenement.

Later she came to think herself lucky that she had at that time very little real idea as to what she was attempting. But life was still wonderfully simple to her, and she expected to make this old woman happy until she died. She even had some wild notion that somehow she would not let Mrs. Watson die.

But what kind of house was this! In renting that miserable little apartment she had not thought of taking anybody to live with her, but merely of using it as a center from which she might view her terrain and do a little bandaging of such cases as came to her. She began to think again of a loft, where she could receive and nurse a number of sufferers.

Mrs. Watson had left the cancer hospital round and rosy. She arrived at Scammel Street — only a couple of months later — thin and pale. Rose would not have known her had it not been for the gleam of the prankish personality under the almost abject humility of the broken old woman. She did not need to tell the friend who welcomed her with such warm understanding that her face was dressed only twice a week now, and that for this she had to walk some distance to the dispensary. As though to make up for this, she was swathed in such oddly assorted clothes, and with so grotesque a veil wound round her head, that the women all down the street stuck their heads out of the window to look. Nor did Rose fail to see the absurdity of her appearance. She understood, however, that misery often does have absurdity for inseparable companion. Her heart went out in compassion.

The swathings in which Mrs. Watson had arrived made her appear almost robust. Seen at close quarters she was very weak, and she had greatly wasted in a couple of months. She arrived without stockings and in slippers. Her cough almost scattered her face in fragments every time it seized her. She had to put up hands shaking with pain to keep the pieces in place.

As that cough had to be dealt with at once, the first thing Rose did was to run to the drugstore. There she spent seventy-five cents on a cough mixture. It was just half of all the money she possessed in the world at the moment. But the money was well spent; Rose ever afterward had a grateful feeling about patent medicines. The entry book reads: "October 17, 1896 — Mrs. Mary Watson, about 65 years old — center of face largely eaten away by cancer — destitute — sent away from New York Cancer Hospital as inoperable after six months' stay, received into my little home."

Rose had to tell her guest the situation. "You had better understand what you are coming to," she said. "You are more than welcome if you'd like to come. But I can't be certain of having fire enough on the hearth for cold days, or enough bread and milk."

The blue eyes smiled at her over the bandages: "That's all right, dearie," she said, "we've always been good friends. With you I'll gladly starve and freeze. Why," she cried, gazing on the bright yellow floor and the wood fire, "this is heaven!"

It was at once tacitly settled between them that Rose was the daughter — she was addressed as such — and Mrs. Watson was the mother who directed and advised in everything. And Mrs. Watson was so gentle and intuitive that there seemed nothing odd about the arrangement — at all events not in Mrs. Watson's eyes. She was most anxious to be of service, and would leap to help and anticipate needs. Rose even decided that those bright blue Irish eyes could see round corners. She it was who took it upon herself to answer the door; and she knew by instinct how to classify and deal with callers.

She was so anxious to help that Rose became anxious in her turn lest the feeble old woman would do too much. Too much could easily bring on a fatal hemorrhage. The day after her arrival Rose said to her, "Now, mother dear, I have to go out for a little while, and I know the floor's terrible, but don't you dare to scrub it. I'll do that when I get back."

"*I?*" said "mother dear," putting on the air of a dowager countess, "*I?* Of course I wouldn't do it. Don't have any fear about that, daughter."

All the same, Rose hurried home, as she had a good deal of fear. There, sure enough, was Mrs. Watson on her hands and knees scrubbing away.

It was a strange life they lived together, making their tea and coffee, like gypsies, on the open fire in a saucepan propped up on bricks. What little food they got came from a loan from Julian. Yet they were not only happy together, but Rose had a radiance of happiness — kindled by a feeling that she was being of use to Mrs. Watson — also in a sense of freedom from the really unnecessary "necessities" to which she had so long been accustomed. It was for her like breathing the clean salt air of mid-ocean.

And Mrs. Watson was such good company. In the evening after supper she used to sit folding and unfolding the corners of her apron while she told some Irish tale with all the skill of her gifted race. She showed herself an artist in her preamble, her pauses, the middle with its little surprises artfully arranged to hold the attention as she went on. Rose sat there fascinated, spellbound. Now and then the storyteller stopped a moment to groan. Then after the pang had safely slipped past, she went on with her story. In later years when smug or gushing people annoyed Rose by commenting on her "wonderful work" she used to retort: "I'm glad you think so. At closer quarters you might think the poor unattractive, the sick poor nauseating. I can't say that I do this work because I get excitement or pleasure out of it." But in the case of Mrs. Watson there was an Irish charm that made even hardships delightful to bear in her company.

One of the two rooms in that little tenement — three, if one counted a tiny kitchen — had to be used as a kind of dispensary. For Mrs. Watson, Rose managed to squeeze in a cot in a bedroom which already seemed too small for one bed. Their only window opened on a stable wall a foot away, though somehow a good deal of air got in. Rose had heard that there was some danger of contracting cancer by proximity, and she knew that she was putting her disbelief to the test in sleeping side by side with Mrs. Watson. She discovered a new joy in proving that she was safe.

Nor was that all. Mrs. Watson saved her life. Working so hard and going out, disregarding possible consequences, in all weather gave Rose pneumonia.

It attacked her suddenly in the middle of the night. Twice she was swept from head to foot with a chilly wave, and afterward she did not think she could have survived a third. But Mrs. Watson was alert.

"You stay there, daughter," she said, "and don't worry. There's a nurse upstairs. Just wait until I can get this old coat of mine on over my nightgown and I'll call her. You'll be all right, dearie. You'll be all right."

Rose Lathrop did recover, but she could hardly have done so except for Mrs. Watson's prompt action; and it is rather wonderful that she survived pneumonia suffered in those cheerless rooms so bereft of all comforts. The nurse would look in every now and then and tell Mrs. Watson what to do, and Doctor Coyle made his visits, but after all, it was Mrs. Watson whose devotion brought her safely through this danger right at the start. The dying woman cared for the woman who had come there to look after the dying.

Every evening now, instead of a wonderful tale of Ireland and in the Irish manner, Mrs. Watson came and knelt beside Rose's bed, in her own suffering, to say the rosary for her. Rose all that time held a relic of a saint in her hand. And there beside the bed was Mrs. Watson's offering of prayer and pain. There seemed to be something holy about the poor, quiet, broken old soul kneeling there in peaceful hopefulness and yet calm resignation to whatever God's love and wisdom chose.

"But Rose," said one of her former friends, who had heard she was seriously ill and who had come to visit her, "how can you possibly endure the sight of such a terrible disfigurement?"

"She has been very good to me."

"I daresay she has. But to hear how affectionately you talk to her! You with your refinement and appreciation of beauty! — how can you look at her without shuddering?"

"Well, I can. Perhaps it's because I love her. Sometimes I wonder whether I am worthy of her love."

CHAPTER IV

First Recruits

In March, 1897, as the city was at last going to pull down the long-condemned 1 Scammel Street, Rose rented four rooms at 668 Water Street, where afterward a second floor of four rooms was taken. It was considered palatial after Scammel Street, and if that is the case the mind reels in horror trying to imagine what Scammel Street could have been like.

The picture before me of the Water Street house shows something that it would be hard to match in any American city today, and impossible to find in New York — a wooden house, very poorly built, of two stories and of a basement that clearly was used to being occupied, as its windows were above ground. There were no shutters on the ground floor, nor any steps leading to the front door. And though, at the time the picture was taken — presumably shortly after Mrs. Lathrop had gone elsewhere — there seem to have been people upstairs, the ground floor and the basement were completely abandoned and were rotting away. One can see that at no time could this have been other than a wretched hovel; yet this hovel was a palace compared to 1 Scammel Street. The dirt could have been cleared away, and that of course was the first thing done. The bedbugs and the rats took a little longer— but sprays and a collection of cats finished that job. But the squalor and the heat in those small rooms under that low, all-but-level roof — from these there was no escape. The work took up so much time that the diary — it really had not been a diary proper before — stopped for nearly a year. Then Rose wrote: "No chance for making these notes has been found between these dates (September 29, 1896, and September 17, 1897); nursing from five to eleven at night, or doing all it involved to set out as a nurse, soon prevented my sitting up till two A.M. to write description of the East Side." Yet one of the first entries – that for September 21st – like many that follow – runs: "I forgot to ring the Angelus, being ill and very busy. Alas, what a scatterbrain I am." Nevertheless by the 29th she was praying for a first-class Remington typewriter for her work. She was putting the finishing touches to her book on her father.

In the account Rose Hawthorne Lathrop wrote later of 668 Water Street she called it "a house now justly torn to bits," and "a place so small and tumble-down that it surprised its friends in serving the few poor sick so well." But for the rest her account is very cheerful, and for her it marked an important stage in her career, because, for the first time, she had, on however small a scale, a hospital, whereas at Scammel Street she had been able to take in – or squeeze in – only two guests. Now there were from the start three patients and, as soon as the other floor was rented, seven.

There was a constant stream of visitors – the poor looking for help, and the more well to do who had come to bring help. All had to enter through a little low-ceilinged kitchen, through which they passed into the sitting room. There, rich and poor alike, stood speechless at the oddity of the scene: it seemed to be a warehouse that had been commandeered by an unusually pious set of ship-wrecked pirates for a place of worship. On one of the walls hung a great black crucifix. There were a couple of small plaster statues – of the Sacred Heart and the Blessed Virgin – on the table, before which a votive lamp hung by a chain from the ceiling.

The warehouse impression was conveyed by several boxes of secondhand clothes – for which there was always a demand – and an office table bestrewn with letters. Another table held their medical supplies – mostly salves and bandages. At almost any time one of the "out patients" would be having a wound dressed by one of the nurses behind a screen. The screen was used because all visitors had to be received in this queer crowded room, which, by having quite given up every hope of conventional dignity, managed to be reasonably comfortable. Everything was perfectly neat and clean; and patients, as well as nurses, remembering Scammel Street, said, "This is heaven!"

These nurses were picked up by Mrs. Lathrop anywhere. None of them were paid of course, and no services — as any kind of help was so desperately needed — could be refused. But except for a few instances, such as everybody in such work has encountered — of a few scatterbrained enthusiasts who oh *do* so much want to help others, and then, when it comes to the point, do nothing at all — this unpaid help was that of the most valuable kind, much too good to pay for.

Even those who couldn't do any actual nursing — like Rose's young nieces Hildegarde and Beatrix, Julian's daughters — were pressed into services within their powers, if only reading aloud to bedridden patients. It is not very safe to get too close to an enthusiast: immediately you have a task assigned to you; you may even catch the infection of enthusiasm yourself.

But, of course, what were needed above all were not people who dropped in occasionally to lend a hand, but people who would devote themselves completely to the work. Of those who did want to help several, like dear, goodhearted, rather sentimental Alice Wheeler, were very quickly overcome when they discovered what it was they had to do. They cannot be blamed. Heroism is a rare quality. And merely to endure the constant odor of cancer calls for heroism — to say nothing of the bandaging of horrible wounds.

One of these helpers — perhaps the first regular helper Mrs. Lathrop had — was Mary Mahoney. She was there waiting when Rose returned from some work that had taken her into the streets.

"I hope you haven't been here a long time," Rose asked. "You see, I'm obliged every now and then to go to my patients, to change their dressings, and make them comfortable for the night."

"I did not mind in the least," Miss Mahoney explained. "Your patient and I have had a nice little chat, haven't we?" she said, smiling at Mrs. Watson. "But to come to the object of my visit: I have had some experience in nursing, and am here to offer my assistance, if you will have me."

"Do you realize what kind of work this is? Early and late — no time for reading or writing — and usually very repulsive work, too."

"I know about what to expect," Mary Mahoney answered, "and I still would like to come."

"Then thank God for answering my prayer."

About the same time came Mrs. Margaret Corcoran. She was very useful but before the end of the year presented a problem by declining into a galloping consumption. Fortunately, as we see by the diary, a Miss Spety, "my dear friend the trained nurse [presumably the one who had come to the rescue when Rose had pneumonia], came and offered some weeks of nursing free . . . just as we were at a loss what to do for some one to nurse, scientifically, Mrs. Corcoran. Praise be to God." Even so Mrs. Corcoran died.

The previous January 6th the diary reads: "Miss ——* came to help me . . . and convinced me that she must stay." And Ellen Ryan had promised to come on February 1st for life. But from the absence of further reference to Miss Ryan she evidently changed her mind about the work; as for Miss ——, Mrs. Lathrop changed her mind about *her*. Not all at once though. Two weeks later the diary reads: "Miss —— appears to be *most* desirable, does quantities of work, *most* thoroughly, and seems to mean to stay always."

But four days later we find: "Miss ——'s inspiration to come

* As the lady referred to is still living, her name is omitted here.

to us has this early seemed to her an unbearable cross, as she cannot endure the smells and sights and turns out to be rather flighty, in spite of her efficiency in cleaning a room. She has been up to Miss Swift and Mrs. McGinley and shown her queer streaks, and I must give her up at once." These disillusioning experiences are common enough in all such enterprises, and there is no doubt that few things can be harder to bear than hard monotonous work among cancer patients, who are never going to get well and whose wounds and their constant odor are very disgusting. Poor Miss ——! She cannot be blamed. She meant well, but it was a bit too much for her.

The general situation — the urgent need for help and the difficulty in securing it — appears in a letter written on July 3, 1898, to Sister Marie Elise of Mount St. Vincent's-on-the-Hudson. This Sister had sent Mrs. Lathrop a young woman who wanted to help.* "Miss ——," Rose Lathrop writes, "charmed us at once, and has now been here to help us one afternoon, and 'does my heart good' by not *balking*. Oh, that is such a provoking failure of most would-be heroines. She does *just* what I ask, even if averse to it, without a trace of aversion: with that good cheer which means a soldier spirit.

"No better life, I am more and more convinced, can be carried on by women of intelligence, and I long to have truly intelligent and noble women adopt it, for I can never myself make it the growth it should be. I am sorry to say, this is true.

"Send me more strong young women, or delicate brave ones! Not that I make bold to assume that any of them will *join us* or stay long, but good might come in reasonable proportions."

Then she explains that the last two sentences were written a

* This is a different person from the one mentioned above. It is she who has given this letter to Georgetown University, but with the stipulation that her name be omitted, as she did not remain at Water Street.

day apart, as she had had to stop to dictate an article to a stenographer friend who had come from up town for the purpose. "So," she continues, "my foolish time is broken up without order hourly, but I am glad I am so foolish as to hasten into everything regardless of the consequences, regardless of system — for a dead stop would occur if I waited for wisdom and a corps of assistants, before beginning our attack upon the cruelty of non-action for cancerous poor. . . . Pray for me, I beseech you, that true charity may take possession of my hard heart."

By the time that letter was written the turning point had already been reached, the survival of the work was already assured. This probably was something that Rose Lathrop did not suspect as yet. For already she had been frequently enough disappointed in those who had come to help not to be discouraged at times. Her own mind, moreover, was still so uncertain as to what the outcome of all this was going to be that she operated merely on a day-by-day basis, performing the immediate task, and leaving the future in the hands of God. She can hardly be said to have had any plans more definite than that.

But on the afternoon of December 15, 1897, a young woman named Alice Huber set out to visit her carrying a letter of introduction from the celebrated Father Fidelis of the Cross, a Passionist, who had formerly been celebrated in other ways. At Dixwell's School and again at Harvard this grandson of Chancellor Kent, the "American Blackstone," had carried off all the honors, even in face of the formidable competition of young Oliver Wendell Holmes, the future Chief Justice. He had married, and was the father of several daughters, and held the presidency of Hobart College, when his wife died. He had joined the Catholic Church, and upon his wife's death had entered the Paulist Congregation and was ordained, with the understanding that, should he ever be free to do so, he would become a Passionist. This door was opened to him by a wealthy Californian couple, the O'Connors, who adopted the children, but with the proviso that their father was to surrender not only his legal but his natural rights — he was not to see his daughters again. President Theodore Roosevelt said of this tall, masterful, and famous man, "that even if he *was* a monk you could hear the clank of his sabre as he strode along."

Alice Huber, the daughter of a doctor in Kentucky, had got to know the Passionists very well in her home state, and through them Father Fidelis, who had sent her a letter of introduction from Rome. She was a painter — and a good one — holding a position as instructor in art in New York. But she had read some newspaper account of Mrs. Lathrop's work for the cancerous poor and felt she would like to meet her. She little realized what was in store for her when she set out for 668 Water Street that December day.

Her diary tells of what happened. She found the dilapidated frame building. There was no bell, but the door was open, and as she stood there hesitating, some children playing in the street called to her, "If you are looking for Mrs. Lathrop, go to that door." They pointed to one at the end of the hall.

She entered, as did everybody, straight into the little kitchen, but went at once into the living room which Rose has described as half warehouse, and half church. It also served as a spare bedroom when a new patient arrived.

A fair, bright-faced young woman — she looked young even at forty-six — dressed in nurse's uniform and with a mane of red hair got up from the floor, where she was kneeling bandaging an old woman's leg and said, "Do sit down until I finish; then we can have a nice long talk."

Alice sat down upon the only comfortable thing she could see in the room — an old green sofa — and took in the scene. She noticed how clean everything was, but also how poor and bare. And it touched her to see Mrs. Lathrop's cheerful and simple manner with her patients, some of whom were clearly very exacting. One of them was a bad-tempered-looking old woman with a stick which she kept firmly planted before her, ready for instant use, while she scowled at her companions. And Alice was to record that the old lady with the stick proved to be, upon further acquaintance, as fierce as her appearance suggested.

Alice had come there with the idea of offering to help a few hours every week. But the horrible wounds she saw being dressed and the pervasive, disgusting smell made her feel inclined to draw back. The contrast between these women, who formed that day a lifelong association, was this: where Mrs. Lathrop's heroism was headlong, carrying all before it like a charge of cavalry, Miss Huber's was of the dour sort that manned the redoubt. To her dying day — over forty years later — the sight of cancer and its odor were repulsive to her. This is very clear from the diary she kept, and it is the measure of her sacrifice.

She agreed to go to Water Street one afternoon each week, and Mrs. Lathrop took her to the street door to point the most direct way to the Grand Street ferry. Turning back, Alice looked at her standing in the wretched, tumbledown doorway, the only bright thing in all that ugliness and misery. And at that moment a feeling of pity and affection for this woman filled her. The grace of God operated through a warm, human love.

The following Tuesday Alice went to help in the dispensary, as she had promised, but felt what seemed to her the very maximum of disgust. As to this her diary reads: "God must have put that feeling into my heart. He wanted me to come and help build up the work, and I didn't want to come and still I had the feeling of wanting to do some good. I came the next Tuesday to help and I must say that I loathed everything about the place and still I forced myself to dress a frightful sore that makes me sick to think of it, even to this day."* But Mrs. Lathrop seemed so cheerful and happy, and looked at her so pleadingly as she was leaving that Alice, who was on the point of saying she could not stand it, said instead that she would come again the following week — and this soon became two afternoons a week.

* Aug. 30, 1901, the day she began her diary.

That Rose Lathrop herself had no idea as to the outcome of that visit is evident from her own diary, in which it is not even mentioned. On December 16th she added a notation later which, without referring to Miss Huber, says: "Letter in answer to two from Father Fidelis"; but on the following January 4th — this also is a note added later — we find: "Alice Huber decided to give her life to the work!" The entry on the 16th contains this: "On the 11th beloved Alice Huber assured me, again, that she would soon be with me, only a previous promise preventing her from staying 'then and there.'" That same day she could write: "Ellen Ryan promises to come on the 1st of February for life. So has St. Anthony, in 3 weeks answered my appeal for 'subjects.' Glory be to God." To complete the good news, Mrs. Cockran — so Rose misspelled the name — assured her three days later that she had decided to stay. The use of the word "subjects" here, even though it always appears in inverted commas, shows that Mrs. Lathrop already regarded her work as that of a religious community.

And so it was, though of course it had no standing as such in canon law. Mrs. Lathrop had a husband. Nobody there was bound by any obligation but did everything as the free offering of charity. But there would have been no work at all except for the religious motive. Very gladly did she accept help, not only in money but in personal services, offered by Protestants or Jews; but even at this stage it was a distinctively Catholic charity. On March 16th she writes: "I promised to love our dearest Lord to the exclusion of all else. Also to work *much harder*. I have begun to realize that our Lord loves me, even me, & every one."

On March 25th, 1898, Alice Huber joined Rose Lathrop.* Not till then did Alice fully realize the hardship of her life. It was

---

* That is her own reckoning. Actually she seems to have gone to Water Street the evening before — according to R. H. L.'s diary.

work, early and late, unceasing work, often far into the night. There was no time for reading, or even to write letters home; and Alice grew very homesick — all the more so as her pious father and mother, who probably would have approved her entering a convent, definitely disapproved of the strange unclassifiable life she was leading.

Her friend, the Passionist Father Edward, however, writing to her from Baltimore on January 21, 1898, said: "Dear child Alice: Your great & heroic resolution did of course surprise, I may say — startle and alarm me at first — in such sort that I know not what to answer, — & feared to write back at once, — lest I should say any but the right thing." But having thought and prayed about the matter, he concludes, "In the name of God continue as you have begun."

A little later an undated letter from him says: "Were I a St. Francis de Sales I would be only too glad to go on and take charge of you two girls." And from Italy on December 17, 1902, he wrote to tell her: "Our soul is not more present to our body than He is to body and soul, or in the words of St. Paul of the Cross, 'He is more present to us than we are to ourselves.' The practical moral of this fundamental truth, dear Alice, is that we can and must be near to each other in God, and that when we go a long journey, we do not leave our friends so far behind."

The coming of Alice Huber was marked by her going with Rose to the 5 o'clock Mass at St. Gabriel's where the Passionists were conducting a mission. They received Holy Communion together, and then assisted at the Mass of Father Edmund Hill at the Blessed Virgin's altar. "He was like an angel," the diary reads, "so simple, so absorbed, so peace-giving. He offered the Mass for Alice and me."

This Father Edmund Hill was another remarkable man. His father was an Anglican clergyman, and, after being educated at Oxford, young Hill was already in deacon's orders when he fell in love with a beautiful Irish Catholic. He followed her to New

York, and there she entered the Society of the Sacred Heart and he, a little later, the Catholic Church and then the Passionist Congregation. It was friends like these that encouraged this heroic enterprise in the slums of New York.

Hardly had Alice Huber gone to Water Street when Rose Lathrop fell ill, so that everything had to be supported by Alice's untrained shoulders. "However," she placidly remarks, "she soon recovered and all went on as usual." But if this was so, it was because of Miss Huber's presence. She had nothing of Mrs. Lathrop's surging enthusiasm, but she brought something without which that enthusiasm might have failed. This was a steady persistence of industry and a cool practical good sense. It was a much needed balance. Here again was the proof that most great projects are brought to success by the co-operation of two or more people, each of whom supplies what the other lacks, while being stimulated or checked (as need be) by qualities perceived in the other partner of the team. Alice did have — and in her diary admitted having — Irish melancholy, derived from her mother, and a kind of halfhearted belief in the superstitions of Kentucky. She could be a bit moody at times, and there is no doubt that she displayed all through life strongly marked idiosyncrasies; but her value to the work Mrs. Lathrop had started is beyond all calculations. She was just the right second-in-command, a gift straight out of heaven.

Everything, so she noted in her diary, was extremely poor. Pine boxes served as chairs. Meals were taken by the nurses with such patients as were able to be up and about. These were eaten, as there was no other place, in the kitchen.

Concerning this there is a piece of paper pasted into Alice Huber's diary on page 7 — in all probability years later. She confessed that she never became reconciled to using the same dishes as the cancer patients. But Mrs. Lathrop noticed this and was watching. On one occasion Alice put a clean glass in a special place where she could get it again for her own use.

"What's that for?" asked Rose.

Alice was cornered. "For myself another time, Rose."

Rose shook her head, "No Alice, you'd better put it with the rest of the glasses."

Alice Huber never made that mistake again.

Nor was that all poor Alice Huber had to accept. After lying awake at night hearing a patient groan, it seemed that all day long in the adjoining kitchen the pots and pans rattled; and then when night came again, if the patients happened to be quiet for once, the people in the neighborhood would be quarrelsome, or a cat start wailing. This incessant assault on her nerves was past all bearing, and yet was borne.

The summer of 1898 was unusually hot, and the Water Street tenement stifling. The old, cracked walls were infested with bedbugs and the roof leaked. The room Alice shared with Rose had pans all over the floor to catch the dripping rain water. And winter was as cold as summer was hot. The patients were comfortable enough in their beds, but Alice and Rose in their little unheated room nearly froze to death. And Alice, unlike her friend, did not have the buoyant resources of gaiety to carry her through difficulties; all she could do was grimly stick it out. Never for an instant did she think of abandoning the work.

Relatives or friends of Rose's would also come around and after having watched an hour in speechless horror would say to her, "But this is impossible! You must stop and come away. I have seen nothing so dreadful in my life."

Others took it lightly, as one of her whims or poetic fantasies: "Well, Rose," these would say, "when you get tired just let us know."

Others again left in a thoughtful silence, without making any attempt to persuade Rose to give up her work. They could not but see how happy she was, and they were moved when they observed what it was she was doing.

To one who wrote begging her at least to move to a less

dangerous district she replied: "I shall never permit myself to deny anyone assistance because of any reason that springs from my own convenience, [but] listen only to the good pleasure of our Divine Master which always advocates the cause of the poor."

If there were moments now and then when, the work seeming even more weary and thankless than usual, she was tempted by thoughts of the pleasantness and ease that she could have by stretching out her hand, always at such times God sent a burst of sunlight to restore peace in her soul. She was discovering that to be one with the poor wholeheartedly brought a sort of joyous inebriation of the energies, something that uplifted body and soul. By that joy she felt herself more than repaid.

As for the difficulties of nursing, she used to get quite impatient with those who used to say, "Oh, but I could never do it!"

"Nonsense!" Mrs. Lathrop used to tell them. "Any woman can be a nurse if she chooses. I'm speaking of any normal woman, of course, not arrant fools; all that's needed is courage and compassion."

"But what do you accomplish, Rose?" her friends protested.

"I'll tell you. If any sacrifice we make causes those who come into contact with us to have even a single layer of their meanly disposed hearts thaw a little — *that* will be accomplishment enough. So much can be done in a minute. Why, it takes only a minute to decide to die to self!"

She used to insist that St. Vincent de Paul had the right idea. "If ten women in every parish," so she declared, "undertook to set themselves apart, free of pay — but with a bank account for the poor — and would look after cases of destitution and severe sickness; and if each of these then tried to win recruits, in a single year New York would have no cases of incurable sickness uncared for in the slums, or any case of a poor person hurried to the Island against her will. There would be no more of those dark sick-rooms — abominations! No hungry invalids! No children sleeping in the family bed with a consumptive! What *couldn't* be accomplished in a year by consecrated women! Yet what does one find on looking around on women? One is thunderstruck. Take the ordinary female out of her home, and you have something so ridiculous upon your hands that you fall into a panic. Put her on a committee and see what happens. I'll tell you — gossip and flattery and back-biting and snickerings and the consuming of refreshments! But one woman with a purpose among them — what cannot she effect! There is a tenacity about a woman's convictions, when she consents to have any, that holds better than her masculine rivals. I daresay our venture in this work may be made with some stupidity, but a general does not send his men home because they are unintelligent. What they have to do is to stand firm under fire. So we, as we realize that this usefulness of ours is largely a matter of menial service, are able to accept our mediocrity humbly and without much grumbling. When God commanded us to love people and to help them, He took our mediocrity into account."

"But just what is it we have to *do*, Rose?" her friends listening to the eager and somewhat scornful exposition, would ask.

"*Do?* Give ourselves! That's all. We must give our compassion as we would give it to our own families, if we were really generous. But of course it does call for the sacrifice of your life. That's why Christ asks it and blesses the simple choice with an unending reward."

But those who saw what was called for marveled. An Episcopalian deaconess came to Rose one day. "Could you come with me, Mrs. Lathrop?" she asked. Rose at once put on her hat, and they went out together.

In the poor house they entered, the suffering woman, whom she had never seen before, seemed to Rose her own sister. She had it brought home to her then: this *was* her sister.

The woman was lying on a tattered, black, horsehair sofa, her head resting on a pillow dark with grime. Over her was thrown a ragged quilt, cheap, soiled, torn. The room stank. A son, about eighteen years old, slipped away as soon as they arrived, obviously glad to leave. The sufferer's breath came in gasps; her face glistened with the swelling and sweat of her agony. Her eyes glared out in horror.

One arm had swollen to an enormous size. Her side, where she had suffered an operation on a heroic scale, had around it bandages left on for a week. These had become like rock, stiff with pus and blood. But two hours later she was at 668 Water Street. They got her to bed, and she smiled up at them and murmured, "This is heaven." It was what nearly all of them said.

Then there was the case of Miss Mason.

So many times a day a knock came at their door. This time they saw a woman tall, ladylike, elderly, pale, and shabbily dressed in black.

"Oh, I am very tired!" were her first words.

"Come in here, then, and sit down."

"No! I cannot come in. Can't you see why?"

"I see you need a good rest," said Mrs. Lathrop.

The woman groaned. "No, let me sit out here. Nobody will let me go near them any more."

They gave her the chair she asked for — out in the passage, and a glass of wine kept for the last hours of the sick. It revived her and she went on: "I need your help. I have read about your nursing the cancerous poor. Well, I'm one of them. But I was too proud to come to you until — until I became so ill and so obnoxious to everybody."

She spoke haltingly, after seeming to be about to faint from weakness and abased dignity. Listening to her, Mrs. Lathrop and Mrs. Corcoran wept.[*]

"What shall I do, if you will not receive me as a patient?"

---

[*] The account of this given in *Christ's Poor* (Jan., 1904) makes it clear that the "other nurse" in this scene was by then dead. So it could not have been Miss Huber. The one answering the description at Water Street when this took place is Mrs. Corcoran.

she exclaimed suddenly. The nurses stood there weeping silently — weeping because they could not take her.

"I didn't know," she went on, "what it was like here — so small, and you, so poor yourselves. You cannot take me, can you?"

Rose sobbed, "All our beds are full."

Miss Mason whitened at this and began to rise from her chair.

"Then there is nothing for me but suicide," she said. "I will go."

Rose put an arm round her.

"Then you are not a Catholic — if you talk of suicide!"

"No, I am not a Catholic. Would that prevent my being admitted?"

"No, indeed. The only difficulty is that we are so crowded already."

Rose beckoned to gentle hearted Margaret Corcoran. They went into the kitchen, and shut the door, leaving Miss Mason in the hall. They were both trembling as they took each other by the hand and looked into one another's eyes.

"We can't let her go, can we?" whispered Rose.

"How can we?" sobbed Margaret.

"Would *you* turn her away, Margaret?" As Margaret did not answer Rose went on. "Of course you could not. Nor will I. We would die instead. It is for such cases that we have started this work."

When they returned to Miss Mason she was crouching against the wall, huddled in a fragile heap upon the kitchen chair.

"We are going to take you," were the words that roused her to joy.

But she surprised them by saying, "Not yet. I can manage for several weeks more. I'll come to you when my money is used up. Oh, thank you for saying I may come!"

It seemed unlikely they thought, as they watched her creeping away, that she would have the strength to creep back. But she did, obviously dying and supported by nothing but her will.

Somehow as soon as she knocked on the door, three weeks later, both Mrs. Lathrop and Mrs. Corcoran knew who was there.

They had no bedroom for her, only a bed in the sitting room behind a screen.

"My heart is so weak!" Miss Mason whispered. "I thought I was going to die on my way here."

Rose had to cut her clothes off. This took two hours, and both patient and nurse were exhausted. Rose had never seen anything so unimaginably terrible. Now for the first time in a year Miss Mason was comfortable. Murmuring her thanks she fell asleep.

The next day she did die. In a suitcase was a Bible with passages marked — those appropriate to the wretched and friendless. In the margins were comments in her handwriting. She had appealed to God and in Him had found a friend.

Also in the suitcase was forty dollars. She had said something about this, but they thought she was delirious. But no, to her last hour she had shown she was a woman of honor whose word was to be redeemed. The money was for her funeral.

In the words written during the first year of her work, though not published until 1902, Rose Hawthorne Lathrop said that sometimes when she stood in her little room with her money almost exhausted, the distance up rich Fifth Avenue seemed as far and as frozen as Alaska. She had to draw upon reserves of courage and develop a new skill to ask the well-to-do for funds to continue. Yet she had always a firm conviction that she only had to explain the need and that immediately the necessary help would be forthcoming.

"What am I trying to do down here among the poor?" she wrote. "To make impossible the homeless condition of incurable cancer patients; to make impossible their semi-neglect in homes that are unfit for them; to take the lowest class we know, both in poverty and suffering, and put them in such a condition, that if our Lord knocked at the door we should not be ashamed to show what we have done."

She continues by saying that she has two helpers at that time — Alice Huber had not as yet joined her — and they had five cancer patients, with another (presumably Miss Mason) expected soon. But she was also helping several other families. And she cheerfully admitted: "I have a reputation among some of those people, who judge one harshly and whose opinion is of less than no consequence, of rather liking to help drunkards. I never do if I know it, though I may some day help a drunkard in some manner, as a matter of high principle. I have looked for it, but cannot find a strict ruling out of sinners from charity." From which it is evident that Rose's compassion is edged — as all charity ought to be — not only with indignation but with scorn.

If one wants to find the motive for this charity one must look for it in Rose Hawthorne Lathrop's love of Christ. And here I must refer to two passages from her diary, written down in as offhand and matter-of-fact a way as anything else that was happening and which therefore are all the more revealing.

On January 16, 1898, she says that about two weeks before, just after Holy Communion, she had had a vision of our Lord. It is mentioned as casually as that. Again on March 24th, about four in the morning when "getting up, I joyfully prayed and saw our Lord, as if upon the Crucifix, not upright, but before being removed from the cross, after it was lowered."

As to the objectivity of this neither I nor any other man can say an affirmative word; but who shall deny the objectivity? There is not the slightest doubt, in my mind, that Rose Hawthorne Lathrop, whether it was with her physical eyes or the eyes of her soul, did see Christ.

And it was not, as one would have expected to see Him, hanging upon the cross, but as One about to be removed from it.

CHAPTER V

The Devil With Golden Curls

George maintained some contact with Rose, and this made her aware that the blow had hit him very hard. Yet what else could she do? Many and many a time had she been about to leave him — and actually did several times leave him for short periods — but each time her pity had overcome her judgment. Now she feared that he might make of the fact that she had gone away an excuse to let go what hold he had so far kept upon himself. He was publishing no books, though he was full of great schemes. Fortunately the opera he had made of *The Scarlet Letter* had been reasonably successful, and a man as proficient as he was, so capable of supplying editors promptly with the commissioned article or story, ought to be able to weather any sea. But when at last he sent her the tale he had written in collaboration with Edison, she saw how pitifully it had dwindled from the grandiose projection of it. What the newspapers had trumpeted as though it was almost an earth-shattering event turned out to be two installments in the *English Illustrated Magazine*. Rose surmised that, when it came to the point, Mr. Edison had somewhat failed George, but she could not help believing that George had also failed himself. His preliminary note ran: "This story is the result of conversations with Thomas A. Edison, the substance of which he afterwards put into the form of notes written for my use. His suggestions for inventions and changed mechanical, industrial and social conditions in the future here embodied, I understand to be simply hints as to what might possibly be accomplished. Mr. Edison assumes no responsibility for them — for the story itself I alone am responsible."

Poor George! Rose could so well remember how often he, though extremely competent, proved somewhat weak in inventiveness and had to turn to her to supply what he lacked. Here, not having her to fall back upon, she could see that he had stolen more leaves than one from Bellamy's *Looking Backward*. She read sadly, noticing the missed opportunity — for surely an opportunity had been missed, though she had never been very optimistic.

It was a tale about a young man placed in a state of suspended animation by a process called "vivification." He remains asleep, as it were, for three hundred years and is awakened about the year 2200. George brought in a great many references to "scientific" improvements in daily life; and she smiled to read that George — sanguine as ever — said that travel was largely by air! He told of all sorts of laborsaving devices and conveniences. She wished she could have a few in these poor rooms at Water Street. Oh, and so communication with Mars had been established! — a visitor from Mars was an intimate friend of George's hero. And of course he had supplied a "vivificated" girl — Eva — who belonged to the hero's (Bemis's) own century. For a while Bemis is inclined to love a girl of the new century, Electra by name, but finally he turns back to Eva and they visit Mars together. It did not seem to lead anywhere in particular. The mountain had brought forth a very small mouse.

Still, George had some interesting ideas. There was a "Federation of the World," which, if stolen from Tennyson's "Locksley Hall" was specified as one in which governmental functions were administered by "small, efficient, and responsible committees," though on a republican plan, instead of by parliaments, congresses, and mobs, as of old. And the supreme control was to be vested, Rose noted, in a world committee of twenty "and the fierce light of honor and responsibility and watchfulness that beats upon them gives them no chance to fool or prevaricate with the race." She read, "It is happier and pleasanter to be honest, and is the highest kind of diplomacy."

She closed the magazine and sat there thinking. If only the world committee would do something for the cancerous poor! How nice for George to be able to luxuriate in the building of his brave new world. She had to be satisfied with these little, shabby, crowded rooms on Water Street. There was Mrs. Watson groaning; Rose was brought down to earth in a hurry from her visit to Mars in the company of Bemis and Eva.

Rose seems to have attempted some literary work, though how she expected to get any done while performing the often endless and exhausting duties she had undertaken is past understanding. But she apparently hoped to keep her enterprise afloat with her pen, and of course the Hawthorne royalties she continued to receive. And it is evident from her having on hand a number of longish articles when she founded her little magazine *Christ's Poor*, in 1902, that they were turned out at Water Street. It may be surmised that she had written them to sell and had failed to do so. In all probability a good many of the unpublished manuscripts of hers still at Hawthorne, New York — stories and poems — were also produced in order to keep the charitable pot boiling. In this case the pressure under which she wrote and the constant interruptions might well account for their having been returned by editors as unsatisfactory.

She did however place a few articles, and it was at Water Street that she completed — by what heroic efforts it is impossible to say — her very charming *Memories of Hawthorne*. For though existing letters make it clear that she had been working on this off and on for some years — making her first sketch of it in her last year at the Wayside* — it was at Water Street that

* At all events she had written an undated letter about 1883, to Aldrich from 39 West Ninth Street, New York City, to complain of the lowness of Mr. Houghton's offer. And George wrote to Aldrich from 80 Washington Square, on Jan. 28, 1884: "[Mrs. Lathrop] was not only unwilling to let him have it on his terms, but extremely indignant at the smallness of

the project was at last brought to completion. This no doubt
explains the presence of "a young woman who helps me with
shorthand and typewriting" mentioned in the account of her
first year.*

We know something more about her *Memories of Hawthorne*.
An article covering part of it appeared in the *Century* in 1894,
and in 1896 four of its chapters were published in the *Atlantic
Monthly*. Rose's editorial methods deserve a word of comment.
As might be expected, she was not very accurate in the matter of
letters, amending freely, so much so that some of the letters
quoted in the *Century* and as given in the book are not quite
identical. Perhaps the explanation appears in a letter she wrote to
Gilder on July 6 [1893] — "My dear Richard: I should wish
to omit anything that might give pain to anyone, for my parents
never gave pain. . . . The extracts I sent you I had not had time to
ponder over, much; & I know that the life in them must not be
wrung out." On the other hand in an undated letter to Scudder
from Wellesley Hills — probably just before she went to the East
Side — she submits to being toned down a bit in relation to
something that she had said about Margaret Fuller: "I cannot
afford," she writes, "to seem more ill-natured than I am, so I
will explain that when I said I expected to print the Countess
d'Ossoli's letters in order to show how badly they could write in
those days, I meant that my father & mother shone the brighter
in their simplicity & culture . . . & I had not been able to resist
the desire to make apparent how much they had to overlook in
even some of the finest minds about them, who certainly dreaded
commonplace naturalness." It would seem that the solution finally
decided upon here was that, as Rose Hawthorne Lathrop could
not bring herself to quote Margaret Fuller's letters without

---

the sum and quite resolved, therefore, to keep the sketch out of his hands
altogether."

* *Christ's Poor*, Vol. I, No. 12 (1902), pp. 15-16.

remarking on Margaret's literary affectations, it would be kinder not to quote them at all.

If she did any doctoring of letters, it must be remembered that Julian did too, and that the practice was common at the time and not regarded as reprehensible. Poor Sophia Hawthorne has been severely criticized for bowdlerizing her husband's notebooks; and it is evident, from a letter to Scudder written a year or two later and which will be noticed at the proper place, that Sophia's daughter approved of what her mother had done. On the other hand there is the undated letter to Houghton, Mifflin and Company, headed 668 Water Street, which takes a somewhat different line when her own father and mother are not concerned. She tells her publishers that Mrs. Melville has been asking to have certain omissions made from her husband's letters in the *Memories of Hawthorne*. "I have argued with her by letter," Mrs. Lathrop tells her publishers, "as well as I know how, but this does not seem to have made her any happier than she was before. If I can or should do anything about having the words erased, will you let me know? Perhaps the opinion of some one else would, if favorable to my idea of leaving a man of genius safely in care of his own expression, have effect in inducing Mrs. Melville to let the printed record stand as it is." However Rose herself did not apply such a principle strictly in the case of her own parents — and Mrs. Melville seems to have had her way in this instance, for on page 156 of the *Memories* a letter from Melville to Hawthorne ends with the three dots that would seem to indicate an omitted passage.* It is probably safe enough to guess that it was another allusion on Melville's part to the anticipated joys of metaphysics over a quart of liquor.

Whatever Rose Hawthorne Lathrop's general principle, her practice appears in a rather touching postscript to one of the letters from Water Street to Houghton, Mifflin: "I believe I spoke

---

* Many of the Melville and Hawthorne letters are apparently being secretly held by some collector or dealer. So there is no means of checking the published text. This is one of those letters.

in my last note in a way to clearly show I feel my father and mother to be aware of all I do and write. I hope you will pardon my obdurance about it."

In all probability Rose had been working hard on this manuscript of hers in the year between leaving George and her commencing the cancer work — one surmises in the quiet retirement of Wellesley Hills. And certainly a tremendous improvement was effected on the preliminary sketches of those chapters which, though they contain omitted material useful to this book, were far below what she finally published. Yet it is clear that the finishing touches to the *Memories of Hawthorne* were given at odd minutes during the day, or late at night, at Scammel Street and her second place of abode in the New York slums. More than ever must the wealth of Rose's experiences and the physical circumstances of her childhood have stood in glaring contrast to the wretchedness and poverty with which she was surrounded. She weighed this as a matter of no consequence whatever. She had found at last her life's work; the book had to be disposed of as a way of clearing the deck for action. When she had discharged her duty to her father's memory, the world could make no further call upon her.

The first patient to be received into her apartment by Rose Hawthorne Lathrop was still with her. This was Mrs. Watson who, until cancer and the morphine she had been secretly taking for some time combined to wreck her, was the pride and comfort of Rose's life. Mrs. Watson was greatly changed from what she had been when she was in the cancer hospital, but while living with Rose she changed even more. Sometimes she would say in a low, sad voice, "When my sight goes, daughter, I shall go insane."

There was another change — experience was to teach Mrs. Lathrop that it was all too common among cancer patients —

which overtook this hitherto good, sensible Irish countrywoman. To be provided for, in conditions better than known before, offers a temptation an untrained mind seldom resists very well. There are many people who come to take what is done for them so much for granted, that they become insolent in their ease and at last unreasonably exacting. Worst of all, they develop craftiness and deceit.

Mrs. Watson was too kind — and also too intelligent — to go to the extremes of some others whom Rose was to encounter, but when she moved out of Scammel Street to the relative luxury — poor as it was — of Water Street, she began to give herself airs as being the first and, as she supposed, the specially privileged patient. By way of asserting her position, she began to invite her relatives around.

Now for the first time Rose discovered about Mrs. Watson's two daughters. When they appeared she saw they were handsome and strong young women; she also noticed that they nearly always smelled of drink. And with their appearance upon the scene their mother began to sink to their level. She was from now on turning over every parcel of secondhand clothes that arrived and begging — hesitatingly, gently, but very insistently — for the best things among them.

"Sure, and me daughters have nothing to put on!" was her explanation. And Rose did not like giving things to women who, she felt sure, at once took them to the pawnshop.

It seemed impossible, yet it was true that the class of people living around them in Water Street was still lower than those they had recently left. Yet even if Mrs. Lathrop had wished — as she did not — to hold herself aloof from the life of the neighborhood, she could hardly have done so. She knew she was at liberty to leave, but as she had gone there to be of service she threw herself, as it were, under everybody's feet.

In Mrs. Watson's case there was a kind of recontamination with the corruption from which she had, for a while, escaped. Now she reverted to her element, and her old tendency to play the clown, as she had an audience again, showed itself. Somehow in the close quarters of Water Street it seemed more out of place than it had been in the large circular ward of the cancer hospital. Though she never asked for whiskey, knowing very well that she would not get it, Rose felt that she was hankering for it in her evening reflections. Yet in a moment, if her help was needed in an emergency, or some little problem came up, Mrs. Watson would completely rouse herself from her lethargy and be bright and noble.

As she was now unable to go to the Catholic protectory to visit her grandson, little Willie of the golden curls, Mrs. Lathrop arranged to have him brought to Water Street — "that angelic child more beautiful than an infant cherub imagined by the greatest artist." And indeed a couple of his silky locks, kept by Mrs. Watson in a little box which hung in a bag carried under her skirt, did show a beautiful gold. "Ah, and the sweet child!" Mrs. Watson would say, gazing at the hair, "if I do say it meself, daughter. . . ." And the fond grandmother would expatiate with Irish eloquence upon the charms and virtues of dear little Willie.

As soon as Rose saw his sharp face a shiver ran through her. The gold had darkened, and the eyes of the boy showed a satanic cunning and effrontery. She saw at once that he was a criminal in the making, that the angel would soon prove himself a little devil.

Even so, Rose decided that to accept him was part of her bargain with Mrs. Watson. The grandmother's pride in the boy, and her joy that he was there, were things that had to be respected. With the reflection, "Well, perhaps now that we've got him we can develop him along other lines," Rose steeled herself to meet what her intuition told her was going to be a difficult situation.

"Now, Willie," she said to him, "I suppose they taught you your catechism at the protectory."

"Yes, ma'am."

"Then let me hear you. Who made you?"

He knew all the answers, rattling them off without hesitation, but with no more interest in the matter than in the multiplication tables. And Mrs. Watson, seeing the good account he was giving of himself, beamed with pleasure.

"He *likes* studying it," she said proudly, "I taught it to him meself long ago."

Rose began to have hopes of him. Perhaps that look of mystic vagueness in his eyes — that was how she thought of it afterward, at the time she thought perhaps it showed a gentle truthtelling nature — impressed her favorably.

But his grandmother was not helping much. She was always hiding food under her bed or behind the green sofa for him — denying when caught that she had done so. The cherub was being stuffed with all the best morsels that came into the house. And when he stole food or money himself, not only did he swear, with the most innocent look in his eyes that he knew nothing about it, but Mrs. Watson swore too. From the secondhand clothing sent in Rose picked him out a suit for everyday, and for Sundays she took him out and bought him a new suit. These disappeared when he went to see his mother — one of Mrs. Watson's daughters, and Rose knew that all she had accomplished was to provide a bottle of whiskey for that handsome harridan.

The neighborhood was a tough one, but the little angel became famous within a few weeks as the very worst boy among all its little scoundrels. The grownups avoided him and, except for the members of his own gang, the boys fled his approach. Water Street had become a suburb of hell.

Rose, when previously looking at the wild excitement enjoyed by the children of the poor — things hardly conceivable among the sedately brought up children of her own experience — regarded them sympathetically; but little Willie went a bit too far. He built fires upon the shed roofs and kept off the other boys — and even their elders — with well-aimed bricks. The dispensary was soon caring not only for cancer patients but the broken heads of Willie's casualties. As for those beautiful lips that always had the right answer in the catechism lessons, they showed themselves even more adept in the use of lurid profanities.

Mrs. Lathrop was obliged to face the question: should she let Willie stay and be the death of them all or be the death of Mrs. Watson by sending him back to the protectory? It really seemed as though her work was held in Willie's grasp — a small boy with the intelligence of a man. She wondered if he was going to destroy it all — this golden-haired, apple-cheeked stripling of Satan with his cold, hard eyes — and yet a heart that apparently could be easily touched were it not for a conscience so petrified that no furnace could have melted it.

Hopefully she would say to him, "Here, Willie, are some pictures of saints. Would you be a good boy if I gave them to you?"

"Yes, ma'am. How beautiful, ma'am!"

But he had learned where she kept these things. The next day Rose found them all gone. Willie had stolen them and had sold them. When she tried to touch his heart, he listened to her affectionate little sermon and promised to "remember," and said he was sorry when he was taken red handed and could not deny his crimes. The photograph that appears as the frontispiece of this book catches her at a moment when Rose, even while dressing Mrs. Watson's face, had to pause to give little Willie a resounding box on the ear. A few more of them would have done him a world of good.

A priest was brought in to see him — it was a last desperate attempt to rescue the boy's soul — and on departing the good Father had guaranteed good behavior in the future. "I'm sure you won't have any further trouble, Mrs. Lathrop, after this. He's just a bit high-spirited."

That same afternoon Willie celebrated his conversion by building the biggest of his bonfires on their woodshed. So though Mrs. Watson was having hemorrhages on account of his misdeeds, Rose decided that it was impossible to do anything more with the little angel. He would have to go back to the protectory.

But this was not easily done. Mrs. Watson got out of bed, ill as she was, and dressed herself. "Now, daughter," she said, "Willie has a good heart. I'll watch him meself and won't let him steal any more or light bonfires. Don't you worry. *I'll* look after him."

She did. She directed his thefts — and little Willie went off to his mother with more clothes than ever for her to pawn. And when Rose got angry and stern to her "mother," the wheedling tone turned to one of injured innocence.

"Daughter," the old lady asked, "why are you no longer a saint?"

At this Rose wept. She loved Mrs. Watson and she noticed that all the joy was being taken out of her life because people failed to appreciate her angelic grandson. In the diary we can read how many novenas Rose offered that she might keep her temper or be more patient with Mrs. Watson. She was reproaching herself with having failed. Here she had a wonderful chance to save a soul, but this needed a hopeful gentleness she could not muster. Brokenheartedly she sent little Willie away.

What happened afterward gave her further cause for self-reproach. One day, while Rose was looking at Mrs. Watson, the old lady suddenly said, "Daughter, it's happened! I can't see a thing." For a long time her blindness had been expected as the cancer crept closer to her eyes, but now that it had actually occurred Rose took it to be somehow her own fault. There was Mrs. Watson turning her face from side to side, whitened with blank amazement. She had so little face left at all, but that little retained an extraordinary power of expression. The arrogance that had been increasing in her for months disappeared at a stroke, and she became humble and cheerful, though unsmiling and rather foolish.

There were times, however, when her bitterness and sarcasm returned. Then she would declare that she was neglected, "And you don't even give me enough to eat. It's starving I am." Her complaints were often half insane. On January 6th we find that Rose had just concluded a novena with Mrs. Watson, that she herself might have patience with the women under her care. Simultaneously she was saying the Litany of the Blessed Virgin that Mrs. Watson might be more patient and resigned. Her most frequent prayer for herself was that she would learn to govern her temper and become like St. Francis de Sales.

For Rose this was a daily grief — that she could not be more magnanimous toward the old woman, and she reproached herself for resenting Mrs. Watson's unreasonableness. Yet it seemed to her that the complaints the old woman made were justified after all, for what were a thousand charitable acts and laborious services when the spirit of love was not made apparent in them?

On May 5, 1898, there is the simple entry in the diary: "Mrs. Watson died on the night of the 3rd." As Rose sat by her black coffin in that shanty room — Mrs. Watson was the first of many poor people whom Rose had to bury after caring for them — her thoughts were full of reproach: she told herself that she had shown herself a poor friend to the poor, a heartless judge of a kinder heart than her own, and a darker failure — because of the greater light she had — than this dead woman who had so often prayed for her. She even brought herself to believe that she had injured Mrs. Watson, who had never injured her. The train of her thoughts as she sat there was: "Well, I see I have failed. All I can hope is that God has special constitutional clauses of mercy for those who try to reach heaven by Alpine climbing — and then fall into a crevasse."

CHAPTER VI

Death Opens a Door

George Lathrop clearly had gone through a bad time of it since Rose's departure. For a while he continued to hope that this would prove to be merely a passing storm, like the others, even though it was, by far, the most severe of them. In the palm he sent her on which he had printed:

> *To Rose with love from George*
> *From New London, Palm Sunday, '95*

one catches a note of hope. It was to let her know that his feelings were unchanged and that he was still holding on to their New London house so as to be able to welcome her there. He no doubt also hoped that this would touch her heart.

It did touch her heart — deeply: she put the palm away among her treasures. But it did not shake her resolve.

In her diary we can see a great many references to the novenas she made "for the complete conversion of my beloved husband." She made the nine First Friday Communions for the same object. He remained always a concern to her, but she knew that she could help him only spiritually.

Then she heard that he had left New London. He had come to see that she would not go back to him, and there was no sense in his trying to keep up the house alone. It was sold — at a loss* — for pink floors and the like probably did not make 27 Post Hill Place any more attractive to prospective purchasers. Once having

* There is no record of any money coming to Rose out of this transaction.

& to holiness. As I stood beside his body, soon after his death, the beauty & nobility & the exquisite gentleness of his life, & the eloquence which breathes from the unbreathing being of one who has died in the Lord, spoke plainly to me of his virtues, & the welcome our Lord had given him into His rest. My own soul was trembling in the dark uncertainty of all unworthiness. Yesterday, early, his soul came, I am sure, to console me, in his loveliest way of forgiveness."*

As a memorial of him Rose kept — presumably taking it from his bedside in the hospital — his prayer book, a volume about three and a half inches by two. This is now at Rosary Hill Home. Another memorial of him was that when she became Mother Alphonsa she always made a practice — very unusual with nuns — of keeping the use of the name "Lathrop." The Westchester village in which she settled changed its name to Hawthorne. This was in honor of her father, though it also recognized her own presence there. But that name was not of her choosing; the "Lathrop" was. She did not forget that she was George's widow.

A few final pathetic touches are in the diary. Scattered throughout, until it ended the following April, to be continued by Alice Huber, are many references to the prayers she is saying for George. Nine days after his death she writes: "Thousands of prayers are ascending for my husband's translation to heaven." On May 1st, the diary reads: "Have last evening, for the first time since George's death, felt courage, & am very cheerful, *in Christ.*" And on February 3, 1899, the entry is: "3rd 1st Friday, finished the novena of 1st Fridays for the repose of my husband's soul." She had begun a similar novena, not finished at the time of his death for his "complete" conversion. The entry continues: "I prayed that he might be received into heaven on Xmas Day; & I then felt that he was in bliss. God bless his beloved soul."

* The press reports at the time said that George's wife, mother, and brother were with him when he died. These may have been given out by old Mrs. Lathrop.

On February 2nd, she began a novena to St. Anne for the recovery of her mother-in-law's lost eyesight. The two women went to visit St. Anne's shrine on East 76th Street together on that day. And as on March 3rd, she writes: "Began second novena to St. Anne for Mrs. Lathrop's cure in conjunction with her," it would seem that old Mrs. Lathrop had become a Catholic or was now under instruction. From her letters to Rose it appears that as early as 1891 she had been having serious trouble with her eyes.

Letters and entries in Rose Hawthorne Lathrop's diary indicate that already she had hopes for a cancer hospital. She even dreamed of one with three hundred beds. And as the first step toward this she managed to buy, with the help of people she now had interested in her work, 426 Cherry Street — something that more than doubled the capacity of beds and gave reasonable comfort and security. The entry in the diary on April 12th says that it was to be called St. Rose's Free Home after St. Rose of Lima. But this was not at all because her own name was Rose, or because the transcendentalist, Elizabeth Hoar, forty years ago in Italy had picked this Peruvian saint as her patron. It came about because they wrote the names of several patrons on slips of paper and put them in a box. The name of St. Rose of Lima was drawn as in a lottery.

The new home was opened on May 1st. It is amazing, considering the poverty in which she began, that Mrs. Lathrop was able to pay $9,500 down and the balance within a year.

Rose Hawthorne Lathrop's method of appeal was that of begging in the newspapers. In later years she occasionally paid for advertisements — some of them like the financial statement of a bank, showing her assets and liabilities — but the method was in general the same at the end as it was at the beginning. The Archbishop of New York would not sanction their begging from house to house, but she felt that her letters in the press were equivalent to an openly outstretched hand.

It is true that in later years the proceeds of a theatrical performance or a lecture were now and then given to her work, and these she thankfully accepted. But she never would countenance bazaars or teas as means of raising money. Nor would she put her poor under the patronage of St. Bingo. It was the hourly mercy of the public that she sought.

The papers were always very friendly to her, both on account of her father and of George, who was well known to most of the editors. Her work was in itself "news" and her mode of appeal, in its simple sincerity, spiced occasionally with humor, made editors willing to print the letters she sent them.

"When the women of a distant land," she wrote in one of these letters (February 24, 1899), "are homeless through the tragic event of war or famine, the Christian heart, wherever it may be, provides assistance, and is only breathless for fear the succor will come too late. Close beside the citizens of New York I know of five women, bedridden from a tragic disease, who will soon be houseless if their fellow-citizens do not remember them. Their need is as sad — though not picturesque — as any in the world. These five cases of cancer under my care are but a handful of those who are equally in jeopardy all over the city."

On March 4th she wrote again, when the answer to the appeal was inadequate, giving a list of names and donations, and adding: "It will be seen that a very different figure must be reached if the charity is to be strengthened, and the fault, which lies somewhere, I am convinced is neither in the charity nor in the public, but very likely in my lack of skill in advocating the work. . . . But I do justly expect the moderate success, immediately, of a gift from the public of $15,000, with which to secure a house devoted to the charity in its small beginning. I ask those who glance at this appeal to send me what they can spare, from a two-cent stamp to a thousand dollars."

An appeal, signed the previous October 18th by four prominent men who vouched for her work, said that it was supported wholly on voluntary contributions and needed about $600 a month. "A personal visit to the house at 668 Water Street," it said, "would, we are sure, open the hearts and the purses of all those who love their neighbors."

Alice Huber, who at this point takes over the community diary — keeping it until her death nearly forty years later, far more regularly than Rose Lathrop did, though without her literary ability — was rather humorous about their arrival in what really was, this time, compared with all that had gone before, a palatial home. Yet it was still poor enough, and they had to beg for old furniture and kitchen utensils, not having any money over after having squeezed out that enormous sum of $9,500.

Alice had sent the patients on ahead and told them to cook supper while she took her last look around 668 Water Street. But when she arrived in the new house, there all the patients were, taking things easy and not a sign of anything being cooked. They all laughed when they saw her face and told her the kitchen range was being repaired. So they had a scratch meal from a small stove upstairs, setting their plates wherever they could find room. After supper Rose went to find her black cat and its three kittens. In this respect she was still little Rose Hawthorne of Concord. But as Alice did not share her liking for cats, she threatened to do all kinds of dreadful things to the kittens if they dared to come into the new house. In spite of this they frisked and jumped about as though she were joking. Even when she gave them a cuff, they seemed to think she was playing. However, in the end antifeline Alice relented and permitted them to stay.

A couple of private letters, undated but written during 1899 or 1900 to Scudder of the *Atlantic*, who had approached Rose Hawthorne Lathrop to see whether she could supply introductions for a new edition of Hawthorne's works, brought only her suggestion that perhaps bits taken from her *Memories* would serve. She explained that she was too busy to write anything new and told him why: "I am overworked at present . . . & am up often at four A.M.! With a long day of ceaseless action, & the entire management of our money concerns, from *good* food *well* cooked for nineteen sick, to cleaning rooms & seeing callers, to say nothing of the dressing and nursing, & I am quite puzzled as to how to sit down to think, but will see if it can be done." Perhaps she was interrupted at this point for she continues in the somewhat vague style which every now and then wraps her eminently practical mind like a golden cloud: "Your patience with me is very encouraging, & would almost put thought and intelligence into a pine-knot, long faded upon the moss at the foot of a singing tree. Sometimes I wonder why it is that war of any kind so destroys the beauty & geniality of what we fight for, be it our nurses or our principles of justice & love.

"God bless you all, in your lovely regions and atmospheres, where you have all testified of God." (Upon this letter some-one had penciled, "Read by Mr. Kimball and H. R. G. — but we do not feel very definitely enlightened.")

In the other letter she tells Mr. Scudder about how pleased she was with the medal of St. Genevieve his wife had sent her from Paris, and says: "It has been one of my hardest sacrifices to let the letters of my beloved ones lie unanswered, because work was to be done of so different a sort. At least a hundred such letters both fill my heart with gratitude, & torment my selfish old mind with longing to speak. You have had indeed a long letter, but it was not doubtful whether I had a right to my time, in this case." She signs herself, "Rose H. Lathrop now Sr. Mary Alphonsa."

In Rose Hawthorne Lathrop there was a very unusual combina-

tion of impulsiveness and good sense. She was disposed to let her
mind go soaring up wildly into the air, like a kite, and then write
or say something vague or even incomprehensible. But her mind
was like a kite, too, in that it was firmly attached to a string and
could always be hauled down to earth from the windy weather
above. And her impulses were, at all events in this last phase of her
life, sound ones. She did not guess at the outset where her work
was going to lead, but she was on the right track from the outset
and she never left it. All that happened was that the way opened
out for her as she went forward.

Even after George had died neither Rose nor Alice had any
idea of forming themselves into a religious community, though
now they were free to do so. That idea was brought to them
from the outside, though as soon as it had been presented they
saw that, not merely did it accord with what they were trying
to do, but served to guarantee its continuation. For of course had
Mrs. Lathrop died before an organization had been effected, her
work probably would have died with her.

Moreover, she saw at once that a religious organization, with a
definite rule, was the only secure way of maintaining that cardinal
principle which she was never tired of asserting and which was,
in fact, printed in every issue of her magazine. It was that her
charity demanded two things of those it helped — that their cancer
should be incurable and that they should be destitute. What she
feared above all else was that a time might come when, in the
great hospital she confidently expected to grow out of such small
beginnings, there should be a temptation to accept a few paying
patients. These she knew would be the cuckoo's fledglings that
would oust the rightful birds from their nest. But if it could be
hammered in that nobody was ever to be accepted who could
pay, then, only then, would her work be saved. How else
could this be brought about except by writing it into the formal
constitution of a religious community? Always she had had a
religious motive — and this motive animated such Protestants as

the admirable Mr. Greene who so loyally supported her. But a religious rule gave force and direction to that motive. The idea therefore of becoming Sisters was at once eagerly accepted as soon as it was suggested. It did not mean, in this case, a change so much as a natural and inevitable development of the idea they already had.

One statement which has been widely publicized must be corrected before proceeding further. It is that Mrs. Lathrop and her friends in their early days called themselves "the Daughters of the Puritans." Regarding this it is enough to say that in her journal Mrs. Lathrop always refers to herself and her associates, even while they were still a wholly voluntary group, under the title which they still bear — that of the Servants of Relief for Incurable Cancer.

In February, 1899, a young Dominican priest, Father Thuente of St. Vincent's on Lexington Avenue and Sixty-Sixth Street, went out in a heavy snowstorm to call on the ladies who had been helping a Mrs. Daly, a member of his parish. His visit, though it marked a turning point in Rose Lathrop's life, was not at the time thought of any special importance and received no mention in Mrs. Lathrop's diary. When the priest came to the address he had been given — 668 Water Street — he hesitated; he could not believe that anybody could be living in so tumbledown a place. Nevertheless he climbed the shaky porch stairs and knocked.

A bright-faced, redheaded woman, looking much younger than her later forties, opened the door and said, "Oh, do come in, Father."

He then introduced himself and said he had come to thank her for looking after Mrs. Daly so well. "Poor soul, she had nobody else to look after her."

"We only do look after women who have nobody else to whom they can turn, Father. Her husband does his best, but he is out all day." Then she asked, "Won't you come upstairs and give the patients your blessing?"

When he climbed to the second floor he found Alice Huber and another nurse and their five patients. To the left, opening out of the living room, was where the nurses slept in institutional beds, so as to save space, in upper and lower berths. He was greatly impressed, and noticed that on a table was a small statue of St. Rose of Lima.

"I belong to the same order," he told them.

"Oh, yes, Father," said Alice Huber, "I know all about the Dominicans. I was educated by them — at St. Catherine's in Kentucky."

"You probably know then that St. Rose was not a nun, but a member of the Dominican third order."

Yes, Alice Huber and Rose knew that.

He glanced at the dress they wore — something midway between a nurse's uniform and a religious habit. At first, when he met Mrs. Lathrop at the door, he had supposed it peculiar to herself. But now he saw these women did constitute a kind of religious community and that this was a semireligious dress. He shot a question at them, "Did you ever think of becoming Dominican Tertiaries? Then you'd be like St. Rose."

They had not. So he promised to send them some books and pamphlets and took his leave.

To piece the story together accurately one has to go back to Mrs. Lathrop's diary, which ended on April 15, 1899, and Miss Huber's which she started on August 30, 1901. The second diary provides a condensed history of the intervening period. Miss Huber writes: "On the 19th of May [1898, and therefore just a month after George Lathrop's death] Mrs. Lathrop announced her intention of cutting off her hair, & putting on a sort of semi-religious dress. I begged her not to do so. She persisted in her design & cut off her beautiful hair & put on a cap something like that worn by the Sisters of Charity." (She refers of course not to the "cornet" Sisters, but the New York group which wears a poke bonnet.) Miss Huber also writes of "a linen dress and a white neck handkerchief. A few days afterward I put on the same dress without, however, cutting off my hair." In this garb they went to see the Sisters of Charity at East Broadway and there Sister Rosalita advised them to call on Archbishop Corrigan to ask his permission to wear the dress. The diary continues: "At first Archbishop Corrigan refused the necessary permission, but on a second appeal granted it, but advised us by all means to consider attaching ourselves to some existing religious order." An inserted page in Miss Huber's diary mentions that they did see Monsignor (then Father) McMahon and he told them that it would be necessary to have permission to wear "the semi-religious dress." She adds: "At first the Archbishop was cross and spoke sharply to Mrs. Lathrop. Her eyes filled with tears."

Following the archbishop's advice, they went to see another lady who had a project he thought the Servants of Relief could join, but it was evident on both sides that their objects were at variance, and from this quarter pressure was brought to bear on the archbishop to suppress St. Rose's Home. "But," says the diary, "he refused to do so, saying, 'If it is not God's will it will go to pieces and if it is God's will it will succeed.' " Miss Huber comments that they were greatly encouraged by these words; "in times when indeed it seemed we had been abandoned by all, the Archbishop was a good friend."

Under May 25, 1898, the entry in Mrs. Lathrop's diary is: "Yesterday Miss Huber and I went to the Cathedral to show the Archbishop the dress we now wear, & obtain his permission to go singly to cases, & to be out till 9 PM in twos. Could only see Father McMahon, but he was very kind & favorable, & advised me to write to his Grace, which I did that evening. The dress is so like a nun's simplest costume that we are taken for Sisters. Many persons & boys take off their hats to us. Alice felt as if she had always worn it, & so do I."

The best — certainly the most reliable — way of telling the rest of the story is by quoting some official documents. On July 7, 1898, Father McMahon, then the archbishop's secretary, advised Mrs. Lathrop not to seek to have a chapel in the house because of the difficulty she would have in maintaining a chaplain. On October 15th, he writes: "In conformity with your desire, I have mentioned the matter to the Archbishop, and it is his opinion as it was mine that it would be better for you to continue your work without any reference to him. He will not disturb you in the least, but you know that it would scarcely be wise for him to do anything just at this stage: but you can rest assured that he appreciates as well as do all who have the welfare of humanity at heart, the work you are doing."

On December 28, 1898, word came from Father Thomas F. Myhan, the archbishop's assistant secretary: "His Grace received your letter and bids me write you in his name. The favor you ask is such an extraordinary one that he feels reluctant to grant it. However, he gives you permission to have Holy Mass offered in the House, *for one time only*, and the request must not again be presented, for he would have to refuse to even consider it."

And on April 20, 1899, the archbishop writes in his own hand: "I take pleasure in testifying that Mrs. Rose Hawthorne Lathrop has devoted herself with great zeal and patience to the task of caring for patients afflicted with cancers and that her efforts, as far as I can judge, have done much to contribute to the comfort of those suffering from that dread disease." In the years ahead there were many occasions when the Servants of Relief felt that many influential clerics were not very friendly — though all such references in the diary may at this date be safely left unquoted. But it is no more than due to Archbishop Corrigan's memory to record that he always stood a friend.

Early in August, 1899, Father Thuente called again — this time of course at the new house at 426 Cherry Street — and advised them to call on Archbishop Corrigan for permission to join the

Third Order of St. Dominic. Strictly speaking, a little more than that was being asked. Merely to become a member of one of the third orders does not require the ordinary's permission, but only that of the superiors of the order itself. But what Mrs. Lathrop and her associates sought was permission to become Tertiaries living in community and permission to wear the habit. The habit may sometimes even be worn by Tertiaries living in the world. And St. Rose of Lima and St. Catherine of Siena were never nuns; though clothed as such, they resided at home, in a way that would not be permitted today. What Rose Hawthorne Lathrop did was to found a specialized group of Tertiaries — the Servants of Relief of Incurable Cancer of the Congregation of St. Rose of Lima, which forms part of the Dominican Third Order, yet is now directly under the control of the archbishop of New York even when working in other dioceses. That canonical status was not as yet fixed or even thought of, but it was all nevertheless clearly implicit in the plans made by this very impulsive but clear-sighted woman.

On September 14, 1899, the Archbishop gave his permission. Father Thuente received them into the Dominican Order — Mrs. Lathrop taking the name of Sister Mary Alphonsa, and Alice Huber that of Sister Mary Rose. Though they were not as yet permitted to wear the Dominican habit, they tried to live a more religious life after this, saying the Little Office of the Blessed Virgin and giving regular times to prayer and meditation.*

On Christmas Day, 1899, Mass was said in the little chapel in Cherry Street — a mere passage between two rooms. It was for this that Father Myhan had given special permission. To those who were bedridden Father Thuente carried Holy Communion; they had been able to hear Mass from where they were.

In the fall of 1900, after they had been Tertiaries for a year, Mrs. Lathrop and Miss Huber — they still had to be addressed as

* It is worth noting that the Office is said by them even today in English, not Latin — a rather unusual arrangement.

such, as, lacking the habit, their religious names could be only for strictly private use — called on the archbishop. He told them they had passed through a long, hard novitiate. A few days later Archbishop Corrigan sent for Father Thuente and told him: "You are interested in the work of those two women down in Cherry Street. Well, go and give them the Dominican habit."

Father Thuente was not expecting this. "Why, your Grace," he said, "this is most extraordinary. In this country we are not allowed to give the habit to Secular Tertiaries."

"I know it's extraordinary," was his answer, "but remember that they are doing an extraordinary work." And he quoted: "If this work be of men, it will come to naught. If it be of God, you cannot overthrow it."

The giving of the habit was accomplished in a very simple ceremony on the Feast of the Immaculate Conception, December 8, 1900. From that date they were officially Sisters Alphonsa and Rose. On that occasion the two Sisters made their vows. The archbishop recognized that they had already completed an extremely rigorous novitiate.

But still they did not have the Blessed Sacrament in the house, though Mass was now said on Sundays and holydays of obligation by a Capuchin Father. But after a visit the archbishop paid them — when he left them an envelope plump with bills — that defect was rectified. On October 4, 1901, the Feast of St. Francis of Assisi, Father Thuente said Mass and left the Blessed Sacrament in the tabernacle on their altar. That time when giving Holy Communion to the patients in their beds he was almost overcome by the odor and had to return quickly to the altar to recover.

Sister Rose had painted a picture of St. Rose of Lima for the oratory.* She also played the little organ and sang a hymn for this occasion.

Writing one of her appeals to the public at this time Sister

* The large painting of St. Rose, now in the chapel at Hawthorne, was painted later by Sister Rose.

Alphonsa, as she has to be called from now on, said: "I am trying to serve the poor as a servant. I wish to serve the cancerous poor because they are more avoided than any other class of sufferers; and I wish to go to them as a poor creature myself. . . . In order to accomplish anything that will be lasting, women must be called who are capable of renouncing ease and pastime, for the sake of that true love of God which shares the sufferings of Christ in a mode of life which He recommended and lived."

CHAPTER VII

A Little Sunshine to Share

That first summer at 426 Cherry Street — the buying of which had cost them almost every penny they had — was a difficult one. And when Mrs. Lathrop fell ill and Miss Huber had to take charge, she was fearful under the kind of responsibility she had never had before, though she was, in fact, eventually to show that she was a better manager of money than the older woman. Mother Alphonsa was excellent in the large design but less good in careful attention to details, the sort of thing in which Sister Rose was in her element.

All this, however, was still new to her, and she felt the strain. As always happens when an old house is bought, a number of things had to be done to make it livable, and the plumber and the carpenter presented large bills and would not wait. In desperation Alice went to Rose, who was lying ill in the lower berth of their room, and wailed, "Let us draw out every cent we have and give it to them; and if we starve, it cannot be helped!" Things fortunately didn't come quite to that pass; a few days later unexpected donations came which not only enabled them to pay the plumber and carpenter but to have enough money over to carry them through to the fall. They had already discovered that the summer was their lean season, so they tried to put by a little to serve for those months. But that they were not doing so badly is shown by the fact that by May, 1900 — a year after buying 426 Cherry Street — they had only two thousand dollars left to pay off.

Some of the patients, however, thought that the Sisters were doing a little too well. At all events such was Mrs. Dwyer's belief, though no doubt hers were somewhat extreme opinions. After being rather queer for some time she suddenly went insane and had to be taken in a hurry to Bellevue.

She had been helped by Sister Alphonsa since the Scammel Street days and, as she became more sick, had several times been invited to join the circle at Water Street. But no. Rose would meet her sometimes hobbling along with her stick on Grand Street and she would submit to be taken into a store and then and there be provided with a shawl and mittens against the cold weather. And to these presents of clothes and groceries she would respond with, "Well, I never did! You are so kind to me. God will reward you! No one was ever so kind to me before. I do love you!" But still she preferred to be independent.

But one day she arrived at Cherry Street and told Sister Alphonsa: "I was thinking — I thought — I dunno — but I am not smart any more. I guess you'll have to take me in, after all."

The Sisters understood her reluctance. They knew that the poor are only too well aware of the bad odor of much of what passes for charity. Mrs. Dwyer accepted even *their* charity only because she had to. But by way of still asserting her independence she brought with her forty dollars wrapped up in a piece of cloth and bound with tape. Would Sister keep it for her?

Upon this Sister Alphonsa asked: "Wouldn't it be better off under your pillow, Mrs. Dwyer?"

"No, dear, I can trust you."

She didn't trust the Sisters very far, though. And every now and then — but especially when anything new came into the house — she got suspicious and demanded her money. Then, much to the disgust of the other patients, she counted her wad of bills before their eyes, grunted as if to say, "well, at least they haven't stolen anything *yet!*" and then had the money put away again. The climax was reached when the little organ was carried into the chapel in preparation for the day when the Blessed Sacrament would repose there. Then Mrs. Dwyer turned to her fellow patients and said: "I've known them longer than any of you have. And when I first knew them they had nothing; now they can buy pianners!"

Many things of course arrived in that house that they did not have to pay for at all. Not one of the present Sisters is a survivor from those early years, but there are still some people alive who remember Mother Alphonsa as far back as her days in New London as the beautiful Mrs. Lathrop. One lady who knew her just a little later, Miss Anne McKenna of Jersey City, tells me how she and Agnes Storer — both of them students at Manhattanville and Children of Mary there, were sent by Mother Ellen White with altar linens for the Cherry Street chapel. It must have been about the time the Sisters had permission to keep the Blessed Sacrament in the house.

The chapel was on the second floor, where there was a passage between the rooms which, like so many New York houses then, had clothes closets on one side and washbasins on the other. It was on the washbasin side that a little altar had been arranged, and sitting or lying in the adjoining rooms the patients could assist at Mass. Upon leaving the two girls asked the way to the Rivington Street Settlement and the policeman directed them: "Two blocks ahead, Miss, then to the right and you'll know Rivington Street by the smell." It seems to have been from that chance errand on the part of his daughter that Doctor Storer of Newport became interested in Mother Alphonsa's cancer work.

From a similar source comes word of how Miss Louisa Morrison, a teacher of music, used to go once a week to Cherry Street to sing for the patients. In days when there was no radio, and one listened to the phonograph through ear tubes, entertainment of this kind meant a good deal to women who were, for the most part, bedridden. Mother Alphonsa never forgot that normally people need a reasonable amount of amusement to keep them from moping.

So far they had been able to do nothing for male patients except dress a few of their cancers in the relief room. Here the "relief" was sometimes paying the rent, or providing money or groceries or secondhand clothes. But though their professed purpose of course was to treat cancers, the nurses found they had to do much more than look after one particular disease. To almost any ailment of a simple sort they gave treatment. And one old lady had almost every ailment from a lame ankle to asthma, earache to brown skeeters. Of all these diseases she considered, so they judged from the minute descriptions she gave, the brown skeeters to be the worst. They finally managed to diagnose it as bronchitis.

From the outset, Mrs. Lathrop became aware that men needed her help quite as much as women did, and were just as likely as women to be destitute. Also she was soon made aware that, though more women than men have cancer, the cases among the men were more often of the internal sort. In those days, when X-rays were not in common use, diagnosis often failed to locate the disease in men where women's cancers, being more frequently superficial, were noticed at once.

While still Mrs. Lathrop she had often pondered this problem, without seeing any solution except in that large hospital she dreamed of having one day. At that time she had the small house on Cherry Street, and just two or three regular helpers. In a place like that she could not accommodate men and though she had thought of an annex for them, this for a number of reasons had not been practicable — a conclusive reason being that she did not have the money. It was as much as she could do to keep things going for her collection of suffering women.

She admitted her advantage in being "untrameled by business acumen and cowardly prudence," and that this fortunate lack had enabled them to plunge ahead so swiftly and improvidently. But there were, after all, limits to her power, and when General Putnam, the president of a western railroad, wrote asking her to take in a male patient, she had to refuse. In that particular case she did not feel so badly about the man involved, for General Putnam would be sure to find him a suitable place. What the application did was to make her think all the more — and regretfully — about men sufferers in general.

About then a lady connected with charity organization called to draw her attention to a case. This often happened, just as it often happened also that Mrs. Lathrop, in the course of her cancer work would encounter cases that fell within the scope of the work of other organizations.

"I want you to come with me," the visitor said, "a poor fellow — nowhere to go!"

"A man!" There was consternation in Mrs. Lathrop's voice. She was still Rose Lathrop, as this happened at the period when they were still wearing their semireligious dress. Only very privately was she Sister Alphonsa as yet.

The visitor nodded.

Mrs. Lathrop looked grave. "But what *can* we do? — just the three of us! Our friends are always begging us to take a little rest now and then, so as to live a few years longer for our work. But the fact is that we *have* no place for men — you know that — and no money to rent rooms for them."

"I know," said the visitor, "all the same something must be done for this man." She was quiet and gentle in her manner — but there was a flash in her eyes, heroism in the set of her lips.

Miss Huber turned to Mrs. Lathrop, saying: "You are the fanatical one, Rose. Why not see the man?"

The fanatical Rose answered: "I can *go,* but what can I do? Even to spend an hour on this visit means giving time I can't afford. I'm driven to death."

Alice Huber smiled, and noted how Rose looked quite relieved when she was told, "All the same, Rose, perhaps you'd better go."

The visitor beamed. "I knew you would send to see him! I myself felt that his case was a hopeless case, but when I saw the refinement of the man I could not resist the pathos of his appeal. I'm sure Mrs. Lathrop will have some inspiration to prevent his being sent to the almshouse on the Island. He's begging to be saved from going there."

Mrs. Lathrop beamed in her turn. If only all charity workers were like this one! Then an iceberg of a problem would begin to melt into spring loveliness. But Alice said — what else *could* she say? — "But it's really impossible. Seeing him is only going to add to our unhappiness at not being able to do anything. And he lives too far away for us even to call upon him often to dress his wounds. It would be dishonest to hold out the slightest hope of our being able to help."

But the visitor turned to the fanatic. "Well then, Mrs. Lathrop, come along."

"But I can't go *now*," said Rose. "I'll go with you tomorrow morning."

"No, *now*. Tomorrow will be too late. Arrangements have already been made to send him to Blackwell's Island. Only my pleading has given him a few hours of grace — until I've seen you."

"Then wait till I get my veil and cloak."

Alice Huber's parting words were: "All right, Rose, but remember — don't you dare to promise to take charge of that man!"

The man had a hall bedroom over a liquor store — and to get to it they had to go through its side door.

The room was almost completely filled by a double bed, but the man was expecting them — he had been assured by the charity worker that she would get somebody to look after him, and so, though he was lying down, he was dressed in a brown tweed suit, ready to leave at once.

One glance at him showed he was a gentleman. Though all but blind and nearly stone deaf and unable to do more than mumble a few words, his manners were beautiful. And his half-dead, pale-gray eyes lit up in a way that restored for a moment their former beauty.

Rose took in the situation at a glance — it was one all too familiar to her. Everybody had been afraid to go near him. Dust and unwashed cups and plates and spoons were on the table, empty milk bottles stood on the floor; a few books and photographs of friends were ossified into the general litter. And yet Rose could see that the dirt was not of his making; he had been totally neglected.

She had already formed a plan — a desperate one to people with no money. They would rent a tenement of two or three rooms close to 426 Cherry Street, trusting to donations to cover the extra expense. Their man who ran errands for them, in return for a room in what had once been their stable, could be moved over to the annex to be an attendant to the patient. She thought of another argument; the Cherry Street house and its back yard were all cluttered up with gifts of old clothes and secondhand furniture. By taking a tenement apartment they would get a badly needed storage room. She was trying to justify what she was about to do, knowing that it really could not be justified.

She found the old gentleman was a former officer in the British army with a pension of eight dollars a month — destitute enough, in all conscience. He had been given notice to leave his hall bedroom, and with a face half eaten away he was too terrible an object for anyone to let him even the poorest room. The doctor who had been looking after him had been advised that he should go to Bellevue.

"But, doctor," he had mumbled: "They won't keep me at Bellevue. I'll get sent to the Island."

The doctor tried to quiet him: "Oh no! They'll keep you there. I have some influence at Bellevue. I'll see to it that the almshouse never swallows you up."

None of them trusted that promise.

The liquor-store keeper came up — a stout, rosy man.

"Yes, ma'am," he said unctuously to Rose. "*I've* been looking after him. And there's not many that would."

"I *see* you've been looking after him," Rose returned dryly.

Unabashed he went on, without troubling to drop his voice, knowing the old officer could not hear him. And his manner suggested that it would not matter if he did, so near was he to death.

"I am his only friend. If you ask me, ma'am, the best thing that could happen is that the doctor would give him an overdose of morphine."

Rose grew hot and scornful. "You have an Irish name," she said, "are you not a Catholic? Catholics usually have a respect for life and believe that each moment is given us by God as another chance for reparation and the purifying of our souls."

The liquor-store friend was still not abashed. He supposed Rose was embarrassed because she thought the old officer could hear. He laughed and shouted at her, "He can't hear nothing!"

Mrs. Lathrop knew better than that. She saw that the old gentleman had been watching their lips, and at a crisis like this, the faculties are sharpened. She saw that he understood that his murder was being proposed, even though she tried to keep a cheerful and indifferent expression on her own face, so as to conceal her horror.

The officer struggled to a sitting posture at the side of the bed and on a piece of paper wrote, with a graceful deliberation and neatness of touch, but with a groan or two that told what the effort was costing him:

"Repeat all you're saying, or I shall imagine everything!"

She sat down beside him and spoke right into his ear. She would tell even a dying man not less than the truth, "I think you'd better go to Bellevue. We can do so little for you. But there's no doubt that they will send you to the Island. You have been a soldier: this would be a valiant act of submission to the will of God."

He roused himself and a little of his soldierly mettle flashed out. Now he wrote vigorously, as a man defending himself with his back to the wall, ready to die, sword in hand. "Take me, please," he wrote, "to *your* hospital. I don't care how poor and humble it is. I want to be under your care."

By way of answer she guaranteed nothing. But she held out her hand. The old soldier understood. She was promising that her best would leave nothing better to be done. His eyes shone and blessed her. He knew he could rely on her unspoken word.

The next morning rooms were rented across the street from St. Rose's Home and were being scrubbed out ready to have some of the furniture in the back yard put there for the old soldier. Just then word arrived that he had been taken to Bellevue. At once Mrs. Lathrop got a cab and, with the errand man, drove to that hospital.

The officer was there still, for a kind doctor had promised to keep him until the next morning, as he said friends would be coming for him. And the old man's eyes shone large and glad. Rose had to bend her head to hear his mumbled, "I thought you'd come!"

Oh, the gratitude of his eyes! Looking at him, Rose felt how small was the act of kindness she was doing, how slight a balance to his weight of misfortune. "O Christ!" she said silently, "why will we not give You all we possess!"

As his room was still not ready for him, she promised to send for him at two that afternoon.

"You'd better not make it any later, Mrs. Lathrop," the doctor told her.

She caught the precautionary hint and answered, "If I have to borrow Cinderella's coach I'll have a carriage here for him then!"

To see this first male patient in his neat room at the tiny annex was well worth the trouble it had cost. The old gentleman arrived very pale and faint after his journey in the cab, but with a heart as light as a child's.

He greeted Rose with the manners of a prince and in his gratitude showed his breeding. He seemed to grow handsome again, and ordered the errand man about like a flunky. He was happy, gentle, stately, and instead of dying in a few days as the doctors said he would, he lived three months — long enough for the male annex to become firmly established.

During those months of suffering — but also of happiness — he returned to his long-neglected religious duties. His beads were always on his wrist, his prayer book was always within reach. The references he made to his faith; the prayers that were said at his bedside; the visits of the priest; his touching pleasure in the little holy pictures Rose and Alice gave him, all showed the sweetness and nobility of his nature. Never did he boast of his past; there was no need for that; they could see that he must have come of a distinguished family.

He liked to be read to, for he could see very little now. But the nurses were too hard worked to sit by him, and the janitor's education was not good enough to please the fastidious old man. Not that he ever said anything. But an eyebrow would lift at a mispronounced word. Some of Julian's children, however, were pressed into service — or other chance visitors. And though his deafness made the reading something of an ordeal to the reader, the old British officer's interest in any item of English news in the papers made the effort its own reward.

It was at this time that Agnes Storer and her friend made their visit from Manhattanville. Agnes came again soon afterward with her father and mother, and now found Mrs. Lathrop and Miss Huber garbed and styled as Sisters.

They were very anxious that Doctor Storer should see the male annex. It was so pitifully small that the hardest heart would melt at the sight of a very sick old man of refinement in such a place —

of which the best to be said was that it was a shade better than nothing. The testimony of so eminent a physician would, they were quite certain, do much to convince the public of the need they were trying to meet.

Sister Alphonsa steered him across the street, down which drays drove full tilt, and up entrance steps crowded by babies, and nursemaids hardly older than the babies, and came to the peaceful little room where the old soldier lay waiting for a death that approached with agonizing delays. Before she opened the door Sister Alphonsa said, "To me, Doctor Storer, he's like a man in a duel that he never wanted to fight. He knows he's going to be killed. And magnanimously he shoots over the head of his adversary. Not a word of complaint."

Agnes Storer's eyes caught sight of something. "Look, father!" she said, "he's wearing a military medal."

The old man motioned to the girl to bend down and mumbled something feebly into her ear.

She turned to Sister Alphonsa and said, "He says the medal is to be yours."

The doctor gave that day a prescription that the Sisters have used freely ever afterward. "You've never tried Bass's Ale, I suppose. Then do, you'll find there's nothing like it to give some relief — especially in cases of face cancer."

A few days later the old officer died and the liquor dealer came down for the funeral and even revealed that his friend was a member of some fraternal society which would bury him. They dressed him in his old British uniform, though it had some moth holes, and his coffin was draped with the Union Jack. Sister Alphonsa carried flowers to the undertaker's parlor, and the hearse drove past the Home on its way to the church. There was only one mourner, the liquor dealer, and he lifted his hat to the Sisters, who tearfully stood at the door of 426 Cherry Street, pausing a moment in their labors, as the body of the old gentleman was carried by.

The annex, however, was only a makeshift, and some of its unsuspected disadvantages soon appeared, making other arrangements imperative. The winter of 1900–1901 passed for their aching hearts under the shadow of unanswered prayers. Yet Sister Alphonsa was sure as to the outcome, though all the printed appeals in the papers and letters to personal friends had brought in only a thousand dollars toward a place for the men. She would have liked to have bought the property on either side of 426 Cherry Street, but even if she had the money, the owner said he did not wish to sell. And it was in vain that she tried to raise the forty thousand dollars asked for another house near by. They certainly did need something, when a man was strangling slowly to death in the annex on the opposite side of the street with nobody to look after him at night but the janitor. It was for him like a long-drawn-out hanging.

Then there were complaints from a neighbor who had gone to the board of health saying that the annex was not kept sufficiently clean. This was an attempt to get revenge on the Sisters' janitor for complaints against him for burning feathers in his basement. But the board of health inspector said he had never seen a cleaner place in his life; so that anxiety was removed.

Another problem came with a new janitor they employed. He had a good heart, but he used to drink frequently, and when he got drunk he let the furnace out. He was remorseful afterward, to the point of tears, but that did not alter the fact that men suffering intolerable pangs had also to suffer from the cold. And now that Rose and Alice were Dominican Sisters they could not run across the street in the middle of the night to see that the furnace was all right. They therefore began a novena to the Sacred Heart — asking for a new home that might be anywhere, so long as it would, in some way, provide for the male cases and give them more room for their women.

No answer at all came to that first novena. And Sister Alphonsa said to her assistant, "Do you realize there is not a ray of hope? Yet I *know* it must come. Our Lord is our only resource, and He will not fail us. He will give us a large, comfortable home; I know it as well as I can see it now."

Into the hand of a statue of St. Joseph, Sister Alphonsa put a scrap of paper. On it she had written: "Glorious St. Joseph, please give to the Servants of Relief a house in which they can take care of many sick in safety for many years."* Then she started a new novena.

In these novena prayers she got the patients to join. There was no room for them all — seventeen now — in the passage that served as their chapel, but those who could not get inside knelt at the open doors and the bedridden said the novena prayers where they were lying.

All of them knew that late at night, when the lights were out, Sister Alphonsa often crept into the little chapel to kneel there upright, without any support, and pray in the presence of the Blessed Sacrament. They could sometimes hear her voice speaking aloud, and they were awed by her fervor: "Lord," she would say, "You *must* give us this new house. We *need* it. And I have nobody to look to but You, dear Lord!"

* This scrap of paper is still preserved at Hawthorne.

CHAPTER VIII

A Home in Westchester

One morning Sister Alphonsa was told that a priest would like to see her. As soon as he had introduced himself as Father Couthenay, one of a group of French Dominicans — of the great Lacordaire's foundation — who were exiled and had settled in Westchester County, he came at once to the point.

"We want to sell our house, Sister," he said, "and we think you might like to buy it. I believe it would be well suited to your work."

She was so staggered at the suggestion that she did not know what to say for the moment, and he enlarged upon the fine location, the beautiful grounds, and the large building.

"Yes," he said, "I admit a little old, but very good for you. And cheap!"

She had sent for the levelheaded Sister Rose. She felt she needed some such calm controlling influence, or she would go floating away into the air. With Sister Rose by her side, she was able to reply fairly coolly: "Of course, Father, we'd like to see the country and of course it wouldn't cost much money to make the trip; and I can imagine we are justified in looking at the property. But as for buying it. . . !"

As she spoke Sister Alphonsa could see in Sister Rose's eyes that the idea was preposterous. Her voice was saying, "But, Father, we have only a thousand dollars!"

The ebullient Frenchman was not in the least downcast. "That's all right, Sister. You pay us for the house when you wish. Go and see it. Please. It is what you need."

After taking him to the door, Sister Alphonsa went back and said to Sister Rose: "After all, this *is* the last day of the novena."

It was a mild day in early May that Sister Alphonsa and Sister Rose took the train to the village of Sherman Park — the present Hawthorne — just north of White Plains. When they arrived at Unionville Station an old carriage, drawn by a very old black horse and driven by an extremely old French coachman, was waiting to take them to the home Father Couthenay said they should buy. Seen from the bottom of the hill, the long, narrow, wooden house, which lay strung out with its line of windows and endless porch, looked like a railway train on top of Mont Blanc.

It was a delightful day — the trees feathery with new energy, the ground scattered over with violets, ferns, and anemones, and birds singing on every branch and bough. Under that blue sky it really felt as though they already owned the place.

The first thing they came to on entering the grounds was a replica of the Lourdes grotto built by the Dominican novices who had been there. A tablet on it commemorated the three priests of the order who were lost in the wreck of the *Bourgogne*.* One was the prior of the house. The chapel was simple and bare, but noble.

The Father who was to show them the property — a man who sighed and smiled at every word, every step — took them to the orchard first.

"These trees, Sisters," he said, "were planted by me — and now I'm going to China and I shall never see them again." At this there was another sigh, then a smile.

"My grape arbor!" he explained — a smile and then a sigh. "And you see my beehives. These bees are either great philosophers — or else very stupid. I do not know. They make the honey and I take it from them, and they are fortified with indifference, or else they do not know what I have done."

* The ship from which St. Francesca Cabrini landed in New York on March 31, 1889.

In the same style he displayed the greenhouses, full of flowers, the garden beds also brimful, and the vegetables. Here the Frenchman's sighs were really profuse, but the two Sisters, in white Dominican wool like himself, laughed so merrily that he was soon smiling again.

He led them up branching wood paths to the grove on the hill behind the house — young oak and beech and maple. From there they looked out on the line of hills, lavender and blue, on the opposite side of the valley. The sunlit fields were pulsing with the shadows of the clouds drifting overhead. It was all such a change from the squalor of the slums that over and over again Sister Alphonsa leaned toward Sister Rose and whispered: "We *must* have this property."

Sister Rose shrugged her shoulders and answered each time, "I know it's all beautiful. But how can we pay the bills?"

As Sister Alphonsa could not find an answer to that question, she said severely, "What a thing to say!"

The Father who had been showing them around was a good psychologist. He had started with beautiful grounds and had let the sight of hills and heavens create enthusiasm before taking them into the house itself. For this was merely a shell, and could they have realized how much they would have to spend on it to make it habitable they would undoubtedly not have had the courage to complete the purchase. The interior looked very austere, naturally enough, after having been used as a friary; but they realized that all that could be easily changed, and it was not part of their idea to make the home they gave their patients anything but as pretty and comfortable as possible. In the kitchen, however, there was a scene that showed them that gentleness had by no means been absent. There a lay brother was petting a box of white chicks — still as small as the egg from which they had just emerged. Obviously these little chirping innocents knew nothing about either austerity or hunger. Their destiny was to grow up to feed the patients.

There were disadvantages in the house they saw at once; others they discovered only by degrees. The most cursory glance revealed that a building like this — not compact but a long strip, almost a string — was going to be hard to run with their mere handful of helpers.

"We could of course," suggested Sister Rose with mild irony, "have a private trolley car and so dash from point to point."

"Or put the Sisters on roller-skates," suggested Sister Alphonsa catching up the suggestion.

"Or when the community gets large enough," went on Sister Rose, "we might station them in platoons at various points. We could meet in the chapel and the refectory!"

They laughed at their fancies but saw the physical layout of Rosary Hill was going to make things difficult. But when they turned and looked out of the porch that ran the whole length of the long building they no longer dreaded the responsibility they were assuming.

"Think what it will be, Sister dear," said Sister Alphonsa, "for our poor old women — and don't forget *poor old men too* in this place! — to gaze upon the fragile color of peach blossoms against a misty distance."

"To take spiritual courage from that camp of hills," went on Sister Rose — "a far-stretching army, prolonged in line as the horizon itself!"

"And see that train down in the valley, puffing through the ravine! It makes one feel that human sympathy is close to our efforts."

The French Dominican listening had stopped sighing, and was all smiles.

They went back rejoicing to the stuffy streets of New York. The Dominican Fathers were willing to let them have those sixty rooms and nine acres for twenty-eight thousand dollars — and to accept the thousand dollars they had as a down payment. They got it so cheap because it was a place suitable for little except a home for convalescent people or (what it had been built for) a summer resort. As such, it had been named "Tecumseh" to make a connecting link with General Sherman. It could never have been very well suited for a Dominican friary.

But the Sisters— even that damper of enthusiasm, Sister Rose — were so enthusiastic that they were ready to buy everything with the house — the vines and the bees, the old horse and the hens, even the old French coachman. Him, however, they did not have to buy; he looked upon himself as a kind of serf who went with the property and refused to budge and did, in fact, turn out to be very useful.

On June 1st, Mother Alphonsa — now that there were two houses and she was the superior general she became "Mother" — and a group of postulants set out to take possession and to prepare the ramshackle building for the patients.

At first, Mother Alphonsa was a bit dismayed by the vast distances at Rosary Hill Home. But she was cheerful about it and said, "Don't worry! We'll soon get used to this. To anybody who has been living in a mousetrap of course the Catacombs would seem bewilderingly large."

But life did seem to be spent wildly on the wing, and the poor women were left at the end of every day exhausted at the amount of dashing about they had to do. But the distances developed the muscles needed to cover the ground and soon they forgot how much they were running about. Then Mother Alphonsa told them: "Didn't I tell you it would be so? The difficulties we anticipate usually turn out to be the most empty nothings in the world. All one has to do is face them frankly — and persist. Then they disappear!" She had to admit that had the Sisters allowed themselves so much as a grain of prudence, or had listened to any of the sage advice they had received, they would not have gone a step further.

But difficulties nobody had told them about soon appeared. One was the wind that always seemed to be blowing on that hill and against which they had no protection in a house all doors and windows. There would be a sudden slamming of them; then they jumped as though a cannon had been fired. One step outside, and they were blown away. They hung on to their wimples and veils and gasped, with heads held down against it, "the wind! the wind!" It blew, they often thought, from all four quarters of the heavens at once. Even in that first summer they discovered what the wind could do there. All the windows had been left open because of the heat when a storm suddenly broke, not only with wind but with hail. The front door burst open and all the pictures — including a painting of George Washington — and the vases in the hall were hurled to the ground by a blast that howled, Mother Alphonsa thought, like March at the North Pole, raging through an avenue of icebergs. If July was like this, they asked themselves, what would the winter be? An order for fifty tons of coal went out by the next mail.

But despite these little troubles, they were more delighted with Rosary Hill Home than ever. George Washington was hung up in a new frame, and he did not appear to be worried, they noticed. Why should they worry?

But they did see that there was going to be a difficulty in that house in winter. One of their boilers broke down and a regiment of new heaters had to be added. They estimated that the coal alone would cost them two thousand dollars. To Mother Alphonsa the one object of life for the moment was to beg that two thousand dollars from friends and forget everything else but keeping warm till springtime, like dandelion seeds.

Then they were told that the water was bad; it was even suggested that it would give them all typhoid. It certainly had an oily taste, though this made them hope that one day they would find a gusher on the property. That hope — but also the nuisance of oily water — disappeared together with the discovery that some oil had been leaking into the water from defective machinery.

A much more serious reason for fear came upon them — and that remained, though toward its removal Mother Alphonsa steadily worked, and before her death, had already provided the solution. This was that the old wooden building was as bad a firetrap as could well be imagined. At any moment for twenty-five years Mother Alphonsa expected to see the whole place a single sheet of flame. Every time a patient died — and every patient went there to die — the Sisters were able to feel that that particular patient at least had won through to safety. The rest of them remained with the constant threat of a fire made all the greater by the constant winds on their hill.

From the patients the Sisters were careful to keep these fears. To the residents of Sherman Park — many of whom thought of cancer as a contagious disease — the establishment of Rosary Hill Home in the village, even though on its edge, was anything but a matter for rejoicing. But the Sisters rejoiced, and so did the patients.

These poor women — and now some men — came mostly from the slums of New York into the fairyland of the Westchester hills. They arrived pale, emaciated, and haggard eyed, but in a day or two were out in the vine draped summerhouse looking out over the peaceful valley and the blue hills. On the surrounding piazzas other patients sat or walked; and the more vigorous climbed the hill behind the Home into the wood, from which they came home with big bunches of wild flowers and glowing spirits. For those who could not walk the old carriage and the very old horse and the extremely old French coachman were pressed into service, and every fine afternoon a group went out for drives in the neighborhood. It soon was proved that the happiness and contentment found in this home often added months or even years to the lives of these doomed people. Even Gustave, the aged coachman, seemed to renew some part of his youth. Instead of limping about like a wounded hare he now almost tripped it like a fairy. If an errand had to be done in rain

or snow, he cheerfully bundled himself up and did what had to
be done. At other times he sat in his blue overalls and with a red
scarf round his neck in the pantry, peeling potatoes and apples.

Sister Rose, up for a visit from Cherry Street, saw him and
beckoned to Mother Alphonsa. As one painter to another, Mother
Alphonsa whispered: "Yes, a perfect subject for a French
watercolorist!"

The circumstances of the life of Rose Hawthorne — as afterward of Mrs. Lathrop — had been such that except for the
Wayside and, very briefly, the house on Post Hill Place in New
London, she had never had a very secure home. The nomad —
once he starts wandering — finds it hard to stop. Yet suddenly
this wanderer did stop — never to roam again, except from the
New York slums to the Westchester hills, for thirty unbroken
years. But if she found a home for herself it was only by providing a home for the homeless. About herself she never thought.
And if she was in charge of the country house instead of Cherry
Street — which was left under the care of Sister Rose — this was
not a matter of choice but necessity. Rosary Hill was obviously
the head house of this religious community now; it was therefore
at Rosary Hill that the head of the community had to reside.
Neither to Mother Alphonsa nor Sister Rose would it have
occurred to ask which of them was getting the pleasanter job.
Each woman gave herself to the cause without thinking about
herself, but did simply, without fuss or question, the thing that
needed to be done.

The only pang that either woman felt — and that was very
keen — was the pang of separation from one another. They had
formed an extremely close personal friendship, and this of course
persisted. In fact, it is not too much to say that the personal
attachment of these women enabled them to bear the pain of their
separation, as to each the cause was more than the individual.

When one reads Alice Huber's diary one sees very clearly that, at the outset, it was the affection and pity she felt for Rose Hawthorne Lathrop at their first meeting that drew her back to a work which was then wholly repugnant to her fastidious instincts. It was upon this natural basis of friendship that the supernatural charity animating their work was built.

That natural repugnance never left Sister Rose, as she confesses in her diary. It was fortunate in a case like hers that she should have been fortified not only by God's grace but the grace she derived from the older woman, whose qualities her own qualities completed and balanced. No better arrangement could have been made, than that Sister Rose should remain in New York and Mother Alphonsa take command of the country house.

But this necessitated a rather unusual arrangement of another kind. Sister Rose was the novice mistress at Rosary Hill. This meant in effect that her duties, as superior in New York, permitted her to see them only every week or so; for all practical purposes therefore these new recruits had to be trained by Mother Alphonsa who was, except in name, their novice mistress. Though sometimes both women came to have misgivings about this matter, and felt that their novices were not receiving due attention, Father Thuente told them they might set their minds at rest. There can be no doubt that he saw plainly that their force of character, the self-abnegation and the spiritual fervor of Mother Alphonsa and Sister Rose much more than made up for what a more regular, conventional, and commonplace novitiate would under the now existing canon law demand.*

* The new canon law making the positions of superior and master or mistress of novices rather incompatible with each other did not enter into force until 1918. On the other hand the Congregation of St. Rose of Lima for the relief of incurable cancer patients among the destitute poor came officially into being as early as the Feast of the Immaculate Conception, 1900. Until the enforcement, therefore, of the new canon law of 1918 the functions of superior and of master or mistress of novices could legitimately be combined in one person. Mother Alphonsa's method of operation, however, was apparently continued by her with due permission until her death, some eight years later.

The first winter was so hard a one for them at Rosary Hill that some of Mother Alphonsa's best friends — hardheaded business-men — thought she had undertaken something beyond her strength and advised her to give it up. She, however, argued that the second winter would be much easier — that they would be freed from the expense of renovation, and would have no heavy charges to meet except those of the mortgage and for heating. What was perfectly true was that few charitable enterprises could have been run so inexpensively as this.

Such arguments nevertheless do not sound very convincing in face of an empty coalbin and the difficulty of paying the mortgage interest when it was due. It so happened that they were saved at the last minute by legacies — in particular the balance of one of ten thousand dollars from Mrs. Mascho-Williams that was paid sooner than was expected. Most amazingly Mother Alphonsa announced in print that the Sisters had decided to trust promises, hope for windfalls, and pray for big donations. And that method seemed to work. It was at the end of a second novena asking for the two thousand dollars they owed in bills that Mrs. Mascho-Williams's estate was settled and overnight changed the entire financial situation.

But when, on December 8th, Mother Alphonsa went to St. Rose's to renew her vows with Sister Rose, everyone there saw how chapped and coarse her hands were. She wouldn't even allow more to be done for them than to have some vaseline put on. "I can't wait," she explained. "I've got to get back to look after the furnace. *That* isn't so bad. But the pipes have frozen, and we had to get snow and melt it for our cooking this morn-ing. That's what's made my hands like this."

She took it all lightly enough, but when she asked Mr. John D. Crimmins to become the treasurer of the institution he de-clined, seeing how bad was its financial position and having learned from past experience that the treasurer's function can be that of paying the bills out of his own pocket. Ten years later, he did consent to act as treasurer at St. Rose's; but this time he was blunt in saying he did not wish to be involved.

But Mother Alphonsa was equally blunt in the letter she wrote him, when in reply to his question as to their position she answered: "I can only say that the financial condition of this charity for cancerous poor is that of a beggar." She told him that she had spent $20,000 in the past year on the two homes and must have shocked all his principles of sound business by adding: "To give you an idea of my point of view, I will frankly state that I am glad we have spent $20,000 . . . and that today we are so urgently begging again. It is the principle which my conscience relishes most in this undertaking, greatly as I personally suffer from the whole principle." She reminded him that Madame Schervier, whose magnificent home and hospital for the aged now stands in New York as a monument to her faith in God's providence, shared her dislike of financial securities. It is, Mother Alphonsa tells Mr. Crimmins, her intention to spend everything they get, except for a thousand dollars or so kept in reserve, without attempting to build up any large investments. No wonder good Mr. Crimmins shuddered to hear such financial heresies and begged to be excused from accepting the treasurership.

Mother Alphonsa was determined to keep the work going by begging, but begging of a kind for which she had special talent — letters in the press and other printed appeals, as well as private letters to those who might be interested.

Already she had issued from Cherry Street her little pamphlet, *Sketch of Aims and Work of St. Rose's Free Home*, but this — eight pages of about two hundred words to a page — attempts only what its title indicates and contains nothing of the intimate and personal details which so strongly appeal to people and therefore make excellent publicity. At that sort of thing she was to show that she excelled. In order to provide a vehicle for it, she founded — with the first number appearing in August, 1901 — a little magazine she called *Christ's Poor*.

Yet she did not describe it as a "magazine." On the title page it is called "a monthly report," and in her letters Mother Alphonsa usually refers to it as a pamphlet. As 90 per cent of all the material that appeared in its rather irregularly issued numbers was written by herself — though she took contributions when she could get them, sometimes even when they had no bearing on her work — this was because it was easier for her to sit down and write an article herself, than to appeal to other people for one. If now and then young Hildegarde Hawthorne's verse, for example, was printed, this was not because it helped the poor in any obvious way but merely because good-natured Aunt Rose wished to give a little encouragement to a budding poet.

Mother Alphonsa saw her objective clearly. She made no attempt to establish a magazine, such as many religious organizations have, in order to help support the organization on its literary profits. Hers was the expectation of a loss, but not of a large one — a loss that might be more than made up by the interest aroused in the work itself. Though the cost was never very much — about seventy-five dollars an issue with very few subscriptions to offset it — nevertheless seventy-five dollars was a heavy enough bill to cause irregular publication.

Further, *Christ's Poor* was offered as a "report" rather than as a magazine because it was all about the cancer work. It is true that in some of the later issues — when Mother Alphonsa was hard pressed for time and could not sit down and write special articles — she would fill up blank pages with almost anything that came to hand. Then a useful stand-by was a report of a recent speech by President Theodore Roosevelt. More than once he appeared as a "filler," though of course this did represent a personal admiration on the part of Mother Alphonsa.

It is just as well that she regarded the magazine as she did.

None of her assistants had any literary talent or could have told about the work with the warmth and humor and charm and vividness at the command of Hawthorne's daughter. The magazine did therefore serve her purpose of keeping interest alive in the work; it also — though this was not in the least part of her intention — became, to some extent, an autobiography and is, in effect, the history of the beginnings of her cancer work.

The magazine, which was at first printed at the novitiate of the Dominican Fathers at Somerset, Ohio — and therefore at special rates — did not look very much like a religious magazine. The first issue — and most of the subsequent ones — had as frontispiece a reproduction of Millet's "Man with the Hoe" and some lines from Edwin Markham's famous poem:

> *There is no shape more terrible than this —*
> *More tongued with censure of the world's blind greed*
> *More filled with signs and portents for the soul —*
> *More fraught with menace to the universe.*

Other lines were used sometimes, but usually from the same poem; *always* from the same poem when Millet's picture appeared. The first issue had only fifteen pages and the subscription was fifty cents. There was an article "Acknowledgment of Kind Help" — which afterward was replaced by a list of donations; this thanked the doctors and the lawyer Mr. Greene. Another (also a rather regular feature) indicated the main needs of the Sisters and their patients. Other items were an article prominent in every issue — so that there could be no mistake — headed "The Objects of the Work"; odds and ends under the title "Record of the Charity"; and "The Real Case in Regards to Cancerous Poor" — this also was an explanation of the purpose of the charity. "It should be made so thorough and affectionately gentle," it concluded, "that even the poor can praise it." Earlier in that same article we are told that "this little pamphlet" seeks to explain and advertise the charity which "has now and then been attacked by opposition on the ground that it is not needed." Before long the magazine was four times and eventually six times as large and was for the most part filled with accounts of specific cases or incidents, but these — broadly speaking — were only added to what Mother Alphonsa said in the first issue and which she kept on saying.

None of the articles in that issue was signed. In fact there never were any signatures except those attached to the few poems and articles by special contributors printed later. Literary reputation was the very last thing the former Rose Hawthorne Lathrop was thinking about; nor did she write for the pleasure derived from creation. All that belonged to her past, and of her past she never spoke — even to those most closely associated with her. She had no other concern than interesting people in her work and so stimulating their support. At the same time the vigor and felicity of much that she wrote shows a very genuine literary gift. And without in the least seeking to do so, she revealed herself. Certainly her best writing appeared in these obviously hastily produced pages — always of course excepting that labor of love, her *Memories of Hawthorne*. But for that matter *Christ's Poor* several times acknowledges her indebtedness to her father, and shows Mother Alphonsa Lathrop as Hawthorne's daughter.*

Two things should be specially noted: one is her capacity for scorn; the other is an amazing forthrightness. Instances of scorn appear — one takes them as they come — in the second issue (page 6) when she speaks of one type of so-called charity worker who "will advise you to uplift the poor, after choosing the nice, clean specimens." And in the following issue she writes scathingly: "That the poor live an infernal life before death is convincing proof to us that they are to blame, and are to be ignored. . . . They are themselves no worse of heart than we are,

---

* She also shows herself to be little Rose Hawthorne still in a spelling which she did not always have time to check with the dictionary.

their sins being even more simple, if more obnoxious to the sight and hearing." Never in this charity worker is there the slightest trace of the characteristic faults of the "socially minded" — a smugness and a sense of superiority. The last thing in the world that this woman wished to be was respectable. Nobody was less of a pharisee than herself. She went to the poor, not only to live among them in the physical sense; she wished to be one of them. "Magnanimous men," she wrote, "whether soldiers, statesmen or benefactors, burn with a superb fire which there is no overlooking or mistaking." Later in the same article she says, "The Gospels were written for giants in sinew and spendthrifts in emotion."

The forthrightness appears in every line, and is sometimes no doubt not very tactful. Never does Mother Alphonsa use guarded or "official" language. She took her public completely into her confidence, in telling them what she hoped to accomplish, and how. In a letter to the New York *Times* she describes her method as "extremely like that of outdoor begging; the hand held out suddenly and insistently; but there is this difference, that the petition is known to proceed from a harmless and truthful poverty, on behalf of the saddest physical suffering and neglect of all."

As it was directly to the public that she made her appeal, she never sought state aid or, for that matter, any allocation from the special funds of Catholic charities. To have accepted such help might have meant some sacrifice of independence. This remains a principle of the Servants of Relief.

In "The Objects of the Work" — that constant feature — she says, among other things, that she means to prove "that the public is willing and able to provide all the money and many articles necessary for such charitable care as we undertake to give." The public was her essential co-operator; upon its "daily mercy" she never wearied in saying she depended. It was in that confidence — and her trust in God — that she went forward. She was utterly imprudent and improvident by all ordinary standards.

And she was to demonstrate that her methods, from which she never deviated by a hair's breadth, could succeed.

Perhaps she did have some advantages. As the daughter of the great Hawthorne, even as George Lathrop's widow, the press was ready to be kind to her. And she made good "copy." But this would have helped her only for the first article or two, after which her news value would have been exhausted. Though free publicity was provided by the press, it was on the tacit understanding that the publicity was put to good use. Moreover if she had tried to make too much use of it, or to capitalize on her advantages, again editors — and the public — would soon have got tired. But she was so obviously simple and fresh and disarming in her naïveté — so little of the professional publicity expert — that her charm never failed. She asked for little; her requests were most modest, if they were also unabashed; she never failed to get what she wanted.

She appealed sometimes to former friends and acquaintances. She knew Mark Twain slightly, from the New London days. And before that George Lathrop had induced him to read for the Authors' League at the Madison Square Theatre. With a delightfully innocent "gall" she wrote to him asking him to send her an article for *Christ's Poor*. The article she failed to get. But he replied to her on October 19, 1901, addressing her as the "Mrs. Lathrop" he had known, assuring her that, if he were not so hard driven, nothing would give him more pleasure "than to try to write something worth printing in your periodical, 'Christ's Poor'; indeed, you pay me a compliment which I highly value when you invite me to do it." Nothing would have been more gracefully put. Surprisingly he added: "I have known about this lofty work of yours since long ago — indeed from the day you began it." He says he has watched its progress, and that "its prosperity will be permanent since it has its endowment banked where it cannot fail until pity fails in the hearts of men. And that will never be."

How far Mark Twain carried out his promise to make the needs of this charity known among his friends, it is impossible to say. But Mrs. Clemens' name is several times found in the list of contributors to the work and on October 2, 1903, when she herself was too ill to write, her daughter Jean did so, enclosing a cheque for two beds that were needed and saying: "[Mother] wishes me to let you know how very much interested in your fine work she is; and you of course know that she is very eager for the success of your institution — possibly as eager as you; but that is not likely, for of course mother is an outsider, and not the originator of the hospitals." Within a year of that letter Mark Twain's wife died at Florence.

A friend of the old days, Mrs. Samuel G. Ward,* often sent contributions; so did Mrs. St. Gaudens, whom she had known at the Gilders' salon; and publishers — Houghton, Mifflin among them — also sent useful cheques. Most of the sums that came in were small — some as small as a quarter — but all were acknowledged both by being listed in *Christ's Poor* and by a personal letter from Mother Alphonsa. Not the most munificent but the most regular of these benefactors was Mr. Warren Greene, the well-known lawyer, who did all their legal business for them gratis. Never did his monthly cheque for twenty-five dollars fail to arrive, and often it was twice or triple that amount.

But not only did Mother Alphonsa print a list of contributions; she also published financial statements. In later years these were offered to the public in a more or less scientific fashion: but the first statements are all the more appealing because they are so very amateurish. In *Christ's Poor* for November, 1901, Mother Alphonsa cheerfully remarks (page 12): "The report of the financial state of our humble Homes is not reassuring, except that we can say we have always escaped disaster, and expect to do so now." But the expenses tabulated on page 10 are amazingly small, though it should be remembered that for that particular month

* A friend of her mother's and a convert to the Catholic Church.

the heavy outlays on the mortgage and for fuel did not occur. To be statistical for once, here is the statement:

Payments Made in September for Rosary Hill Home

Feed for live stock	38.30
Plumbing and boiler setting	36.70
Bread, expressage, and stamps at village depot	45.26
Clothing	7.10
Carpentry	15.38
Drugs	20.68
Man on farm	5.00
Engineer and general worker	55.00
Barber for male patients	2.75
	226.17

Amount Spent in St. Rose's Home, Cherry Street for September

Groceries, fruit, and vegetables	31.27
Meat bill	22.80
Bread bill	4.60
Rolls and cake	2.80
Small sundries	14.30
Woman to help	7.40
	83.17

Under this appears the note: "Vegetables, sent from the farm of Rosary Hill Home, lessened expense."

Further explanations are made in the January, 1902, number: "There being No necessity, in the care of incurable cancer, for OPERATIONS, the paraphernalia of a hospital is not necessary in our hospital homes. . . . Moderate effort alone is in demand, so far as instruments and surgical relief go." It may be added that the doctors at Cherry Street gave their services free and charged only nominal fees at Rosary Hill. "In spite of this simplicity and economy," Mother Alphonsa ventures to say, "it is often said that the patients fare better than those often do in institutions where large sums are paid." With justice she took special pride in that fact that the Homes served very good food very well cooked. "The reason probably is that no self-interested or careless person intervenes between the market and the meal when served." Anybody who has had much experience of institutions — whether of colleges or hospitals — will know that this is a good deal to be able to claim.*

After remarking that most patients had small insurance policies that relieved the Sisters of the expense of burying them, she continues: "On the other hand, there are certain large outlays. In the city Home, there is a Relief Room, to which people come in their hunger and eviction, to whom food and rent are given — after careful investigation — seldom in ready money, but by direct communication with the grocer and landlord; except for small donations to persons already known to be trustworthy." Apart from the cost of heating Rosary Hill and the payment of the mortgage, she says that she does not expect the outlay there to

---

* "To the casual observer, who is not familiar with our work, it might appear from a survey of our yearly expenditures that the patients and sisters are receiving only the barest necessities. The truth is, however, that each year our homes receive large donations of canned goods, meats and vegetables and other necessities which materially reduce the expenses. In the past, we have not included these material donations in our yearly statements but in the future we plan to give a more accurate picture by not only including donations but also the value of the nursing services of the Sisters. If we were to include our Sisters' services at even a minimum of their worth, the total cost of operating our Homes would be tremendously increased.

"We would like to point out, while we are on the subject of expenses, in order to correct any views to the contrary, that our patients receive the very best that we can procure for them in the line of food, medication, etc. We always purchase the first quality and if there is any little dainty that will add to the comfort or pleasure of the patient, we do not hesitate to procure it. The Sisters have a vow of poverty which obligates them to be careful of the goods entrusted to them, but this does not infringe in any way on the requirements for the general comfort or happiness of the patients." — *From Minutes of Meeting of Board of Trustees, May, 1946.*

be large, after a few absolutely necessary renovations have been completed. In the issue for the following May she summarizes everything. During the past year the charity had housed 65 patients, of whom 28 had died. They had 15 nurses — all of course Sisters — and the per capita cost of all expenses in the two Homes, allowing for deductions on account of death, was $300 a year. "In St. Rose's Free Home," she adds, "now paid for, the average is actually much less, as will be the case in Rosary Hill Home, when it is finished and paid for." Really it is not possible to see how things could have been conducted more economically — especially when the economies were never at the expense of the patients. It all boiled down to this — no reserve fund was (on principle) laid by for a rainy day. But the public was candidly informed: "The Sisters at Hawthorne need almost anything that a human being could use." Sitting at the little desk which was her editorial office she dared to dream of what she called "epics of charity" — of work of this sort as an outlet for genius — "the great bloom from seeds sown by Christ and His friends in the Spring of compassion." Never did she think of her own work as more than a very small thing — but she did at least see that it was in this work that she had effectuated the creative gift she had always known she possessed but that had amounted to so little, after all, when she had attempted artistic expression. How very true it was, she thought, that only in losing one's life can one find it.

CHAPTER IX

The Guests

As far back as the start at Scammel Street when Mrs. Watson was received by Rose Lathrop into the dingy slum tenement whose only attractive feature was a floor painted marigold yellow, all the patients had been treated as guests. What was offered to them was of course charity of the sweetest and tenderest kind, yet one hesitates to use a word which the world's acquaintance with "do-gooders" has fixed in the derisive proverb "as cold as charity." The experience of the poor with most charity workers has convinced them that only too often such people cannot truthfully say they are constrained by the charity of Christ. Therefore a less resounding word, but one not so abused, serves the purpose better — "hospitality." The poor whom Mother Alphonsa took in were her guests — not merely people whose minimum needs were provided for but men and women whose whims were humored, so long as these were not too unreasonable and it was possible to give them what they fancied they would like.

In the little talks she would make from time to time to the Sisters — especially to those being trained in the novitiate — and which she sometimes used afterward as articles in her magazine — Mother Alphonsa was emphatic: "The one thing I am really anxious about," she used to tell them over and over again, "is the *quality* of our kindness." She did of course tell them, "we hope to grow into a large band of women devoted to this and other incurable diseases among the poor." In any organization they would have been told something of the sort. And perhaps in many novitiates they would have heard: "We must be so humble in our spirit and in our labor that no women could be more humble." But nowhere could be heard such words spoken with a more passionate conviction. The thing that startled and electrified was to be told: "Unless we can really forget our own material, unspiritual interests, we are as miserable in our folly of sham assistance as the poor are in their disease, as useless in our false delicacy as the poor are in their ignorance, and so the world has but one more class of fools the more, and still another class of morally sick people — those who attempt to be kind without being devoted."

Another day she would say: "Possibly we enter religion with the idea that we are going to pray vocally all the time, or at least remain in peaceful contemplation of God; then we are appalled to discover that we must scrub, cook and obey as to forms of prayer, and as an evidence of religious sincerity, whereas the prostrations and ecstasies which we had regarded as signs of grace are received as dubious testimony." She laid it down as an axiom: "It is an absolute physical and mental necessity that persons who pray much should work actively with the body."

She assured her novices — what indeed they saw to be the truth — that they were not to be among those who enter a convent sturdy, rosy, and cheerful, and in a few weeks, become pale and languid. "Oh, yes," she exclaimed, "their prayers may become purer and their patient resignation is often beautiful to see, but there is surely no point in letting them fade away when they could work for the public good! We shall be pure spirits quickly enough; but I'm not wanting to see any little angel — perhaps only a nervous and acid little thing — developing a cough and then have her superiors wonder why some of their best subjects last such a little while. Nursing does not flourish upon bodily asceticism — though I don't need to tell you that our mortifications should be hourly."

Another day she would tell her novices: "God is so generous that even when we merely act harmlessly He is sure to reward us. What then when we try to be heroic? Why, nothing pays such dividends! What we should be humble about is that we can do so little for the gift God is sure to give us. We might as well stop thinking how generous it would be to do something for God without looking for any return from Him. That may be virtue, but it is very stupid and mistaken virtue. You can be sure of one thing — you will get a reward from God for every act worthy of reward, and if you are not rewarded by Him, that is a certain sign that you don't deserve it. Undoubtedly in the past, as now, there were relatively few really noble souls, but it does seem to me that there were in the past fewer complacent triflers. A mechanical usefulness — that, to be sure, never disturbs routine, but it never evolves the slightest ability to act nobly when left to itself. How many people enter the religious life whose heroism never leads them higher than to be a pharisee. How are we going to move mountains unless we start trying?"

But then another day she would balance this with: "There is a rather fantastic estimate in the world about the sacrifice that nurses of the cancerous poor must make. And certainly there is an element of courage in befriending the kind of people whom we befriend. But everybody who lives a vigorous kind of life has to exercise courage. It takes courage even to live — unless one is a lizard! There is no need, though, for us to exaggerate what we are doing. The great saints are as dead as Baldur! What we do have to show is compassion; for that there is no substitute. The time may come when, with the discovery of a cure for cancer, this work of ours will become a fossil. But we haven't got there yet. Our function in the world is to do something for the terrible sorrow those know to whom no pity is given."

But this of course could not be left entirely to little talks to the Sisters or little articles in the magazine. It had to be carefully set down in the constitutions of the Sisters of Relief, and though their stringency has recently been somewhat mitigated, their provisions are, in the main, those laid down at the outset.

Like all Dominicans, the Servants of Relief of the Congregation of St. Rose of Lima follow the Rule of St. Augustine. The distinctive regulations of this particular group — its constitutions — are therefore all that need be glanced at here. Two unusual features are the constitutional insistence upon plenty of good food for the Sisters, as this is necessary because of the nature of their work, and that the Little Office of the Blessed Virgin Mary be said in English not Latin.

To summarize these constitutions — of which the most interesting concerns the relations of the Sisters to the patients — it is expressly laid down (page 52) that "only the very poor who are suffering from cancer in its last stages" be received; that "no pay patients be received," or any donations be accepted in connection with them. If anyone who brings a patient says, "You will not receive money but I will make it all right," that person must be made to understand that such a patient "is not a subject for our work, for when such persons come in, the work is in more or less danger, and persons who can well afford to pay elsewhere will take the place of the poor."

The constitutions further insist that those received shall always be treated with the utmost consideration, but that the aim of the charity is spiritual good even more than the alleviation of physical suffering. There is to be no harsh speaking to any patient, and no shrinking on the part of any nurse from close contact. To emphasize this the Sisters are forbidden to wear rubber gloves when dressing cancers. There are to be no experiments with the patients, no use of knife or even of radium is allowed. There were occasions when Mother Alphonsa could have obtained large contributions if only she had relaxed this rule. She much preferred poverty. Indeed, in order to emphasize unworldliness the constitutions lay down that all future foundations are, like the first two, to begin in poverty and in a poor part of the city.

To implement this it was laid down that no paid nurses were to be employed, except a male orderly for the men. In the pamphlet issued in 1906, Mother Alphonsa declared that all hired help is bound to be inferior and, in the *Report* for 1923–1924, that "it is best not to employ professional substitutes to carry on our compassion for us." And though it is perhaps rather strong to speak of "the diabolical nature of most orderlies," Mother Alphonsa soon discovered that, as a class, they were somewhat given to drink, though it is only fair to add that the luck of the Servants of Relief in this respect has been very good. Even so, the employment of any male nurse or orderly was looked upon as an unavoidable evil. Mother Alphonsa made, as we shall see, constant efforts to solve that problem in a different way.

But that not all the orderlies were of an undesirable type is made clear by a letter written by Mother Alphonsa on January 4, 1909, to Miss Mary T. Kivlon of Fitchburg, Massachusetts. It also unintentionally reveals the writer's kindness and runs, in part, as follows: "I know that you & your lovely friends will pardon my delay in writing, unseemly as it is, when I tell you that our male nurse has been ill with pneumonia, and it has been my duty to nurse him, so that I have watched his breathing & symptoms constantly, by day & night. As he is a most devoted servant of our sick men, & was overtired when he fell ill, we feared he could not live through the strain. But now he is apparently out of danger. I leave you to judge whether this mainstay of our male department did not necessitate great work for us all, & our less feeble patients among the men, by falling out of the ranks for a time, & I really had to let my letters go, for I had scarcely a moment's sleep . . . since a life hung on the fidelity to the nursing."

Yet good as were the services of this particular man, he was, after all, only a servant working for wages, and not part of a corporation that would continue even should he die. Mother Alphonsa's hope therefore continued to be that she would obtain the help of a group of men who looked upon nursing as part of a religious vocation. Only from those making a complete sacrifice of themselves would the higher devotion, or even any real efficiency, come.

The patients were from all walks of life, and had nothing in common except their incurable disease and their destitution. In the last of her *Reports* Mother Alphonsa wrote what would have been equally true at any other time: "It seems as if in no section of human existence could persons be more admirable, on an average, than cancer patients as the Sisters see them; indeed, it seems as if no class held such brave, devout, nonsense-free human beings."

Before looking at individuals, the aspect of the group as such should be noted.

There has never been any distinction in these homes on account of race or religion.* It is of course natural enough that in a home under Catholic auspices Catholics should predominate. But this is only because the homes are better known inside than outside Catholic circles. In the Georgia home the Catholics do not number 10 per cent of the patients, and elsewhere the Catholic predominance is not overwhelming. No religious test of any sort is applied; all that counts for admission is need.

No members of religious orders — male or female — are accepted, as these have a claim upon their orders and so cannot be considered as destitute. But a few secular priests, without means, have been accepted, and though Jews are usually well taken care of by their own charitable organizations, they are by no means ineligible for these Homes.

Whatever the faith of the patient, it has been proved over and

* The home, recently founded at Atlanta, Ga., could not function at all, unless it did separate whites and Negroes. That concession has regretfully to be made there; it is made nowhere else.

over again that they come closer to God in the spiritual atmosphere these Homes provide. It seems almost like getting a ticket to heaven to be admitted. But though the number of conversions to the Catholic Church has been large — so large that Mother Alphonsa never would publish it — her work was in no sense a proselytizing agency. Yet its motive was religious, as it tried to aid Catholics to be better Catholics and to help all the patients to make their peace with God. Never was it Mother Alphonsa's way to tabulate statistics; but in a letter written, in 1918, to the editors of *Dominicana* at Washington, she told them: "The number of conversions at the city home of the Sisters continue to be remarkable under the spiritual influence of the Reverend John T. McEntyre, P.R., of the not distant St. Teresa's Church. And sometimes as many as three converts a week are received."

It was the knowledge of the spiritual good that was being effected that sustained these Sisters. As for the patients, they grew holy in bearing their sufferings. It reminds one of the verses Mother Alphonsa's childhood friend, Louisa Alcott, found under a wounded soldier's pillow when she was nursing during the Civil War at the Georgetown Hospital.

> *I give a patient God*
> *My patient heart.*

That was what made it all so well worth doing. "Mother," a visitor once said to the superior of Rosary Hill, "I wouldn't do what you're doing for twenty thousand dollars a year."

That visitor got the instant answer, "Neither would I — for twenty thousand dollars a year!"

Many of those received at Rosary Hill, as at St. Rose's, had no idea what was the matter with them. Of course they usually found out quickly enough, and the Sisters never attempted to deceive them. These hospitals were somewhat exceptional in permitting no lies. But there was no reason, as a rule, for *forcing* grim knowledge upon the patients, and some actually died without knowing that their malady was what Mother Alphonsa used to call the insanity of the flesh. Over and over again this happened: a patient would beckon a passing Sister and say in a horrified whisper: "Do you know what is the matter with this man you've put me in with?"

Instead of playing with the man and asking, "No, what *does* he have?" she would answer instead, "Yes, he has cancer."

"But Sister, if you put me in with him *I'll* get cancer too!"

It was hard to make them believe the disease was not contagious. All that was attempted was to make them happy, and to bring them, if possible, to God. The Sisters all hoped that some time a cure would be found for cancer. But they were not concerned with speculative possibilities but the practical considerations to which they limited themselves.

Whether these men and women knew it or not — and most of them of course knew it perfectly well — they had all gone there to die. But though doomed, they were received into a home full of love, whose one concern was making their last days a little easier. Indeed it was for all of them days that were made immeasurably easier because of the tenderness they received. Their physical sufferings were considerably lessened, and the mental anguish of feeling themselves abandoned and unloved — *that* was removed altogether. A very gentle old lady spoke for hundreds when she told Mother Alphonsa, "I felt when struggling up the steps of the house that I was coming home, and a great peace filled my heart."

This being so, they very often lasted a long time — years when the doctors had given them weeks. But in the early part of the century, when the knife and radium were not so freely used — often, in the case of the poor, merely experimentally — the general longevity was considerably more than it is now. Few patients who arrive at any of these houses today live out their year. At that time several of the patients who were received still had seven or eight years before them. This, however, was usually true only of those with face cancers; even at that time others lingered only for months or even weeks.

The pervading atmosphere is one of cheerfulness. It is not always twilight. Many of the patients, these "wounded" men and women, are better off — except of course for their mortal malady — than they have ever been in their lives; and all are made comfortable. Even the characteristic odor of cancer can be reduced by frequent attention until it is almost unnoticeable. All is made sunny and pretty for them and their sufferings are not constant. The cares of the world have fallen from them; they no longer have to worry as to whether or not they will be cured, they can therefore address themselves undisturbed to mortal life's main business, life eternal. Passing into one of these homes after neglect they said — how many times did not Mother Alphonsa hear it said? — "This is heaven!"

What particularly delighted Mother Alphonsa was the good done to the men patients she was able to receive into a real home no longer that makeshift annex on the other side of Cherry Street. Sad as the physical condition of these men might be, she noticed that they showed a most extraordinary capacity for rebounding from being poor, pale, bedridden, or (at best) chair-ridden invalids to brave hearts, who, though doomed, were glad to help lift the furniture or work in the garden. The manly character, she decided, was so brave and good that generosity and courtesy brightened every circumstance of the day. The Sisters were gladdened by the golden and silver praise these men showered upon them.

They had a favorite spot on the shady side of the porch that completely encircled the long narrow house, and there they gathered and talked and read the papers and smoked. Every now and then a couple of them would slip away for some chore that needed doing, and so anxious were they to show their gratitude in this fashion that Mother Alphonsa tried to stop them. "You're doing too much; it isn't good for you," she would tell them. She did not say that work that heated the blood was very bad for cancer, for she did not wish them to be reminded of their condition, but rather to forget it as far as possible. Even apart from this, too strenuous work was liable to send them to bed for a day or two with a belligerent headache.

Her indulgence extended to their smoking — something distinctly dangerous in that firetrap. But she realized that it would be hard for these men to be deprived of tobacco, and that if she attempted the prohibition, some of them would certainly try to evade it. So she and all the Sisters kept their eyes open for possible dropped matches and cigarette butts, and hoped for the best.

Some few rules are of course unavoidable in an institution. But there could never have been an institution run with fewer regulations imposed on the patients — those imposed on the Sisters were plentiful. No doubt it was often a cause of inconvenience to the staff when a patient decided to stay in bed, or go to bed early. But Mother Alphonsa's principle was that the patients should, as far as possible, be allowed to do as they liked. What was the Home founded for except to make them happy? And was it not almost the definition of a home that it was the place where one may behave as one pleases? She even humored the men when she found that the little room she gave them to be their smoking room — feeling it safer that the smoking be always done in one place — for some reason or other did not suit them. The men continued, as before, to choose, like birds, their own perch. Anybody else might have gone and said, "Now listen: you *have* a smoking room. I'm going to ask you to use it and *not* come out on the porch to smoke!" But not Mother Alphonsa. As they did not use their smoking room she let them follow their own devices. The smoking room was turned into a bedroom.

A happy solution — at all events for fine weather — was presented when Miss Anna Martense Wilbur came one day and said: "Mother, I'd like to give you a thousand dollars."

Immediately Mother Alphonsa's mind began to wonder what she would spend it on — a ceiling looked as though about to fall — and some new plumbing was needed; but Miss Wilbur went on, "As I'm giving it in memory of my brother Gerrit, don't you think it would be best to use it for your men?"

"Yes, my dear, I'm sure I can put it to good use for our men in some way. That's very kind of you."

What she decided on was a summerhouse built in the men's pretty embowered garden and whatever was left over could be spent on making the greenhouse more usable in the winter. So there in the summerhouse, with three arches on each side — so many frames for the blue hills and the green trees — the men could sit and smoke while listening to the birds which seemed to have a special fondness for that spot. When Father Thuente was shown the summerhouse he exclaimed, "Why, you're treating the men better than the women!" Previously the men, when they had gone to this garden, hobbling there with pillows and shawls, or, if they were too feeble for that, followed by a Sister or the male nurse carrying these articles, had been badly drenched whenever a sudden storm came. They were not nimble enough to get back to the house in time. But now they were quite secure.

As for the women whom Father Thuente accused Mother Alphonsa of neglecting, they got their summerhouse only a little later. There under a grape vine in the arbor a Sister would read to the patients who were sufficiently well to go there, while they looked at the Home's three sheep in their little meadow where a young shepherd dog frisked about learning to take charge of them.

All kinds of cases arrived there — pathetic, interesting, and even amusing. There was an impresario and his actress wife, both afflicted with the disease — admirable people they were too. There was the ancient old man who, like rain on an old roof, seemed to come through at every point — in the guests' parlor, or the Sisters' refectory, anywhere where there was a door. One day he even got into a peach basket, and when the Sister pulled him to his feet, he walked along quite placidly with the peach basket sticking behind. There was the former sea captain who when dying told the Sister, "If any of my friends come to see me, tell them that I have set sail, but I shall remember them when I pull into port." And there was the queer old lady — "Aunt Kate" as they called her — who spent the last eight of her seventy years there, who had a still queerer hat which she valued as something priceless, which, as an antiquity, it may have been. Her greatest worry was deciding upon whom to bestow this treasure before she died. One day, when she thought her end near, she made up her mind at last. Then the Sisters had to use consummate tact in getting the beneficiary to accept the old hat. Later in the day she decided she was not going to die just then after all — and so wanted her hat back. Now a tact even more consummate had to be used, so that the recipient could be induced to show a decent sense of reluctance in returning that priceless monstrosity for a little longer to its owner. In startling contrast to her was Helen, an eleven-year-old girl — they had children of two in the Home with cancer — who had had twenty-four operations and who was so happy that she would never have to have another. Charlotte, still younger, soon joined her, and they had the greatest fun together with Jack and Jill, their Australian doves, and the canaries Helen raised and the farmyard chickens and ducks. In the spring, these two girls were the first to find the early anemones, violets, and columbine in the wood behind the house.

In one of the first numbers of *Christ's Poor* Mother Alphonsa wrote: "The atmosphere of economy is very precarious to the health. . . . I believe no economy is kind in charity, except what is provided by the will of God in circumstances over which the giver has no control, because the will of God is unmistakably perceived. Obligations that must obviously be met control obligations which we would generously like to meet. We should not voluntarily throw away a penny of our funds. But if by a too careful investigation we throw away charity instead of coin, we shall be asked for the multiplication of the talent without having accumulated it. . . . What shall be said, then, of the reckless elegance of buildings, and the reckless apportionment of salaries, in institutions, organizations, and hospitals, and of the severe economies in these places which are enforced on behalf of the poor, for whom these places are founded?"

Her precept certainly accorded with her practice, so much so that she used at times to alarm the people round her by giving too freely. Once Sister Rose fell ill just as summer approached, the season of the year when funds were always low because so many people were out of town. To provide for this at the city house, Sister Rose had put a few hundred dollars in reserve, and as she knew that Mother Alphonsa knew where she kept the key to her cashbox, she gave the key to one of the Sisters, so that the money would be safe from depredations. But that Sister fell ill too, and put the key in its usual place. Mother Alphonsa seized upon it in triumph and went straight to Wanamakers, where she bought something for everybody, except herself, a hundred and fifty dollar radio for the patients, and even a dog for one of the men she had once happened to hear say he was fond of dogs.

In the *Buffalo Express* for May 30, 1903, there was published a delightful letter she wrote to Mrs. Reed and a group of women in Buffalo who had helped her from time to time. And this shows the delicacy of her kindness to her guests. "You cannot know," she said, "how my hours of chance are wrested from me to prevent my writing letters. Housework, sewing, guests, new cases, deaths hurry me from one hour till another. You are so kind and make us feel so safe and befriended in your unwearying efforts to keep discomfort away from our much shadowed life. The offer of towels and sheets in the near future is seized upon. The pretty new cups and saucers were so needed. I find that many of the patients, especially the women, were once pretty comfortable, and our big, heavy cups have sometimes taken away their appetite. So now we gladly use the pretty ones on the trays of the most sensitive folks, as I know God does not want me to remodel their minds and tastes, at this late day in their suffering. In regard to a photograph of me, I am as prosaic as any other old servant. Besides, I think a nun ought to look like every other nun, unless she is a saint of superlative magnitude. Even then, though I love their faces, I cannot see that my devoted admiration pleases God or them a bit, whereas a fervent 'Hail Mary full of grace the Lord is with thee' in the words of God's messenger, would be listened to with respect in heaven. Perhaps your dear mother would like a photograph [sic] of our Catherine of Siena to show her what a Dominican should look like, and I am going to see if I can get a copy of an authentic print of her glorious face. Sanctity is such a limner! No art can fathom its touch and light."

From the long letter to Miss Mary T. Kivlon from which quotation has already been made, another passage might be given at this place: "Well, dear friend, now let me tell you how happy the box made us all! It . . . made us exclaim with our gratification as we unpacked it. I assure you that we find such gifts a real delight because we are too driven with hourly work to broadcast the appeals for them . . . & as we have for a long time printed less in the papers about our Homes, fewer people notice our great opportunity for giving clothing to the sick poor both in & outside of our domiciles. . . . The linen & cotton were fairly hugged with satisfaction, for though not exactly charming like the gifts of more definite shape, they mean successful 'dressings' that are comfortable for our sick. Of course when a patient gives a sigh of relief & thanksgiving after a dressing done by a Sister, that Sister is in a seventh heaven. You told me not to expend any outward show of gratitude to you in my busy life, but I cannot help wishing to speak from my heart of my devoted thankfulness to you." She signs herself "Your loving and devoted M. Alphonsa (Lathrop, O.S.D.)."

There we perceive Mother Alphonsa's real warmth of heart, united to the sort of delicacy that proves kindness and courtesy to be almost synonymous. The same qualities appeared in her being willing — indeed anxious — to leave her patients in the belief — which they nearly all had — that their families were paying for them. Many of these patients were aware that their relatives could have paid. Mother Alphonsa knew in how many instances those capable of this would not pay. For such patients themselves this was fortunate, for the offering of money was an impassible barrier to admittance to either of her homes. But where relatives or friends failed, she did not, though then her scorn flared. "It will be conceded," she wrote of such a case, "that he was destitute enough to belong to a charitable home, being without means and without love, and alas, without honorable friends." On the other hand, over and over again, she helped a poverty-stricken family not only because of its own need, but perhaps even more to relieve the anxiety she knew that the patient would otherwise feel.

The tramps who appeared so plentifully in spring also were her frequent guests, if only overnight ones. It is of course a tradition at Catholic religious houses to give food and shelter to those who ask them, but Mother Alphonsa's indulgence toward these "bluebirds" was something special, and almost anticipated the activities of those Anglican Franciscans at Graymoor, a little to the North, who afterward became Catholic Franciscans. She often had nine or ten tramps at a time for dinner, and would scold herself for this with the reminder, "You'd better remember that this charity was not founded for tramps but for people who can't walk!" She was always vowing to throw the next one that came on the ash heap. But she felt she had to ask him a question first, and she found that if she asked a question, she was lost. Why, the man turned out to be a human being, not a piece of tin or old scrap iron! At her second question she would be feeling as sorry for him as she had felt for anyone in her whole life. She believed that they had all come to this pass through drink, and no doubt that was frequently true. If they admitted it, she could forgive the weakness, but if a man denied it, she at once set him down as an arrant liar.

One day one of the tramps tried another kind of humbug with the Sister who was giving him a lunch in the kitchen.

"Over at White Plains," he told her, "there are ever so many murders that never are discovered."

"Is that so?"

"Yes, ma'am, — ever so many."

She took the wind completely out of his sails with, "Were you ever present?"

"*What!*" he demanded staring.

"Did you ever see one of those murders in White Plains?"

He looked cautiously to left and right and stammered out, "Of co-co-course not."

Never again did that man go to Rosary Hill.

But many of the tramps proved to be fairly decent fellows, and were glad to do a day's work for three big meals and fifty cents. The French Fathers had advised Mother Alphonsa, "Be nice to the tramps. But not *too* nice." And she discovered that the good food at Rosary Hill was news in the peripatetic grapevine. But like her father, even when she knew she was being imposed on, she suffered it — that is, of course, so long as the imposition was not carried too far.

She thought of the view of the Westchester Hills as conducive to peace, and therefore as an aid in the treatment of her patients. A little gardening — so long as it was only a little — or a few light chores on their farm also was good for morale. Nobody, however, was obliged to do anything, for they were all guests, but they were free to do what they wished, as this was their home.

Even the farmyard animals were almost regarded as guests, though in their case they ended up on the plates of the other guests. The patients liked to watch what went on in the barnyard, and so did Mother Alphonsa — when she could spare the time. A hen bringing up ducklings greatly amused her. She thought she noticed that it was "the most honest and generous-hearted hen [that] is always selected for this trying role." The pathos therefore made it perfect. She watched how the poor, black hen good naturedly followed her brood to the water and then stood gazing bewilderedly at their unaccountable propensities.

The doves were as beautiful as lyrics, and Mother Alphonsa never tired of watching them. At four in the morning the tattoo of their small, hard feet began on the roof. At once she felt that something noble had been added to the waking dawn.

Though she had no geese, she did not wonder that they saved Rome when she looked at their cousins the ducks swimming in their tank. The hens came to the water and took from it a kind of cup of tea; the doves lighted on the rim, looked at their images and had a sip. But the ducks were in their element — with nothing of the grace of swans but with a kind of plain sturdy efficiency that pleased her.

Money was still hard to get and went out very quickly. The items of expense given often seem ridiculously low, and then are suddenly offset by some huge items. In May, 1903, for instance, she had to pay out $4,637.10, but this included $1,311.51 for meat and groceries (going back for over seven months), $215 for four funerals, $1,500 for a new heater and radiators, and $874 to Lord and Taylor for a year. The following month only a little more than a quarter of that was expended, and it would have been little indeed except for $230 for coal and $260 for mortgage interest and $200 for a plumber's bill. The food in both houses together cost less than $150. In July, the total expenses were less than $1,000, including $300 paid off on the new heating system. August was got down to $555.69. The expenses for both houses seem to have averaged about $1,000 a month. This was managing very well. But as Christmas, 1903, drew near, the bills had mounted alarmingly. Not only did the Sisters have payments to meet for fire insurance and on the mortgage and for coal, but there was a bill at a general store for about $2,000. Mother Alphonsa saw no merry Christmas for the Sisters or her guests. Yet in the February issue of *Christ's Poor* she was able to announce that $1,500 had come in, so that some of the bills had been paid and even little Christmas presents provided. "But," she added, almost gaily, "the large creditor who needs payment is still waiting, and all the coal piled in the cellars of the country Home is unpaid for." So the Sisters still needed prayer to unravel the tangled mystery of their financial affairs. She goes on: "January brought the welcome young year; and he turned out to be a regular baby." In the fierce cold the pipes froze and the hydraulic engine broke down, and the local talent only made matters worse. However, experts from New York appeared, just when Mother Alphonsa feared all her patients would get pneumonia, so she was able to conclude: "Never had baby year been so cunning and satisfactory. God grant that he may grow up to be very good; and especially attentive to the Servants of Relief, who are always asking for attentiveness."

The patients were Mother Alphonsa's guests in life; they were often so even in death. For though most of them had some little insurance that would provide for their burial, many had nothing at all. At first Mother Alphonsa wondered whether it was right to spend upon the dead money that she had collected for the living, but she reminded herself that she helped all kinds of distressed people — some of them not ill at all — regarding these as "the pensioners of the poor," whose prayers would bring a blessing to the cancer work.

Then one poor woman begged to be taken to the home simply that she might die there and be buried from Rosary Hill chapel. The promise was made, for so piteous an appeal as hers was something Mother Alphonsa could never resist. But by the time they had arranged for a large carriage and a stretcher — as they had no ambulance — the woman could not be moved and was dying bitterly disappointed. The word had not been kept after all.

Almost at the last moment Mother Alphonsa sent her promise that she would be buried from the Sisters' chapel, though she felt that this time she had gone too far. But what would God, she asked herself, wish for this poor woman? Why should she be denied the consolation she had sought? "Our own poor," she wrote, "welcomed the sacred body, the temple of the Holy Ghost, thankful that they could pray around it and rescue it from ignominious neglect, when she could no longer eloquently plead for herself."

They had their own burial plot — it could almost be seen from Rosary Hill — in the All Souls' cemetery at Pleasantville. There the daughter of Longfellow, the wife of Milmore, the sculptor, had donated a granite cross where the Sisters and their patients were to repose. As Mother Alphonsa often used to say, it completed their home for them.

CHAPTER X

Friends and Neighbors

The arrival of the daughter of Hawthorne in the neighborhood had, in one way, the effect of a very mild and quiet bomb. Before 1901 was out, the name of the place, which had hitherto been Sherman Park, with Unionville as its railway station and Neperan as the post office, became Hawthorne. It was professedly named after the writer, but of course it happened only because of Mother Alphonsa's settling at Rosary Hill. She gazed with a rather amused eye at the hot battle raging at the foot of the hill between the "Hawthorners" and the "Neperaners," but took no part in the village controversy. At least what happened indicated that the good will of the community had already been won; at the time of her first coming the establishment of a cancer hospital there had been received with consternation by some of the inhabitants.

There was no resident chaplain until 1912, but they relied on the service of temporarily resident priests, or on one of the French Dominican Fathers, who were still in a neighboring house. But Father McEntyre, their good friend of St. Teresa's Church, was conspicuous in the help he gave, and later served as spiritual director and as member of the Board of Trustees. This office he retained even after being appointed rector of the seminary at Dunwoodie. And Bishop Cusack, the auxiliary in charge of religious orders, also showed himself a firm friend, at a time when some influential members of the archdiocesan clergy were inclined to be critical. Anything, of course, at all out of the ordinary is certain to receive the disapproval of the conventionally minded, whose ideas (useful enough no doubt, in their way) can only move in the groove of set routine. It is worth while noting, however, that Archbishop Corrigan, and then his successors Cardinal Farley and Cardinal Hayes, always upheld Mother Alphonsa and the Sisters.

The novitiate was at Rosary Hill, with the novice mistress, Sister Rose, living elsewhere — in itself a sufficiently unusual state of affairs to give a handle to those who wished to complain. And the novitiate consisted of a good deal of hard work; so much so that willingness to work was the first thing looked for. Regarding this one finds rather caustic comments at times from Sister Rose in her diary. And Mother Alphonsa had to tell the young women who had joined her: "I know it's all a breathless routine of work here. But remember that Mass and the recital of the Little Office and your spiritual reading and the reading aloud during dinner give you periods of refreshment far more than working women ever find in the world, or than women of leisure usually permit themselves. Our particular group of Sisters undoubtedly do accept work that is more exhausting than most nurses know — except during epidemics or in time of war, or in the mission field perhaps. Well, what about the calm of conventual life? That, my dear Sisters, has to be for us in our interior peace, which is the highest and best form of peace. It is not to be acquired by the insincere or the lukewarm, those who must have exterior peace when they enter a convent. Here you can expect hard work, often turmoil. Let your peace be in your hearts."

But the situation of the novices sometimes troubled Mother Alphonsa and Sister Rose, until Father Thuente — who had become prior at St. Vincent Ferrer's on Park Avenue — wrote the novice mistress a reassuring letter. It was dated January 16, 1912, and read in part: "Your objection does not seem solid. I believe the older sisters would look upon it just as I and you do — a step onward to make the community happy. It happens very often in private families that the oldest children receive a poorer education and that the younger ones enjoy much greater advantages. The older ones, seeing that, thank their parents for what they gave and cheerfully help the parents to give the others more than they received.

"You and Mother Alphonsa have in no way neglected your novices. You have brought extraordinary sacrifices to give them their spiritual training. The Sisters, I am confident, understand that and appreciate that. If they should feel that the community in its infancy did not give them just all that might be desired they will certainly rejoice to see the younger ones get all that can be given. They love the work and the community and they want the community to progress. You seem to fear when there is no fear. Think less of what this or that Sister may think or say. Ask yourself what does God want us to do."

A young Sister, joining them just about that time and now superior-general, said to me more than once: "When I used to see those two women, I was in awe of them, so holy were they." With good reason did she feel awe: an example was being set such as far more than made up for the formal training about which these two women sometimes had unnecessary qualms of conscience.

Being women of such complete dedication, and never having had any other novitiate than the work itself, it is possible that they were inclined to be stricter than superiors commonly are whose zeal has been moderated — usually very wisely — in their training. But for work in its initial stages, when enthusiasm counts for so much, strictness, even a somewhat excessive strictness, has much to commend it. The fainthearted, for whom ordinarily a useful enough place can be found, tend to drop off; but those who remain have their fervor and devotion intensified. Yet Mother Alphonsa, though she may have been quick to reprimand, was equally quick to go to any subject toward whom she felt afterward that she had been too severe and ask forgiveness. And though the Sisters sometimes felt she was exacting — demanding for instance that the brass lamps then in use at Rosary Hill should always be burnished to a dazzling brightness, and that the flowers in the vases before the pictures and statues in the wards be renewed every day — at the slightest sign of wilting she would demand, "What are these withered things doing here?" — the Sisters soon recognized that she spoke in the fervor of charity and not because she was a martinet. Over and over again she told them, "If I am strict with you, it's because I want you to be perfect." They could not but notice the contrast between the rooms provided for them — simple but sufficiently comfortable — and the superior-general's room. In *her* bare cell there was nothing but a truckle bed, a couple of stools — not even a table — and a candle. A single shelf contained three or four spiritual books. She never spoke of her past life, but if any of them had read her *Memories of Hawthorne* they would have discovered there that she had been brought up in comfort and had, at times at least, known luxury. To ordinary comfort she was utterly indifferent. It was not that she laid upon herself any physical austerities; it was rather that she was so consumed by what she was doing that she was not even conscious that some little practices of hers were hard to emulate even on the part of strong young novices. Never, while she was alive, were they allowed to kneel at Mass with anything to lean upon. And when Bishop Cusack was undergoing an operation for cancer, she kept all of them — except those who went out to look after the patients — an entire hour on their knees erect before the Blessed Sacrament praying. The urgency of prayer did not even permit an interval for dinner. She probably had no idea what a really painful penance she was imposing. But though the Sisters suffered at such times, they knew they were learning a lot. Nobody could be close to her without seeing her fervor, or catching some part of it.

One day a young Sister — she admits that she probably had it in mind to impress Mother Alphonsa with her zeal — finding unexpectedly that she had twenty minutes to spare went up and asked, "Mother, is there anything I can do now?"

"Do? Of course there is, there's always something to do. Bring a pail of water."

And out to a rosebush in the garden she took her guileless little novice, carrying a pail of water herself, and there together they picked off all the caterpillars they could and drowned them.

But they all understood how kind she was to them as well as to the patients. She always kept a basket at hand full of their stockings and these she would darn at any spare moment, or when she was ill. If the Sisters protested she said, "Oh, nonsense, all of you are much too busy! This is about all a poor old woman like me can do." These darned stockings would be distributed by her in the cells on Saturday night.

For Sister Rose, 1908 brought sorrows that served to detach her the more fully from everything but her work. In that year died not only a younger sister but both her parents. When she went home to Kentucky to attend her father's funeral she remarked that the same leaves that had been budding at the time of her mother's burial were then falling mournfully on his grave. That showed poetic feeling, and even if she did not display a great deal of artistic temperament, she showed more artistic capacity than her more temperamental friend. She was the organist on special occasions, and also had a real, if somewhat somber, power as a painter. Her picture of St. Rose of Lima is an excellent piece of work; so are the stations of the cross which she did for the Rosary Hill Home as a memorial to her father and mother. It was she who now took the lead in developing the city house to what it should be.

Yet the building of a large new home in the city was Mother Alphonsa's doing, though it appeared to have come about by accident. She always worked very much on a day-to-day basis, in spite of her large dreams of the future. But when on December 8, 1909, she and Sister Rose took their final vows, they thought

it was about time to take stock of their work. They found that
in the two houses they had received about a thousand patients,
nearly all of whom had died with them. Nobody had ever been
refused admission who qualified as being destitute with an incurable cancer. There had been times when every cot was occupied
and Morris chairs had to be used as beds. They had even had
patients give up their beds to newcomers more sick than themselves, saying they were glad to do this after all that had been
done for them. This sort of thing had made it clear for sometime
that the Cherry Street house was quite inadequate; and though
Hawthorne had room enough, not every patient was strong
enough to endure the journey there.

Still no definite move had been made to obtain a larger city
house. But when in May 10, 1910, Mother Alphonsa had published
one of her letters of appeal in the New York *Times* for funds for
current expenses, Monsignor McGean of St. Peter's Church wrote
saying that a family in his parish had offered twenty-five thousand
dollars for a new St. Rose's home if Mother Alphonsa could raise
the same amount. At once she started looking for a site and
settled on the lot at the corner of Front and Jackson Streets. To
make sure that she got it Mother Alphonsa used the "white magic"
so useful on such occasions, and buried a medal of St. Joseph
there. She did not know it at the time, but this was the site of
the home of the Dominick Lynch who first brought Italian opera
to New York. He regarded it as the most desirable spot in the
small city of his day; to Mother Alphonsa its location seemed
good because it was opposite Corlaers Park and close to the East
River as it turns round the expanse. Facing it on the other bank
was the Brooklyn Navy Yard.

As usual she had cold water thrown on their plans by sensible
people. "But, Mother!" she heard, "you have hardly enough
money to buy food for the patients you've got at present!" She
smiled at the good advice — and then smiled very broadly when
Mr. Cornelius F. Cronin came forward with the second twenty-

five thousand dollars. He had heard a Sister using a drugstore telephone to make arrangements for the burial of a patient.

This was just before Christmas, and Sister Rose records in her diary of how Mother Alphonsa took her out to do Christmas shopping. "Mother Alphonsa is an indefatigable shopper and I was simply exhausted." A day or two later, after they had deposited the $50,000 in the bank, the diary reads: "We went shopping, not because we had $50,000 and in any case, that could not be used — but because Mother Alphonsa had received some money specially for Christmas. She shopped six times harder than before, until I sat down in a chair, too tired to walk or talk." But on December 28th, Sister Rose, when she went to Rosary Hill, found even the indefatigable Mother Alphonsa "in a collapsed condition."

By the end of 1912 the new St. Rose's Home was completed and ready for occupancy. The *Report* for January, 1908, to October, 1912, is able to announce that of the $148,110.92 which it had cost (including the $37,000 paid for the lots) all but $19,682 had been paid. It is worth noting that of the money which had come in, $3,000 was obtained by the Lenten lectures given by Dr. Walsh in 1912.

Further statistics given in this *Report* for the two homes for the sixteen years of the cancer work show that of the 1045 patients received: 652 had been Catholics; 363, Protestants; and 30, Jews. Again, to analyze these figures, 884 of these patients had died in the homes, 70 had left for various reasons, 16 had been sent away,* and 75 remained at the end of 1912.

Meanwhile the mortgage on Rosary Hill also threatened to reach a collapsed condition. This situation was saved by a Carnegie Hall lecture given by the famous orator, Morgan J. O'Brien. It brought in no less than five thousand dollars. As so often happens in such cases unobserved work insured the success

---

* Occasionally this happened. There had been two or three cases of insanity; the others were asked to leave because of a quarrelsome disposition or drunkenness.

of the spectacular event. In this case it was the preliminary organization conducted by Mr. Edward J. McGuire, the legal counsel of the Emigrant Savings Bank, and the overtime labor contributed gratis by his secretaries, that brought about the desired result. We hear of similar efforts that raised sums almost as large: a benefit performance by George M. Cohan, and also, Dr. James J. Walsh's lectures — by now an annual event that was an important item in the Homes' yearly income.

The first of the lectures by this very genial and clever man, who had what he himself cheerfully described as "an Irish gift of the gab," was made a social occasion at Rosary Hill. All kinds of celebrities came there and sat on the grass or in the summer houses while Dr. Walsh held forth on the subject of St. Francis of Assisi. And it really did seem that the setting was charmingly Franciscan. Among those there was an old acquaintance of that first Catholic summer school at New London, when it was poor George who lectured so well. How great had the changes been since then! But Mrs. Mosher was just as beautiful as ever, and though seeing her gave Mother Alphonsa a pang, she was much too busy with her work — much too busy that day presiding as hostess for so many well-known people who had come to hear Dr. Walsh — to have time for more than a passing glance at the past.

To mark the opening of the new St. Rose's Home, in 1912, a booklet was sent out containing photographs of the building and a financial statement, besides notes about various benefactors whom Mother Alphonsa liked to style her "co-workers." It was the precursor of the *Reports* which are much more than financial statements, but lively and amusing accounts of this or that aspect of her work. *Christ's Poor* had proved too costly to print every month, even though the bill was for only seventy-five dollars or so. An occasional pamphlet could be better printed and served her purpose almost as well.* Not only that, the getting of it out took a good deal of time, especially as Mother Alphonsa wrote virtually the whole of every number herself. And just as she had cheerfully admitted that her spelling was at times a trifle eccentric, she was quite cheerful about the lapse in publication when writing in the issue for January, 1904. (This, by the way, has printed on the cover "Vol. II, No. I." It should of course be Volume III.) "It was," she says, "a spasmodic breathing of communication with the world, followed by what seemed interminable silence." Every month she had hoped to resume editing the little magazine in the little dove-haunted turret where it was put together; but in addition to the question of finding time and money, she had fallen on the ice, and concussion of the brain had been feared. Then the new archbishop of New York, the future Cardinal Farley, when asked about the magazine, had made the routine answer that he was willing for her to continue it, but that he would have to ask his consultors — following which, the whole matter slipped his mind. When she next saw him and asked about it, he said, with a casual cheerfulness almost equal to hers, "You don't mean to say that I forgot to tell you you could continue!"

Even then there was an obstacle: though a friend had given her seventy-five dollars to pay for the next issue, she was just at the moment so close to bankruptcy that "it seemed wiser to keep the Homes alive than to print a pamphlet over their remains." All of which, without much apology, Mother Alphonsa records in an editorial. This, like the frank and cordial and intimate tone of the magazine, is characteristic of her. It was most unlucky that the revived Volume III only lasted half a year. She had, however, succeeded in making her aims very clear and in providing stories and articles which constitute the early history of the work and — though this was not her intention — are an excellent picture of her own forthright, warmhearted self.

* It need hardly be said that, from this biographer's point of view, the discontinuation of the magazine was an immense loss.

Some breaks came with the past, though the past had really been broken with quite decisively from the moment Rose Hawthorne Lathrop took up her cancer work. So it was much more than a dim memory when she heard that her brother-in-law, Frank Lathrop, had died. She had liked him, but he, even without the excuse of an unhappy marriage, had shown something of his brother's weakness. But like George, he had made something of a name for himself and had both charm and talent.

Then shy little Emilie Learned appeared one day from New London. After Bunner's death her sister had gone back to live in the old town, and they told Mother Alphonsa they had a room waiting for her. She told her friend, "But, Millie, though it's dear of you and Alice to ask me, of course I can't go. You see how busy I am."

"Yes, I see that, Rose," Emilie persisted, "that's just why you should take a nice long rest with old friends."

Nor would a letter shake her resolve. She explained that she might perhaps get away if she could leave Emilie herself in charge. What they needed most of all were capable women for positions of authority. No, she could not accept the invitation. At New London, Emilie reported, "Well, Alice, I can tell you one thing. Rose is now where she belongs. She never was that here."

Then, in 1904, she was invited to a Hawthorne celebration at the Wayside. It was now occupied by Mrs. Lothrop who, as a writer of the popular children's stories about the Five Little Peppers, felt herself to be part of the house's literary traditions. This time Mother Alphonsa was tempted, and though she would not take part in what turned out to be a gathering of aged transcendental shadows, along with such venerable literary gentlemen as Colonel Higginson and a few others of that sort, cracking their so very transcendental jokes that creaked almost as much as their arthritic joints, still she did nonetheless write a couple of letters about her father. The second of these, which Mrs. Lothrop told her guests was written by "Mrs. Lathrop" — of course Concord did not acknowledge her as Mother Alphonsa — "from her summer home" concluded: "The clearest picture in my mind, always, as I look back to that time between 1860 and 1864, is that of my father and mother stepping side by side about the grounds, looking at a branch here or a vine there. He talked then. Her head was almost always lifted; she was looking straight forward or up at a height of summer loveliness. He was usually looking down, though not without a ready willingness to follow her command, and also look at some simple grace of the verdure or sublimity of the sky. But he did not forget the grass blade or the pebble or the mystery of our earthly sojourn."

One of the oldest of her friends, giving the least spectacular of services, but a service of incalculable value to her, was Henry Reel. He conducted a drugstore on Henry Street when Mrs. Lathrop first settled in the slums, and very often this kind man gave his wares to the poor. Often in their relief room at Cherry Street Mother Alphonsa and Sister Rose had heard poor people who needed medicines say, "Oh that's all right; Mr. Reel will put it up for us for nothing!" When he retired from business ten years later he continued to compound medicines for the patients of the two houses, being able to buy drugs at cost price and contributing his own skill and time free. Not only that, but he helped organize the auxiliary for drugs with six hundred members, each of whom contributed a dollar a year. Also he acted as one of the trustees for the homes. It was a characteristic of Mother Alphonsa that she could win the devoted friendship of such good men and then not merely use them for what they were worth but show her complete confidence and trust. Her generosity called forth their generosity, and then her generous recognition of their friendship bound them the more securely to her. In this, as in other matters, she showed that cold caution is not real prudence.

One of the first friends made after going to Westchester was Brother Julian of St. Joseph's Normal Institute at Pocantico Hills, on the hill opposite the one she had settled on. He was always popping in and out. If there was a bad storm he would be over immediately afterward with a group of students to see that everything was all right.

"I see that you're still on your perch," he would say by way of congratulation.

Whenever the protectory band was in the neighborhood to play at some function, he saw to it that the boys came to Rosary Hill. Big vans would come creeping up the steep road; then there would be a burst of music under the patients' windows. He brought over his own choir whenever there was a special celebration, or to give the patients a concert. They were able to do everything from Irish jigs to Gregorian chant. If there was a notice in the papers that the Sisters had been left a legacy he would be the first to notice it and telephone the news. On both sides there were all kinds of charming little amenities — including presents of cakes and bottles of wine — such as often mollify the austerities of religious life.

Similar amenities were exchanged between Mother Alphonsa and the Maryknoll Fathers, whose first home was hardly a stone's throw away. And the group of secretaries who had come from Boston to help Father Price and the future Bishop Walsh in the editing of the *Field Afar* — known at that time locally as the "Pious Women" and afterward, because they occupied St. Theresa's Lodge, as the "Teresians" — later became the Maryknoll Sisters. From Mother Mary Joseph, the present superior general, who was one of that first group, come extracts from the community diary kept at that time.*

* As a footnote to history, which will of course take care of them in rather more than a footnote, their names may be inserted here. Mary Josephine Rogers became first Mary Joseph and then Sister Mary Joseph and then first superior. She is now the mother general. Mary Louise Wholean died, in 1917, as Mary Xavier — not strictly speaking "Sister" as

At first these young ladies were known just as Miss Rogers
and Miss Wholean and Miss Sullivan and so forth. Afterward,
even before they became Sisters, they took religious names, but
of course did not use them except privately. Then Miss Rogers
was just Mary Joseph and Miss Wholean (who kept the diary)
Mary Xavier. And when Mary Louise Wholean had to undergo
a serious operation, Father Walsh wrote, in April, 1912, asking
prayers for her recovery. Mother Alphonsa wrote on the envelope: "Rapidly recovering. Novena is made to St. Gertrude."*

One of the notes, written by one of the secretaries and signed
— as Father Walsh usually signed — "The Maryknolls," tells
Mother Alphonsa: "You will never know how much we have
enjoyed and appreciated your cordiality and kindness — not only
have you been a 'benefactor,' we have come to regard you as a
personal friend." The unstamped envelope is marked "basket
mail." Some of the other letters from "The Maryknolls" obviously
were sent in the same way.

As to the attendance of the group at the Mass in the Rosary
Hill chapel, there is this entry: "The cancer patients seem to
share Mother Alphonsa's delusion that we are a 'holy group.' This
morning one of them, whom we have named 'the boss,' forcibly
removed an outsider who dared to kneel in our midst, throwing
us thereby into an ecstasy — of laughter!" However "holy" they
may or may not have been, they were evidently a merry group
of girls.

One of the earliest references in the rather sketchy diary
kept in those days by the incipient community is: "This noon
the girls returned from the chapel at Rosary Hill, with a basket

---

the approval of the congregation did not come from Rome until 1920 — an
extremely short period of waiting. Sara Theresa Sullivan is now Sister Mary
Teresa. Nora Frances Shea died, in 1940, as Sister Mary Theophane. Anne
Agnes Towle died, in 1944, as Sister Anna Maria. Margaret Anne Shea
became Sister Mary Gemma but did not persevere. All these women came
from New England but, as their names indicate, were of Irish stock.

* From this operation (on March 29th) Miss Wholean never did fully
recover, however. She died in the community in 1917.

containing a dozen and a half of eggs. Mother Alphonsa has given orders that the eggs shall keep up an uninterrupted procession toward Maryknoll." This was the "basket mail" in which letters — and perhaps fruit and vegetables — were left by one of "the girls" on the chapel steps. On coming out they would find their offerings removed and eggs in the basket.

Nor were eggs the only things sent. "It was a splendid surprise," reads the diary, "when after lunch, Mother Alphonsa's man appeared with the reward which we had not earned — three bricks of ice cream and a loaf of cake. We welcomed the treat with exclamations of joy and ran for plates and spoons. Then we sat on the front lawn, each with the third of a brick. The picnic lasted until the last bit of cream had disappeared. Meanwhile Thomas had been sent for to carry the third brick to the Fathers and Brothers." This sort of thing was all the more helpful because the secretaries were without a permanent cook in their cottage, so the arrival of ice cream relieved them of the work of making a dessert.

The reference to their not having "earned their reward" should be explained. The secretaries had promised to give a little concert for the patients; then a message had come from Mother Alphonsa asking them to postpone the concert until Thursday. Just as they were preparing to go to Rosary Hill, however, they heard its bell tolling, "and decided that one of the patients must have died from the mere anticipation of the coming ordeal!" Afterward they discovered that they had been expected and that the bell had tolled for nothing more dreadful than to announce that confessions were being heard as the next day was the First Friday of the month.

When the fall came, another kind of service was rendered, noted in the diary for October 1, 1912: "Mary Joseph borrowed some farm implements from Mother Alphonsa and with two of the others spent the morning digging potatoes. By noon the three of us had qualified as first-class gardeners, having harvested the

entire crop of our five gardens." Until "the Maryknolls" located
seven miles away, every evening at dusk Father Price could be
seen making his visit to the Lourdes grotto at Rosary Hill. But
even after distance came to intervene, cordial friendship continued between the two communities. When Mother Alphonsa
died it was Bishop Walsh who preached at her funeral.

But the closest of all of Mother Alphonsa's friends was also
the most distant — a man she never saw. This was Brother Dutton,
who had worked with Father Damien in the leper colony on
Molokai, and who was still working there. His script even at
eighty was beautifully clear and firm but he seems to have been
almost totally inarticulate — at any rate in his laconic letters. One
can nevertheless still feel the warm heart in them, and Mother
Alphonsa's expansiveness, on her side, made up for anything he
may have lacked. Perhaps some readers of her letters to him may
feel as some few people also do about the letters Mother Seton
wrote to her friend Antonio Felicchi.* The conventionally
minded naturally feel a little surprised at such warmth of expression in letters written by nuns to their men friends. And in part
the explanation may be that both of these women had been
married, and neither had gone through the molding process of a
novitiate. The truer explanation, however, is that a largeness of
heart demands a largeness of utterance. Those who fail to
recognize this are a bit inclined to think of such expressions as
gush. Nothing could have been further from the character of
these great women. It may do some people good to know that
Mother Alphonsa wrote to Dutton as "Beloved Brother" and
signed herself "with love and reverence" not just "Sister M.
Alphonsa Lathrop, O.S.D.," but "Your Sister." My heart is

---

* I am referring more particularly to the letters in photostat at Emmits-
burg, which have not been quoted except for the few in my book, *The
Reed and The Rock.*

warmed when in her letter of July 27, 1914, she tells him, "I welcomed and kissed your gifts to our poor."

"How I love the thought of you; indeed I always have," she says in the same letter to this aged man who on his fortieth birthday (which he spent in retreat at the Trappist Monastery in Kentucky) decided to devote the rest of his life to the poor. "Never for a moment," Mother Alphonsa tells him, "have I ceased to lean upon you as a model." She says she has lost the gift of writing — it would hardly seem so, though what letters she does write have to be penned at midnight at the end of an exhausting day — "so that I, myself, have ceased all this time to talk to my friends with the pen, except when charity demanded." But she has a definite reason for this letter of July 22, 1913: "It seemed as if in all the world there could not be anyone who knew so absolutely what we are trying to do, and why, as yourself; and so, with your blessed kind words, I felt that you were our Brother indeed. . . . I felt that if I wrote to you, I should ask you to come and help us. I felt that you would inevitably hold us in contempt if I did so, for at that time you were an absolute necessity to your poor lepers."

Then she comes to the point. She now invites him to settle in New York, "gathering around men who did not feel called to the priesthood, but are willing to give their lives to God in tending the sick. These cancer cases need you, as the Lepers did, whom you have now established in perfect safety, as a class, for devotion from their fellow beings. We have long nursed an average of fifteen men at a time [this was in 1913], with the assistance of a paid orderly. You can imagine what that means. The doctors all tell us that no paid orderly is temperate, and few of them kind. . . . I want for the men, who always have a department in our Homes, the same honorable devotion of attendance that we give the women. . . . I want you to come and found a charity for them, in connection with our charity for the women. . . . I beg you to remember that God has given you the capacity and the exalted reputation which will enable you to do for these others, despised, avoided, loathed, but tender of feelings, and deeply humiliated, and frequently unconverted souls, the supreme act of causing to exist for them a charity that can never die. . . . All would rise up to help you, and there is no question of the means for it all."

In the last issue of *Christ's Poor* (June, 1904) she had written a long article on Molokai and had said that the Servants of Relief "would never have gone into action had it not been for Father Damien," and earlier issues of that little magazine refer to him enthusiastically. When they were sent two pieces of his cassock, Mother Alphonsa wrote: "Tears and prayers alone can speak at the sight, and at the presence, of a relic so humble, and so heroically sprung." Here, explicitly acknowledged, was one of the main inspirations of her own heroic work.

Brother Dutton could not accept her invitation. He was too old to start a new work. Moreover he had dedicated his life to the lepers. So in reply to her appeal he used to send her, from time to time, pictures of himself with notes scribbled on the back, and the briefest of cards, promising letters that he never wrote. He calls her his "Dear friend," he asks when her birthday is and how old she is — he guesses that she was born about 1850. "Anyway we are all jogging along. Hope we are doing well, what may be pleasing to God. Am hoping St. Joseph helps you — as he does me. A great saint, and wonderful are his doings." The letters are touching because of their inarticulateness. But Mother Alphonsa understood perfectly. He was praying for her. She went on praying that Brother Dutton would change his mind.

CHAPTER XI

The Dream of the New Hospital

Though the little magazine, *Christ's Poor,* had ceased publication suddenly for the second time in the middle of 1904, Mother Alphonsa several times thought of reviving it. About this she wrote on April 13, 1905, to a Mr. Billings, who had let her know that he would like to have a complete set, to say: "The little print stopped for want of funds, a year ago, & then could keep going only for six months. It costs about a hundred and fifty dollars a month,* everything included, & we cannot always manage the bill promptly. I hope to print it again very soon, however." It would even appear that at the very moment of its demise she was thinking of something a bit better, the extra cost of which would be covered by six issues a year instead of twelve. For on June 23, 1904, she wrote to Robert Underwood Johnson, whom she had known in her days at the Gilder's salon, inquiring about something to be printed by the Century Press, "accurately and with a certain distinction."

At that time the magazine was thought of simply as a means for raising funds for current expenses, but as she managed to provide for these in other ways, the idea was allowed to die. Not until a very large sum of money had to be raised for the replacing of the ramshackle wooden firetrap at Rosary Hill with something more serviceable and safer, did the need of a pamphlet become urgently necessary. That was how the first of *Reports* — that for July, 1920, to July, 1921 — came into existence.**

* This was in its enlarged form. Earlier it had cost $75 an issue.
** In 1912 there had been a *Report* issued, but not until later were these *Reports* thought of as regular publications.

It was of course just like Mother Alphonsa to lose no time in coming to the point. The first article in it is entitled "A Fireproof Country Home." It lays the emphasis just where it belonged, upon the fact that the old building was very hazardous.

But before coming to that article, some of the other contents of the *Report* might be noted. The mortgage of $60,000 on St. Rose's Home had just been reduced by two legacies, each of $20,000 — one from Mrs. Russell Sage, the other from Daniel J. Carroll. That home had cared, during the year, for 355 patients, of whom 115 were male and 240 female, 327 white and 28 colored, 273 Catholics, 70 Protestants, and 12 Jews. During the year 242 patients had died, 23 had left, and 90 were still there. The total expenses for the year had been $29,674.07 — or less than a hundred dollars per capita. And this included an item of $6,034.93 for improvements, mainly in connection with the fire escapes. Rosary Hill Home, on the other hand, had had only 94 patients during the course of the year, yet had cost $35,939.65. This much higher cost of maintenance was due to a number of reasons. Over $10,000 had been spent on repairs and improvements and furniture. And there were doctor's fees which the city house escaped, and the luxury of a resident chaplain. At St. Rose's Monsignor McEntyre continued to give his ministrations free.

But when all necessary allowances have been made — the greatly disproportionate cost in running the two houses is probably the difference between Mother Alphonsa and Sister Rose. The one could make a little money stretch a long way. The other sometimes had to do so, but she seems to have had a good time spending when money was there. Her great gift lay in raising money, a gift that was soon to be called into play. She realized her talent and wrote in this issue: "There is no end to the variety of methods of startling and catching and forcing people into 'giving.' We choose at once the old-fashioned way of asking outright in a few words; though we were obliged to do so in the daily press; for we are not permitted to utter our petitions at doorways. The papers were kind as fairies to us." However, she admits: "No doubt we are grotesque and contemptible to many because we do not have the jaunty forms of veiled mendicancy. We do not want endowments, even if they were offered (which they have not been). We do not want to be rich; but we do nevertheless want to have plenty of donations for the benefit of the poor. . . . Some people think that the inspiration about poverty was a matter of epoch, and not for all time the most precious bulwark against vanity and spiritual leakage. At any rate, if we were to receive a great legacy or a great sum in another form, we should not invest it in any way, but let it lie at the bank at the usual moderate interest, until it was used up."

The *Report* is less personal in tone than the magazine had been; otherwise the following letter, which had been received just at that time, probably would have been included. But there is no reason why it should not be included here as showing a typical case of Mother Alphonsa's work. It was dated April 24, 1922, and came from Pauline Louise Titus, a lady who had been a social worker for eighteen years. "Never, never shall I forget," writes Miss Titus, "that terrible August noon when I stood at the door of Hawthorne, having literally been 'turned down' by the twelve institutions in and around New York where I had tried to place my cousin & in my excitement and discouragement having left my letter of recommendation from Father Payne in the New York hotel. I told my story to the Sister who answered the door, & she asked me to wait. She disappeared – & I knew it was another hopeless quest. Finally she returned to the doorway & said, 'Yes, we will take her. When will she come?' I thought I did not hear correctly – that the sun had been too much for me, & I asked her to repeat it. When I finally grasped it all – (I am not irreverent) – I seemed to hear Our Lord's own words: 'Come unto me.' There are no words to tell you the effect it had on me; it was the nearest approach to the divine that man could achieve. I went down to the station and telegraphed just your words to Dad — and he has since told me that the message had the same effect on him, 'Put off thy shoes, the place where thou standest is holy ground.' And in the two years which followed — no words can ever tell what you did for such a difficult case." She signs herself "in undying gratitude and reverence."

The people received at Rosary Hill were given a comfortable home amid beautiful surroundings. But it had never been a safe home; and the danger that there could be in a fire on that windy hill was all too evident. And there *had* been fires. Once, in 1904, Mother Alphonsa was showing a visiting priest Sister Rose's fine painting of St. Rose of Lima when she lifted her eyes and saw that the roof of the chapel was in flames. Though it was soon put out, there could be no certainty that this would happen the next time. And there were serious threats — one which in a letter to Sister Rose she called a "near tragedy" — when the burning brush in a March wind showed what would have happened had the wind blown in the other direction. "I really think," she concludes, "I shall have to cut down a lot of trees on the north and make the ground an earthen affair, for it is something to wonder at when a big wind and fire get together on this hill."

On December 10, 1917, they did get together at Columbus College, which was conducted by the Salesian Fathers, at Hawthorne. This made Mother Alphonsa more alarmed than ever. "If this modern brick building in the valley could be so quickly and so completely destroyed," she wrote, "what would happen to our helpless patients, if this wooden shell of a building, open to the fury of the four winds on the hilltop, were to take fire? A fireproof building must be provided, at least for the bedridden patients."

For more than eighteen years, that first and most important

article of the *Report* for 1921–1922 tells us, the Sisters had been praying that their big, wooden house would not burn down; now Mother Alphonsa tells us that they had made up their minds to build "the impossible hospital-home." The only consolation they had in the pine clapboard where they were was that it was better for the destitute cancer sufferers to be inside than outside.

She, herself, had already picked out the spot for the new home — and later she had to fight for it against all the practical men who had been telling her that it would be well-nigh out of the question to get the building materials so high up along so steep a road. But there she had been buying, a couple of lots at a time, whenever she could scrape the money together. Her idea was to use the old house for the training of new Sisters — which sounds as though she thought it did not matter if they burnt to death, but which really means that she supposed they could get out. After all, the house might "stand intact as long as those indomitable wooden houses in which George Washington established his headquarters throughout the land." But dying men and women required something better than clapboards.

She felt that there would be a contest of generosity among the benefactors of the work once the need was made known. Not even excepting lepers, she called the cancerous poor the most destitute of creatures. Moreover leprosy was very rare in our own land, whereas "[the] cancerous poor are at our side anywhere in America and they are being thrust into the night."

She felt sure that her patients on that hill found that the beautiful scenery had a curative effect, even though they did not realize it. "The men and women," she went on, "sit on the benches of the terraces or the chairs of the balconies, and look and look. When we ask them what they are looking at they say, 'The cows on the farm across the valley'; but the trees and misty colors and the enormous breadth of sky and clouds must soothe them unbeknown." But this did not alter the fact that, unless they got another house, they might all be roasted alive.

She herself had already designed the home she wanted, and her sketches may be seen showing that the house, when it was built, followed her design. It was, she decided, to be plain and simple — in the Spanish mission style, but of course not of adobe but of fireproof brick covered with cement, and with a roof of red tiles.

"We," she said firmly, "are Servants of Relief, and the money we beg for the harborage of our patients is given to our Lord's Poor, and not to us. The house would have to be completely furnished as well as built, but, unlike other hospitals, it would not need expensive equipment for observation and radium treatments." Allowing for recreation rooms and a few guest rooms, she estimated she would need $200,000 — a very small sum for what she meant to give. To get it she said, "We are going to beg in that calmly industrious manner with which a bird builds its nest. It is not on record that the bird stops before the nest is built, unless it dies in the attempt."

There was another matter — one that had always been pressing but that weighed heavier than ever now that they were planning for extension — and this was the need for recruits. Rose Hawthorne Lathrop had not asked for even one assistant when she first went to the slums, in 1896; in fact she had thought of her little effort, in her modesty, at first as a "one man show." But she soon discovered the need of help — any sort of help, even that of an hour or two a week was welcomed — and it was wonderful when she obtained the perfect coadjutor in Alice Huber. They were still working together as a wonderful team, but the two houses already called for a considerable staff. And only Sisters who gave everything and who asked nothing would do.

Yet it was not easy to find suitable Sisters, except among those people — who are fortunately more numerous than the world supposes — to whom the prospect of hardships and heroism is a positive inducement. Some of the young women, who were accepted in the novitiate at Rosary Hill and who left after a time, probably would have done well enough elsewhere. And perhaps some of the caustic comments in Sister Rose's diary on the novices who said after a while that the work was too much for them, did not allow enough for mediocrity. "I never knew that they ever did anything, except look at other people work," Sister Rose confided to her diary, concerning a couple of postulants who gave up. Still, good as those young women may have been in their own place, that place was obviously not among the Sisters of Relief. The obtaining of recruits for the two hospitals was of course even more important — immeasurably more important — than being able to build those hospitals. The most constant prayer, therefore, was that women should be given the grace of this particular and difficult vocation. In the appeal printed in the *Report* for 1921–1922, we read that the main requirement is "the self-consecration which enables the human being to dare all that God wills, and that recognizes that it is God Who succeeds, not the weak creature who is laboring in the act of love." "O Sisters, as yet unseen," Mother Alphonsa writes, "come, with your many gifts of different capacities, and your compassion, to Him Who lives among these sufferers."

In the next *Report* (for 1923–1924) Mother Alphonsa returns to this theme, elaborating more fully. "The work of the Servants of Relief cannot grow much without a large affiliation of Sister-nurses to take charge of foundations in other cities besides New York." This shows that already the work is projected on a nation-wide — perhaps a world-wide scale. Since her death advances have, in fact, been made to Philadelphia, to Fall River, to Atlanta, and to St. Paul.

Now Mother Alphonsa explains what she needs in the way of helpers. "It is very often supposed," she writes, "that our work is the last word in detestable conditions, and therefore, that anything is good enough for us; whereas, for the sake of our patients both as to body and soul, the best is barely good enough." So as to guard against frightening good prospective Sisters away, she elaborates: "Our circumstances are infinitely more easy than those of leper-nurses and (perhaps a synonymous matter) foreign mission Sisters; and no doubt we ought to be sorry to say, that there is nothing queer or rare about us, nothing that should make young women with mettlesome powers conclude that our ways are sublimely brave and our vocation too hard and abhorrent." She remarks that it has been said that the Servants of Relief are martyrs. This she calls a "rather hysterical opinion"; they are commonplace enough and have "very many ameliorations such as a saint would abhor." She therefore fears that unless her work is better understood, "it might tempt women of potential courage to decide that it is unthinkable to be as brave as all that." It boils down to this: Only the brave are wanted, but she does not want to terrify people by exaggerating the degree of bravery called for.

A few other things should be noted about this *Report* and those that immediately follow it. One is that Mother Alphonsa remains as fixed as ever against accepting any pay patients. She has seen it happen so often: a bed is endowed, and one would suppose by that made secure for the poor. Then — with the excuse that this is only for the time being and until a destitute patient comes along — a paying patient is put into it. What he pays, it is argued, can be used afterward to support a destitute person. Once admit that compromise, she felt, and the hospital for the poor is ruined, except perhaps financially. "Pay beds and free beds," she declared, "are in eternal enmity." That there should be no doubt about this principle, she wrote it into the constitutions of her community — irremovable except at the cost of changing the whole character of its work.

Another principle, very closely connected with it, was that all the work — with the exception of a few jobs left to a male orderly — should be done by the Sisters themselves. It is certain that the best work in every department of human activity is disinterested work. Most of us of course have to be paid for what we do, in order to be able to do it, but to allow the profit motive to be anything but secondary is a death warrant to first-class achievement.

The services of doctors were thankfully accepted and were — at any rate at St. Rose's — usually given gratis. But even at Rosary Hill, out of the $35,991.69 spent between July, 1920, and July, 1921, only $1,253.19 went on doctors and drugs. Mr. Reel was continuing to contribute his own time and bought their drugs at wholesale prices; but one would surmise that at least half that amount went on the pharmacy. This would mean an average of forty to fifty dollars a month for doctors.* No resident physician was ever employed in these hospitals. A doctor would make the rounds and look at the patients, but the chief purpose was that the patient should be able to look at him. It was good for their morale to know that there was a doctor available and of course, it was a good thing for the doctor to keep an eye on them.

The greater number of experienced nurses were those stationed at 71 Jackson Street. For in the city house not only were there always about seventy-five patients — as compared with the thirty-five or forty which was then Rosary Hill's maximum capacity — but the worst cases were kept there, those who could not endure the ordeal of going by train or car thirty odd miles into the country. The difference between the two houses is given eloquently in the statistics: where one out of every two of Rosary Hill's patients died, two out of three died at St. Rose's. If this disproportion gradually seems to have lessened, this is only because the expectancy of life of those now received also has lessened. No doubt the knife and the use of radium have saved many sufferers from cancer, but those who unsuccessfully under-

* I find in the financial statement of the Rose Hawthorne Lathrop Free Home of Fall River, Mass., for 1936 this item: "Physician's salary, $300" for the year. A merely nominal charge, of course.

go operations have their lives shortened. The stay of the guest in
these Homes is not, on the average, as long as it used to be.

Mother Alphonsa who, one might almost say, had from the
start kept her work going by means of appeals in the newspapers,
now turned again to the papers — but this time for the obtaining
of the large sum she needed for the building of the new Rosary
Hill Home. And Maurice Francis Egan, a nationally known
figure, not very long back from his post as American Minister
to Denmark, came forward to write an article for the New York
Times book review and magazine section. Mother Alphonsa had
known him as a young man at the Gilders', and he had lectured
for George Lathrop at that first session of the Catholic summer
school at New London. Nobody could have been a better choice.

Egan, as wisely as modestly, let Mother Alphonsa write the
article herself, except for a few paragraphs at the beginning
and the end. But as he had known Emma Lazarus and her sister,
Josephine, and realized that with the Jews of New York their
names would be very impressive, he played them up for all that
they were worth — and perhaps a bit more.

This, however, is not to say that Emma Lazarus had little to
do with the matter. For here, thirty-five years after the death of
Mother Alphonsa's friend, whom she called a mind "lofty, brilliant and pathetically unsatisfied," due tribute is given to "this
young woman of fairest promise and exalted perceptions," a
victim to cancer in her prime. "But," Mother Alphonsa continued,
"though I deeply grieved for her, I would not pity her, for she
never knew unaided suffering, but every amelioration." It was
not to cancer sufferers as such that Rose Hawthorne Lathrop
had ever felt her mission to be, but only to the destitute among
them; for theirs was the utmost in destitution. As she had done
before, she lays a much greater emphasis upon the unnamed
seamstress as the inspirer of this work. "A fire was then lighted

in my heart," she said, "where it still burns, to do something toward preventing such inhuman regulations [being sent to Blackwell's Island] for those who are too forlorn to protest. I set my whole being . . . to bring consolation to the cancerous poor."

Other influences were noted as in the pages of *Christ's Poor.* These included that of Una with her settlement work in London. And proudly once again Rose Hawthorne Lathrop indicated what she owed to Nathaniel Hawthorne, writing: "The first influence came from the attitude of my father's mind toward both moral and physical deformity and corruption. Some critics call his mental inclination morbid, using the word in the wrong place. It is the sinner who is morbid, not the man who pities him and devotes his abilities to helping others to sin no more as he did, even if the sinner himself is beyond reclaim. Extraordinary sinners . . . came to my father with their woes of conscience (much to his innate horror) because they knew from his writings that he was full of compassionate insight, and at the cost of his equanimity he consoled them, in so far as this life holds consolation for enormous wrongs." Here she was most his daughter: like him fastidious and sensitive, her compassion had conquered her repugnance.

The editor of the New York *Times* Magazine at this time was Clifford Smyth, and he used to go to Water Street with Beatrix Hawthorne (whom he afterward married) and her sister, Hildegarde, the daughters of Julian. He used to be roped in to read aloud to the first of Aunt Rose's male patients, the old British officer in the annex, while the girls made bandages on the other side of the street. His acquaintance with Mother Alphonsa therefore went back to her "Mrs. Lathrop" period, and she was very fond of her "dearest Clifford," while he, for his part, entertained the idea of writing her biography. There was always a room for him at Rosary Hill when he wanted to go there for a few days;

which he very often did. But he was not a Catholic and, in fact, was inclined to think of Catholicism as something merely incidental to this admirable work, instead of understanding that Catholicism was its essence. It was because of him, however, that the Maurice Francis Egan article appeared; and his wife's aunt — to him, too, still "Aunt Rose" — reluctant though she was to have any personal publicity, submitted to it when it was a question of helping the project of her fireproof home.

But Clifford Smyth, in 1912, had run up against something he did not quite grasp, though it was stated in the 1906 pamphlet, and in other places: "From the first, the charity has been regarded as a religious work, since no inducement outside of religion could be sufficient to give it life." He in the goodness of his heart was thinking how best to present its case to the public so as to receive the maximum of financial support, but his well-meant suggestions brought "dearest Clifford" a very long letter, dated May 26, 1912, which may have shocked him a little, though he could hardly have failed to admire Aunt Rose's forthrightness. "I think a little differently from what you do," she tells him, "as to the Catholic side (which is all of it) of our charity. I say *all of it*, but do not mean that the Protestants do not gain very much by the Protestants we receive, & I think they *should* help and uphold us. The Jews seldom apply, & usually under some deception on the part of their people or some hospital, & usually go away soon. . . . So I do not feel that the Jews owe us anything, though their kind help has been much appreciated. But I do not want to *plead* with Protestants or Jews to help us as I would with Catholics. I think your idea of asking Protestant ministers and Jews of standing to write letters of endorsement, would be opposed to my instincts, & I have used only those Protestant letters which come to me of their own accord. We have crowds of such friends, but I would not do more than print a letter which had already come spontaneously.

"In regard to Emma Lazarus's effect upon my choice of the

work, it would not be more than that of four loved friends, who
died of cancer, all as well off for money as herself, & it would
seem to be bidding for Jewish favor to make more of it than I
did in my letters about my beginning. . . . The *person* who made
an immediate and lasting effect upon me, as the reason for taking
up this line of usefulness, was a poor young seamstress whose
story was tragic (in my eyes) and for her connection with it no
one would care but a fervent Catholic. . . . I must have given
you an exaggerated idea of the influence of dear Emma, so that
you wish to use it for our benefit more than I honestly can."

How utterly unwilling she was to permit any kind of compromise is shown by her referring, in that same letter, to a telephone conversation she had had with Clifford Smyth. He had
rung her up very excitedly to tell her, "Aunt Rose, I know a man
— he is of great importance — who is willing to help you."

"That's very nice, Clifford," she said.

"But I must tell you this, though, Aunt Rose. He says that he
wants an assurance that the money would not be absorbed by the
Catholic Church in some way."

Now it would have been very easy for her to have said, "Tell
your friend that we'll account for every penny as being spent
on our cancer patients — and that we make no religious distinctions among them." But no, what she did say was, "Then tell
your friend that we don't need his help." In the letter she explained her attitude: "Any slur of such sort upon our fealty to
the Church's prelates or interests would make a gift positively
unblessed to us. . . . Now, Clifford, you have come bang up
against one of my very disagreeable sides. . . . Just tell the man
who is afraid to help us lest the true Church will gain by it, that
he does not yet know what the spirit of *this* Catholic charity is,
& that his money may keep him chained to a small rather than
a large magnanimity."

With these noble and scornful words she dismissed her ignominious opportunity.

CHAPTER XII

The Honors

Mother Alphonsa was getting old, and few people now remembered her as Rose Hawthorne Lathrop. But she did not forget, and usually signed her name as Mother Alphonsa Lathrop. Rarely, or never, did she mention her past, and she was too busy as a rule to think consciously about it; but it was always at the back of her mind, whatever other things were occupying it.

Once she said to Dr. Walsh, "I never really wanted to write about life; I wanted to live it." And that was what she *had* done — in supernatural terms — for her middle years had been filled with one failure after another, and only when she was turned forty-five did she at last discover what it was God had sent her into the world to do. Though in Julian's praise of her literary productions there probably was a certain amount of delicate flattery, he was nevertheless sufficiently discerning: she *could* have been a writer — but of course only on condition that she had cared enough about it to be one. She never had cared enough. And she knew from her father's case, if in no other way, that art, if one is going to do more than trifle with it, must absorb one.

Nothing had ever absorbed her until she had flung herself headlong into charity. That marriage of hers had never engaged her interest very deeply. She had always been restive — not so much because of poor George's inadequacy as because she had soon discovered that marriage was not her métier. In the end she hardly had any other choice but to leave George, but she could see that had he only yoked himself to somebody else, his development would have been rather different from what it was.

Oh, well, she reflected sighing, all that was a long while ago! George was at rest and she would be soon at rest too — after she had brought the job she had in hand to completion. A little more and she would be ready to depart, with a wonderfully rounded out life.

Honors — unsought but not to be refused — came to her. In 1914, she was given the medal of the National Institute of Social Sciences. Eleven years later her father's college of Bowdoin had a celebration and President Sills, in giving her an honorary M.A., embarrassed her a little by quaintly calling her "the saintly daughter of the Puritan novelist." But of course he meant well. In the following year the Rotary Club gave her its medal, which its president, Pirie MacDonald, hung around her neck. That day she permitted photographs, at all events photographs were taken of her by the press photographer, though even for them she would not "pose." These were the only pictures ever taken of her in the religious habit. Two months later she celebrated her seventy-fifth birthday.

Two years before this, on September 14th, she and Sister Rose celebrated their silver jubilee. "All along," wrote Sister Rose in her diary, "we had opposed any celebration, but finally consented to have one. However, the decision was made too late to send out invitations. So Mother sent the invitations through the press. Many old friends of the work responded and a large crowd gathered for the occasion."

Monsignor McEntyre, that old friend of theirs, said Mass, and Father Thuente, an even older friend and the one who had first suggested their becoming Dominican Tertiaries, preached. Afterward, luncheon was served to the guests under a canopy in the novitiate garden. It was then that Mother Alphonsa was able to announce that the Smith brothers had sent a cheque for $50,000 — $25,000 to each of the jubilarians, or $1,000 for each year of faithful service to the poor. These were the benefactors who gave $25,000 for the building of the new St. Rose's Home. They were George and John who, under the name of Edward Smith, conducted a business of wholesale confectioners at 154 Greenwich Street.

This was the largest single contribution they received at any time. But already, on New Year's Day, 1923, Mr. R. J. Cudahy, the Manager of the Funk and Wagnall Publications, had arrived with a group of cheques and some cash, given by himself or collected by him from his friends. The total was $17,500.

Large sums of this sort were very welcome, of course, but were not looked for. What Mother Alphonsa did count on were quite small donations. And all kinds of little schemes had been tried to draw such a stream in steadily. She preferred widespread interest — "the hourly mercy of the public" — to two or three munificent benefactors. In 1904, Dr. Storer and his wife and daughter had given their names (and the first dollars) to a "shield of honor," on which was to be emblazoned the names of those who gave a dollar a month. "The benevolence of the public," Mother Alphonsa said, "towards these Homes is their only safeguard from bankruptcy and defeat." She was always saying things like that. She had started this work with nothing at all, and had never put anything by prudently for a rainy day. Yet somehow she had managed.

The building of the fireproof home, however, was so important a matter, that even from the general gifts that came in — intended for day-by-day maintenance — she now managed to slip a good many dollars into the building fund. Two packets of letters from her to typical supporters, and kept all these years by those to whom they were addressed, have come into my hands. Mr. Edward A. Braniff of Tulsa, Oklahoma, in sending me what he has, expresses his amazement that one so old and sick should have the courage and strength to write these letters for the little sums she received. It was indeed amazing. Anybody else would have thought the matter adequately dealt with by sending a receipt. Not so Mother Alphonsa. The indomitable old lady personally thanked everybody, and often enclosed snapshots of the patients or the grounds or the buildings. With very few exceptions all such letters are in her own hand.

On May 8, 1922, she tells Mr. Braniff: "I have put the matter of a new Home of fireproof materials here, into the care of Our Lady of the Immaculate Conception & her Miraculous Medal is in the ground." On August 23, 1924, she apologizes for being so late in thanking him — each time it was for five dollars — because of a severe illness, "several of these attacks making it doubtful if I could survive. It took long to become strong enough to write a letter, & I have not fully recovered." Yet she goes on for two closely written pages. On April 27, 1926, nine days after she was given the Rotary medal — which she never even thinks of mentioning — again she writes Mr. Braniff two closely written pages. "The five dollars," she says, "will help us to become safe in this place of ours, to which the brush fire the other day was driven by a fierce wind, but the local fire company rushed up the hill to save the dear old wooden building. . . . Our new home is promised for the Autumn, having been delayed in several ways wholly unexpected. Now all is clear sailing with it. The weak heart from which I have suffered for so long has made my especial work for the charity a limping effort, but I am getting better again, since [I am] able to go out into the garden. I remember that at one time I failed to write to several of the benefactors you found for me and failed to remind them of our work & need, & so I lost the rich help they all gave. Imagine my regret! But sickness is the greatest despot of all."

Similarly Mr. Michael A. Coyle of Westport, Connecticut, is thanked for five dollars on January 17, 1923, but is told, "I have been very ill for a long time and am only able now to begin answering letters." The following April 4th he is again thanked for five dollars and is told that she has a fourth of the sum needed for the fireproof Home. On December 12, 1924, he hears, "we expect to build during 1925," and on the following April 1st:

"All is well with us — the sick ones better, including myself, for whom you so kindly wish better health." And on March 16, 1926, she writes that his five dollars is doubly welcome "because our Superiors hold us carefully to what we have already raised before allowing us to plan for the whole structure. We expect to have half the Home ready by the Feast of the Sacred Heart, the 11th of June." In a postscript she says: "My health is better & better all the time, but I am not a day younger than 74."

At the trustee's meeting in May, 1923, it was agreed to make a start on a building because everybody was so sorry for Mother Alphonsa when she was told that the funds were not sufficient as yet to permit actual work on the new Rosary Hill Home. The result was a perfectly plain structure of hollow tile covered with concrete, which though in no style in particular, would fit in well enough with the Spanish Mission hospital when it went up, and with which it was to be connected by an overhead passageway on arches, which was used as a smoking and radio room.

This new St. Joseph's House as it was called, was blessed on April 24, 1924, by Monsignor McEntyre, though without any public ceremony. And the following day the very sick patients were transferred there from the old wooden hospital. They at least were safe. In her letter Mother Alphonsa refers to it with a good deal of satisfaction. It housed twenty-five people very comfortably in large wards, and she tells Mr. Braniff: "This first portion has cost a good deal, but not more than an architect was planning to ask for it, if connected with well, electric laundry, etc., aside from his fee. We were given permission to build it without architect or contractor, & have been very careful about it. . . . I only wish we could show you our contented patients in their new quarters (that is 25 of them), which you partly built."

By the time the *Report* for 1923 came out she felt herself almost in a position to put up the dreamed-of hospital-home. "Since

December 1st," she writes, "the Fund asked for has grown rapidly, owing to extensive advertisements in the papers, which give the public a knowledge of the state of the case that nothing else could, and to-day we count $120,000 as the total received, while $30,000 has been promised from reliable sources. Forty-five thousand dollars of this money has been used to erect . . . [St. Joseph's House] and all that is connected with it; the great electric well to supply the future main Home with water, and the old home, too; and the electric machinery for a large laundry to do the work of the whole number of persons on the property." She continues to state her expectations, which do not really seem to be equal to her needs and no doubt account for the fact that, in the end, she was only quite sure of the $40,000 for the building fund in the bank. Yet cheerfully she announces: "The construction work will proceed as far as is permitted, by a total as yet unknown."

Not till the spring of 1926 was she able to publish in the papers (as her custom often was) a balance sheet for the past four years. This showed that she had just over $150,000 in hand. That was considered sufficient by the ecclesiastical authorities to permit her to start. "Our patients," these advertisements read, "who are of all creeds and nationalities, pay nothing because their pockets are empty, and we are their connecting link with their friends among the public. Give us this fireproof house."

It had been a hard struggle, but it was now coming near a close — the crown of her life, something vastly more important than medals and honorary degrees. She had thriven on work, and had worked even when ill, and had, after all, lived to a very vigorous old age. All people of her type can take as their motto: *In coelo requies* — there'll be rest enough in heaven.

She could be sure now, not only that the new Home would go up — she was about to give the order to the contractors for the digging of the foundations — but that the foundations of the Congregation of St. Rose of Lima, the Servants of Relief for Incurable Cancer, had also been well laid. In the hands of Sister Rose and the other women whom she and Sister Rose had trained all would be well. At seventy-five, Mother Alphonsa knew she must be nearing her end, but she meant to work to the last. The new hospital was her pet project: and the raising of money by letters in the papers was her special department. She continued to busy herself with it, very happy but increasingly weary. She kept scribbling away at her letters — five dollars more for the fund, two dollars more; all these friends (and most of them she never met) she thanked herself, usually adding some little personal word. She understood that some of the smallest donations meant the greatest amount of sacrifice.

One day an elderly couple called and asked to see the superior. The Sister at the door told them: "She has gone to Pleasantville to do a little Easter shopping. Do you mind waiting? I'm sure she will not be long."

"You will do just as well," the man assured the Sister, as he handed her an envelope. "I saw in the papers that she wants two hundred thousand dollars for a new home for her patients. When she comes back tell her she needs only a hundred and ninety-nine thousand."

CHAPTER XIII

To His Beloved, Sleep

Meanwhile, life went on as usual in the two Homes, and hardly a week passed in either place without a visit from death. At the end of any year the houses would be as full as they were at the beginning, but at least half the people who were there in January were gone by December.

Yet everything was very cheerful, and even the doomed were treated as though sure of living a long time. For the young patient, Helen Steiger, as she was interested in music and said she would like to go on with her violin lessons, Mother Alphonsa provided a teacher. At the other end of the scale was Miss Costello who was eighty-six. She was bedridden, but on Christmas morning insisted upon getting up. So the Sister dressed her in her nicest bed jacket and wheeled her out into the sun parlor where the presents were spread out. When Miss Costello was given hers, her eyes filled with tears as she said, "God bless you all, good Sisters." Then when she started to sing *Jingle bells* in her little cracked voice, the eyes of those who heard her were wet.

Then there was Miss Cooke who was dying, and who knew she was dying, in August.

"I hope you'll live till the Feast of the Assumption, Miss Cooke," said the Sister. "That's a lovely day to die." (That was the way they talked about death there.)

"Yes, Sister, I wish I could," returned Miss Cooke, "but suffering like this, I can't live for three more days."

"Try and be patient and thankful. Remember you are having

your purgatory in this life. Offer your sufferings to the Blessed Mother. She won't forget you."

"Thank you, Sister, I'll try."

August 15th came and Miss Cooke was still there. At five in the morning the Sister went to give her her medicine and was told, "Oh, I'm burning from head to foot. Here's the Assumption and God is not going to take me today!"

"Cheer up, Miss Cooke — the day is young yet."

A friend who came to see her in the afternoon was only just in time to join in reciting the prayers for the departing soul beside her bed.

Much the same point was made, more roughly, by an elderly priest who called one day. To one of the male patients who was complaining he said, "Cheer up, you're not in hell yet."

From St. Rose's Home there came a crop of stories. One was of a little, dried-up old man with a bad face cancer. He retained one fresh sentiment — a fondness for his shoes so great that he refused to take them off when going to bed. The Sisters and the men in his ward tried to break him of this habit, but not with much success. Almost a week after his arrival two friends called to see him.

"Well, Pop, how do you like it here?" they asked.

"Oh, it ain't so bad," he told them in his shrill treble, "only when I go to bed with my shoes on they raise hell."

Another old fellow there, though very sick, had a remarkably cheerful disposition and did much to make his companions cheerful too. He took upon himself the duty of calling the men on Sunday when it was time to go to the chapel. Then he used to stand at the elevator and shout, "All ab-o-o-a-rd!" And many who responded to his call took the trip across the dark river.

Friends continued to depart — Mr. Warren Greene, almost the first friend they had, and Monsignor Flood who, at their request, had been appointed their ecclesiastical superior, and George McEntyre, Monsignor McEntyre's brother, and the brilliant and versatile Father John Talbot Smith. Five years before Brother Dutton had written, on the back of a snapshot of himself: "Here I am at seventy-eight years, and you are only seventy. Now you begin to live on borrowed time and have my best wishes for your sanctification." The laconic Brother added as postscript: "I ought to write you a letter one of these days — or nights. Your unanswered letters are among my treasures."

And there was that other Brother, who is still with us — he was a good deal younger than Father Damien's assistant — Brother Julian. Mother Alphonsa had sent him a bottle of medicine but also (as the next day was St. Patrick's Day) a bottle of Sherry. The previous year (on August 19th) she wrote to him: "I am very much broken down, and only at times able to mingle with the happy greetings that are going on around me. However, I may grow better at 74, and be able to call upon you, & see the beautiful pictures you have had painted both inside and outside your dwelling. Please greet Our Lady's Statue for me, Our Lady of the Immaculate Conception in the Boys' Chapel!" But on September 27th she had to ask him to forgive her for being so ill: "I beg pardon for being so very stupid when I spoke to you after the ceremonies on our day of clothing, but I was in a daze then, & had to strain every nerve to speak at all. . . . The dear boy you introduced was of course surprised to find me dumb as a fish. I wondered many times why you called him to me, and pray that God will bless his fine candid soul — for he looked to me one of your best boys."

Her own brother, Julian — now eighty, but still hale and hearty and looking very distinguished with his long white mustaches, something like the son of their father's old friend, Oliver Wendell Holmes, in appearance — dropped in unexpectedly for a visit. He had written to her thirty-five years before this to tell her that *she* was the real Hawthorne. It was true.

They talked of the old days at Mrs. Blodgett's and at Rock Ferry, of Mr. Squarey and Mrs. Roundey, and of Mr. Bennoch and Henry Bright, and of Rome and Florence, and of the Brownings and Storys, and of Concord — Emerson and Thoreau and dear, absurd Alcott. They rambled on, as elderly people do in their reminiscences, seeming to dwell more upon the distant past than nearer things. George was not mentioned. He was so far removed from all this; besides he and Julian had often not got along well together. But when she showed him Giovanni Cephas Thompson's picture of her, he laughed and said, "Well, it's just what you used to look like, Rose, my dear! And do you know? — oh, I must tell you this — I ran into Giovanni Cephas's son, young Hubert. You remember Hubert, don't you? This picture reminds me of the incident. I was at some banquet or other and was introduced to a Mr. Thompson, a political boss. Not only that, but he was a huge man, weighing at least three hundred pounds. As we were talking, something about his eyebrows recalled long forgotten days and things. I knew his name was Thompson, and I had the impression that his initials were H. O. Suddenly I swung on him and demanded, 'Are you little Hubert Thompson?' 'Why, of course I am,' he said — 'all that's left of him!' "

Mother Alphonsa threw back her head and laughed at the memory. So that was what had happened to the little ten-year-old boy, rather small for his age, and not at all robust!

"Not funnier than what happened to little Rosebud Hawthorne!"

They sat on the porch together and looked over the blue Westchester hills. She was five years younger than he was, but still old. Tired certainly, but just as certainly vigorous. The octogenarian sighed. How he envied her! Upon the whole he had been a rather successful man. But it was clearly this sister of his, who had failed at music, and then failed at painting, and had really nothing to boast of in literature except that book on their father — what a resounding success she had made of her life!

It was, he reflected, queer how success came to people. Hers had come because she had thrown her chances away — or was it that she had laid her life down? She had never been one he could argue with, though they had had lots of arguments — some rather heated ones. People like this had found the real secret. One looked at their hands and their feet, and if one had any discernment at all one saw there the marks of the nails.

Then the old man rose stiffly, and said good-by to his sister, and got into the car that was to take him to Hawthorne Station. In a few days, he said, he was going back to California.

Though Sister Rose was never heard by any member of the community to attribute anything that had been done to her own efforts, but always gave all the credit to Mother Alphonsa, Mother Alphonsa herself was well aware how much the work — and she herself — owed to Sister Rose. Over and over again in her letters, especially those written on anniversaries, she wrote: "How can I ever thank you enough for casting in your lot with mine, or thank God for sending to this work so great a treasure."

When Alice Huber went that afternoon, in 1897, to help for an afternoon at the old Water Street tenement, she had been deeply moved with pity and affection for Rose Hawthorne Lathrop. These feelings served to take her back again, but of course they would never have served to keep her in a work which, to the very end, was repugnant to her feelings, as she confessed in her diary. For such fidelity, only a supernatural motive sufficed. But things which become supernaturalized originate in the natural. Nor need they lose any particle of their natural goodness, but, when passing beyond, heighten it rather. The strong friendship between the two women only grew deeper, the more complete was their dedication to God. For each the greatest sacrifice that had to be made was the separation that resulted from the founding of Rosary Hill Home. That they had accepted this separation without repining shows how far they placed their cause above merely personal inclinations. But their affection had grown because of — and within — the work in which they were co-operating. Each year they grew closer together.

They continued to meet, however, very frequently. And when Sister Rose was not on a visit to Hawthorne, Mother Alphonsa was on a visit to New York. Nothing of any importance was ever done without their consulting one another, and they worked in perfect harmony, being almost like the two lobes of the single brain. That was necessary for the success of their work.

What are called special friendships are wisely discouraged in religious orders, but the reason for this is obvious; there is the danger that the private friendship will be to the detriment of the religious life or the work of the community. The risk of enclaves of two or three has to be guarded against. And the affectionate and endearing terms these friends used in writing to one another are not ordinarily met in the correspondence of nuns, yet their mutual affection, it must be remembered, was profoundly based upon their mutual love of God, in whom they lived and moved and had their being. They were drawn so intimately toward each other because both were possessed so profoundly with the one supreme motive of an heroic love of the neighbor for the love of God — something of that Pauline love for an intimate fellow laborer.

A letter dated merely August 29th, but which must be 1901 because the address is given as "Neperan" instead of Hawthorne, reads in part: "My darling Sister: This letter contains a love for you that is growing more true than when you felt I loved you first, and which partakes more than ever of the light & security of God's love. But you see day by day how imperfect all that I do & feel still is, & you will have much occasion to instill generosity into your true & beautiful love for me. If I seem harsh, & am harsh at times, it is the imperfect effort of a poor wretch to bring to your soul & mine a greater share of God's truth. . . .

"May St. Rose of Lima, our great & beloved American, help you & me to a complete union of intention & action, that our work may flourish, but still more that our souls may come to Paradise, one of these days, hand in hand, & simple & gentle as two little doves that move shoulder to shoulder over the sward.

"My darling, we all love you as few women are loved."

And on September 3rd (still 1901) there is a letter beginning: "My darling Sister & friend," and full of a sense of the writer's inadequacy. "But soon," she goes on, "I shall be able to rest, I hope, in a mere longing to be absorbed in Christ, & then I shall at least become a gentle & harmless sphere, waiting to be dissolved out of the 'body of this death,' which confines us in a seeming life. . . . Do not worry about me, sweet dear, for as you say, I am really strong & I faithfully promise to be *careful* of myself. . . . I will hope to live; — impatiently waiting for the moment when God wills that I should cease to struggle against my evil ways, yet patiently staying at my post in order perhaps to gain some little victories over myself, & be not so far — so utterly far from my dear Lord when I have quite finished my poor course. I have quite ceased to hope for anything in usefulness to others. That is all a delusion. But my attempt has brought me to know you & be with you, dear. It is a great jewel in a heap of faded flowers."

As Christmas, 1925, drew near Mother Alphonsa wrote to Sister Rose admitting that she had most reprehensibly taken a peek at her present before Christmas day. And early in January she made what proved to be her last visit to St. Rose's. Sister Rose was ill but Mother Alphonsa, who declared that she herself had not felt so well for months, sat by her bed and talked of her plans for the future. "When the new house is completed, I intend to give more of my time to the Sisters; at present I'm just rushed to death."

In the spring, when Sister Rose, now quite recovered, went to Hawthorne, she found that the excavations for the new building really had been started. A few days later, Mother Alphonsa wrote to say that the lumber had already been carried up the hill. In her enkindled imagination she was already drawing plans for the chapel — in fact it was already laid out, she said — and she was about to design the convent. Sister Rose read the letter and passed it over to Sister Paschal. "Read that," she said, "and tell me if anyone can stop Mother from working."

Sister Rose wrote in her diary for May 24th that she had spent the 20th — Mother Alphonsa's seventy-fifth birthday — with her. "Mother looks young," she wrote, "her eyes are clear and her voice sounds like a silver bell; there is nothing in her face to indicate age. I feel she will live to be very old." It was, she noted, a perfect day and the spring was in full bloom at Rosary Hill. But on June 22nd, when Monsignor McEntyre saw her, he told Sister Rose over the phone, "Mother does not look well. It is the first time I have seen her looking badly. I do not think she is well."

Whether she was well or not, she was very happy, now that the steam shovels were at work and the workmen's sheds going up. And when this new house was built — it was to her design and on the spot selected by her, in defiance of all that the architects and contractors had said — she had so arranged it that there would be sunshine in every room. At that thought there was sunshine in her heart.

In the bank statement she had checked on June 1st, she read with immense satisfaction that there was a balance of over $150,000. Then there would be a couple of thousand dollars interest, and legacies that would bring in $30,000, and a special donation for beds of $11,000. There was a nice little windfall too. At Christmas she had received more than $11,000 over the amount she had asked for in donations. Not all of this could be used of course for the new building. They had to support the two houses as well — and that meant a yearly outlay of $35,000. But it would go a long way toward covering the $317,000 provided for in the specifications.* She had every right to feel immensely pleased.

On July 5th Sister Rose went up to visit Mother Alphonsa again, taking with her a young girl who was to enter the novitiate. When they rang the bell it was Mother Alphonsa herself who let them in.

"Oh, Mother," Sister Rose said, "why did you come down?"

"I want to welcome this child."

She *was* only a child, wearing her high school graduation dress to show Mother Alphonsa.

"How lovely, dear!" was the comment. "I feel that the Lord has indeed blessed us when He inspires little girls like you to come and work for the poor."

The girl went into the novitiate and the two old women sat on the porch, talking of the past and planning for the future. While they sat there, a flock of pigeons flew in groups several times around them and then settled on the grass. Mother Alphonsa watched them and then said, "How lovely they are! And though I know they do some damage, I love to see them flying about. When I first came here and everything was so hard, I often felt lonesome. Then they were a consolation to me."

Sister Rose stayed there with her friend until the 7th, and when she said good-by she had no idea it was a final parting. On the evening of the 8th she rang up Rosary Hill to ask how Mother Alphonsa was.

"Why, she was fine," the voice said over the wire. "She went to Mass and received Holy Communion, and after she had looked over her mail she went to the new house. She does so like to watch the men pouring concrete. After that she went to look at the flowers and told us she hadn't felt so strong for a long time."

That news was very good, so when early next morning Sister

* What they actually had to pay, after the completing of the basement, was $345,691.29. It was paid to every penny, without any mortgage being taken.

Rose heard the telephone ringing she supposed it was about a patient who was very sick. She was accustomed to getting these calls at dawn.

The Sister at the telephone desk said, "It is from Rosary Hill and Mother is very ill."

Sister Rose said at once, "There must be some mistake. I rang up only last night, and she was feeling fine."

Then the Sister whispered, "Mother died in her sleep last night."

It was as her father had died. And this painless death was a fitting reward to one who had given thirty years to the poor who suffered from the most painful of diseases.

"When the house is built," so runs the proverb, "death enters in." For her, death had not waited for the house to be built.

On a bronze tablet at the entrance of the house she had designed but had not lived to see finished, these words are cast: "This Home is a memorial to Mother M. Alphonsa Lathrop, O.S.D., who died on July 9, 1926. We who have completed the Home must bear in mind that she who laid the foundation stone braved many hardships and difficulties. We have only finished what she commenced and made secure. This is her last gift to the poor. May her name be held in everlasting remembrance. R.I.P."

Bibliography

The main source for this biography is to be found in documentary materials now made available for the first time. These comprise the diaries of Rose Hawthorne Lathrop (Mother Alphonsa) and her coadjutor and successor, Mother Rose, also a mass of Hawthorne material, most of which has never seen the light and upon which unfortunately I can draw in this place only for general background. Mother Alphonsa was to a great extent her own biographer and the historian of the Congregation she founded — though she intended to be neither — in the magazine she edited intermittently between 1902 and 1904 under the title of *Christ's Poor* and in the *Reports* which were issued in subsequent years. To these should be added the various pamphlets descriptive of the aims of her work. Some of this material had been incorporated into a manuscript history of the order written by Sister Joseph, O.S.D., and placed completely at my disposal. I have, however, gone very much outside that manuscript to avail myself to the full of the documentary material at Hawthorne, New York. These priceless things I was allowed to bring to the sanatorium in which I had to produce this book. Mr. Robert L. Straker of Longmans, Green & Company, who has a book in preparation on Horace Mann and has acquired by purchase a large number of Mann and Hawthorne and Peabody letters, most generously supplied me with copies of the many that related to my subject. And from the Maryknoll Sisters came a transcript of passages from the early diary kept by their budding community.

Other letters have been supplied by the Houghton Library of Harvard University, for which I must thank Mr. William A. Jackson; The Talbot Collection of Georgetown University, for which I have to thank Father Gerard F. Yates, S.J. My thanks are also due Mr. Robert W. Hill of the Manuscript Division of the New York Public Library for letters used from the Century Collection and Dr. John D. Gordan for the letters used from the Henry W. and Albert A. Berg Collection in the New York Public Library. Still further letters have been supplied by Mrs. Clifford

Smyth of Armonk, New York, one of Hawthorne's granddaughters, and Mrs. Hawkins, her daughter, and by Mr. Manning Hawthorne, a Hawthorne great-grandson of Woodstock, Connecticut, for the use of which I have obtained permission from Professor Manning of Kenyon College. The Dominican House of Studies at Washington also sent letters. The Reverend Jerome Dee, O.S.B., of St. Anselm's Abbey, Manchester, New Hampshire, supplied me with his unpublished Master's dissertation at the Catholic University of America on George Parsons Lathrop. Scattered letters have been sent by Mr. Ferris Greenslet of Houghton, Mifflin Company; the Rev. C. P. Biglin of Old Town, Maine; Miss Mary T. Kivlon of Fitchburg, Massachusetts; The Catholic Lending Library of Philadelphia; Miss Charlotte M. Meagher of Buffalo; Mr. Michael A. Coyle of Westport, Connecticut; and Mr. Edward A. Braniff of Tulsa, Oklahoma. Valuable information has been supplied from various sources, especially by Mrs. H. C. Bunner and her daughter Mrs. Dimock of New London, Connecticut.

Arvin, Newton, *Hawthorne*, Boston, 1928.

Bacon, Theodore, *Delia Bacon: A Biographical Sketch*, Boston and New York, 1888.

Bridge, Horatio, *Personal Recollections of Nathaniel Hawthorne*, New York, 1893.

Brooks, Van Wyck, *The Flowering of New England*, New York, 1936.

Burton, Katherine, *Sorrow Built a Bridge: A Daughter of Hawthorne*, New York, 1938.

Cheney, Ednah D., *Louisa May Alcott: Her Life and Letters and Journals*, London, 1890.

Egan, Maurice Francis, *Recollections of a Happy Life*, New York, 1924.

—— "A Legacy of Hawthorne," *New York Times Book Review and Magazine*, April 16, 1922.

Dominican Cancer Homes for the Destitute: A Brief Summary of Data, New York, 1906.

Fields, James T., *Yesterdays with Authors*, Boston, 1897.

Fields, Mrs. James T. (See Howe, M. A. De Wolfe).

French, Lillie Hamilton, "Hawthorne's Daughter," *Ladies Home Journal*, Feb., 1893.

Gilder, Jeanette, *Representative Poems by Living Poets* (with an introduction by George Parson Lathrop), New York, 1886.

Gilder, Richard Watson, *Letters of Richard Watson Gilder*, ed. by his daughter, Rosamond Gilder, Boston and New York, 1916.

Hall, Lawrence Sargent, *Hawthorne Critic of Society*, New Haven, 1944.

Hawthorne, Julian, *Shapes That Pass: Memories of Old Days*, Boston and New York, 1928.

—— *Hawthorne and His Circle*, New York and London, 1903.

—— "A Daughter of Hawthorne," *Atlantic Monthly*, CXLII, September, 1928, pp. 372–376.

—— "Such is Paradise: The Story of Sophia and Nathaniel Hawthorne." *Century*, CXL, Dec., 1927, pp. 157–179.

—— *Nathaniel Hawthorne and His Wife*, 2 vols., Boston and New York, 1893.

Hawthorne, Nathaniel, *Our Old Home*, and *English Notebooks*, 2 vols., Boston (see also Stewart, Randall).

—— *Passages from the American Notebooks:* ed. by Sophia Hawthorne (see also Stewart, Randall).

—— *The Marble Faun*, Boston, 1862.

—— *The Hawthorne Diary of 1859*, ed., by William L. Reenan, in manuscript, Freelands, 1931.

—— *Passages from the French and Italian Notebooks*, Boston 1872.

Hawthorne, Sophia, *Notes in England and Italy*, New York, 1870.

The Hawthorne Centenary Celebration at the Wayside, Concord, Mass., Boston and New York, 1905.

Higginson, Thomas Wentworth, "Una Hawthorne," *Outlook*, July 2, 1904, LXXVII, pp. 517–524.

Howe, M. A. De Wolfe, *Memories of a Hostess: A Chronicle of Eminent Friendships*, drawn chiefly from the Diaries of Mrs. James T. Fields, Boston, 1922.

Howells, William Dean, "Recollections of an Atlantic Editorship," *Atlantic Monthly*, vol. C (1907), pp. 594–606.

James, Henry, *Hawthorne*, New York, 1880.

Jensen, Gerard E., *The Life and Letters of Henry Cuyler Bunner*, Durham, N. C., 1939.

Lathrop, George Parsons, *A Study of Hawthorne*, Boston, 1876.

—— "Orestes A. Brownson," *Atlantic Monthly*, vol. LXXVII (1896), pp. 770–780.

—— (see Gilder, Jeanette).

—— "Edison's Kinetograph," *Harpers Weekly*, vol. V (1891), pp. 446–447.

—— "Talks with Edison," *Harper's New Monthly Magazine*, Feb., 1890, vol. LXXX, pp. 425–435.

—— "Hostility to Roman Catholics," *North American Review*, vol. CLVII (1894), pp. 563–573.

—— "Loyalty of Roman Catholics," *North American Review*, vol. CLIX (1894), pp. 218–224.

—— "An Author Who Could Not Help It," *Lippincott's Magazine*, vol. XXXVIII (1886), pp. 423–430.

—— *The Rose and the Roof-Tree*, Boston, 1875.

—— *Dreams and Days*, New York, 1892.

—— *Spanish Vistas*, New York, 1883.

—— "The Hawthorne Manuscripts," *Atlantic Monthly*, vol. LI (1883), pp. 363–375.

—— (in collaboration with Edison, Thomas Alva) "In the Days of Time," *English Illustrated Magazine*, March, 1897, vol. XVI, pp. 679–693; April, 1897, vol. XVII, pp. 89–91.

—— (in collaboration with Rose Hawthorne Lathrop) *A Story of Courage: Annals of the Georgetown Visitation Convent*. Boston, 1894.

Lathrop, Rose Hawthorne, "The Hawthornes at Lenox, Told in Letters by Nathaniel and Mrs. Hawthorne," *Century Magazine*, vol. XXVII (1894), pp. 86–98.

—— "Some Memories of Hawthorne," *Atlantic Monthly*, vol. LXXVII, pp. 173–186, 373–387, 492–507, 649–660, Feb. to May, 1896.

—— *Memories of Hawthorne*, Boston and New York, 1897.

—— (in collaboration with George Parsons Lathrop), *A Story of Courage: Annals of the Georgetown Visitation Convent*. Boston, 1894.

—— *Along the Shore*, Boston, 1888.

Lazarus, Emma, *Selections from her Poetry and Prose*, ed. with an introduction by Morris U. Schappes, New York, 1944.

Meigs, Cornelia, *Invincible Louisa*, Boston, 1933.

Morris, Lloyd, *The Rebellious Puritan: Portrait of Mr. Hawthorne*, New York, 1927.

Osborne, John Ball, "Nathaniel Hawthorne as American Consul," *Bookman*, Jan. 1903, vol. XVI, pp. 162–163.

Porter, John Addison, "The 'Dr. Grimshawe' MSS," *The New Englander*, vol. XLII (1883), pp. 339–353.

Rideing, William H., *Many Celebrities and a Few Others*, Garden City, N. Y., 1912.

The Rule of St. Augustine and the Constitution of the Servants of Relief for Incurable Cancer, rev. ed., Hawthorne, N. Y., 1944.

Salem Gazette, "A Noble Mission Beneficent Work in Which Mrs. Lathrop Is Engaged," issue for Nov. 12, 1897. (Has a large picture of R. H. L. at work in her hospital.)

Sketch of Aims and Work of St. Rose's Free Home for Incurable Cancer, New York, 1910.

Stewart, Randall, Ed., *The American Notebooks by Nathaniel Hawthorne, Based Upon the Original Manuscripts in the Pierpont Morgan Library*, New Haven, 1932.

—— *The English Notebooks by Nathaniel Hawthorne. Based Upon the Original Manuscripts in the Pierpont Morgan Library*, New York and London, 1941.

Stewart, Randall, "Editing Hawthorne's Notebooks: Selections from Mrs. Hawthorne's Letters to Mr. and Mrs. Fields, 1864–1868," *More Books*. Sept., 1945, vol. XX, pp. 299–315.

—— "Hawthorne's Last Illness and Death: Selections from Mrs. Hawthorne's Letters to Mr. and Mrs. Fields," *More Books*, Oct., 1944, vol. XIX, pp. 303–313.

—— "The Hawthornes at the Wayside, 1860–1864: Selections from Mrs. Hawthorne's Letters to Mr. and Mrs. Fields," *More Books*, Sept., 1944, vol. XIX, pp. 263–279.

—— " 'Pestiferous Gail Hamilton', James T. Fields, and the Hawthornes," *New England Quarterly*, vol. XVII, 1944, pp. 418–423.

—— "Mrs. Hawthorne's Financial Difficulties: Selections from Her Letters to James T. Fields, 1865–1868," *More Books*, Feb., 1946, vol. XXI, pp. 43–52.

Tate, Alfred O., *Edison's Open Door*, New York, 1938.

Ticknor, Caroline, *Hawthorne and His Publisher*, Boston and New York, 1913.

Walsh, James J., *Mother Alphonsa, Rose Hawthorne Lathrop*, New York, 1930.

Index

Academy of the Assumption, Wellesley Hills, 255–256
Alcott, Abby, 118, 119
Alcott, Bronson, 7, 27, 107, 108, 125, 424
Alcott, Mrs. Bronson, 107, 108, 113
Alcott, Louisa, 90, 107, 110, 118, 125, 156, 194, 371
Aldrich, Thomas Bailey, 149, 187, 192 n, 198, 199, 203, 213, 306 n, 317
Aldrich, Mrs. T. B., 184
Alphonsa, Mother, see Lathrop, Rose Hawthorne
American Copyright League, 209
Angel in the House, The, 57
Arnold, Edwin, 28, 157
Arnold, Mrs., see Channing, Fanny
Atlantic Monthly, 102, 128, 130, 137, 172, 176, 178, 179, 181, 192, 193, 197, 199, 204, 307

Bacci, Constantino, 87–88
Bacon, Delia, 47–48
Bailey, Miss, 115
Barrymore, Maurice, 211, 317
Bartlett, Dr., 120
Bartlett, Ned, 152
Bath, 103 f
Bennoch, Francis, 3, 4, 13, 43, 44, 45, 46, 51, 129, 424
Biglin, Maggie, 232, 242
Blackheath, 44, 46
Blackwell's Island, 261, 265, 337
Blodgett, Mrs., 9, 42
Bowdoin College, 8, 91, 415
Bradford, George, 31, 114, 152
Braniff, Edward A., 416, 417
Bremer, Frederika, 71–72
Bridge, Horatio, 124, 135, 137
Bright, Annie, 156
Bright, Henry, 13 ff, 25, 42, 99, 156, 424
Brook Farm, 233–234

Brooks, Van Wyck, 103
Brown, Miss, 53
Browning, Elizabeth Barrett, 76, 79–81, 92, 95, 96, 135, 424
Browning, Robert, 57, 79–81, 92, 192, 424
Browning, Robert Wiedemann ("Penini"), 81, 156 n
Brownson, Orestes, 230
Bryant, William Cullen, 71
Bull, Ephraim, 139
Bull children, the, 139
Bunner, Henry Cuyler, 196, 211, 213, 214, 215, 317, 393
Bunner, Mrs. H. C., 393; see also Learned, Alice

Campbells, the, 11
Cancer Hospital, 262 ff
Carnival, the Roman, 70, 89, 90–91
Carroll, Daniel J., 402
Catholicism, the Hawthornes' attitude to, 29, 30–31, 32, 61 ff, 84 f, 193 f, 123
Catholic Summer School, the, 232, 243, 244
Century Magazine, 198, 199, 205, 307
Channing, Ellery, 109
Channing, Fanny, 157
Channing, Dr. William Ellery, 28, 229
Channing, W. H., 28
Chappell, Alfred, 230–231
Cherry Street, Number 426, 320 ff, 328, 332, 338, 342, 343, 352, 362, 364, 373, 389, 394
Christ's Poor, 280, 300 n, 356 ff, 361, 376, 391, 392, 401
Clapp, Miss, 158, 159, 160
Clarke, Eliot, 141
Clarke, Lilian, 141
Clarke, Sarah, 72

437